Praise for *Written in Blood*

"It is difficult to find fault with this book. . . . *Written in Blood* is a marvelous contribution to the study of modern Russian culture and should be required reading for anyone interested in Dostoevskii, terrorism, or the Russian intelligentsia."

Slavonic and East European Review

"Destined to find readers far beyond Slavic departments and enthusiasts of Russian literature."
Choice

"A superb model of interdisciplinary scholarship: highly original, subtle, thought-provoking, and a pleasure to read. Analyzing both word and deed, Patyk rewrites the history of modern terrorism showing why the Russian case was pivotal. A gripping story."

Susan Morrissey,
author of *Suicide and the Body Politic in Imperial Russia*

"A wonderful book, full of original insights on the intersection between Russian literature and the birth of modern terrorism. Challenging usual ways of thinking, *Written in Blood* is sure to become a classic in Russian cultural studies, to be read and appreciated by scholars, students, and general readers alike."

Anthony Anemone,
editor of *Just Assassins: The Culture of Terrorism in Russia*

Written in
Blood

Revolutionary Terrorism and Russian Literary Culture, 1861–1881

LYNN ELLEN PATYK

THE UNIVERSITY OF WISCONSIN PRESS

Publication of this book has been made possible, in part,
by a grant from the First Book Subvention Program
of the Association for Slavic, East European, and Eurasian Studies
and through support from Dartmouth College.

The University of Wisconsin Press
728 State Street, Suite 443
Madison, Wisconsin 53706
uwpress.wisc.edu

Gray's Inn House, 127 Clerkenwell Road
London EC1R 5DB, United Kingdom
eurospanbookstore.com

Copyright © 2017
The Board of Regents of the University of Wisconsin System
All rights reserved. Except in the case of brief quotations embedded in critical articles and reviews, no part of this publication may be reproduced, stored in a retrieval system, transmitted in any format or by any means—digital, electronic, mechanical, photocopying, recording, or otherwise—or conveyed via the Internet or a website without written permission of the University of Wisconsin Press. Rights inquiries should be directed to rights@uwpress.wisc.edu.

Printed in the United States of America

This book may be available in a digital edition.

Library of Congress Cataloging-in-Publication Data
Names: Patyk, Lynn Ellen, author.
Title: Written in blood: revolutionary terrorism and Russian literary culture, 1861–1881 / Lynn Ellen Patyk.
Description: Madison, Wisconsin: The University of Wisconsin Press, [2017] | Includes bibliographical references and index.
Identifiers: LCCN 2016045013 | ISBN 9780299312206 (cloth: alk. paper)
Subjects: LCSH: Russian literature—Political aspects. | Terrorism—Russia—History—19th century. | Terrorism in literature. | Alexander II, Emperor of Russia, 1818–1881—Assassination. | Dostoyevsky, Fyodor, 1821–1881—Political and social views.
Classification: LCC PG2975 .P38 2017 | DDC 891.709/35847081—dc23
LC record available at https://lccn.loc.gov/2016045013

ISBN 9780299312244 (pbk.: alk. paper)

On the cover, clockwise from upper left: portrait of Alexander Pushkin (1827) by Orest Kiprensky; portrait of Fyodor Dostoevsky (1872) by Vasily Perov; portrait of Nikolai Gogol (c. 1841) by Fyodor Moller; *Explosion at the Winter Palace 5 February 1880* by Pyotr Petrovich Sokolov

In memoriam

DAVID A. J. MACEY

In completion of an incomplete

Contents

Acknowledgments   ix
A Note on Translation, Transliteration, and Other Technicalities   xiii

Introduction   3
Prologue: "Just You Wait! (Uzho tebe!)"   18

Part One: Enigmas of A-synchrony

1. What Do Nihilists Do?   43
2. "Very Dangerous!"   52
3. Extraordinary Men and Gloomy Monsters   60
4. "Daring and Original Things" (Assez causé!)   67
5. "Vous trouvez que l'assassinat est grandeur d'âme?"   73
6. Spoiling One Idea to Save Another   82
7. A Gloomier Catechism   93

Part Two: Apparitional Terrorism in *Demons*

1. "Again, Like Before"   105
2. "The Only Possible Explanation of All These Wonders"   110

3. Tarantulas with a Heart? ... 118
4. Dostoevsky's Counterterrorism: "The First Step" ... 125
5. Dostoevsky's Counterterrorism (Continued): Laughter through Fear ... 134
6. The Unity of All Terrorism(s) ... 141

Part Three: "The Little Devil Sitting in Your Heart"

1. A Change of Heart ... 151
2. An Original Plan ... 155
3. Emotions on Trial: Witness Testimony and the Prosecution ... 159
4. Emotions on Trial II: The Defense ... 167
5. Whose Rebellion? ... 176
6. False Christs and Little Devils ... 181
7. "That Is the Whole Answer" ... 192
8. The Khokhlakov Principle: Russian Society in the Mirror of Revolutionary Terrorism ... 197
9. Again, Like Before (Again) ... 202

Part Four: The Beautiful Dead (Deed)

1. Writing in Blood ... 211
2. An Icon with Death ... 215
3. Celebrity Icons ... 224
4. Terror in Search of a Face ... 236

Epilogue: "All of Europe Thrills to the Horror" ... 247

Notes ... 263
Bibliography ... 309
Index ... 323

Acknowledgments

It seems like I have been writing this book all my life, or even longer, and so the debt of gratitude I have amassed is understandably enormous. For the sake of argument, let's begin with Mr. Redding, my sixth grade social studies teacher, who affirmed that "yes" Russia was a European country and acquiesced to my desire to do my final report for our Europe unit on Russia. That was a coup. And then there was my seventh grade English teacher, who did not report me to the FBI for writing a story about a socially conscious terrorist who planted bombs in public restrooms. Times were different then. Skip ahead years to my good fortune in meeting Jessica Stern at the Hoover Institution at Stanford University. Jessica offered kindness, inspiration, expertise, and research work on her book, *The Ultimate Terrorists* (2000), which rekindled my interest in terrorism as I embarked on a Ph.D. in Russian literature.

Enter the angels of my destiny: professors Monika Greenleaf, Gregory Freidin, and Gabriella Safran in the Slavic Department at Stanford. Each of them contributed in their own way to my intellectual development, and all were models of brilliant writers and original thinkers. Their unflagging support and friendship sustained me during challenging years when it seemed unlikely, at best, that I would finish my doctorate. If they ever doubted, they never showed it. Dan Edelstein also joined, at a critical moment, in helping me think about terror/ism in a French revolutionary context, and my very collegial and talented cohort (Anne Eakin-Moss, Amelia Glaser, Luba Golburt, Elif Batuman, Sarah Pankenier-Weld, and Martha Kelley) was a great boon. For my daily bread during these years, I want to acknowledge the support of a Mabelle McLeod Lewis fellowship, a Whiting fellowship, and a Mellon postdoctoral fellowship, and for my spiritual bread, I will always treasure the friendship of Gabriella Bockhaus, Andrea Orzoff, and Robin Lyday.

Another spin of the Wheel of Fortune landed me at the University of Florida in Gainesville. Galina Rylkova, Alexander Burak, Frank Goodwin, and Galina Wladyka were warm and welcoming colleagues, and Ingrid Kleespies, Conor O'Dwyer, and Michael Gorham were both wonderful colleagues and next-door neighbors! I am especially grateful to Michael, for his ceaseless encouragement, and to Joseph Spillane in History, for leaving no stone unturned in his quest for my hire. In the European History section, Sheryl Kroen, Alice Freifeld, Howard Louthan and Andrea Sterk also shared ideas and made me feel like a valued colleague, rather than a "trailing spouse."

The Russian Department at Dartmouth College plucked me from the swelling ranks of non-tenure track faculty in 2012. I am grateful to Deborah Garretson, John Kopper, Victoria Somoff, Mikhail Gronas, and Alfia Rakova for their warmth, collegiality, and mentorship. The German Department is something of a second home, with Irene Kacandes, Yuliya Komska, and especially Petra and Michael McGillen offering invaluable advice and unstinting friendship. The book that you hold in your hands assumed its current and final form during these years, thanks to Dartmouth's resources, its impressive undergraduates (including my research assistant, John Howard), and generous writing and research time. I am grateful to those who graciously agreed to read portions of the manuscript, especially to Susan Morrissey, Randall Law, Derek Offord, Randall Poole, Martin Miller, Andrew Chapman, and John Kopper for their insightful and generous comments. The University of Wisconsin Press's readers, Susan Morrissey and Anthony Anemone, offered thoughtful and judicious suggestions and heartening encouragement. I am also grateful to a third, anonymous reader, who alerted me to how it was possible to read this book.

Gwen Walker at University of Wisconsin Press deftly shepherded this book through the review and publication process, asking thoughtful and thought-provoking questions when necessary. Where would I be

Acknowledgments

without editorial assistance? I am grateful to Adam Mehring and Judith Robey of University of Wisconsin Press and to Avram Brown, for his astute editorial assistance. Carla Marolt provided fantastic options for the cover design. The index was prepared by J. Naomi Linzer.

An initial version of Part Four Chapter 3 first appeared in *The Slavic Review* under the title "Remembering 'The Terrorism:' Sergei Stepniak-Kravchinsky's *Underground Russia*" (68, no. 4 [2009]: 758–781).

There are those who had almost nothing to do with the book, but without whom . . . I'm proud and delighted to have as my lifelong companions my sisters, Lisa and Laura. My in-laws, Fran and Larry Finkel, provided every type of support and sustenance imaginable, from childcare to beef brisket and beyond. By proofreading this manuscript, Fran has exceeded anything in the annals of mother-in-lawhood, and I am deeply grateful. My funny and adorable boys, Max and Leo, are grateful to my book for the hours of extra screen time when Mom was happily occupied, and Mom is grateful to Nintendo. Chloe, our Golden Doodle, is also grateful to the book for long, meandering walks and the absentminded second dinners. But there is someone who has no reason to be grateful to this book; my husband, Stuart Finkel, who has sacrificed months away from his family every year to return to the University of Florida, so that I could enjoy the benefits of a tenure-track position at Dartmouth. I am inexpressibly grateful for his love, support, research assistance, and sacrifice.

My most enthusiastic and uncritical readers—my parents—long ago passed from the scene. I hope heaven has a good interlibrary loan. This book is in memory of Gloria Patyk née Czarnecki (1941–2002), Gary Patyk (1939–2008), and Jean Patyk (1915–2016), all of whom I love, miss, and see in my dreams.

A Note on Translation, Transliteration, and Other Technicalities

Many of the works cited are classics of Russian literature that have been translated by professional translators and scholars. Where such outstanding translations exist, I use and cite them. Where I have relied instead on the original Russian in order to underscore a particular nuance, I cite only the original in the notes. If no translation is cited, that means that I have provided it. For the convenience of the Anglophone reader, I have anglicized familiar Russian proper names; otherwise, I used the Library of Congress system of transliteration. The word "nihilist," which occurs frequently in this text, presented a particular problem. In contemporary Russian sources "nihilist" is not capitalized; in Anglophone sources that refer much more specifically to Russian radicals consecrated to revolutionary violence, "Nihilist" is capitalized. I have observed this distinction to the best of my ability.

Written in
Blood

Introduction

> If we postulate as polar opposites "natural horror" (earthquakes, ecological disasters, death by prolonged illness) and "art horror" (the genre that includes Dracula and Stephen King, thrillers as well as Artaud and Beckett) terrorism would be somewhere in between.
> ZULAIKA and DOUGLASS, *Terror and Taboo*

The Great Bequest

In July 1877, in the course of a lengthy review of his great compatriot Leo Tolstoy's latest novel *Anna Karenina*, Fyodor Dostoevsky struck an unexpectedly plaintive note: "If we have literary works of such power and execution, then why can we not *eventually* have *our own* science as well, and our own economic and social solutions? Why does Europe refuse us our independence, *our own* word? These are questions that cannot help but be asked. It would be absurd to suppose that nature had endowed us only with literary talents."[1]

Yes, absurd, even at the zenith of literature's social relevance in mid-nineteenth century Russia, even to a writer such as Fyodor Dostoevsky. For a great nation such as Russia, literary talents—however big—were too little. Dostoevsky took the absurdity of this proposition as proof in advance that Russia was destined to make an even greater bequest to the world than mere words, and encouragement that his literary project was sure to work out precisely what this bequest might be. Arguably, Dostoevsky's quest was cut short when the writer died without producing the capstone of his career, the planned sequel to *The Brothers Karamazov*. But some two months later, on April 11, 1881, what may be taken as a confirmation that Dostoevsky's ambition for Russia had in fact been realized came from an indubitable source. In a letter to his daughter, Jenny, the aging Karl Marx inquired: "Have you been following the trial of the assassins in Petersburg? They are sterling people through and through, *sans pose mélodramatique*, simple, businesslike, heroic. Shouting and doing are irreconcilable opposites . . . they try to teach Europe that their *modus operandi* is a specifically Russian and historically inevitable method about which there is no more reason to moralise—for or against—than there is about the earthquake in Chios."[2]

In 1881 Marx was struck by what became one of Russia's most momentous contributions to political modernity, a new "modus operandi," a strategy of political violence that would become known as "terrorism."[3] Marx was most taken by its laconic heroism and unpretentious stoicism—and by the fact that it did not upset his theory of revolution too much. This form of flagrant voluntarism was, Marx temporized, ultimately inevitable in Russia and no more subject to moral judgment than a natural disaster. As far as Marx was concerned, Dostoevsky needn't have worried, much less moralized.

My study begins, in any case, with the point on which the two men converged: the valorization of the deed over the word. Even for Dostoevsky, there were words and then there were *words*, by which he meant something entirely different than those produced by even such literary talents as Tolstoy. *Written in Blood* in fact argues that revolutionary terrorism was just as much Russia's (literary) word as its (revolutionary) deed, and that it issued from the bourn of a literary culture whose marks it indelibly bore. This is why there must be a literary history of terrorism. Without Russia's far from negligible "literary talents" it is by no means certain that there would be any historical terrorism at all.

Terrorism: A Story about the Violence

"The assassins" whom Marx praised were six members of the first revolutionary organization that devoted itself to terrorism, the People's Will (Narodnaia volia). After eighteen excruciating months and six failed attempts, they had achieved their ultimate goal: the assassination of Tsar Alexander II on March 1, 1881. The three-day trial of the conspirators, Andrei Zhelyabov, Sophia Perovskaya, Nikolai Rysakov, Timofei Mikhailov, Nikolai Kibalchich and Gesia Gelfman, was covered more thoroughly in the international press than in the severely censored Russian media, and Karl Marx, along with the rest of the world, was duly apprised of the efficacy of this innovation from the depths of a backward "oriental despotism," as the Russian Empire appeared to "Western eyes."[4]

Marx was struck by this peculiarly Russian "modus operandi," but the "Russian Method," as it came to be known, was just one strategy of sub-state political violence to mature in the last third of the nineteenth century. Other—possibly more innovative—means were employed by the Irish-American Fenians agitating for Irish independence from England. The Fenians commenced a dynamite campaign in January 1881 with an attack on a military installation in Manchester, but followed by planting bombs at key symbolic and strategic locations (Scotland Yard, the offices of *The Times*, the Tower of London, the Nelson Column), heedless of London's bustling crowds.[5] Yet the Fenians did not win comparable recognition for their modus operandi from the likes of Karl Marx or from historians of terrorism, who with few exceptions have conferred the dubious honor of inventing terrorism upon the Russian revolutionaries—or "Nihilists," as they were called—of the mid-nineteenth century.[6] In fact, the title of "first" has gone to the Russians less on the basis of actual chronological priority (the movements were roughly contemporaneous, as was Ku Klux Klan terrorism in the Reconstruction South) than because Russia as the birthplace of modern terrorism is a *better story*, as opposed to other stories that would locate the birthplace of modern terrorism in the United States (as would be the case with both the Irish-American Fenians and the Ku Klux Klan).[7]

How, then, did Russia win this unenviable distinction? If histories and chronologies of terrorism are parsed, the Russians' priority is justified on two counts: their "spectacular successes" (above all, the assassination of Alexander II) and the fact that the Russians wrote.[8] A case in point: Sergei Nechaev's 1869 pamphlet *Catechism of a Revolutionary* invariably figures as a seminal *event* in all chronologies of terrorism (no matter that Nechaev's actual deed was anything but a "spectacular success"), even while Dmitry Karakozov's failed tsaricide in 1866 and the Fenian-linked attempt on Queen Victoria in 1872 are frequently omitted.⁹ Without question, the *Catechism* is a notorious manual for waging terrorist warfare that would school subsequent generations of the most diverse national backgrounds.¹⁰ Yet the pages of the *Catechism*, especially its first sections dealing with the revolutionist's "attitudes," are torn directly from Russian literature, and Nechaev's Revolutionist is immediately recognizable as only the latest model of "gloomy monster"¹¹ to roll off the literary assembly line following Turgenev's Bazarov, Chernyshevsky's Rakhmetov, and Dostoevsky's Raskolnikov.¹²

In his foundational *The Age of Terrorism*, Walter Laqueur noted this special relationship between terrorism and Russian literature, observing that "[it] was easier for Russian [writers] to understand their own terrorists" than for Western writers to understand theirs, and concluding that terrorists "emerge as credible human beings from Russian literature."¹³ Of course Laqueur means that Russian writers succeeded in making their terrorists fully believable, three-dimensional characters, but his syntax creates an ambiguity that allows for another reading; namely, that terrorists emerged from Russian literature in a sense similar to the claim, attributed to Dostoevsky, that "All of Russian Literature emerged from beneath Gogol's overcoat."¹⁴ As I will argue at greater length over the course of the book, there is considerable—and even some *literal*—merit in the metaphor that Russian literature served as revolutionary terrorism's "overcoat," whosoever's the generative overcoat is said to be—Radishchev's or Pushkin's or Gogol's or, most fittingly, Dostoevsky's. From Radishchev's *Journey from St. Petersburg to Moscow*, to Pushkin's *The Bronze Horseman*, to Nechaev's *Catechism*, to Turgenev's "The Threshold," Russians wrote their terrorism into being in every available genre—travelogue, pamphlet, lyrical poem, novel, prose poem, profile, sketch, and memoir—in addition to writing it in blood.

For those outside of Russian studies, the assertion that *literature* played a critical role in the historical emergence of terrorism may seem an overblown and at the same time transparently opportunistic attempt to claim some contemporary relevance for my chosen field of study. And so I submit that in addition to and inseparably from terrorism, Russian literature *at the same time* set forth a new ethos of nonviolence, the old ethos having been long since established (and long since ignored) in the Gospels.¹⁵ Terrorism and nonviolence were two branches of the same tree, two sleeves of the same overcoat.

Introduction

It is no coincidence that the advent of what Walter Laqueur has called "the age of terrorism" coincided with the "age of literature," an age on the threshold of a mass, global media in which literature—particularly in the form of the great realist novel—enjoyed a particular intellectual caché and social relevance.[16] Literature enjoyed an especially authoritative *moral* status in Russia because, as the *doyen* of the radicals—Alexander Herzen—so eloquently put it, "in a country where the people is deprived of social freedom, literature is the sole pulpit from the height of which the cry of the people's indignation and conscience makes itself heard."[17] Literature offered a public forum for the discussion of politically charged social and economic issues, although this discussion often proceeded obliquely, by allusion in various forms (the famous Aesopian language). Readers therefore approached literature with the utmost seriousness, expecting and demanding that it offer solutions to the "accursed" and "eternal" questions, the most pressing of which was how to live.

Literature was not shy about providing the most detailed models on that score. As Russian pioneers in the semiotics of behavior have demonstrated, beginning already at the dawn of secular literature in the eighteenth century, it offered behavioral codes for emulation in the day-to-day life of educated Russians.[18] If Russians were more receptive to such artificial models than Western Europeans, it was because a series of "natural disasters" in the form of cataclysmic political overhauls initiated from above (Peter the Great, the Great Reforms) disrupted traditional behavioral models. Old ways were rendered obsolete, "reactionary," or just plain nonsensical, and the behavioral wheel had to be reinvented. In addition to models for discreet behaviors, literature offered for imitation (not only in Russia) what Lydia Ginzburg has termed "historical personalities" that resonated with an epoch: a Werther or a Childe Harold or a Chatsky.[19] However, it was literary realism—a style that laid claim to unmediated mimesis—that was charged with cutting the New Person from whole cloth at the most fraught moment, at the dawn of Russia's post-feudal order in the late 1850s.[20] As the historian Susan Morrissey put it, "The 'new person' was born on the boundary between literature and life," with the literary critic as midwife.[21] It should little surprise that this was a double birth, and that "the new person's" fraternal twin, the terrorist, was born at the same time. As Herzen remarked, "this mutual effect of people on books and books on people" resulted in some strange things; certainly, cautionary tales about the perils of "unnatural" births, the unholy offspring of "art [horror]" and "life [horror]"abound, and this is one of them.[22]

Fantastic Realities

No study of terrorism, however, can progress very far in its narrative before running up against the definitional problem, the problem that there is no consensus, and much contention, about what "terrorism" is. The deep roots of the controversy lie not in how one characterizes the violence (as random, symbolic, extranormal); the underlying problem is whether terrorism is in fact *the violence*, or whether it is something else. The positivist or actor-based approach that has long held sway in terrorism studies assumed that an actor (usually an individual or non-state group) committed an act of violence that was essentially, self-evidently terroristic. Actor-based approaches concern themselves overwhelmingly with identifying the causes of terrorism for the ultimate purpose of preventing it: what causes terrorism on the social, economic, political, and individual psychological level? By contrast, the social constructivist or "critical" approach to terrorism took flight on the truism that "one man's terrorist is another man's freedom fighter," and that the "terrorist" exists in contemporary discourse only as a pejorative, designating those whose violence one opposes. From the critical point of view, "terrorism" is largely a discursive product that "lacks any ontological fixity." Instead, it "only exists as the outcome of a complex, ceaseless dialectic between acts of violence and those witnessing, describing and interpreting those violences."[23]

These approaches are hardly mutually exclusive; both are in fact necessary to account for the emergence of terrorism in revolutionary Russia. Whereas the social constructivist approach is a latecomer that has been most fruitfully applied in the post factum analysis and deconstruction of terrorism discourse, here I will argue that in Russia terrorism existed as a "social fact" before it manifested as a "brute fact"—as concrete acts of violence committed by revolutionary actors—and before it was designated by the neologism "terrorism."[24] In Russia, the attribution of exceptional events (whether actual or anticipated) to political actors with political intent was independent of the actual existence of those actors and, in the context of revolutionary hopes and fears, conjured those actors. In short, terrorism and terrorists existed in fantasy before they manifested in reality, and to the extent that terrorism is always an interpretation of an act (of violence), it hovers on the boundary of the real and the imagined. The hallmark of the fantastic, according to the literary theorist Tsvetan Todorov, is the reader's irresolvable hesitation as to the reality of narrated events, and it is precisely this hesitation concerning whether an act (of violence) is terrorism or not that lends it a fantastic quality.[25] Ultimately, to the extent that terrorism enthralls our emotions and imagination and derives its power from them, it is "fantastic."

It is no coincidence, I think, that from the 1840s Russia onward, the "fantastic" and all such phenomena associated with what detractors categorized as the non-real (German idealism, philosophical abstractions, the imaginary) were in retreat. In the context of the heated polemics of the following decades, the word "fantastic" became a pejorative, used to discredit and stigmatize one's opponents' most fundamental ideals as ludicrous and absurdly unreal—and to stigmatize literature as itself a confection suitable only for adolescent minds. With the additional impetus and luster lent by positivism and materialism, the "fact," the "real," and "realism" became the radical intelligentsia's touchstones and relentless mantra, so that we might say that the literary history of terrorism in Russia is one in which the fantastic becomes horrifyingly real.

In Russia the political ground for such fantastic apparitions was provided by the concept of *kramola*, which is most often translated as "sedition" but refers much more broadly to any kind of open or conspiratorial revolt against the established order. In the original Old Church Slavonic, it denoted a revolt against God, and its more modern figurative usage referred to something prohibited or forbidden.[26] In key respects, *kramola* is a fitting counterpart to our modern "terrorism" in that the term is a pejorative rhetorical (rather than legal) term denoting an abstraction, but one that can be reified as the *kramol'nik*, the "seditionist." When terrorism and revolutionary terrorists appeared in Russia, they were first experienced as part of this long familiar, intractable *kramola*, and *kramol'nik* was used interchangeably in contemporary discourse with other words, such as *fanatik* (fanatic), *zlodei* (villain, evildoer), or *zloumyshlennik* (villain, or literally "evil-thinker") to denote the figure that ultimately became known as the *terrorist*.[27]

It is worth emphasizing that in Russian "evil thinkers" are indistinguishable from "evil doers." Russia's first "modern" law code, the *Ulozhenie* of 1649, held word, deed, and intention of harm to the divinely anointed tsar equally culpable and punishable by excruciating death. Most infamously, though, the *Ulozhenie* required anyone with knowledge of such words, deeds, or intent on the part of another to inform the authorities. The resonant phrase for declaring such knowledge and initiating an investigation (in which torture was the primary means) was "Word and Deed" (slovo i delo).[28] Whereas in the West these two concepts became increasingly separate and distinct in legal, moral, and ontological terms, such distinctions remained hazy in Russia, providing the atmospherics for fantastic realities. With the boundary between word and deed thus blurred, depending upon "those witnessing, describing and interpreting," the suspect word could easily cross the line to become a sinister deed—to become, in other words, terrorism.

Despite these preexisting conditions, the terrorist and terrorism were something new and unprecedented.[29] The symbolic center of modern terrorism was the individual subject/actor, precisely that crucial component missing from terrorism as a "social fact." And Russian literature fleshed out this center not only by default, because the individual is the focal point of modern fiction and the bearer of the heroic, but because the writer as emblematic of the modern subject was on a collision course with the autocratic state, predestined by the nature of his craft for sedition. Therefore, the search for prototypes for the modern terrorist leads not only to the early modern *kramol'nik*, but also inevitably to the writer himself.

A Moral Monster

Historians certainly cannot be accused of neglecting the role played by the writer and Russian literature in the genesis of the revolutionary movement, but they have generally subsumed literature under the history of ideas, and terrorism under the history of the revolutionary movement. Moreover, histories of the revolutionary movement have quite understandably foregrounded the contribution of radical writers to radical thought, without inquiring how non-radical texts—how indeed literary culture as a whole—might be implicated in the emergence of revolutionary terrorism.

As a literary history of terrorism this book does not attempt to trace direct lines of causality, or identify points of one-to-one correspondence between a literary model of the terrorist or of terrorism and actual historical terrorists. To do so would be to begin our story too late:

terrorists were not explicitly portrayed in Russian legal literature until after 1905, by which time a "second wave" of revolutionary terrorism was already breaking upon the shore. Nor should my argument be mistaken as a monocausal explanation "Russian literature caused terrorism" or a denial that the brute violence of terrorism in fact existed, and exists. Instead, I attempt to describe a subtle and intricate feedback loop between art and life, between cultural representations—many of which preceded the actual manifestation of terrorism—and political violence. The tropes for conceiving and interpreting violent political opposition and its agents crystallized in literature, and along with extra-literary factors, shaped the modus operandi that won international notoriety as "the Russian method."

In their seminal study of terrorism discourse, *Terror and Taboo*, Zulaika and Douglass observe that in contemporary discourse "the terrorist" has taken the place of the "wild man," "savage," or "barbarian" as the monstrous new enemy of the human race (hostis humani generis).[30] Like these early modern existential threats to civilization, "the terrorist" is spun from dehumanizing and demonizing rhetoric, rhetoric that not coincidentally mirrors the terrorists' own. As a liminal figure who unleashes chaos and destruction from the margins of society, this concept of the terrorist exhibits a formlessness that lends itself to dichotomies and the ability to encompass "the seemingly contradictory functions of hero and criminal, guardian angel and demon, martyr and murderer" in the social imaginary.[31]

As a literary history (or better, genealogy) of terrorism, my narrative traces the interplay of formlessness and form—and therefore also the wide variety of forms that terrorism and the terrorist assume over the period of my study. Despite its misleading "ism," terrorism does not constitute an ideology but is a method that can be wielded in the name of any ideology, from radical populism, to Christian fundamentalism, to Islamism. At its most basic structural level, terrorism is "a frontal assault on any norm, moral, political or social."[32] In a political context, terrorism becomes a violent contest over political legitimacy, one best understood not as a one-sided tactic but as a *dynamic* that involves "the antagonistic interplay between state official and insurgent leaders."[33] This interplay has social/discursive and brute/physical dimensions, which together determine the way in which terrorism is historically actualized.

If the most salient feature of modern terrorism is the targeting of "the noncombatant public and soft civilian targets of opportunity," then the form that terrorism in Russia ultimately took begs the question of whether the "first modern terrorism" was "modern" or not.[34] The fact that in autocratic Russia power was still personally embodied by the tsar conditioned the emergence of what the historian Manfred Hildermeier has called populist political terrorism, in which a self-elected revolutionary elite targeted the tsar or other officials held responsible for the regime's malfeasance.[35] In the face of government arbitrariness and absence of rule of law, the terrorists presented themselves, to borrow Herzen's resonant phrase, as "the unwritten moral check on power" that was otherwise lacking.[36] Russian revolutionaries effectively adapted the model of tyrannicide, a legible and valorized form with no native antecedents, as the centerpiece of a systematic tactic of political violence underwritten by legitimating modern ideologies (the will of the people) and the most modern of destructive technologies—dynamite. After the assassination of Alexander II, the Executive Committee of the People's Will addressed an open letter to his heir, Alexander III, demanding precisely the import of those rights and civil liberties necessary for the unimpeded development of the individual. Thus the People's Will parlayed "backwardness" (absolutism) and "imitativeness" (tyrannicide) into originality—and murder into martyrdom.

Historians have wondered at the terrorists' oversight or naïveté in 1) lacking an endgame for a political overthrow of monarchy; and 2) assuming that the murder of the tsar would dispose his son and heir to accede to the murderers' demands. The resources at the People's Will's disposal were obviously insufficient to accomplish the revolutionary transfer of power. Instead, their hope was that their deed, in rending the fabric of the established order, would create the conditions for a radical socio-political transformation. That proved an unrealizable fantasy; nonetheless, even after the organizational demise of the People's Will, its legacy in the form of terrorism's powerful representations inspired "national liberation fighters" in revolutionary and anti-colonial struggles across the globe.

A Literary History of Terrorism

Possibly the most incisive definition of terrorism available is the one offered by David Rapoport, as "the use of violence to provoke consciousness, to evoke certain feelings of sympathy and revulsion."[37] Historians

Introduction

of terrorism have recognized that it is not so much grievance but the *consciousness* of grievance that gives rise to terrorism.[38] Consciousness and its provocation were the province of Russian literature and the métier of one writer in particular—the great novelist Fyodor Dostoevsky. Every major Russian writer of his era wrote about terrorism, whether explicitly or obliquely, yet Dostoevsky stands out for his remarkable attunement to and synchrony with revolutionary terrorism. In a feat of dialectical virtuosity, Dostoevsky had reclaimed the pejorative "fantastic" as his peculiar badge of honor, to later arrive at a synthetic literary method of "fantastic realism"—a method ideally suited to discern and anticipate such "fantastic realities" as terrorism. The core three parts of this book are dedicated to what I refer to as Dostoevsky's "terrorism trilogy": *Crime and Punishment* (1866), *Demons* (1870-72), and *The Brothers Karamazov* (1878-80), works that coincided with watershed moments in the historical evolution of terrorism. These novels far surpass the anti-nihilist novels of his contemporaries both in their artistry and in the deeper, more nuanced, and more prescient representation of political violence. Through close readings of these works and their immediate historical context, I track Dostoevsky's dynamic understanding and complex relationship to this still unknown, unfolding phenomenon. As will become amply clear, Dostoevsky possessed unique insight into the discursive construction of terrorism, the vicious circle of revolutionary and state violence, and terrorism's trajectory in the modern world.

While Dostoevsky is generally considered a loyal monarchist and political conservative with little sympathy for nihilist ideas, my readings uncover the deep-seated reasons for his unusual attunement to those ideas, as well as the surprising alignment between Dostoevsky's own literary method and "the Russian" one. This is in no way to suggest that Dostoevsky lent explicit support to radical ideas or tactics, or that his writings served for young radicals as Nikolai Chernyshevsky's *What Is to Be Done?* did, but that is not because Dostoevsky did not aspire to such influence. Rather, my point is that Dostoevsky was preeminently both creature and creator of the same literary culture whence terrorism issued. Moreover, unlike his peers Tolstoy and Turgenev, he never ceded the field and was ceaselessly engaged in literary and journalistic work on political themes from the advent of the Great Reforms to his death in 1881. No less than his radical contemporaries, Dostoevsky himself longed for the advent of the "new Russian man," and his literary art provided the venue for the creation of this image according to his own specifications—specifications that strangely mirrored those of his ideological opponents.

Finally, it would be remiss to ignore the fact that Dostoevsky's own self-conception as a writer rested on audacity and that his literary aspirations led him to alight on the same method that enticed the revolutionaries: murder. In the three novels under discussion, Dostoevsky employs a sensational act of violence with political implications to rivet his audience's attention and provoke "sympathy and horror." Yet this was all in the service of a higher goal, which for Dostoevsky consisted in pronouncing a "new word": a momentously field-shifting utterance that would have the transformative efficacy of a deed.

Terrorism, like Dostoevsky's "new word," was a long time in coming. In the spirit of a genealogy, the prologue of this book, "Just You Wait!" (Uzho tebe!), begins before the concept (Begriff) and tactic of terrorism do and marks the time between terrorism's appearance as a literary-discursive phantasm and its actual historical manifestation. This offers fertile ground for probing terrorism's "lack of ontological fixity" and observing that with terrorism, as with ghost stories, the ghosts'/terrorists' reality is beside the point: the *stories* are what scare. In fact, the first blow struck against autocracy was not a bomb, but a book: Alexander Radishchev's *Journey from St. Petersburg to Moscow* was construed as an assault on the sovereign by no less than Catherine II herself, who meted out exemplary punishment. The writer Radishchev's word/deed and Catherine's reaction to it, I argue, provides the schema for revolutionary terrorism, and Russia's most celebrated writers, Alexander Pushkin and Nikolai Gogol, subsequently offer revisions and variations of this scenario, driving it more deeply into the Russian cultural imaginary. Moreover, Radishchev models the ethos and pathos of terrorism via his surrogate narrators and ultimately offers the moral/legal justification for retributive violence based on natural right. The prologue remains a prologue, however, and the waiting doesn't end soon enough for Fyodor Dostoevsky, who in December 1849 suffered a repeat of Radishchev's fate and was arrested and sentenced to death for incautious words. Luckily for everyone, Dostoevsky's true culpability remained undiscovered so that his sentence was commuted, and he lived to write another day.

Part One, "Enigmas of A-synchrony," examines the befuddlement in store for contemporaries and posterity thanks to the historical advent of terrorism without "terrorists" and terrorists without "terrorism," in

1862 and 1866, respectively. In the St. Petersburg fires of 1862, a narrative of terrorism was fanned equally by Peter Zaichnevsky's incendiary pamphlet "Young Russia" and by rumors emanating from "literate spheres," while the presumed terrorist-arsonists were nowhere to be found. In the meantime, writers and critics set the stage for the appearance of "a man of action," "an extraordinary man" suited to the peculiar conditions of an uneven struggle against an internal enemy. Yet when Dmitry Karakozov lurched out of the shadows on April 4, 1866, to commit the first act of revolutionary terrorism, he failed to be the first "terrorist."[39] By contrast, Rodion Raskolnikov, the hero of Dostoevsky's *Crime and Punishment*, is the first fully—too fully—imagined terrorist in Russian literature. Dostoevsky crams all of terrorism's contradictions into Raskolnikov, whose practice falls short of his theory so that he commits an ordinary murder instead. This blunder becomes the source of Raskolnikov's self-recriminations in the second half of *Crime and Punishment* and drives him to take his theory of political murder to the "outermost pillars." I then conclude by pointing to the ways in which the revolutionary agitator, Sergei Nechaev, might have benefited from the mistakes of his fictional predecessor, had he heeded Raskolnikov's lessons.

Part Two, "Apparitional Terrorism in *Demons*," begins with the premise that the historical incident upon which Dostoevsky's novel was based, Sergei Nechaev's murder of the student Ivanov in November 1869, was not apprehended by contemporaries as "terrorism." Rather, it was Dostoevsky who made terrorism visible in his novel before it had historically appeared. This accounts for the paradox that *Demons* simultaneously is and *is not* about terrorism. Dostoevsky consistently undermines the actual existence of a terrorist plot and an international revolutionary conspiracy, the better to illustrate terrorism as a "social fact" constituted by the town's reception of Stavrogin's and Peter Verkhovensky's outrages. Nonetheless, Dostoevsky's prescience and penetration extends to all forms of terrorism, and Part Two considers *Demons* as both a project of preemption and a pioneering study of the phenomenon. In addition to anticipating the symbolic and aesthetic dimensions of the individual terrorist as they would evolve in "the Russian Method," *Demons* exposes the sentimental tropes that underlie the novel's narratives of (self)destruction and the reciprocally constructing fantasies of the "terrorist" and the "counterterrorist." Ultimately, *Demons* (re)presents a fantastic menagerie of types of political violence that have been called "terrorism," and Dostoevsky offers unusual insight into the fundamental discursive mechanism underlying terror/ism in all of its forms.

Historians have long regarded the trial of Vera Zasulich in March 1878 for the attempted assassination of the governor of St. Petersburg as inaugurating the first wave of terrorism that culminated in tsaricide in 1881. While literary scholars have noted the influence of Zasulich's trial on Dmitry's trial for parricide at the end of *The Brothers Karamazov*, its far-reaching influence in the novel has not been fully appreciated. Part Three, "The Little Devil Sitting in Your Heart," therefore begins with a close reading of the Zasulich trial in order to demonstrate how her lawyer, Peter Alexandrov, presented Zasulich as a sentimental subject and her act of violence as "a cry of the heart." Dostoevsky's own literary debt to the trial becomes clear in the pivotal chapter "Rebellion," but also in the children's plot, where Dostoevsky recapitulates the dilemma of outraged feeling and the desire to retaliate in order to show that the little devil of terrorism sits in even the most innocent of hearts: it is in crucial respects the reaction of innocence to evil in the world. Yet the solution to retributive violence that Dostoevsky proposes through the elder Zosima, as well as Alyosha's foundational speech at the stone, mirrors in important ways the phenomenon of terrorism that the novel seeks to overcome.

Part Four, "The Beautiful Dead (Deed)," commences the story of "the Terrorism's" afterlife, when the party of the People's Will had been decimated in Russia. Only then does the terrorist's image emerge from obscurity to be broadcast to the world. Writers and visual artists in Russia and abroad, such as Ivan Turgenev, Ilya Repin, Vsevolod Garshin, and the émigré revolutionary Sergei Stepniak-Kravchinsky, sought to create the terrorist's body and face as legible signs, and yet the moral duality implicit in their crime/deed of heroic martyrdom immensely complicated the task of rendering an unambiguous image. The image also posed a challenge to the writer's word, and Part Four examines the anxiety inspired in writers and government officials alike by the mimetic power of terrorism and the terrorist.

The Epilogue, "All of Europe Thrills to the Horror," sketches the reception of Russian Nihilism cum terrorism in Western Europe in the 1880s as a preliminary investigation of how and why the Russian brand won the distinction of being the first manifestation of "modern terrorism." In conclusion, I come full circle by showing how Nihilism and terrorism were instrumental in arousing Western interest in Russia more generally, and especially in Russian literature, which was regarded as the privileged source for understanding this new scourge. On more than one level, then, terrorism succeeded as "the use of violence to provoke consciousness, to evoke certain feelings of sympathy and revulsion"; in this case, to awaken the West to Russia as the birthplace of the men—or "monsters"—of the future.

Prologue

"Just You Wait! (Uzho tebe!)"

> As in Hamlet, the Prince of the rotten state, everything begins by the apparition of a specter, more precisely, by the waiting for this apparition. The anticipation is at once impatient, anxious, and fascinated: the thing ("this thing") will end up coming.
>
> JACQUES DERRIDA, *Specters of Marx*

Karl Marx's *Communist Manifesto* famously begins with an act of political prophecy that is cast as an act of ghost seeing. "A specter is haunting Europe," intones the manifesto, but in the ironic rather than Gothic mode.[1] For the inveterate materialist, Marx, there could of course be no "real" specter. Instead, "the heads of Europe... Pope and Tsar; Metternich and Guizot; French Radicals and German Spies"— all alike are spooked by what amounts to "nursery tales" of communism that they themselves have fabricated. Marx's sly intention is to debunk these tales by turning on the lights and "manifesting" the real thing!²

Since the excesses of the French Revolution had unsettled European imaginations, Gothic tropes had been marshaled to frame the menace of revolution and terror in terms of all the horrors—natural, supernatural, historical—known to man: demons and monsters, diabolical secret societies and the Spanish Inquisition.[3] Marx's spectral metaphor, however, was certainly better suited to the acts of proto-terrorism that punctuated the first half of the nineteenth century than to the proletarian revolution that he heralded. Throughout the first half of the century, individuals or small conspiratorial bands had materialized suddenly, seemingly out of nowhere, and wreaked a terrible vengeance only to suffer an equally terrible punishment. But they continued to live on in popular memory and lore.[4] These "specters," wielding daggers and, more devastatingly, "infernal machines," haunted the nightmares and waking hours of the heads of Europe.[5] Napoleon I, the ultimate usurper, political assassin, and "enemy of the human race," himself constituted one of the most frequent targets of assassination plots, as did the succession of restored Bourbon monarchs.

The emergence of terrorism in Russia is unthinkable without this larger European context of social revolution and national liberation. Indeed, *la Grande Revolution* was the fountainhead of the revolutionary *imaginaire*, and revolutionary leaders such as Robespierre and Marat served as the models and idols for Russian radicals, as did the charismatic leaders of national liberation movements such as Garibaldi and Mazzini. Yet quite possibly the only thing that "the Russian Method" owed directly to the French Terror was its very general means— violence—and the dusty epithet "terrorist" that was used primarily to refer to the historical actors of 1793 but had no real contemporary salience until after 1881, for reasons that will become clear.[6] In other words, it would be a mistake to view Russian revolutionary terrorism in a direct line of descent from the French rather than as a phenomenon arising from a Russian cultural ground that had absorbed and adapted those influences.

Debates about the old or new provenance of terrorism are not, in fact, new. In Russia the People's Will's "Emperor Hunt" in 1880-81 generated vigorous public debate about the causes and genealogy of terrorism/*kramola*, with some commentators harking back to Dmitry Karakozov's attempted tsaricide in 1866 and others to Vera Zasulich's attack on F. F. Trepov in 1878, and still others all the way to back to antiquity, to the tyrannicides Harmodius and Aristogeiton and Brutus.[7] As is so often the case, this debate among contemporaries presaged the still unresolved debate among scholars about terrorism's historical origins. This prologue stakes an intermediate position by beginning before the first actual occurrence of Russian revolutionary terrorism—Karakozov's—and illuminating the way in which presentiments and prefigurations of terrorism both in and around literature laid the ground for its moral-symbolic matrix long before the first shot was fired.

Presentiments

In June 1790, when a travelogue entitled *A Journey from St. Petersburg to Moscow* by an anonymous author was placed in the hands of Catherine II of Russia, a few pages sufficed for her to recognize its true nature.[8] "The purpose of this book is clear on every page: its author, infected and full of the French madness, is trying in every possible way to break down respect for authority and for the authorities, to stir up in the people indignation [negodovanie] against their superiors and the government."[9] Even while the identity of the author and his intentions remained obscure, for Catherine the case was cut-and-dried. Her private secretary recorded that the empress in an unguarded moment "was graciously pleased to say that he [the author] is a rebel worse than Pugachev," referring to the audacious Cossack leader Emilian Pugachev, who in the early years of Catherine's reign had threatened her empire by claiming to be the legitimate sovereign, Peter III, and leading a vast and bloody rebellion in Southwest Siberia.[10] Pugachev was ultimately betrayed, captured, and brought to Moscow in an iron cage, where the empress's sovereignty was reasserted when the pretender was decapitated, drawn and quartered before the massed public on Bolotnaya Square.

As a matter of fact, the author turned out to be one of Catherine's own protégés, the upstanding chief of the St. Petersburg customs office, Alexander Radishchev. While the mystery of the *Journey*'s authorship was expeditiously solved, the mystery of the author's motivation, intentions, and above all abysmal timing baffled contemporaries and posterity.[11] The *Journey*, begun as early as 1780 and submitted to the censor in May 1789, appeared in Petersburg bookshops in June 1790 at precisely the moment when the political turmoil in France spurred Catherine to drop the pose of enlightened monarch and revert to the more tried-and-true forms of despotic rule. For whatever reason, Radishchev failed to heed the signs and plunged ahead with the laborious printing of the *Journey* and its distribution to local booksellers as well as to close friends and associates, who were not as oblivious as its author to the folly and danger that it represented.[12]

Catherine's intensely dialogic reading of the *Journey* is preserved in ten pages of notes, written in her own hand in the book itself. Her conjectures about the author and his motives are a model of police hermeneutics and are worth quoting extensively for the profile of the late eighteenth-century *kramol'nik* that they produce. "He is probably a Martinist or something similar." (Radishchev rejected Martinist mysticism and quietism but dedicated the *Journey* to his close friend, the Martinist Alexei Kutuzov). "He has learning enough, and has read many books." (Radishchev had been handpicked as one of a select group of young noblemen to study abroad at the University of Leipzig.) "He has a melancholy temperament" (Radishchev's narrator frequently succumbs to tears and recriminations) "and sees everything in a very somber light; consequently he takes a bilious black and yellow view of things."[13] Catherine repeatedly notes, in conjunction with specific passages, the author's unorthodox metaphysics and his dispositional indisposition that lead in the end to "unbridled" (neobuzdannyi) pages reflecting an "unbridled mentality" (neobuzdannoe umstvovanie). Ultimately, of course, Catherine gravitated toward the explanation that made the most sense to *her*. From the point of view of the Machiavellian empress who had led the Imperial Guards in a coup that deposed (and later murdered) her husband, Radishchev's writings presented a classic case of frustrated ambition and envy, or in Nietzsche's terms, "ressentiment." "He seems to have been born with unbridled ambition, to have prepared himself for the highest offices, but since he has not yet attained them, the gall of his impatience has poured out over everything established."[14]

In short, the writer/*kramol'nik* was a gloomy intellectual with a rebellious, impatient streak whose frustrated dreams of grandeur led him to lash out against the established order.

Once in prison and in the hands of Catherine's notorious chief of the Secret Chancellery S. I. Sheshkovsky, Radishchev was required to write a confession, and then another, and finally a third, all of which failed to satisfactorily account for his "crime" in the eyes of his persecutors as well as his historians. Yet the first confession, deemed the most implausible, is revelatory for what Radishchev thought he might say to mollify the empress's wrath, to deemphasize the *Journey's* political content, and, most importantly, to portray his "deed" as mere words, and highly unoriginal words at that. To that end, Radishchev confessed to being motivated by literary ambition and under sway of first Laurence Sterne's *Sentimental Journey Through France and Italy* (1768) and later, the Abbé de Raynal's *Histoire des deux Indes* (1770). "I began reading it [*Histoire*] in 1780 or 1781. I liked his style (slog). I admired his rhetorical tone as eloquence, his audacious expressions I considered to be in excellent taste, and seeing him universally esteemed, I wanted to imitate his style (slog).... And so I may truthfully state that Raynal's style, drawing me on from delusion to delusion, led to the completion of my insane book."[15] Significantly, Radishchev did not plead insanity for himself, but for his book. Instead, he pleaded guilty to literary ambition and attempted to divert attention from the *Journey's* political content to its style. Historians and literary scholars, following the lead of contemporaries such as Alexander Pushkin, have taken Radishchev to task for his "barbaric" style and have singled out his sentimental excesses as the most objectionable element.[16] Yet as Radishchev's personal correspondence attests, these sentimental excesses were scarcely imitative literary window dressing, but they were integral to Radishchev's language of the self, its perceptions, appraisals, values, and goals.[17]

For the record, though, it is necessary to note that Radishchev's travelogue is wildly heterogeneous and boasts a number of styles, genres, and surrogate narrators. Radishchev's own narrator presents a rather incoherent personality, somewhat schizophrenically alternating between the two antipodes/"antimodes" of the Enlightenment: satire and sentimentalism.[18] Scholars have recently underscored the problem of saying what, exactly, satire is and have expanded the concept to encompass an aptitude, faculty, or even a disposition.[19] The biggest misconception about satire is that it must be funny, when in fact its most fundamental requirement is that it be lethal.[20] Historically, satire has been a powerful and double-edged weapon, demolishing its targets while endangering its practitioners if their victims were capable of retaliation.[21] Centuries and even millennia abound with examples of representational defamation in satire and caricature that laid the groundwork for actual physical annihilation.

Quite clearly preferring its satirical aspect to its sentimental one, Pushkin characterized the *Journey* as "a satirical call to *vozmushchenie*," a word that originally denoted political "revolt" but by the late eighteenth century had been interiorized as an emotion—"outraged indignation." Radishchev's satire targets petty demons—corrupt bureaucrats, fawning courtiers, and Prince Potemkin's oyster fetish—and certainly arouses contempt and derision, but is nothing so galvanizing as a "call to revolt." By contrast, the emotional charge of Radishchev's sentimental effusions lights the fuse of indignation that would explode into political violence.[22] After languishing in critical ignominy, sentimentalism was rehabilitated by literary and cultural historians who challenged the truism that its tropes invariably served conservative values such as duty, honor, and filial piety. Instead, scholars were struck by the way its overtly emotional language and the supreme value of *sensibilité* at its core coincided with progressive shifts in political, social, and cultural norms.[23] The historian of emotions William Reddy went further and argued that sentimentalism's lachrymose tropes offered a potent means of converting benevolent feelings such as generosity and pity into anger at tyranny and injustice. Thus sentimentalism led to self-sacrifice and political action.[24] In his study of French revolutionary rhetoric, Reddy observes that it was a truism for "sentimentalist" Jacobins that it did. Revolutionary publicists, most notably Jean Paul Marat, employed what Reddy refers to as a "conceptual structure" in his daily diatribes for *L'ami du peuple*, which began with graphic and heart-rending depictions of misery and atrocity and ended with a rousing exhortation to violence in the name of justice.[25]

The Peter and Paul Fortress where Radishchev was imprisoned as of July 1790 did not subscribe to *L'ami du peuple*, so it is likely that Radishchev discovered this "conceptual structure" long beforehand, possibly thanks to Raynal's anti-slavery invective. In any case, Radishchev's purpose was not to incite mobs of hungry Petersburgers to hang aristocrats from lampposts; his project was more subtle and far-reaching. Much like his heirs, the Men of the Sixties, Radishchev intended to create new men, not *ab ovo*, but from the indifferent material at hand—namely, his own readers.[26]

Radishchev's challenge was two-fold: first, he had to substantially renovate the framework, such as it was, of emotional and moral norms, so that it incorporated Enlightenment ideals of human dignity and autonomy; and second, he had to create citizens who would respond with moral indignation to their violation. Critics have bewailed the *Journey*'s repetitiveness as a stylistic flaw, but it is better appreciated as a conditioning device aimed at the reader. In the first several chapters of the *Journey* the narrator, or his like-minded surrogates, recounts dramatic experiences that repeatedly rehearse the same "conceptual structure" or sequence of perception, appraisal, physiological response and feeling that are the constituents of consciousness.[27] The reader must enter into the immediacy of experience entailed in the first-person narration, to be drawn into the fictional simulation of the proper response. This would be all well and good, were it not for the fact that the chain reaction inevitably ends in violence. Through the repetition and intensification of this conceptual structure, Radishchev lays the groundwork for the moral, emotional, and legal sanction of political murder.

The first and most basic task of Radishchev's traveler is to direct attention and awaken perception to the injustices that have hitherto remained invisible to him and his compatriots. No sooner does the traveler take tearful leave of his dear ones in St. Petersburg, than he notices a peasant serf plowing his land on Sunday. After making inquiries, the traveler discovers the extent of the peasant's exploitation by his master. Radishchev's narrator is subsequently overcome by visceral feelings of outrage and indignation ("This thought made my blood boil!" [Siia mysl' vsiu krov' v mne vospalila!]),[28] whereupon the boiling blood provokes an unexpected outburst that gleefully prophesies popular retribution: "Tremble, cruel-hearted landlord! On the brow of each of your peasants I see your condemnation written."[29]

The traveler and his reader are now primed for an even more shocking perception and appraisal, which follows forthwith. "I happened to notice my servant, who was sitting up on the box in front of me, swaying side to side. Suddenly, I felt a chill coursing through my veins, sending the blood to my head and mantling my cheeks with a blush. I felt so ashamed of myself that I could scarcely keep from bursting into tears. 'In your anger,' I said to myself 'you denounce the proud master who wears out his peasants in the field: but are you not doing the same or even worse yourself?'"[30]

The physiological experience of shame (the chill, the blush, the tears) accompanies the narrator's realization of his own hypocrisy.[31] As a social emotion, shame entails an alienation from the self and the internalization of the other's view of contempt and opprobrium. This intersubjective understanding of the self as an object of another's righteous indignation and hostility leads Radishchev to sanction that very violence, but this time against *himself*. "Do you know what is written in the fundamental law, in the heart of every man? He whom I strike has the right to strike *me* [italics mine]."[32]

A notion of reciprocity underlies all sociability as one of the primary moral foundations, and the traveler's maxim is recognizably a hybrid of Biblical formulations of reciprocity (the Old Testament "An eye for an eye" and the New Testament "Do unto others as you would have them do unto you") but receives a secular update through the Enlightenment language of rights. At the next station, Chudovo, the circuit repeats itself, but this time through the narrative offices of the traveler's friend, Ch__. Whereas the traveler's reflections at Lyubani took the form of an internal monologue, Ch__'s account achieves its emotional intensity through the riveting tale of mortal terror of shipwrecked sailors facing imminent death and Ch__'s outrage when subordinates refuse to wake their sleeping commander to mount a rescue operation. Ch__'s indignation is a full-body affair that requires multiple outlets (trembling, spitting, tearing his hair) when he finally is admitted to the commander. "I trembled with the anger of outraged humanity. 'If you are a hard sleeper, you should have yourself waked with a hammer on your head when people are drowning and crying for your help. . . . I was unable to finish my speech, almost spat in his face, and walked away. I tore my hair with rage. I made a thousand plans to wreak vengeance on this beastly commander, not on my account but on behalf of all humanity."[33]

Radishchev reiterates the proposition, this time through Ch__, that one who does harm or allows harm to happen ought to be harmed himself—better yet, by his own hand (hammer). What is new is the spur to Ch__'s indignation; it is not merely a case of individual injustice, but of one done to "all humanity." His "thousand plans to wreak vengeance . . . not for myself, but on behalf of all humanity" [ne za sebia, no za chelovechestva] go beyond any petty scheme for individual revenge. Radishchev's surrogate narrator relents only when he realizes that his humanitarian vengeance was doomed to illegibility. "But when I came to my senses, I realized, from many similar instances, that my revenge would be fruitless and that I would only be taken for a madman [beshenyi] or an evildoer [zloi chelovek]; so I reconciled myself."[34] Yet far from reconciling himself, after Ch__ discovers that society shares neither his moral framework nor his acute sense of indignation, he abandons St. Petersburg in search of something resembling Rousseau's "state of nature."

Clearly, Radishchev's circuits are not mere repetitions, but elaborations in which narrative detail, emotional intensity, and moral claims/imperatives mount. They culminate at Zaytsovo, in the account of another of the traveler's old friends, the judge Krestyanin. An exemplar of Enlightenment humanitarianism, Krestyanin presided over a case that involved an exploitative landlord and his equally abusive family. In Krestyanin's extended telling, the entire family gleefully participated in devising increasingly refined ways to oppress and torture their serfs. Krestyanin (Radishchev) heaps abuse upon abuse and detail upon detail so that the reader's indignation and horror reach a pitch. In the end, the landlord's family schemes to commit the ultimate outrage—the abduction and rape of a beautiful serf girl on the eve of her wedding. Radishchev orchestrates a scene of nail-biting suspense and emotional tension as the girl's fiancé and his old father are first flogged for trying to intervene, then forced to flee for their lives, and finally cornered while they fend off their masters' attack. At this point, the peasants (and the reader with them) are primed to join the melee. "They sympathized with the young peasant and, infuriated against their masters, they gathered around their fellow to defend him. Seeing this, the assessor himself ran up, began to curse them, and struck the first man he met so violently with his cane that he fell senseless to the ground. This was the signal for a general attack. They surrounded their four masters and, in short, beat them to death on the spot."[35] This is not the end of the story, for Krestyanin tells how he scandalized local society by taking the peasants' side. "The peasants who had killed their master were guilty of murder. But was it not forced upon them? Was not the murdered assessor himself the cause of it? . . . The innocence of the defendants was at least for me, a mathematical certainty" [matematicheskaia iasnost'].[36]

Krestyanin first frames the peasants' murder of the landlord as an act self-defense: "am I guilty if I draw my sword in self-defense and deliver society from a member who disturbs its peace?"[37] But later he elaborates an argument based on Enlightenment ideas of the equality of all individuals and the priority of the law of nature over positive law, insisting that by the commission of his heinous acts, the landlord placed himself outside the jurisdiction of positive law: "Then natural law [zakon prirody] was born, and the power of the insulted citizen, who receives no redress through positive law, became a reality."[38]

Krestyanin/Radishchev drew on natural right theory that was well established in Western Europe and had an avid following among Girondists and Jacobins alike (As Catherine observed: "The French venom is poured out").[39] Natural law is the ultimate foundation of the citizen's right to kill, to exact justice outside the positive legal framework of the state, and Krestyanin articulates its foundational premises:[40] "whosoever dares wound him [the citizen] in his natural and inviolable right is a criminal. Woe to him, if the civil law does not punish him. He will be marked as a pariah by his fellow citizens, and may whosoever has sufficient power exact vengeance against him for his evildoing."[41] The notion that "whosoever has sufficient power" may rectify wrong and exact vengeance has a long genealogy, extending back to ancient justifications of tyrannicide.[42] The malefactor who stands in violation of natural law is in violation of nature itself, is condemned to the status of "pariah" or in the Latin formulation to *hostis humani generis* ("enemy of the human race").[43] As such, he loses not only the protections of positive law but the status of citizen and may be killed by anyone with impunity. The discourses of natural law and sentimentalism share fundamental premises, and in its Enlightenment incarnation, natural law is in many respects the rationalization of the *feeling of what is right*, as Krestyanin's formulation so pithily illustrates: "On rational grounds my heart finds them not guilty, and the death of the assessor, although violent, just."[44]

Catherine's initial response to these passages was a coolly commonsensical rebuttal: "But this whole argument can be easily overthrown by a single question: If someone does evil, does that give someone else the right to do even greater evil? Answer: of course not."[45] This "dialogue" between Catherine and Radishchev established the terms of the debate that was to go on for more than a century. On the one hand, Krestyanin's peasants were "guilty but not guilty": guilty of murder, yes, but not guilty according to the head, the heart, and natural law. On the other hand, reciprocity in the form of vengeance is neither more moral nor legal within the framework of the state's positive law. Catherine recognized that Krestyanin's disquisition was founded on principles "completely destructive of the laws and which have turned France upside down," and her observation, "It would not have been surprising if the governor had arrested the loose talker," leaves no doubt that *she* would have.

It is difficult to say what influence Radishchev's own "loose talk" had on his direct contemporaries, although his legacy is beyond dispute.[46] According to his own uncertain estimate, he printed several hundred copies of his *Journey*, and once the incendiary content was discovered, supposedly all but twenty-two copies were burned. Both before and after they were, the *Journey* was a hot commodity in the Russian capital, and multiple dispatches of foreign envoys attest to the fact that Radishchev had become a cause célèbre in Russia and in Western Europe.[47] In the short run, Radishchev's attempt to reform his fellow men by micro-engineering their responses bore little fruit. Many of Radishchev's social peers and even his closest associates were dismayed and alarmed by the content of the *Journey*, even if they regretted his harsh fate (some did not).[48] Pushkin declared, perhaps for the censorship's sake, that Radishchev's sentimental histrionics bored him and made him laugh—undoubtedly not the reaction that Radishchev had hoped for.[49] It seems, however, that Radishchev hoped for very little. In the end, his outraged humanitarians reject acts of violence because of their futility and illegibility, not their immorality. In the meantime, Radishchev has done all he could to make such acts legible, moral, and exemplary.

When Radishchev was charged for his crime, it was not under laws governing speech or the press, since Catherine had legalized private presses in 1783 and Police Chief Ryleev, Catherine's lackadaisical censor, had passed the innocuous-seeming travelogue without, apparently, bothering to read it.[50] Instead, the prosecution threw the book at Radishchev and marshaled every law from the archaic *Ulozhenie* of 1649 and Peter's Military and Naval statutes that applied to disorderly conduct, disturbing the peace, and open revolt against the sovereign.[51] It goes without saying that none of these statutes were remotely applicable to writing a book. In trying Radishchev, the St. Petersburg Criminal Court proceeded with extraordinary precautions, as if Radishchev were the resurrected Pugachev himself rather than an unassuming customs officer. Fettered and under heavy guard, Radishchev was not told the crime with which he was charged, nor was he given an opportunity to defend himself. The text of the *Journey* was considered so inflammatory that the chancery clerks were dismissed while excerpts of his book were read out in court, and the sentence was a foregone conclusion: exile to faraway Nerchinsk (on the Chinese border) bound in irons, followed by death by beheading.[52] However, thanks to the timely conclusion of peace with Sweden on September 4, Catherine was provided the necessary pretext to indulge her love of mercy, and Radishchev's sentence was commuted to ten years exile in faraway Ilimsk, in Siberia. This mitigation did not prevent Radishchev from becoming the first martyr in a two-fold martyrology of Russian literature and the Russian revolutionary movement, as Alexander Herzen, echoing the traveler's sentimental idiom in the preface to his 1858 edition of the *Journey*, enthused, "How can the memory of this martyr be anything but dear to our hearts?"[53]

Apparitions

In 1836 an unprecedented vision crystallized for the poet Alexander Pushkin. Less than a year before his death in a duel, Pushkin made his final attempt to produce a publishable version of his narrative poem *The Bronze Horseman* (Mednyi vsadnik), and he wrote one of the first exemplars of secular biography for inclusion in the *Contemporary*, a biography of Alexander Radishchev. Neither work could appear in print as written: Pushkin was able to legally publish only the Prologue of the *Bronze Horseman*, and the biography of Radishchev had to wait until 1857 to see the light of day.[54] Scholars have recognized that the two texts are linked by factors besides their frustrated publication histories and in fact present distinct visions of the same phenomenon, seen from different angles and with varying degrees of ambivalence.[55]

For his biographical sketch, Pushkin assumed the role of historian and made use of all the available documentary material, including oral histories with prominent contemporaries such as Anatoly Speransky.[56] He begins by rehashing the official explanation for Radishchev's deed as author(iz)ed by Catherine. In this version, Radishchev fell under the influence of the Martinists, and the "mysteriousness [tainstvennost'] of their conversations inflamed his imagination."[57] However, through a series of subtle rhetorical moves, Pushkin arrives at a completely different picture. Pushkin asks his reader to recall "the political circumstances of 1791, the severity of the laws, the cruelty of the people who surrounded Catherine."[58] When the positively brutish spirit of the times is recalled, Radishchev's crime "will seem to us the act of a madman" (pokazhetsia nam deistviem sumasshedshego). Pushkin has insured that the opposite will be the case, and Radishchev's "crime" appears more than justified. Here begins a carefully calibrated shift from a profile of the seditionist as "madman" to a profile of a morally and psychologically competent agent.

> An inconsequential person [mel'kii chelovek], a person entirely without power, entirely without support, dares to take up arms against the general order, against autocracy, against Catherine! And notice: a conspirator relies upon the united forces of his comrades; the member of a secret society, in the case of failure, prepares to win mercy with a denunciation, or, given the multiplicity of the like-minded, relies upon their impunity. But Radishchev is alone. He doesn't have comrades or any like-minded. In the case of failure—but what success could he expect?—he answers for everything, he alone presents himself as the victim of the law. We never honored Radishchev as a great man. His act always seemed to us a crime, something inexcusable, . . . but with all of that, we can't not acknowledge in him a criminal with an unusual spirit; a

political fanatic of course, but acting with unusual selflessness and with some kind of chivalric conscientiousness.[59]

For Pushkin it is tremendously significant that Radishchev was a lone and "mel'kii" individual (he was neither the member of a political conspiracy nor a military uprising) who "dared" not just to oppose Catherine, but to tilt against the entire established order. While accepting and even exaggerating Catherine's perception of Radishchev's book as the ultimate attack ("dares to take up arms against the general order, against autocracy, against Catherine!"), he reverses her valuation. Pushkin cannily evades authorial responsibility for his new vision with formulations that suggest the consensus of polite society ("it will seem to us," "we never honored," and "we can't not acknowledge"), but these same phrases enable him to mint a newly authorized image of Radishchev. This new image retains the requisite condemnation (indicated by the expressions "crime," "inexcusable," and "political fanatic") but is tinged with admiration—Pushkin even implicitly concedes the possibility of considering Radishchev a "great man!"—and the unmistakable aura of the heroic. Like all of Pushkin's famed characterizations, this image is distilled to its essence: an "inexcusable crime" committed by a selfless and moralistic political fanatic who is a martyr for his cause. Yet it bears repeating that Radishchev's "inexcusable crime" *took place entirely within the symbolic order and consisted of writing a book.*

A similar, equally symbolic assault forms the climactic episode of Pushkin's *The Bronze Horseman*, when the poem's protagonist, Evgenii, challenges the looming equestrian statue of Peter I. The *poema* begins with a Prologue that is an ambivalent paean to Peter the Great's creation of a new, Western capital hewn from the primeval wilderness, but it shifts quickly to the story of his protagonist, Evgenii, in the devastating flood of 1824.[60] Evgenii, as Pushkin takes pains to emphasize, is a new type of literary hero. He is not the noble grandee or the Childe Harold manqué, but the "householder" who seeks contentment and meaning within the sphere of work, love, and family happiness.[61] As natural disaster strikes and the flood waters rise, Evgenii is thwarted in his frantic quest to reach his fiancée on Vasilevsky Island. Stranded atop the life-saving perch of a stone lion, Evgenii watches helplessly while the islands are engulfed. Pushkin's emphasis is on his captive position as a helpless witness unable to tear his eyes from the scene of destruction, while the monument of Peter I "turns its back" on Evgenii's plight.[62] When the storm abates, Evgenii discovers the city's and his own life's devastation. The flood has swept away the last trace of his loved ones and hence of his own identity.

Doomed to wander Peter's city as an addled vagabond, Evgenii becomes something ontologically indeterminate and unnatural: "in this way he ekes out his unfortunate life, as neither beast, nor human; not this and not that, neither denizen of earth nor lifeless phantom."[63] With the return of time (the season of the flood) and to the place of his tortured helplessness, the madman experiences a moment of lucidity in which he grasps the unnatural cause of his and the city's disaster and mounts his challenge to the autocrat.

> Around the idol's foundation
> The poor madman circled
> Throwing wild glances at the countenance
> Of the ruler of half the world.
> His chest contracted, and he laid
> His brow against the cold bars.
> His eyes grew dim but his heart was inflamed.
> His blood boiled. He became morbid
> And, grinding his teeth and clenching his hands,
> As if possessed by dark forces,
> "Fine, wonder-working builder of marvels!—
> He whispered, shaking furiously,—
> "Just you wait!"[64]

Pushkin alters our perception of Evgenii, who no longer appears as an innocuous "insignificant man," but as a menacing madman. For all his fury and derangement, he does nothing more bizarre than say a few words to a statue. So few, in fact, that the act as gesture matters no less than the words themselves. So few, in fact, that the poem demands the reader's active collaboration to make his words signify. Within the context of the poem, Evgenii's outburst telegraphs a narrative of blame and retribution. The autocrat is the creative destroyer and the architect of unnatural disaster—the founder of a city that is a deathtrap for his subjects—but it is only a matter of time until the roles are reversed (Just you wait!). Evgenii, however, knows better than to wait, and not a moment too soon, he bolts.

> It seemed to him that the terrifying tsar
> Quietly turned his face,

> engulfed by wrath, toward him.
> And he runs across the empty square
> And it seems he hears behind him
> The thunderous hoof-beats
> . . . .
> The Bronze Horseman pursues him
> On a resonantly leaping steed,
> And all night the poor madman,
> Wherever his footsteps carried him,
> Behind him the Bronze Horseman
> Pranced with a heavy tread.⁶⁵

Since the flood Evgenii has been afflicted by terrors as formless as he himself. Now his audacious act gives them sculptural but equally monstrous form. Nonetheless, Pushkin has carefully engineered it so that the ontological status of Evgenii's terror is indeterminate: either Evgenii is hallucinating in his madness, or the monument has come to life.⁶⁶ By treading this fine line of the fantastic and inducing hesitation, Pushkin emphasizes that terror is quite independent of any reality. "It seems to him," "it seems he hears"—the actual agent of terror may not exist because terror, once evoked, possesses its own agency. Whether or not the Bronze Horseman in fact pursues Evgenii is completely irrelevant. Evgenii was already a terrorized subject; now he is an effectively subjugated subject. After the night of terror has passed,

> ... from that time, when it happened
> That he had to walk by that square
> His face expressed confusion.
> He quickly pressed his hand to his heart
> As if to ease its pain
> Doffed his worn cap
> Did not lift his chastened eyes
> And gave it wide berth.⁶⁷

Pushkin's vision in *The Bronze Horseman* is both more complex and ambivalent than his vision of Radishchev. While in the latter he deals with the fate of the individual subject, in his poema he contemplates the history and fate of Russia. This wide angle allows Pushkin to see terror/ism as a generative as well as destructive force. It also brings into view the cyclicality, specularity, and fantasticality of terrorism. Peter's creative destruction calls forth that of nature, Evgenii, and Peter. This cyclicality is based in turn on specularity, on the mirror-symmetries between architects of unnatural disasters. As Kevin Platt succinctly observes: "the crowned revolutionary is as much a ritual prototype for the rebellious modern individual as he is for the later autocrat . . . the autocratic state that crushes its people in the name of their well-being, the rebel who seeks to overthrow the past but ultimately reenacts it, the individual who should be the beneficiary of cultural and political progress yet instead becomes its victim."[68] Yet scholars who equate state and insurgent terrorism often make too much of this symmetry. The unappeasable wrath of the bronze colossus overwhelms the futile outrage of a tattered vagabond, just as the Neva's floodwaters had overwhelmed Peter's city.

Pushkin had begun *The Bronze Horseman* at Boldino in October 1833 and in December of that year submitted the final draft version to his personal censor, Tsar Nicholas I, who unsurprisingly struck out this entire episode, along with other details offensive to his highness. While Pushkin did consent to publish only the Prologue of the poem, he worked ceaselessly to restore the climactic scene of Evgenii's challenge in a way that would be acceptable to his royal censor. He died without succeeding, but ironically, the fully restored *Bronze Horseman* was published by Apollon Maikov in 1880, when the People's Will had appeared to make good on Evgenii's threat.[69] Yet even—and especially—in 1880, Pushkin's much earlier and bolder poems, which constitute the outstanding Russian examples of the pan-European "cult of the dagger," could not see the light.[70] Scholars have seen the *Bronze Horseman* as a reflection of the crushed Decembrist uprising in 1825, and Evgenii's gesture could be read as a pale shadow of the overconfident challenge mounted by the Decembrists in both life and literature a decade earlier. Among his intimate friends, Pushkin counted those who participated in the Decembrist uprising against Nicholas I, the only actual challenge to sovereign authority that transpired outside of court circles between the Pugachev uprising and Karakozov's attempted tsaricide in 1866.[71] As Yuri Lotman and others have observed, the Decembrist cohort drew their models for historic/heroic behavior from literature, both neoclassical and Romantic (Byronic), and there was nothing innocent about their preferred choice of plots that hinged upon the heroic violence of regicide and martyrdom; in fact, the "literary plot" provided a ready-made assassination plot, as Lotman observes: "Pushkin's exclamation, 'Here is Caesar; where then is Brutus?' can easily be deciphered as a program for a future act."[72]

Ghost Stories

Less than a decade later, at the height of Nicholas I's stifling reign, the even more insignificant hero of Nikolai Gogol's *The Overcoat* (1842) suffers a fate similar to Evgenii's when he is "roasted" by "an important person" (znachitel'noe litso), a bureaucrat who delights in terrorizing subordinates and petitioners alike.[73] When Akaky Akakievich's new overcoat, acquired with much scrimping and sacrifice, is stolen, the "important person" reacts to Akaky Akakievich's direct appeal for help in recovering the overcoat as nothing short of sedition. "Where did you pick up such a spirit? Where did you pick up such ideas? What is this rebelliousness (chto za buistvo takoe) spreading among the young against their chiefs and higher-ups?"[74] Confronted with this allegation, and with the important person's assertion of his identity as an insuperable authority, "Akaky Akakievich was simply stricken, he swayed, shook all over and was unable to stand. . . . He was carried out almost motionless."[75] Like Evgenii, Akaky Akakievich dies a victim of *terror*, not from the loss of his overcoat.

The story doesn't end there, however, because Gogol proceeds to shed the most prescient and piercing satirical light on the birth of revolutionary terrorism from state terror's corpses. Rumors begin to circulate about the nocturnal depredations of a dead clerk (presumably, Akaky Akakievich), who on the pretext of his stolen overcoat, terrorizes St. Petersburg officialdom by stripping the overcoats from all shoulders, regardless of rank. There is no better satire of a government's hysterical and counterproductive counterterrorism than what Gogol gives us: "An order was issued for the police to catch the dead man at all costs, dead or alive, and punish him in the harshest manner, as an example to others."[76] The absurdity of an order that elides the ontological distinction between living and dead results in the inability of law enforcement to tell the difference—and renders the authorities equally terrified of both. Ultimately, the "important person" gets his comeuppance when he is accosted by Akaky Akakievich's ghost, demanding this time not the return of his *own* overcoat, but the "important person's" overcoat. Not only does the "important person" "nearly die" of fear and hasten to give the ghostly avenger his overcoat, but thereafter he substantially modifies his despotic behavior.

As Gogol's *The Overcoat* so clearly demonstrates, terrorism is easily narrated as poetic justice. Ghosts, after all, have historically obliged as society's default avengers when worldly authorities fail to serve justice; with their supernatural métier, they are the literal first terrorists. But *The Overcoat* is rare because while it is clearly social/political satire, terrorism itself is emplotted here as comedy, in the traditional generic sense of a narrative with a happy ending. In *The Overcoat* precisely *terrorism* secures redress for the denuded and downtrodden and successfully achieves its political goal of bringing a tyrant to heel. "He [the 'important person'] even began to say 'How dare you, do you realize who is before you?' far less often to his subordinates."[77] Only the fact that Akaky's ghost so insistently demands the "important person's" overcoat ("It's *your* [italics mine] overcoat I need") and that the phantom becomes at the end of the story a much more formidable figure than the puny Akaky Akakievich ("The phantom, however, was much taller now, with an enormous mustache . . .") suggests the eventuality that insurgents, having wrested the "overcoats" of those in power, will become despotic VIPs in their own turn.

Thus, before the historical emergence of terrorism as a strategy and a practice it existed as a narrative in the cultural imaginary, in stories that not only portrayed the asymmetrical confrontation between state power and an avenging little man (in the altered state of madman or ghost), but also grasped that terrorism is (per the formulation of modern critical theory) as much a "social fact" as a "brute fact."[78] It bears emphasizing that Akaky's "ghost" is neither an actual ghost nor the actual terrorist; the *stories* (rumors) about "Akaky's" "ghost" are. Terrorism in *The Overcoat* is the specter conjured by a collective narrative that interprets completely opportunistic robberies by completely ordinary thieves as retribution for social/political injustice. If it were not for this narrative, the acts themselves (tearing the coats from official shoulders) would have neither their emotional nor their political effects. Terrorism is precisely the specter that rises not from the deed, but from the story about the deed.

In that same year, 1842, an article entitled "The Reaction in Germany" by Jules Elysard anticipated Marx's occult visions, and the revolutions of 1848, by six years. "All people and all men are filled with a kind of premonition, and everyone whose vital organs are not paralyzed faces with shuddering expectation the approaching future which will utter the redeeming word. Even in Russia, the boundless snow-covered kingdom so little known, and which perhaps also has a great future in store, even in Russia dark clouds are gathering, heralding storm. Oh, the air is sultry and pregnant with lightning."[79]

Elysard was the pseudonym under which the Russian nobleman Mikhail Bakunin wrote, and "The Reaction in Germany" marks his definitive turn from Hegelianism to a brand of revolutionary radicalism that he would create in his own image: anarchism. "The Reaction in Germany" channels a heady mixture of German Romanticism à la Goethe's *Faust* (1808), Hegelianism, and Christian apocalypticism. In Elysard's reading of Christian teleology, freedom is the ultimate realization of Christian love and justice, and the revolutionaries, although they are tarred as "enemies of Christ," are alone his true apostles. Not only are they to act, but to bear the redeeming word. This word, however, is negation, for, as Bakunin explains, "Revolutionary propaganda is in its deepest sense the *negation* of the existing conditions of the State, for, with respect to its innermost nature, it has no other program than the destruction of whatever order prevails at the time."[80] In *Faust*, Goethe's Mephistopheles introduces himself with the words "I am the spirit of perpetual negation" (Ich bin der Geist der stets verneint), but paradoxically, he also claims to be "A portion of that power that always desires evil, but constantly accomplishes good."[81] Enamoured with Romanticism's love of paradox, its fascination with dark forces and valorization of individual creativity, Elysard/Bakunin equates the spirit of negation with Christian love and ends by resoundingly affirming negation: "The passion for destruction is a creative passion, too!" To Bakunin, therefore, goes the credit for establishing destruction as a common denominator of art and revolution, a principle that had to await the advent of modernism to be most fully appreciated.

"The Innocent Cause of Fear"

In 1849, an official of the Interior Ministry, I. P. Liprandi, believed that he had uncovered a secret conspiracy to overthrow Russian autocracy. At the home of the refined but eccentric nobleman Mikhail Butashevich-Petrashevsky, well-educated young men from St. Petersburg's best families gathered late into the night to wine and sup, and, less innocently, to discuss "how to arouse indignation against the government in all classes of the population, how to arm peasants against landowners, officials against their authorized superiors; how to make use of the fanaticism of the [religious] schismatics—but among other groups, how to undermine and dissolve all religious feelings."[82] At least that is how the zealous Liprandi characterized these meetings to the sovereign, Nicholas I. After the revolutionary upheavals of 1848, Nicholas required little convincing that it was "an important matter, for even if it were just a lot of idle talk, it would still be criminal and intolerable."[83]

On April 22-23, when the young men who became known as the Petrashevtsy were arrested and incarcerated in the Peter and Paul Fortress, St. Petersburg society reacted with shocked disbelief and disavowed "anything adult" in the matter, insisting that their actions were only "schoolboy pranks, petty skylarking."[84] Nicholas I pulled his own prank nine months later, when on a frigid December morning, the prisoners were taken from their cells, led in shackles to a soldier-lined scaffold on Semyonovsky Square, and read their sentences. "The Field Criminal Court has condemned all to death sentence before a firing squad, and on December 19 his Majesty the Emperor personally wrote 'Confirmed.'"[85] Three men from the first row were tied to stakes before the firing squad, when the drums beat retreat and the tsar's messenger galloped onto the scene bearing the tsar's pardon and the real sentences.

"The retired lieutenant and litterateur," as Fyodor M. Dostoevsky was identified in the indictment, stood in the next row of prisoners to face the firing squad, and his sentence was commuted to Siberian penal servitude and service in the army. Among the formal crimes with which Dostoevsky was charged that merited the death penalty in the view of the High Military Court were: "attending meetings" at Petrashevsky's; "hearing criminal opinions expressed" about the emancipation of the serfs; himself taking part "in discussions about the severity of censorship"; and most damningly of all, reading aloud at Petrashevsky's gathering the critic Vissarion Belinsky's correspondence with the writer Nikolai Gogol.[86] Belinsky had launched the young Dostoevsky into the literary firmament as the "new Gogol" with his effusive praise of Dostoevsky's debut novel, *Poor Folk*. Since then, the two had grown estranged due to ideological, spiritual, and artistic differences. Nonetheless, when given the opportunity, Dostoevsky had eagerly read the dying Belinsky's last testament, his *Letter to Gogol*, before the appreciative audience at Petrashevsky's Friday gathering. Convalescing in Western

Europe and therefore safely out of reach of the tsarist secret police, Belinsky lambasted Gogol for his reactionary *Selections from Correspondence With Friends*, emphasizing that his opprobrium did not stem from personal insult, but "from an outraged sense of truth and human dignity."[87] Belinsky's letter was the most impassioned denunciation of serfdom and autocracy since Radishchev's *Journey*, although it did not contain any incitements to revolutionary violence, only a declaration of hatred for his former literary idol: "why if you had made an attempt on my life I could not have hated you more than I do for these disgraceful lines."[88]

Without knowing the precise nature of the charges, Dostoevsky was made to write an explanation in response to three broad questions that revolved around the kind of man Petrashevsky was, the kind of gatherings he held, and the kind of danger he presented ("does he pose a threat to society?"). Insisting that Petrashevsky was an "honest and noble man," Dostoevsky also stressed his "eccentricities and peculiarities," admitting that these had made Petrashevsky more attractive and interesting to him, along with his lack of practical sense ("he has more brains than sense").[89] But Dostoevsky was more interested in exposing the conditions that could lead to the suspicion and arrest of upstanding young men than in exposing the upstanding young men themselves. He turned the tables on his interrogators and himself demanded an "explanation." "And, in fact, why should the righteous man be fearful for himself and what he says? For this is tantamount to supposing that the laws do not sufficiently protect the individual and that one can be ruined by mere words, by careless phrases. But why is it that we ourselves have so conditioned everyone to regard *as an eccentric act any remarks* . . . that in any way resemble an opinion and are made openly and out loud?"[90]

Once again, we have the same scenario: the "righteous man" puts himself in danger when he commits "the eccentric act" of expressing an opinion in public. Fear is the conditioning factor, and as we have seen, it is double-edged. Of particular concern to Dostoevsky as a writer was the fear of censorship, which he ascribed to the censor's own conditioned fear of *words*. "In the most innocent, clean sentence the most criminal of thoughts is suspected, the censor obviously pursuing it with great intellectual exertion as an eternal, immutable idea that cannot leave his head, that he himself, shaken by fear and suspicion, created, that he himself incarnated in his imagination, that he himself colored with fantastic, terrifying colors, ultimately destroying his phantom together with the innocent cause of his fear—the writer's sinless original sentence."[91] Dostoevsky's "explanation" turns out to be a very precise explanation of how terrorism and terrorists will be born of words, of how an interpretative context transforms the most ordinary remark into not only an event, but a catastrophic happening. "The most ordinary remarks, spoken out loud, gain inordinate significance, and the event itself—the fact that the remarks were ever made—by reason of its perceived eccentricity, often takes on colossal proportions and are bound to be attributed to extraneous (extraordinary) causes rather than to actual (ordinary) ones."[92]

It comes as no surprise that in his explanations and under interrogation, Dostoevsky was a stubborn and wily suspect who refused to implicate his fellow accused or allow himself to be pinned down. Who but the author of the *Double* (and in the future, other such enigmatic heroes) would insist that an individual can not ever be finally and totally known? "Who has seen into my soul?" Dostoevsky defiantly demanded of his accusers. "Who has determined that degree of perfidy, harm, and revolt of which I am accused?" However much Dostoevsky sought to deny that his innermost self was accessible to his accusers, his arrest on charges of sedition made plain the violability not merely of his physical person, but of his very identity, which he passionately defended. "I am not afraid of evidence because no accusation in the world can take anything from me or add anything to me; no accusation can cause me to be other than I am as a matter of fact."[93]

But who was Dostoevsky "as a matter of fact?" Dostoevsky's protestations sound remarkably like the hero of his *Double*, Golyadkin, who insists that others wear masks, while he does not, and that others' views of him are not who he is—but his social existence (or non-existence) is determined precisely by others' views. Dostoevsky's protestations of innocence and indignation *in fact* masked a political conspirator, a member of the secret Speshnev group that had planned to lithograph prohibited literature as the first step to overthrowing autocracy and abolishing serfdom. While the leaders of the secret circle, Speshnev and Filippov, confessed to the existence of the lithograph, they did not implicate Dostoevsky or reveal further details of the scheme. In other words, while Dostoevsky was sentenced for a phantasmal (i.e., nonexistent) conspiracy, the real conspiracy remained undiscovered. As Dostoevsky set off to Siberia in shackles, he had certainly already glimpsed a fantastic reality in which words were (mis)taken for deeds and phantasmal realities for real ones, while real realities remained unperceived.

Part One

Enigmas of A-synchrony

But that's an immoral individual! A villain, a monster!—I hear from all sides the exclamations of indignant readers. Well, good, a villain, a monster: curse more, vilify him with satire and epigrams, with the outraged lyricism and indignation of public opinion, the fires of the inquisition and the axes of the executioner—and you will not destroy or kill that monster, you won't place him in a bottle of formaldehyde for the astonishment of the respectable public.

DMITRY PISAREV, "Bazarov"

I

What Do Nihilists Do?

The easing of repression marks the most dangerous time for an authoritarian government, and Russia in 1861–63 is an object lesson. Even in advance of the Emancipation, rumors of uprisings, upheavals, and a revolution at the gates were rife and struck fear into already apprehensive hearts. When the long-awaited Emancipation was finally unveiled on February 19, 1861, its primary beneficiaries, the peasantry, greeted its terms with disappointment and outraged disbelief. Between 1861 and 1863 the Empire was convulsed by eleven hundred disturbances deemed "political," and the first oppositional organization, Land and Freedom (Zemlia i Volia), made its shadowy appearance.[1] The most prominent radical literary critic, Nikolai Chernyshevsky, used his critical pulpit at the left-leaning journal *The Contemporary* to belabor the Emancipation's inadequacies and rallied indignant students to the cause. Politically motivated student disturbances began in earnest in autumn 1861, and educated society (obshchestvo) proved a fickle ally, as sympathy with the students' aspirations and tactics waned while anxiety waxed.

While still under a cloud of political suspicion, Fyodor Dostoevsky returned to the capital of the Empire on the exuberant—if jittery—eve of a new era. Eager to resume his place in the thick of literary life, Dostoevsky launched a new journal, aptly entitled *Time*, with his brother Mikhail as collaborator. The times had indeed changed since the ascension of the liberalizing Alexander II in 1855, but Peter's city remained in many respects the same. Yet as a self-avowed fantasist, Dostoevsky was able to detect new stirrings beneath the petrified masks of old types, so that when an insignificant and downtrodden clerk appeared in his feuilleton, *Petersburg Visions in Verse and Prose* (1861), the plot had a new and unexpected twist. "But one day, overcome by laments and reproaches of his brood of children and shrewish wife, he suddenly lifted his head and spoke out like Balaam's ass, but spoke out so strangely, that he was carted off to the madhouse!—It has somehow entered his head that he was Garibaldi!"[2] Like Gogol's Poprishchin, who in *Diary of a Madman* (1835) imagined himself the King of Spain, Dostoevsky's deranged clerk became obsessed with the Italian fighter for national liberation Garibaldi, to the point that little by little he convinced himself that he was Garibaldi "the filibuster [flibust'er] and destroyer of all things."[3] The hapless madman is fatally struck by the gravity of his crime, which consists simply in *being* Garibaldi and the challenge that this identity posed to the order of things. "All of God's world slid before him and flew off somewhere, the earth slid from beneath his feet. He only saw one thing everywhere and in everything: his crime, his shame and disgrace."[4] Neither a social fact nor a brute fact, "Garibaldi's" crime is not a fact at all, but only a *fantasy* of identity. Nonetheless, the clerk's only salvation lies in a grand gesture of self-unmasking and repentance, so that "Garibaldi" falls on his knees before his highness confessing, "'I am Garibaldi, do with me what you want!' Well, and they did with him . . . what had to be done."[5] Dostoevsky's final sentence with his signature ellipses betrays some reticence—whether from discretion or ambivalence—about "what has to be done" with someone possessing the effrontery (even if mad) to imagine himself Garibaldi.

Dostoevsky's St. Petersburg vision stands at a critical juncture in his career, in Russian national life, and in the emergence of revolutionary terrorism. Riding the crest of Alexander II's liberalizing reforms, Dostoevsky returned to St. Petersburg with the knowledge that the extent of his involvement in political conspiracy had remained undiscovered: technically, at least, *he* was "Garibaldi" behind the mask. In lieu of a demonstrative public confession, Dostoevsky launched a journal with a moderately progressive tendency that sought to mediate between the radicals and conservatives. Aside from his own personal political peccadilloes, Dostoevsky had good reason to sense that the "destroyer of all things" was at hand. With his penetrating "Petersburg vision" he also revealed the embryo of a novel that constituted the first volume of his terrorism trilogy—*Crime and Punishment*.

If, as the introduction to this book argues, "terrorism" refers not to the act itself, but to the interpretation and reception accorded an act, then it might reasonably be argued that 1862, and not 1866 or 1878, was the year in which terrorism made its first appearance in Russia. In mid-May 1862, Dostoevsky arrived home to find a copy of a proclamation entitled *Young Russia* wedged into his door handle.[6] The proclamation began by stentoriously announcing the advent of a new era ("Russia is entering into the revolutionary period of its existence") and appeared mysteriously throughout Petersburg, not only on door handles but tucked inconspicuously into programs of the capital's most exclusive theaters. As if on cue, on May 15 and 16 a series of fires broke out in the poorer districts of St. Petersburg and burned catastrophically for two weeks, destroying the property of and rendering homeless thousands of the city's most vulnerable citizens. When the fires culminated on May 28, consuming the city's biggest markets and trading points, the Apraksin Dvor and Shchukin market, Petersburgers were awed and terrified by the apocalyptic sight while government officials were at a loss to cope with the panic and destruction. "The sight was terrific. Like an immense snake rattling and whistling, the fire threw itself in all directions, and right and left, enveloped the shanties and suddenly rose in a huge column, darting out its whistling tongue to lick up more shanties with their contents. The authorities had lost their heads."[7]

The menace of fire was certainly nothing new to Russia's largely wooden cities and towns, nor was suspected arson that stemmed from socio-political protest or pecuniary motives. What *was* new were the suspected agents behind the fires. Ivan Turgenev, whose novel *Fathers and Children* (Otsy i deti) had been published to great controversy just two months previously, in March 1862, recalled the general consensus: "When I returned to Petersburg on the very day of the notorious fires in the Apraksin Market, the word 'Nihilist' had been caught up by thousands of people, and the first exclamation that escaped from the lips of the first acquaintance I met on the Nevsky Prospect was: 'Look at what your Nihilists are doing! They are setting Petersburg on fire!'"[8] Without question, Turgenev's reminiscence from nine years later may be considered self-congratulatory. In May 1862 the word "Nihilist" had not yet gained currency to denote either radical fanatics or someone who believes in nothing; instead, a host of other archaic terms were used to designate political radicals with revolutionary designs, among the most common of which was simply "evildoer" (zlodei).[9] What is certainly true is that the fires were not attributed to an act of God or nature, but precisely to students like Turgenev's Evgenii Bazarov in *Fathers and Children*, who embraced an uncompromising materialism and utilitarianism. Bazarov clarifies what it is, in fact, that nihilists do in his first confrontation with the bastion of traditional values, Pavel Petrovich Kirsanov.

> "We act on the strength of what we recognize to be useful," said Bazarov. "At present, the most useful thing of all is negation—we negate [otritsaem]."
>
> "Everything?"
>
> "Everything."
>
> "What? Not only art, poetry—but also—it's terrible to say it . . ."
>
> "Everything."[10]

What is "terrible to say" remains unsaid, but what Bazarov does say is that for the nihilist, the most useful deed is the word, or more specifically, what J. L. Austin famously referred to as a speech act, in this case, to render nonexistent by means of the word.[11] Pavel's more mild-tempered brother, Nikolai, is nonplussed and seeks clarification concerning the nihilists' ultimate aims: "But allow me to say . . . you negate everything, or to put it more precisely, you destroy everything . . . so it will be necessary to build, too."[12] From the point of view of the established order and order more generally, its negation *is* destruction. Let it be noted, however, that Bazarov, as the first and towering representative/representation of nihilism, explicitly refuses to *do* anything and hews to the destructive word, as he confirms for Pavel Petrovich nihilism's ultimate project: "not to undertake anything." "'Just curse [rugat'sia] everything?' 'And just curse.' 'And that's called nihilism?' 'And that's called nihilism,' Bazarov repeated again, this time with marked insolence."[13]

To some extent Bazarov was plagiarizing the fiery and brilliant literary critic Dmitry Pisarev (1840–68), who was the "nihilist" camp's most compelling spokesperson and unceremoniously presented its "ultimatum" in the iconoclastic and highly polemical essay "The Scholasticism of the Nineteenth Century" (1860). "If authority is deceitful doubt will destroy it, and properly so; if it is necessary or useful, then doubt will turn it over, examine it from all angles, and put it back in its place. In a word, here is the ultimatum of our camp: what can be broken should be broken; what resists the blow is worth keeping, what flies to pieces is rubbish, in any case, strike right and left, no harm can come of it and no harm will come."[14] Pisarev's article was a no-holds-barred attack on all established social, cultural, and aesthetic authority that championed instead free inquiry, personal preference, and individual self-realization. His rhetorical fireworks were designed to shock, and duly shocked, Dostoevsky jotted down in his notebook, "Now Pisarev has gone further."[15]

Both Pisarev's and Bazarov's teardown, however, remained entirely in the symbolic realm of ideas, norms, and cultural institutions. By contrast, the anonymous author of *Young Russia* pledged his party expressly to political action: "We studied the history of the West and the study was not for nothing: we will go further ['my budem posledovatel'nee'—literally, 'we will be more thorough/methodical'] not only than the poor revolutionaries of 1848, but also than the great terrorists of the 1790s."[16] The most distinctive feature of *Young Russia* was not the radical tenets of its program for a Russian social democratic republic, nor its polemic with the émigré radical Alexander Herzen, but its striving for effect, its clear desire to intimidate and terrify. This striving was not gratuitous, but a deliberate product of the author's belief that previous revolutions (1793, 1848) had failed primarily because they had not been ruthless and bloodthirsty *enough*. The author(s) of *Young Russia* did not intend to make the same mistake, and so they made terror a central pillar of the revolution as well as the episode that would inaugurate it—its baptism in blood.

> The day will soon come when we will unfurl the great banner of the future, the red banner. And with a mighty cry of "Long live the Russian Social and Democratic Republic" we will move against the Winter Palace to wipe out all who dwell there. It may be that we will only have to destroy the imperial family, i.e. about a hundred people. But it may also happen, and this more likely, that the whole imperial party will rise like a man to follow the tsar, because for them it will be a question of life and death. If this happens, with full faith in ourselves and our forces, and in the support of the people and in the glorious future of Russia—which

destiny has ordained shall be the first country to realize the great cause of Socialism—we will cry "To your axes" and then we will strike the imperial party without sparing our blows just as they do not spare theirs against us.[17]

What is striking about this vision, aside from its crude horror and brutality, is its sheer originality. While citing the French model as a precedent, *Young Russia* in fact definitively departs from the model of legalized terror and instead imagines mass participation in collective carnage at the signal of "To your axes!" (K toporam!)

Needless to say, the incendiary manifesto fanned the flames of public apprehension, fright, and panic. The letters of St. Petersburg's inhabitants bear witness to the sense of ubiquitous threat that M. G. Kartashevskaia conveyed to V. S. Aksakova in a letter dated May 26-27, 1862. "We have such terrible fires, that the entire city is in a panic [v volnenii]. Up to seven fires a day. Wherever you turn, there is smoke and flames. There is not a bit of doubt that it is arson; it is even said that many of the arrested are armed with incendiary shells [zazhigatel'nye sniariady]. Such fires are not for nothing. . . . You can't save yourself from arson."[18] The end of May to the beginning of June marked the height of press reports that authoritatively cited rumors as "social consensus" or "fact." For example: "The whole city is consumed by rumors of the political nature of the fires"; "a well-organized, numerous gang [shaika] of arsonists . . . is connected to the recent appalling proclamation"; and (as the June 9 issue of *Our Times* reported) "all estates blame the fires on political actors—this is a general certainty!" Members of the public like Kartashevskaia found it completely plausible that arsonists were in the pay of the radical émigré Herzen, whose diabolical conspiracy supposedly extended to other Russian cities (Novgorod was next on the list). Herzen, for his part, turned the tables and suggested that the fires were a police provocation designed to drive a terrorized society into the arms of the government and political reaction.[19] In the meantime, editorials and the public imagination together conjured images of axe-wielding arsonists leaping like tongues of flame from a revolutionary conflagration.

In an article entitled "The Fires" earmarked for his journal *Time*, Dostoevsky sought to intervene in the mounting hysteria and captured the scene in his inimitable way. "The people are loudly talking about them [the fires]; there are rumors about captured scoundrels [moshenniki], about some kind of numerous gang, that with diabolical intentions burns the capital from all sides. A panicked terror has overcome everyone. For every inhabitant, every householder, it is only a matter of time until fire is discovered in some corner or another."[20] The dissonance between alarmist media reports, panicky letters like Aksakova's, and Dostoevsky's article is striking. Dostoevsky treats it all with sardonic skepticism—not, of course, toward the fires themselves and their very serious economic and human toll, but toward the terror and specifically toward the existence of *malign agents or terrorists*. In order to dispel the mystique and fear surrounding the manifesto, he casts its anonymous authors as "three smooth-talking schoolboys, of whom the oldest is probably not older than thirteen, [who] printed and tossed around the most stupid sheet, without even decently coming to grips with the foreign books from which they filched and giftlessly distorted [bezdarno perekoverkali]."[21] Dostoevsky's strategy for countering the onus of sedition is familiar from the Petrashevsky affair: to cast it all as profoundly unoriginal and juvenile folly. Ultimately, though, Dostoevsky aims his polemical fire at the media as the guiltiest party, not only for its fear-mongering, but for unconscionably insinuating the idea among the common people that progressive students were behind the fires. In Dostoevsky's mind, these rumors were unlikely to have originated among the common people themselves and instead bore the unmistakable impress of literacy and the stamp of higher spheres—perhaps even governmental ones. The real crime, for Dostoevsky, consisted in sowing discord between two underprivileged and harassed elements of society—the peasant masses "consistently remaining in darkness and ignorance" and the students, "since time immemorial humiliated and insulted"—and opportunistically setting them against one another.

There is no doubt that Dostoevsky's was a principled intervention, but he also had a significant personal stake in the matter, since in the public's overheated imagination, Herzen's plot of revolutionary arson was considered a realization of "Petrashevsky's program." ("It is also being said that in Petrashevsky's conspiracy there was a program for fires and that program is being realized.")[22] In other words, even though Nikolai Chernyshevsky was considered more immediately to blame, Dostoevsky and his cohort, as the progenitors of both the revolutionary ideas and the tactic of revolutionary arson, were also held responsible for the "terrorism" that was harrowing St. Petersburg.[23] Both this first article "The Fires" and a second shorter article demonstrated that Dostoevsky possessed a keen understanding of the workings of terrorism as a social fact, and both were—unsurprisingly—suppressed by personal order of the tsar.[24] Equally predictably, Dostoevsky's repeated calls for "openness" (glasnost') in the investigation and trial of the apprehended arsonists, and his demands for "facts, facts, facts," were all in vain. Nothing of the sort was forthcoming, and the government expressly refused to confirm that among those arrested, there was not one student, much less the likes of Bazarov.[25] Scores of individuals were arrested in conjunction with the fires (with rampant rumors of summary executions), but most of these suspected arsonists were taken into custody to save them from hysterical lynch mobs.

While too literal-minded agents of the Third Section questioned Mikhail Dostoevsky about the identity of the "three smooth-talking school boys," the real author of *Young Russia*, Peter Zaichnevsky, was *already* in prison and probably had nothing to do with the fires. Barely more than a school boy, Zaichnevsky was nonetheless an inveterate and singularly irrepressible "preacher and confessor of Socialism." On the grounds of a single perlustrated letter, Alexander II had deemed him so dangerous that he was immediately arrested and imprisoned, but managed under the lax prison regime to gather something of a literary circle and arrange for the printing and distribution of his manifesto.[26] Thus, the smoke and flames twined with the manifesto's incendiary words to raise the specter of terror/ism, and society quiescently accepted the government's repressive measures as necessary to combat the perceived threat. Terrorism as a "social fact" existed palpably, not despite but *because of* its agents' elusiveness. As Alexander Herzen described that summer in *The Bell* (Kolokol): "In St. Petersburg there is terror—the most dangerous and mindless kind of all, that of cowardice confused. Not the terror of the lion but that of the calf, a terror in which the demented government, not knowing the source of danger, knowing neither its strengths nor its weaknesses and hence pontificating nonsense, is helped by society, literature, the people, progress and regress."[27]

Herzen's impersonal construction is key. "There *is* terror" but terror that is amorphous and agentless, terror that has no identifiable source except those who are subject to it. Instead, like a fantastical Moloch, the collective fantasy of revolutionary arson feeds very real state terror. The actual existence of terrorist-arsonists or an anti-government conspiracy was completely irrelevant. More important than (f)actuality was: 1) the perception of threat or danger; 2) a context that fostered this perception (saturated as it was by revolutionary expectations and post-Emancipation anxieties); and 3) coincidence. In this case, the appearance of the word (*Young Russia*) and deed (the fires) and their mutual amplification was indeed a coincidence. Nevertheless, a pattern of reception, interpretive paradigms (including the possibility of government provocation) and patterns of reaction were set: all that was wanting were actual political actors in place of specters conjured by smoke and mirrors.

2

"Very Dangerous!"

What could be more innocuous than a placid and well-fed country squire, lounging indolently on his divan, sunk in pleasant reverie? Nothing, and this was precisely the problem, according to the radical young literary critic Nikolai Dobroliubov (1836-61), the tireless advocate of literature's power to generate new social types. In his review of Mikhail Goncharov's 1858 novel *Oblomov* (entitled "What Is Oblomovism?"), Dobroliubov obligingly answered his own question. Oblomovism (oblomovshchina) is epic inaction accompanied by existential inertia. Oblomov does nothing because he can do nothing because he doesn't want anything because he doesn't know how to do anything because he knows nothing.

If this were an isolated case, that would be one thing, but Dobroliubov diagnoses a national syndrome. "Oblomovshchina" is an epidemic that knows no boundaries, least of all the one between life and literature, which promiscuously re-infect one another. "This is our native national type... repeated several times in the best of our literary productions.... Even today there are people who seem to be copies of Onegin, Pechorin, Rudin and the others."[1] In lieu of effort and a productive occupation, Oblomov indulges in "bellicose and heroic" dreams of grandeur ("sometimes he liked to picture himself an invincible general, compared with whom not only Napoleon, but even Veruslan Lazarevich was a non-entity"), but only dreams. Instead, of compassion and humanity, he nurtures contempt for "the human ant heap," and worst of all, he is a literary dilettante, but barely even that.[2] According to Dobroliubov, Goncharov captured the signature type of an era, the last iteration of the "superfluous man" immortalized by Ivan Turgenev in his 1850 novella *Diary of a Superfluous Man*. For Dobroliubov, the fact that the Oblomovs' days were numbered was grounds for guarded optimism: "even today, thousands of people spend their time talking and thousands of others are willing to take this talk for deeds. This is because the time for social activity has arrived or will soon arrive.... And that is why we said at the beginning of this essay that we regard Goncharov's novel as a sign of the times."[3] Yet if Oblomov remained the title character, it was because the new men, and no less important, activity befitting them, did not yet exist. Stolz, Oblomov's friend and foil, who wins the love of Oblomov's former fiancée, Olga, is commendably active, "but," laments Dobroliubov, the deeds of such Stolzes, "whatever they may be, remain a mystery to us."[4] In the end, not Stolz but Olga is the exemplar. She "stuns us with the unusual clarity and simplicity of her logic and the stunning harmony of her heart and will."[5] When it becomes clear that Oblomov will never rise from his divan to become the Oblomov she and Stolz have created in their imaginations, "the Oblomov of the future," Olga gently and matter-of-factly breaks with him and transfers her affections to Stolz. Dobroliubov concludes that it is Olga who is battle-ready and confidently predicts that "we may expect to hear the word that will consume Oblomovshchina with fire and reduce it to ashes" from *her*.[6]

Unlikely as it is that Dobroliubov envisioned Goncharov's heroine as a future arsonist ready to torch Oblomovshchina (with *a word*, no less!) Alexander Herzen nonetheless entitled his response to Dobroliubov "Very Dangerous!" (in English). Literary-critical polemics were by their very nature dangerous. A form of war by other means, they were the place in which conservatives and progressives pulled no punches in ideological battles waged via the plot, characters, and themes of Goncharov's or Turgenev's or whoever's latest novels. Readers and critics alike imputed to literature an unquestionable reality, discussing situations and characters as if they were real people, albeit often imagined in terms of a social type rather than in terms of psychological nuance. Critics' interventions not only influenced readers' reception of the work and its characters, but seemed to usher the characters (in altered form) into reality itself. As Irina Paperno explains, "A necessary part of this process is the literary critic, who mediates between the literary work and its actualization in reality. The radical school of aesthetics, the real criticism [real'naia kritika] advanced the idea that an author can reveal things in reality (such as future types) that are independent or even contrary of his intentions. On this view, the critic is full co-author of the text (even though his presence is frequently uninvited and unwelcome)."[7]

As an example of just such an uninvited and unwelcome co-authorship, Paperno cites a notorious episode involving Dobroliubov to which we will shortly return. Another point requires even stronger emphasis. Real criticism held that authors' intentions were largely irrelevant and that their texts, thanks to the literary critic's superior insight, might reveal something independent or "even contrary" to them. Hence, the real critic's role hovered on the boundary between the impudent and the occult. At the same time, however, as the critical dynamos at the *Contemporary*, Nikolai Dobroliubov and his mentor, Nikolai Chernyshevsky, exercised this astonishing power and authority over life and literature, they subtly denigrated their medium's importance. Chernyshevsky, as Belinsky's heir, had fired the opening salvo in his master's thesis, "The Aesthetic Relations of Art to Life" ("Esteticheskie otnosheniia iskusstva k deistvitel'nosti," 1855), by declaring his goal "the defense of reality as against fantasy, the attempt to prove that works of art cannot possibly stand comparison with living reality."[8] At best, art could hope to be an accomplished but always inferior *copy* of life, and the production or consumption of art was a pale substitute for living: "art seems to be a pastime too sickly sentimental for adults and not without dangers for young people."[9] Chernyshevsky's protégé, Dobroliubov, developed these thoughts in different directions and with different emphases. The first entailed making a decisive break with the generation of aristocratic liberals of the 1830s and 1840s (the "generation of the fathers"), who from Dobroliubov's point of view were completely enthralled with imaginary constructs, with principles and abstract logic, whereas Dobroliubov insisted on the concrete, the empirical, and the living: "Facts, facts, that's where we must begin!"

Not one to stand on ceremony in any sphere of life, Dobroliubov performed his interventions with unparalleled skill and gusto, hewing to Vissarion Belinsky's insistence on type as the fulcrum of literature's intervention in life. Not only should writers portray the social types that they observed in reality, but literature should engineer new and improved types, not seen in nature, for Russian soil had thus far managed to produce only the weak and the stunted.[10] The crucible for the creation of the "new type" would be precisely this furious polemic between Turgenev and his arch-nemesis, Dobroliubov. Arguably, the most influential "types" produced in Russian literature in the era of the Great Reforms were not even Russian at all, but based on the immortal literary creations of Shakespeare and Cervantes. In January 1860 Turgenev gave a public reading of his essay "Hamlet and Don Quixote" to the Society for the Assistance of Needy Writers and Scholars. The piece was published subsequently in *The Contemporary* (No. 1, 1860). In it Turgenev essentially outmaneuvered his rival by rehabilitating the two archetypes that the real critics belabored as the old, indecisive and ineffectual types that inhabited Russian reality. Instead, the essay argued that the two archetypes were in fact the Janus-faced embodiment of heroism in the modern world.

Turgenev began his delineation of the two types with the premise that "all people live—consciously or unconsciously—according to their principle, their ideal, that is according to that which they esteem as truth, beauty, good,"[11] and he presented the characters of Hamlet and Don Quixote as exemplifying two fundamentally opposite orientations of the self. The first, Hamlet's, regards the self as the ultimate touchstone and value whereas the second, Don Quixote's, strives selflessly to realize a goal outside of himself or perform communal and transcendent good. A reader of Cervantes's original would be astonished by the gravitas and the sanctity that Turgenev confers on the "knight of the rueful countenance." Instead of delusional folly, Turgenev redefines quixotism as an "archetype of self-sacrifice" and insists that the ultimate idealist, Don Quixote, "typifies . . . faith, first of all belief in something indestructible, in a truth that is beyond any single individual, which is not easily attainable, but only demands devoted service and sacrifice."[12] He "lives wholly (if one can express it so) outside himself, for others, for his brothers, to eradicate evil, to oppose the forces inimical to humanity."[13]

Only after elevating Don Quixote to these sublime heights of morality and martyrdom does Turgenev admit that Quixote's image belongs to the "fantastic world of chivalric Romance" and land the more familiar motley of comedy (and madness) lightly on his shoulders.[14] Lest we take the absurdity of Quixote at face value, Turgenev suggests another interpretation: to appear ridiculous is a form of self-sacrifice. "The ancients called their gods jealous, and in case of necessity considered it useful to render them a voluntary sacrifice.... Might we not consider that what appears farcical in the actions and characters of those called to perform a great new deed as just such a tribute to placate the jealous gods? In any case, without these ridiculous Don Quixotes, without this eccentric vanguard, humanity would not progress—there wouldn't be anything for Hamlets to contemplate."[15]

But if we still laugh at Don Quixote, Turgenev cautions, we do so at our own peril, oblivious to our shared plight. Quixote's image, radiant in its earnest questing and undimmed righteousness, begs the question of whether "one [must] actually be crazy in order to believe in truth, or is it possible that the mind, having gained control of itself, for precisely that reason loses all of its strength?"[16] Is truth, and even more fundamentally, belief in truth, only vouchsafed to the mad? Turgenev's answer is to default to a deeply unsettling skepticism and subjectivism, arguing that since we cannot know whether our convictions rest upon a sound basis of perception (whether what appears a golden helmet is in fact a brass wash basin), what matters most is the steadfastness of conviction. Only "fate can reveal whether we have waged war against specters or real enemies, and with what armour we have covered our heads. Our purpose is to arm ourselves and fight."[17] With this affirmation, the inveterate Hamlet, Turgenev, locks arms in solidarity with the fanatical Don Quixotes to come.

By contrast, the singularly unfunny Hamlet is the ultimate egoist who cherishes and simultaneously disparages his "I" and who subjects everything, including himself, to the acid of skeptical inquiry (he "spies upon himself"). For all his worldly advantages and panache, he is unappealing because he is barren and unable to love, to act, or to create. There is irony even in Hamlet's redeeming positive quality, which is negation. Comparing the negation of Faust's Mephistopheles to that of Hamlet, Turgenev argues that Hamlet's "negation is not evil—it is itself directed against evil. Hamlet's negation doubts the existence of the good, but it doesn't doubt the existence of evil and enters into a merciless battle with it."[18] His doctrine of negation is directed against evil but even more fiercely against enemies hiding behind the mask of sham good. His inveterate skepticism lends him an impartial clarity that does not muddle distinctions but instead demands irreconcilable enmity toward false truths so that he becomes, ironically enough, "one of the chief vindicators of a truth which he himself does not fully accept."[19]

It is worth recalling that "Hamlet and Don Quixote" preceded *Fathers and Children* by two years, making Turgenev's Hamlet the base coat for the negating "nihilists" of *Fathers and Children*. In Turgenev's rendering, Hamlet and Don Quixote are equally heroic types who struggle ceaselessly against evil and for truth by opposite means—Don Quixote by means of his selflessness and folly (idealism), Hamlet by means of his selfishness and skepticism (realism). The destructive aspects of both are unmistakable. Hamlet's negation can raze everything in sight, including himself, while Don Quixote, for the sake of his ideal, may ultimately sacrifice himself and those he intends to save.

As a final note, at the beginning of his essay, Turgenev was very keen to point out the concurrence of the works, both of which appeared in first editions in the same year, 1600. But he leaves the implications of this coincidence unexplored, and another coincidence entirely unremarked. Both of the works unceremoniously dispatch sovereign authority, either with literal regicide as the center and denouement of the plot (*Hamlet*) or at the very point of entry, in the Spanish proverb that Cervantes uses to unseat traditional literary authority in order to give the reader full sovereignty in judging his novel: "*al rey mando*" "I give orders to the king/under my cloak I kill the king."[20]

Turgenev's essay was his last work published in Nekrasov's *Contemporary* before the definitive break two months later, when Nekrasov published Dobroliubov's review of Turgenev's novel *On the Eve* over Turgenev's objections. "*I earnestly urge you*, dear Nekrasov, *not to publish this article* [emphasis in the original]. It can cause me nothing but unpleasantness, it is unjust and sharp—I shall not know where to hide myself if it is printed."[21] From Turgenev's pleading, one would think that Dobroliubov had mercilessly panned the novel. In fact, he did something much worse: he elevated a secondary character, the Bulgarian nationalist Insarov, to the status of the novel's hero and cast the novel itself as a call to revolutionary action. In this regard, Dobroliubov's 1860 essay "When Will the Real Day Come?" (Kogda pridyot nastoiashchii den'?) follows in logical progression from "What Is Oblomovism?" two years previously. As he scours the horizon of Turgenev's most recent novel (*On the Eve*), and the literary scene more generally for some hopeful indication, Dobroliubov commends only its heroines, especially Turgenev's Elena, whose "whole soul longed to do good, and at first this desire was satisfied with customary acts of charity that were accessible to her. 'The poor, the hungry, and the sick held her attention, stirred and pained her; she saw them in her dreams, she questioned all her acquaintances about them.' . . . Her father calls this 'banal sentimentality' [poshloe nezhnichan'e], but Elena was not sentimental [santimental'na], for sentimentality is characterized precisely by an abundance of sentiment and words accompanied by a complete absence of effective love and sympathy."²²

But as attractive and commendable as her actions and character are, they are relatively inconsequential. "Elena could not find sufficient outlets for her strength and was unable to satisfy her strivings"—this despite the fact that Elena was based, according to Turgenev's open admission, on Anita Garibaldi, the wife of the Italian freedom fighter whom Turgenev deeply admired.²³ Turgenev, Dobroliubov charges, obliged his heroine to display lofty stirrings in a trivial manner, not because she lacks courage, but because she fears doing harm. The question is then two-fold: how does one overcome this aversion to "doing harm," and what kind of action is it worthwhile to undertake when "one's soul longs for action and seeks for a great mind and a strong hand to lead it?" Not rescuing kittens, certainly, but violently opposing the "enemy."

Only Turgenev's Insarov has this option readily available. As a Bulgarian enslaved by Turks, Insarov has been shaped from infancy (he has "imbibed hatred for enslavers and discontent with the present state of things with his mother's milk") to fight to liberate his nation from external oppressors.²⁴ External oppressors, it turns out, are far preferable to internal ones, as Dobroliubov explains: "An external enemy, a privileged oppressor can be attacked and vanquished far more easily than an internal enemy, whose forces are spread everywhere in a thousand different shapes, elusive and invulnerable, harassing us from all sides, poisoning our lives, giving us no rest, and preventing us from surveying the battlefield. The internal enemy cannot be combated with ordinary weapons."²⁵ Instead, the enemy he describes calls for a different sort of struggle with new, unconventional tactics created in the same image. The terroristic struggle momentarily becomes visible in Dobroliubov's tropes, yet he quickly retreats from martial language and cloaks the nature of the struggle in hazy atmospheric metaphors: the raw, foggy atmosphere must be dispelled and replaced by one in which the internal enemy "will be unable to breathe."²⁶

What would it take for an Insarov-type hero, as opposed to Hamlets and Don Quixotes, to blossom on Russian soil? In the first place, Dobroliubov admits that an inauspicious reception would await such a type. "He would be perceived as some kind of bandit [razboinik], a representative of the 'anti-social element' about whom the Russian public already knows so much."²⁷ Ultimately the crux of the problem lies in what a Russian would have to do to him/herself given the conditions of struggle against an internal, rather than external enemy. As Dobroliubov explains, "The Russian hero, who usually stems from educated society, is himself connected by blood with that against which he should rise up." He is in the same position as a son of a Turkish sultan who undertakes to liberate the Bulgarians from the Turks—"if such a son were to appear to us as something other than a stupidly spoiled fellow, it would be necessary for him to renounce [otrech'sia] everything that connected him to the Turks: religious faith, nationality, and their circles of family and friends, and the material advantages of their privileged position... that is, the renunciation [otrechenie] of the entire mass of conceptions and practical attitudes which bound them to society."[28] Dobroliubov distills the dilemma to a single evocative metaphor: "They are reluctant to put the axe to the tree on which they themselves grew."[29]

Despite these acknowledged obstacles, the review ends in pining but optimistic expectation of a true Russian Insarov: "We shall not have to wait long for him; the feverishly painful impatience with which we are expecting his appearance *in real life* [my emphasis] is the guarantee of this. We need him; without him our lives will be wasted."[30] In fiction, at least, Dobroliubov did not have long to wait. Turgenev obligingly supplied Bazarov, who was (mis)taken for a caricature of Dobroliubov in the two men's tit-for-tat exchange. The insult was even graver given the fact that Dobroliubov had died of tuberculosis in 1861, and it remained for Dobroliubov's incensed colleagues at the *Contemporary* to fight another day. Externals excepted, Bazarov bore a much closer resemblance to the scorchingly provocative Pisarev (Hamlet), who in fact embraced Bazarov as a faithful representation of his cohort and, at the same time, an exemplar worthy of imitation.

A note on semantics puts a finer point on an important distinction. The Russian Insarov must create himself first through a speech act: he renounces (otrekat'sia). The Russian nihilist, already a *fait accompli* (though perhaps in reality only a "stupidly spoiled fellow"), destroys through a speech act: he negates. "To renounce," with the root "rech'" (speech) at its core, is also a speech act, but in Russian it is an intransitive verb with significant implications for the subject of the act, whereas "to negate" is a transitive verb that is directed exclusively at its object. English translations of Turgenev's *Fathers and Children* often translate Bazarov's categorical "My otritsaem" (we negate) as "we renounce." Turgenev's Don Quixote renounces; Turgenev's Hamlet negates. Dobroliubov's fantasy Russian Insarov renounces; Pisarev/Bazarov negates. In fact, renunciation as an act of (self) creation and negation as an act of (world) destruction are two sides of the same coin, two branches of the same tree.

3

Extraordinary Men and Gloomy Monsters

The conflagration that consumed not Oblomovshchina but the market quarter of St. Petersburg in the late spring of 1862 seemed confirmation that Dobroliubov's "real day" had finally come, or so Alexander II's government was convinced. The radical journals *The Contemporary* and *The Russian Word* were forced to suspend publication while Nikolai Chernyshevsky and his younger colleague Dmitry Pisarev were arrested (on July 7 and July 2) and incarcerated in the Peter and Paul Fortress. While Chernyshevsky was charged and convicted based on fabricated evidence, Pisarev had actually done—or rather written—something deeply incriminating, a pamphlet in response to Schedo-Ferroti's "stupid little pamphlet." Schedo-Ferroti was the pen name of the government agent and apologist Baron F. I. Firks, who had calumnied the exiled Herzen, and Pisarev concluded his evisceration of Schedo-Ferroti with an ill-timed call for the revolutionary overthrow of the Romanovs that contained echoes of both "The Scholasticism of the Nineteenth Century" and "Young Russia": "What is dead and rotten must of itself fall into the grave. All we have to do is give a last push and cover with dirt their stinking corpses."[1]

By contrast, the shy, awkward, and self-effacing Chernyshevsky took care to stay within bounds of the permissible, but the fires provided the government with the perfect pretext to finally net this most wanted of literary men, on the basis of a case that had been prepared well in advance.² However, his prison sojourn provided the tediously workaholic Chernyshevsky with respite from his journalistic responsibilities during which he could pursue his more ambitious projects, and after five months in prison, "public enemy number one" requested and received permission to write a novel, which was serialized in the reinstated *Contemporary* in the spring of 1863.³

If it seems highly improbable that a state criminal should be allowed to legally publish a novel from prison, what is even more improbable is the effect that this somewhat clunky, hastily written and unrevised, but undeniably original novel had. "No novel of Turgenev and no writings of Tolstoy or any other writer ever had such a wide and deep influence upon Russian society as this novel had," avowed the renowned anarchist Prince Peter Kropotkin.⁴ On the surface, there was nothing political about *What Is to Be Done?*, yet every moment of the novel challenged or subverted accepted socio-political, moral, and aesthetic norms. *What Is to Be Done?* envisions the transformation of life in all its minutiae from the bottom up, from the cellar to the rooftops. This thorough *renovation* would seem to preclude the necessity for violent *revolution* since happiness can be achieved simply by rationally remaking oneself to achieve optimal well-being. Nonetheless, a revolutionary conspirator did slip in and slip by the censorship, "the extraordinary man," Rakhmetov. Rakhmetov is not one of the novel's central protagonists: he is mentioned fleetingly in the chapters prior to the one devoted to him before disappearing from the novel entirely. For Chernyshevsky's intended readership, the matter was crystal clear: Rakhmetov was an "extraordinary man," as the title of the chapter devoted to him signals, and though it could be stated only obliquely—a revolutionary. "People like him are in their sphere and in their place only where and when they can be historic figures.... It is difficult enough to explain how they work and what comes of their efforts, because they started work only recently, no more than fifty or seventy years ago."⁵ Simple subtraction allows the reader to date the appearance of people like Rakhmetov as coterminous with revolutionary events in France, in the 1770s–1790s. Thus with Pisarev's laudatory review of *What Is to Be Done?*, entitled "The New Type," Rakhmetov received the official, if necessarily oblique, nihilist stamp of approval as the prototypical revolutionary.

It stands to reason that any literary history of terrorism would take its cue from the countless histories of the revolutionary movement that have seen Rakhmetov in precisely this light, as the literary prototype of the real revolutionary, and reflexively begin here, with Chernyshevsky, *What Is to Be Done?*, and Rakhmetov. In fact, Rakhmetov occupies an extremely important position in the evolutionary chain. The challenge comes in reading *all* of Rakhmetov's parts, instead of fixating on a single aspect, as Chernyshevsky clearly anticipated that his ironically named "sapient" or "perspicacious" (pronitsatel'nyi) readers would do.[6] Formerly, Rakhmetov was read as a steely proto-Bolshevik who modelled a rationalist asceticism; with the collapse of communism and the toppling of its idols, however, Rakhmetov has been demoted by revisionist readings in which the "extraordinary" now appears only "peculiar" or parodic, and the formidable—"funny."[7] Yet it is worth recalling the very obvious literary sources of Rakhmetov's oddity and the narrator's voluble amusement. Chernyshevsky's narrative stance owes much to Cervantes's vis-à-vis his quixotic hero, as well as to the long-established tradition (strategy) of viewing dangerous freethinkers (Radishchev, Chaadaev, Petrashevsky) as, at best, eccentrics—at worst, mad men. From the reading binge that serves as a catalyst for his conversion, everything that Rakhmetov is—barge-hauling *bogatyr*, ceaseless champion of the Cause and of others' affairs (he has no affairs of his own), noble rescuer of a damsel in distress, incognito knight-errant in Western Europe who gives his fortune (anonymously) to prominent unnamed revolutionary philosopher—coupled with his demeanor, including his rueful countenance when he is called a "rigorist"—is à la Don Quixote and thus evokes the narrator's helpless mirth. Especially in light of Turgenev's reading of Don Quixote, it becomes clear that Rakhmetov's apparent ridiculousness is the necessary "sacrifice to the gods"—and one of many.

In fact, Rakhmetov is both ridiculous (but only to the narrator) and terrifying (to almost everyone else). "With the exception of Masha and those who were her equals or superiors in simplicity of soul or dress, everyone was somewhat afraid of Rakhmetov. . . . Even Lopukhov, Kirsanov, and all those who feared nothing and no one at times felt some trepidation before him."[8] So frightening does Rakhmetov generally appear that Vera Pavlovna, upon discovering his lighter side, exclaims: "You're not at all what you seem to be. Why do you always appear to be such a gloomy monster [mrachnoe chudovishche]? And why are you such a nice, agreeable fellow now?"[9]

In this novel in which characters and readers are divided into categories according to their ability to perceive true realities behind deceptive appearances, Vera Pavlovna, like the narrator, gets a privileged glimpse of the "other Rakhmetov" as a "nice, agreeable fellow." Rakhmetov confirms that this is, in fact, the case, but that this does not preclude his being a "gloomy monster." "As a general rule, you see things about you that are not happy. How can you help being a gloomy monster?"[10] It is hard to imagine a more laconic distillation of the tradition of civic grief (grazhdanskaia skorb') from Radishchev to Nekrasov than this.

Of all of Rakhmetov's nicknames and sobriquets, "gloomy monster" is the most frequent, and here, at this critical juncture where the narrator reveals the purpose of the scene and of Rakhmetov, it acquires a special status, especially because it is repeated three times in four sentences ostensibly denying that Rakhmetov is a gloomy monster. Although "gloomy monster" is in scare quotes, Rakhmetov himself uses it without scare quotes, in the same way that Pisarev embraced Bazarov while fully acknowledging that from the point of view of the respectable public, Turgenev's nihilist appeared to be "an immoral individual, a villain, a monster!" In other words, Rakhmetov *owns* his sobriquet as the "nihilists" and later the "terrorists" would theirs, and, at least instrumentally, his monstrousness.

That brings us to Rakhmetov's role in the novel, which Chernyshevsky goads the perspicacious reader to "guess." Most readings of Rakhmetov focus on how the "extraordinary man" has become extraordinary—the charismatic story of his ideological conversion and unusual regimen—yet the narrator very pointedly directs the reader's attention to Rakhmetov's conversation with Vera Pavlovna. Here, Rakhmetov seems to take all the guesswork out of it by robotically stating his purpose several times: "the general outcome of my visit will be consoling."[11] Simply put, Rakhmetov's purpose is to end suffering. This was in fact Pisarev's understanding of Rakhmetov's role "because the main requirement of their being [people like Rakhmetov—i.e., revolutionaries] is to do something to relieve human suffering."[12] In this particular case, his method consists in inculcating the same emotional discipline in the devastated Vera Pavlovna (who has been led to believe that her husband has committed suicide) that he himself exercises and that makes him so perfectly suited to carry out his many missions. This emotional discipline is enacted physically as Rakhmetov makes Vera Pavlovna read Lopukhov's letter without touching it or the table, while he holds fast to one corner in anticipation of her impulsive reaction. From the outside, admits the narrator, the scene is comic, but for Vera Pavlovna it is "excruciating."

But there is an even darker side to Rakhmetov where his formidable emotional control and his gloomy monstrousness combine to produce something genuinely terrifying. His ability to perform any task, without being swayed by "emotion or entreaties," outfits him nicely for the role of executioner. No sooner does Vera Pavlovna determine that Rakhmetov is a "nice, agreeable fellow" than he interrupts the consolatory program and slips on his monster mask to conduct an investigation and mock trial of Vera Pavlovna, announcing: "And now, so that you can more easily conceive of me as a gloomy monster, we must continue our investigation of your crimes."[13] Though it is all done in jest and with the requisite playfulness, with sherry and cigars to take the edge off, the trial is in fact deadly serious and Rakhmetov ultimately levels the gravest political charges against her. "So here are two great crimes on your part: heartlessness and despotism! But the third one is still more serious. An institution that more or less corresponds to very sound ideas about the organization of daily life [i.e., the sewing cooperative]—this same institution you subjected to the threat of destruction. . . . You would have provided the defenders of darkness and evil with an argument against your own sacred principles. I'm not even talking about the fact that you might have destroyed the well-being of some fifty people. What do fifty people matter? You have harmed the cause of all mankind and betrayed the idea of progress!"[14] Vera Pavlovna, the putative "new woman," is unmasked as a "despot," an enemy of humanity, and a "traitor!" "Isn't it true that you are a criminal?" her inquisitor cajoles. Fortunately, her guilt is mitigated by the fact that the crimes were committed "only in . . . imagination" not in actuality—thanks to Rakhmetov's timely intervention, though, as we have seen in "Garibaldi's" case, imaginary crimes warrant punishment, too. The gloomy monster has bared his claws, but at his allies and comrade-in-arms—not, as we might have expected, at his ideological enemies. Rakhmetov is the Russian literary prototype of the revolutionary tribunal, the agent of internal or state terrorism. Hence, he's not such a "nice, agreeable fellow" after all.

But if, after all of this, we see only *that*, then truly we belong to those whom the narrator proclaims will never see Rakhmetov because he is not only a monster, but the ultimate Romantic monster (demon), one whose gloomy monstrousness and his consciousness of it are sources of personal suffering, but suffering voluntarily assumed in order to rid the world of suffering. In the end, what is most striking about Rakhmetov is not his extraordinariness, but his literariness. Perhaps Chernyshevsky invested some of the eccentric radical Bakhmetev or even some of himself in Rakhmetov. (Indeed, his adversaries viewed Chernyshevsky as peculiar and ridiculous.) But this is only speculation.[15] What is certain is that Chernyshevsky sutured together various and contradictory literary models of heroism: the religious ascetic Alexei, Man of God; Don Quixote (Turgenev's, rather than Cervantes's); and the Romantic monster/demon to conjure a compelling image but one that, though conjured in a fortress prison, defies capture. The narrator's ambiguous attitude—now laughing (but never mocking), now exalting with Biblical metaphors—reflects an ambivalence toward the heroic and *"what must done"* that Chernyshevsky shared with his contemporaries, an ambivalence that could not overcome, in the end, his longing for it/him.

What Is to Be Done? ought not to have been written, and the tsarist government had every means at its disposal to ensure that it never was.[16] The traditional scapegoat in this story has been the bungling, inept censors, who subsequently took the fall and were forced to resign from their positions—albeit with full pensions.[17] But the censors did not hand Chernyshevsky pen and paper. It now seems undeniable that the tsarist government abetted the novel's writing, but why? To demonstrate their humane treatment of the prisoner, when he was refused more basic rights, such as visits from his family? In the hope that Chernyshevsky would discredit himself with his talentless novel of outlandish ideas?[18] The reasons will likely never be uncovered, and perhaps it is enough to say that whatever the scheme, it blew up in the government's face. The novel was a colossal sensation, an unprecedented literary event that forced a response from writers in all camps, to say nothing of the government, who in time-honored fashion rendered the novel precious contraband by banning the work and confiscating all copies. For the younger generation who already looked to Chernyshevsky as their lodestar, it served as a new secular Gospel, a manual for living that was immediately put into practice to unpredictable effect.

Of Russia's prominent men-of-letters, Tolstoy and Dostoevsky were most restrained in their response to *What Is to Be Done?*[19] In particular, Dostoevsky's initial critical silence is deceptive, or rather, it is the silence of deep impact, reflection, and assimilation.[20] Although Vladimir Lenin and Dostoevsky might agree on little else, Dostoevsky would surely concur that *What Is to Be Done?* "provided inspiration for a lifetime."[21]

At least it did in Dostoevsky's case: the publication of *What Is to Be Done?* coincided with the transition to the themes and literary aesthetics that constituted the mature phase of his career and produced his greatest novels. His first response to the novel came in the form of the 1864 novella *Notes from the Underground*, which received little attention at the time but which is the primary means by which modern readers know Chernyshevsky's work, so tightly is *What Is to Be Done?* knit into its fabric. And this response, two years in the making, was only the beginning of a long reckoning with something that Dostoevsky knew when he heard it but had not yet said: a new word.

Chernyshevsky paid dearly for his "new word." He was essentially punished for the censor's laxity by the severity of his sentence of hard labor and Siberian exile until 1883, when the terrorist organization the People's Will negotiated his repatriation to European Russia with the promise to abstain from violence during the long-delayed coronation ceremonies of Alexander III.[22] Whereas hostage taking has been a perennial tactic of warfare, using hostages to bargain for the release of imprisoned comrades became a tactic of international terrorism only in the 1970s.[23] In this inaugural case, the life of the ascendant tsar, Alexander III, was bought and paid for by the release of Nikolai Chernyshevsky, whom the People's Will regarded as one of their own. What the government did not yet realize was that the People's Will no longer posed any real threat: the organization had lost its leading cadres to arrest and emigration after the assassination of Alexander II. Unbeknownst to the authorities, the People's Will was a ghost of its former self, but the repatriation of Chernyshevsky was one of its last victories.

4

"Daring and Original Things" (Assez causé!)[1]

Although almost a decade had passed since Goncharov's *Oblomov*, the point of departure of Dostoevsky's *Crime and Punishment* is essentially the same. It is the bed of the protagonist, Rodion Raskolnikov, and the "fantastic nonsense" that he dreams up there. "'I want to attempt such a thing, and at the same time I'm afraid of trifles!' he thought with a strange smile. 'Hm . . . yes . . . a man holds the fate of the world in his two hands, and yet, simply because he's afraid, he just lets things drift—that is a truism. . . . I wonder what men are most afraid of . . . Any new departure, and especially a new word—that is what they fear most of all . . . But I am talking too much. That's why I don't act, because I am always talking. Or perhaps I talk so much just because I can't act. I've got into the habit of babbling to myself during this last month, while I have been lying in a corner for days on end, thinking . . . fantastic nonsense.'"[2] Raskolnikov contemplates the conundrum so familiar from the critical polemics of the early part of the decade: an excess of talk caused by or symptomatic of the inability to act. The conundrum is old, and so is the conflation of word and deed. But in Raskolnikov's case the word/deed must mark a break, must constitute a "departure." "Any new departure, and especially a new word—that is what they fear most of all." For good reason, as it turns out.

"And nonetheless for a start I need at least three thousand now. I'm trying in every corner to get it—otherwise I'll perish. I sense that only chance can save me. Out of the whole stock of my powers and energy all that's left in my soul is something disturbing and vague, something close to despair. Alarm, bitterness, the coldest vanity, the most abnormal state for me and in addition, I'm alone."[3] The reader of *Crime and Punishment* will be excused for mistaking these words and the plight they describe for Raskolnikov's when they are in fact his creator's, Dostoevsky's. With the exception, perhaps, of his fictionalized memoir of prison camp life, *Notes from the House of the Dead*, none of Dostoevsky's works is more autobiographical than *Crime and Punishment*. Dostoevsky's letters of 1864-65 reveal how closely his situation and state of mind paralleled that of the protagonist of the new novel that had begun to germinate.[4] That fateful year was perhaps the emotional and financial nadir of Dostoevsky's life: he had lost his estranged but strangely beloved wife and his most intimate companion, his brother Mikhail, in the space of a few months ("And suddenly I was left alone, and I was simply terrified. My whole life had been broken in two at once"),[5] assumed a massive debt incurred by their failed journalistic enterprise, as well as responsibility for the financial support of his brother's family. And his *Notes from the Underground*, as the rebuttal of Chernyshevsky's *What Is to Be Done?*, passed completely unnoticed. Thus, when Dostoevsky sent a prospectus peddling his novel-in-progress to Mikhail Katkov, the conservative publisher of the successful *Russian Messenger*, describing a former university student "expelled from the university, petit-bourgeois by social origin, and living in extreme poverty who [had] decided ... to get out of his foul situation at one go," he knew whereof he spoke.[6]

Dostoevsky wrote out of desperation and with a sense of urgency, but with undiminished confidence. "Now I'll start writing a novel again from under the stick, that is out of need, in haste. It will turn out to be striking."[7] "And meanwhile, if I'm given time to finish it, the story that I'm working on now may be the best thing I've written."[8] As Parts I and II were published sequentially in January and February of 1866, public response fulfilled Dostoevsky's hopes. In a letter to his close correspondent Alexander Vrangel, he triumphantly reported: "About two weeks ago the first part of my novel came out in the January issue of the *Russian Herald*. It is called *Crime and Punishment*. I've already heard many enthusiastic reactions. There are bold [smelye] and new things in it. How sorry I am that I can't send it to you!"[9] Dostoevsky's literary colleague and friend N. N. Strakhov confirmed that Dostoevsky's assessment was correct but recalled in his memoirs the unusual effect of the novel on the reading public. "Only *Crime and Punishment* was read in 1866. Only it was spoken about by lovers of literature, who often complained about the stifling power of the novel and the painful impression it left, which caused people with strong nerves almost to become ill and forced those with weak ones to give up reading it altogether."[10]

This constitutes a rather peculiar commendation and recipe for success, but as Konstantine Klioutchkine has compellingly argued, it resulted from Dostoevsky's keen attunement and ability to adapt to the rapidly changing media environment. As of 1864, metropolitan newspapers had overtaken the once dominant thick journals as the most widely read and influential medium; feuilletons became the favored genre for recounting evocative street scenes and engaging in provocative polemics alike; and sensational crimes captivated the reading public and boosted sales.[11] Dostoevsky's "willingness to open his novel to the influence of the press" as well as his "journalistic intuition" "allowed him to focus on sensational items charged with high generative potential" and enabled him to produce work that "featured the components of a successful product."[12]

Yet to achieve the distinction and success to which he aspired, Dostoevsky had to go beyond what had already been done. When Raskolnikov finally commits the murder that he has been contemplating for the first fifty pages of the novel, it is narrated from the point of view of Raskolnikov himself, who is filled with horror, disgust, and fear as he overcomes his vacillation to commit his act. Even more horrifically, he goes on reflexively, in sheer panic, to commit a second murder when his victim's unsuspecting younger sister discovers him *in flagrante delicto*. If the naturalistic description of the axe murder of two women and its aftermath were not enough, *Crime and Punishment* draws upon all the sensational melodramatic clichés taken to hyperbolic extremes. The murder is committed by an "educated and well-disposed" (in Dostoevsky's words) young man to save his virtuous sister, Dunya, who is the victim of slander and has no options but a loveless marriage to a capitalist boor. Meanwhile, Raskolnikov becomes involved with a pure and self-sacrificing young woman, Sonya, who had been forced into prostitution by her family's dire circumstances. These become still more dire when her alcoholic father is killed in an accident, leaving a tubercular widow and hungry orphans. In the midst of all this, the suspense turns upon two points: why, in fact, did Raskolnikov commit the crime and what will be his fate—will he be caught, confess, commit suicide, or kill again?

As the final installments of *Crime and Punishment* were published in late autumn of 1866, Dostoevsky wrote Katkov's assistant, N. A. Liubimov, to express special concern that the novel's initial impact be sustained.

> But I ask whether we couldn't do the following: do a notice for the public in the October issue that *the conclusion of Crime and Punishment will definitely follow this year*, and print the conclusion in the November and December issues? I ask for that exclusively because the novel's impression on the public will be much fuller and more sensational—incomparably so; forgive an author's vanity and don't laugh at him, because this is a quite forgivable matter. Perhaps there won't be any sensation at all, but it is quite forgivable (and I think even obligatory) for me, now, working on the novel to count on a success. Otherwise, I think an author ought not even dare take up the pen. In a word, I would like to finish the novel in such a way as to renew the impression, so that people talk about it just as they did at the beginning.[13]

If Dostoevsky was concerned that the sensation of his novel might have waned, he had multiple good reasons. In the first place, the media environment in Russia was absolutely unique, the product of the sudden eruption of modern conditions into a still recalcitrant social and political order. The undeniably beneficent liberalization of the press brought with it the negative effects that Klioutchkine so evocatively describes—namely, stiff journalistic competition and the concomitant cheapening of the word, as stories and ideas were unabashedly plagiarized and bowdlerized in the mad dash to produce marketable copy. At the same time, the continued existence of the censorship—albeit one discombobulated by its revised role—insured the undiminished significance of the writer and the literary word, even while radical writers persisted in their unabated attack on conventional literary aesthetics.

So the writer in the mid-1860s navigated the Scylla of an unpredictable censorship and the Charybdis of the insatiable market, which craved a steady infusion of novelty but was so inundated with media twaddle that anything truly new might simply go unnoticed. This was

Dostoevsky's experience with his *Notes from the Underground*, an experience he shared with his protagonist, Raskolnikov. When at the beginning of the novel Raskolnikov is musing on how difficult it is to say a "new word," he has in fact already said his. His ground-breaking article "On Crime" had appeared three months prior, unbeknownst to him, in a marginal journal but almost no one—neither his best friend, family, nor even those with a compelling professional interest (except, apparently, the police investigator Porfiry Petrovich)—read it until *after* he commits his double-murder. The message is clear: if you want your "new word" heard, write it in blood.

But then suddenly someone did, just as Part III of *Crime and Punishment* was due to be serialized in mid-April 1866. The twenty-five-year-old ex-student Dmitry Karakozov made his "unheard of" attempt to assassinate Tsar Alexander II. Karakozov's indisputably more sensational crime and punishment—he stepped out from the crowd, fired a shot at the tsar, missed, was arrested and subsequently hanged—not only "interrupted" *Crime and Punishment*, as the historian Claudia Verhoeven has observed, but threatened (at least in the mind of its anxious author) to diminish its impact.[14] An eccentric loner who had had been loosely associated with a quasi-conspiratorial circle led by his cousin, Nikolai Ishutin, Karakozov seems to have acted on his own initiative, without the support or benediction of his comrades.[15] Suffering from evident depression and hypochondria (as well as genuine physical ailments, such as venereal disease), Karakozov was ready for death, not the media. For the attempt, he awkwardly disguised himself as a man of the people and had tucked two copies of a proclamation entitled "To My Brother-Workers" inside the pocket of his peasant overcoat, along with pharmaceutically prepared packets of morphine, strychnine, and hydrocyanic acid.[16]

Neither the proclamation nor the cyanide served its intended purpose. The media, however, was ready for Karakozov and with hyperbolic rhetoric made the most of his atrocious crime, despite the fact that M. N. Murav'ev's tight-lipped Investigative Commission withheld all pertinent information, and a government crackdown on all forms of public expression immediately followed Karakozov's attack. Numerous scholars have emphasized the symbiosis of terrorism and the media and have gone so far as to argue that mediatization—the international telegraph, the daily newspaper, and sensationalism—was the necessary condition of the first wave of modern terrorism.[17] All of these elements were in place for Karakozov's precocious attempt, and in the spring and summer of 1866, the media sustained the public's interest with tales of a supposedly far-flung revolutionary conspiracy (a theory propagated by Dostoevsky's own publisher, Mikhail Katkov, in the *Moscow Gazette*), as well as with heroic accolades for Osip Komissarov, the loyal subject and man of the people who had ostensibly saved the tsar's life.[18] The trial first of Karakozov, then of the Ishutintsy, occupied public attention through October 4, 1866, with the Petersburg newspapers *The Northern Post*, *The Senate Gazette* and *The Gazette of the St. Petersburg City Police* running daily reports.[19] Working steadily on *Crime and Punishment* while he summered with friends outside of Moscow, Dostoevsky was not in attendance for Karakozov's execution in St. Petersburg—where he himself had faced a firing squad almost seventeen years earlier—on September 3, 1866.[20] Dostoevsky's letter to Liubimov expressing his concern that the sensation of his novel would not be sustained was penned precisely two months later, on November 3, 1866.

To avoid that eventuality, Dostoevsky did something absolutely counterintuitive and not without risk. Whereas his initial strategy, as the literary critic Philip Rahv speculated, may have been to "depend on the sleight of hand of substituting a meaningless crime for a meaningful one"[21] and to thereby obscure the political significance of Raskolnikov's crime, his strategy after Karakozov's "interruption" was to enhance the identification as a political criminal and this time himself to go "further," in the process suggesting that his hero was or might be (since the possibility certainly remains open) an "extraordinary man," were it not for the *wrong* crime and punishment.

5

"Vous trouvez que l'assassinat est grandeur d'âme?"

In the Epilogue of *Crime and Punishment*, after Raskolnikov has confessed and been tried for the double murder, there is a niggling discrepancy between the crime as a "brute fact" and as a "social fact." To all appearances, the crime was an ordinary one, but the criminal, on the other hand, "did not quite resemble the ordinary murderer, outlaw, or robber, but . . . here was something else."[1] The perplexity turns upon that "something else," that excess that makes Raskolnikov something other than an ordinary criminal. The problem, however, is that that excess is excessive. Critics have struggled valiantly with this excess in trying to solve the enigma of Raskolnikov. Some, such as Vladimir Nabokov, have thrown up their hands and blustered that Raskolnikov has simply too many and too contradictory motives to be psychologically plausible.[2] Others have repeated the same procedure that Raskolnikov performs in his confession to Sonya, when he produces and then rejects ("That's not it!")[3] one explanation after another, proceeding from the most altruistic motivation (he killed for his mother and his sister, to save them from "grief" and "offense")[4] to the most egoistic ("I simply killed, killed for myself, for myself alone").[5] The mistake here is to assume that this procedure constitutes a process of elimination, whereby all the other reasons and motives are systematically excluded (like suspects exonerated), leaving the last, often least suspected suspect as the guilty party. Whether this is a legitimate investigative technique, it is standard narrative practice in crime and detective fiction, but in *Crime and Punishment* we needn't mistake technique for the truth of Raskolnikov, the novel, or of the indefinite, unresolved "something else" to which Dostoevsky referred.

Dostoevsky himself was perturbed by the excess and in his notebooks for *Crime and Punishment* gave himself a harsh ultimatum: to clarify Raskolnikov's motive, one way or the other.[6] However much Dostoevsky might have liked to strike from the record certain inconvenient facts, "the record" was the product of a third person omniscient narrative technique that he had developed expressly for the purpose of "seeing into Raskolnikov's soul" while at the same time maintaining the necessary distance for crucial technical maneuvers. In other words, to adequately delineate the "something else" would necessitate reproducing the complexity of the entire novel, a complexity that Dostoevsky himself apparently regretted but could not avoid. In the interest of striking a balance between the opposing inclinations for the single and reductive versus the multiple and complex, I propose that the most fruitful approach to Raskolnikov's "something else" is through Raskolnikov's questions.[7] In the novel, these questions, undeniably, are urgently relevant to Raskolnikov, to his personal situation and identity. They are all introduced with varying degrees of elaboration in Part I, in accordance with the necessities of the unfolding narrative. This renders moot the genesis of any single question, its external source or point of origin in Raskolnikov's biography or psychology, and for that matter, the question's original form. But as the narrator notes, "none of the questions was new or sudden, however, they were all old, sore, long-standing."[8] These are indeed the old, sore questions regarding identity (the type of man) and action (the type of deed) that Turgenev, Dobroliubov, Chernyshevsky, et al. had been posing for almost a decade, and that constitute the coordinates of an image that was coming into sharper focus. The questions undoubtedly have a familiar ring to them: 1) Is he mad? 2) Is he an extraordinary man? 3) Does he dare? 4) Is there justice in it? 5) Can he endure it?

Ultimately, or so the narrator tells us, Raskolnikov's questions coalesce "into a horrible, wild, fantastic question that tormented his heart and mind, irresistibly demanding resolution."[9] In a signature move, Dostoevsky gives us ellipses rather than the question. Only much later, in Part V, does Raskolnikov put it in words "AM I a trembling creature, or do I have the right . . ." Ironically, even though he did it, he cannot say it: it is the "pure" Sonya who must say it for him. "To kill? The right to kill?"[10] In what follows below, I will show how each question establishes a critical component of *he who would claim the right to kill*.

Is He Mad?

As we have seen, sedition, political rebellion, any challenge to the established order bore the stigma of madness, which could be turned to the advantage of the accused (with madness or eccentricity as a mitigating factor) or to the government (as a means to silence pesky nonconformists, like Peter Chaadaev). Raskolnikov's surname, denoting as it does the zealous and politically rebellious Old Believers (raskol'niki), reeks of fanaticism, and the word *fanatik* in Russian was virtually synonymous with "madman" (bezumets).[11] To rebel against the God-anointed tsar and the divinely sanctioned order was to rebel against God, and thus to enact the very definition of madness, an affliction that in Orthodox and popular thought was associated with demonic possession visited upon wayward souls for their sins.[12] Yet with the advent of Western biomedical paradigms, madness was understood to have natural, organic causes rather than supernatural, moral, or spiritual ones.

The dramatic irony of the first part of *Crime and Punishment* derives from the fact that Raskolnikov suffers from a malaise foretold in his article "On Crime" in which he argues that most criminals are afflicted by a "darkening of reason and the will" that leads to careless mistakes and their ultimate self-incrimination. As confident as he is in his diagnosis, Raskolnikov is undecided with regard to the etiology. "The question whether the disease generates the crime, or the crime somehow by its peculiar nature is always accompanied by something akin to disease he did not yet feel able to resolve."[13]

Through Raskolnikov's irresolution, Dostoevsky mounts a challenge in two directions: to the Western medical explanation of madness and to the deeply ensconced association between madness and political crime by implying that (political) criminals may be initially and fundamentally sane, and that if they go mad, it is because their idea has driven them mad. In the Epilogue "the latest fashionable notion of temporary insanity" serves to mitigate Raskolnikov's sentence, but the narrator's dismissive tone suggests that the *fashionable* (i.e., Western) theory of temporary insanity is not, in fact, the right one.[14] Sonya, upon listening to the preamble to Raskolnikov's "gloomy catechism" (mrachnyi katekhizis) styled as a confession, involuntarily asks herself the same question ("Can he be mad?") but comes to the conclusion that the epilogue reiterates: "no, there was something else here."[15]

Is He an Extraordinary Man?

Precisely the addendum (and loophole) to Raskolnikov's theory of temporary insanity is actually the main theory, the one that critics have typically cited as the "true motive" for Raskolnikov's crime, as well as the motive that renders his crime political or political-philosophical. This theory is only "hinted at" at the end of Raskolnikov's article "On Crime," and Dostoevsky withholds its full elaboration until his first encounter with the savvy police investigator Porfiry Petrovich in Part III. The theory divides people into two groups—the ordinary and the extraordinary—the latter being innovators in the most diverse fields of endeavor (Newton, Lycurgus, Muhammed, Napoleon) whose contribution to humankind warrant their disregard of ordinary human laws and norms.

Raskolnikov's interlocutors deny that there is anything particularly new or original in Raskolnikov's "Napoleonic idea": it had numerous sources, both in and outside of Russian literature. The most frequently cited is Pisarev's review article "Bazarov," which followed the publication of *Fathers and Sons* by only a month. Pisarev set the agenda for much subsequent Russian literature of the 1860s and 1870s—and certainly for Dostoevsky—by asking "What is Bazarov?" ("Chto takoe Bazarov?") and by answering this with reference to Bazarov's unique morality. Whereas for the vast majority, morality was constituted by the social norms of the society into which they were born, a small minority (Bazarovs) not only questioned in words but separated themselves "with deeds, with habits, with their entire way of life" from the masses and thereby achieved "complete self liberation, complete individuality, and complete self-sufficiency [samostoiatel'nost']."[16] In Pisarev's view, if "the Bazarovs" had the proper field of action, their energy and original genius destined them for historical greatness.

Pisarev names George Washington, Garibaldi, Copernicus, Heinrich Heine, and Herostratus as examples. Napoleon's name is conspicuously absent, as is the idea of political assassination, but Count Leo Tolstoy explicitly linked the two in his latest novel, then under serialization in Katkov's *Russian Messenger*. Tolstoy is rarely if ever mentioned as an intertextual source or match for Dostoevsky's Napoleonic idea, although his is by far the most famous literary instance. In the very first part of Tolstoy's *The Year 1805* (later renamed *War and Peace*), the unlikely "Jacobin" Pierre Bezukhov scandalizes the monarchist company by defending murder for the sake of the common good.

> "The execution of the duc d'Enghien," said Pierre, "was a necessity of state; and I precisely see greatness of soul in the fact that Napoleon was not afraid to take upon himself alone the responsibility for this act."
>
> "*Dieu! Mon dieu!*" Anna Pavlovna whispered in a frightened whisper.
>
> "*Comment, monsieur Pierre, vous trouvez que l'assassinat est grandeur d'âme?*" said the little princess, smiling and drawing her work towards her.
>
> "Ah! Oh!," said various voices.
>
> "Capital!" Prince Ippolit said in English and began slapping his knee with his palm. The viscount merely shrugged.
>
> Pierre gazed triumphantly at his listeners over his spectacles.
>
> "I say that," he went on desperately, "because the Bourbons fled from the revolution, abandoning the people to anarchy; and Napoleon alone was able to understand the revolution, to defeat it, and therefore, for the sake of the common good, he could not stop short at the life of a single man."[17]

Pierre's argument appears at first not to be a theory in any strict sense but simply a defense of his idol, Napoleon, and a single act of political murder. Not only does it name Napoleon explicitly, but the cardinal points of Pierre's defense and Raskolnikov's "theory" are essentially the same: Napoleon was "not afraid to take upon himself alone the responsibility for the act" and "for the sake of the common good, he could not stop short at the life of a single man." Although Pierre portrays Napoleon as "defeating" the revolution, he in fact represents its most complete realization. Even the less astute members of the company perceive the shocking implications of Pierre's ideas. (Princess Lise: "Monsieur Pierre *vous trouvez que l'assassinat est grandeur d'âme?*" Anna Pavlovna: "Revolution and regicide a great thing? . . . After that . . . wouldn't you like to move to another table?") Tolstoy clearly has great fun satirizing the shocked reactions of the royalist company to these explicitly revolutionary ideas, though uttered safely in the historical past by the benign, innocuously roly-poly Pierre. By contrast, the lean and hungry Raskolnikov with the unmistakable profile of a nihilist engages in various circumlocutions and euphemisms; nonetheless, it is clear that the necessity of "stepping over a dead body" pertains less to scientific than to political fields of endeavor. In any event, only where sovereign power is at stake would it be possible, in the event of "triumph in their own lifetime," to turn the tables and go from being punished and hanged "(more or less)" to "doing their own punishing," in other words, from insurgent to hegemonic murder.[18]

Does He Dare?

"Oh, come, who among us in Russia doesn't think himself a Napoleon now?" taunts Porfiry Petrovich, intimating that Raskolnikov's pretensions to extraordinariness are in fact rather ordinary (recall that even the lolling Oblomov also liked to imagine himself a Napoleon). So there can be no mistake—a possibility that very much concerns Porfiry Petrovich—there must be a litmus test, or better, two. The first is the more fundamental "to see if you can." "I wanted to have the courage, and I killed. . . . I only wanted to dare [ia tol'ko osmelit'sia zakhotel], Sonya, that was the only reason!"[19] This bare-faced admission comes at the very end of Raskolnikov's confession to Sonya, after he runs through all the other reasons for his act, but it is the first to be alluded to in the novel. "Hm . . . yes . . . man has it all in his hands, and it all slips through his fingers from sheer cowardice."

In Russian, the verb "to dare" has the same root as the adjective "brave, courageous" (smelyi): to dare means "to brave." At issue is the conquest of fear, always a synecdoche for fear of death. As with the daredevil Decembrist described by Yurii Lotman, "the point of the action was to accomplish something unheard-of, surpassing the person who no one had yet been able to overcome, . . . crossing the limit that no one has yet crossed."[20] (The "person-who-no-one-had-yet-been-able-to-overcome" was of course the sovereign.) But the cerebral Raskolnikov elaborates this essentially Romantic praxis into a political theory of audacity. It is not simple might—crude force—that makes right, but audacity. "The man who dares much is right in their eyes. He who can spit on what is greatest will be their lawgiver, and he who dares the most will be the rightest of all!"[21] Audacity, in other words, confers legitimacy. Audacity cannot be reduced to physical or moral courage alone, but—and this is nihilism's contribution—exhibits a moral shamelessness, the willingness not only to flout society's norms but to violate what it holds most scared. This theory is perfectly suited to the exigencies of asymmetrical warfare, where the risky and atrocious are the poison arrows in the quiver of the lesser force. For Raskolnikov, who chafes unbearably at his own powerlessness, the connection between power and audacity is the heart of his idea and constitutes its claim to originality. "Power is only given to the one who dares to reach down and take it. Here there is one thing, one thing only: one has to dare! And then I had a thought then that nobody had ever had before me! Nobody!"

To do, to dare—this is a hurdle that Raskolnikov actually clears, trembling all the while. The other hurdle is an impediment to daring and nearly its opposite: conscience. When Raskolnikov divides people into what are essentially Pisarev's two categories, the ordinary ("by nature conservative, staid, live in obedience, and like being obedient")[22] and the "extraordinary," the extraordinary are initially described in terms of their creative and beneficent activity but later almost exclusively as "transgressors and destroyers." But to carry out creative destruction one must reckon, one way or another, with conscience. And despite Razumikhin's impression that Raskolnikov has reckoned it away the precise role of conscience is unresolved in Raskolnikov's mind, and that is his undoing. First, he asserts that an "extraordinary" man may "allow his conscience to . . . step over certain obstacles, and then only in the event that the fulfillment of his idea . . . calls for it."[23] Later, this very tentative and qualified "permission" attains the implacability of a "duty": "it would even be his duty . . . to remove those ten or a hundred people."[24] This is a qualitatively different idea: the moral *mandate* to kill for his idea. Ultimately, however, a qualification is reinstated. "But if such a one needs, for the sake of his idea, to step even over a dead body, over blood, then within himself, in his conscience, he can, in my opinion, allow himself to step over blood, depending, however, on the idea and its scale—make note of that."[25] Again, it is a matter of just one single "dead body." Ultimately, however, Raskolnikov arrives at the opposite pole. "'Let him suffer, if he pities his victim. . . . Suffering and pain are always obligatory for a broad consciousness and a deep heart. Truly great men, I think, must feel great sorrow in this world,' he suddenly added pensively, not even in the tone of the conversation."[26] Just as the etiology of the criminal's "temporary insanity" is unresolved, so is the role of conscience.

Is There Justice in It?

There is scant evidence that Raskolnikov pities his victims or feels particular remorse on their behalf, at least not *after* the murder. The pawnbroker Alyona Ivanovna never becomes more than "a louse" who "doesn't deserve to live" in Raskolnikov's or the reader's eyes; by contrast, Lizaveta, Raskolnikov's other, accidental victim is pitiable in a far more general sense, as one of the world's unresisting victims, along with Sonya and Mikolka's horse. Yet precisely Raskolnikov's dream of Mikolka's horse presents pity and justice as, paradoxically, the emotional and moral motives for the murder itself. Raskolnikov's nightmare of Mikolka's horse springs from the soil of his suppressed but vivid childhood memories and his child-self's distress at the sight of coachmen beating their dray horses as they pulled heavy loads past his home ("he would be so sorry, so sorry for the poor horse that he almost cried, and mama used to take him away from the window").[27] In the grotesquely intensified dream scenario the child, Rodya, watches with mounting horror and desperation as the drunken peasant, Mikolka, beats his scrawny mare in front of a raucous crowd, first from idle sadistic sport and then in a murderous rage that grows the more murderous out of frustration at not being able to kill. "'It's my goods!' Mikolka cries, holding the crowbar in his hands, his eyes bloodshot. He stands there as if he regretted having nothing else to beat. 'Really, you've got no fear of God in you!' many voices now shout from the crowd. But the poor boy is beside himself. With a shout he tears through the crowd to the grey horse, throws his arms around her dead, bleeding muzzle, and kisses it, kisses her eyes and mouth. . . . Then he suddenly jumps up and in a frenzy flies at Mikolka with his little fists. At this moment his father, who had been chasing after him all the while, finally seizes him and carries him out of the crowd. 'Come along, come along!' he says to him. 'Let us go home.'"[28]

In the dream, Raskolnikov's identification is wholly with his child-self, but upon wakening he identifies with Mikolka. "God, can it be that I will really take an axe and hit her on the head and smash her skull . . . ?" Without question, the nightmare represents the final rearing up of Raskolnikov's moral conscience, galvanized by the outraged compassion of his child-self. But it also reveals a shocking truth: the child and the murderer are one and the same. "Then he suddenly jumps up and in a frenzy flies at Mikolka with his little fists."[29] Mikolka's hyperbolic violence provokes the child Raskolnikov's infantilized ("with his little fists") retaliatory violence. Conscience is double-edged, as likely to compel violence in the very act of deploring it.

In the dream, Raskolnikov is intercepted by his father and ignominiously "carried away" without reaching his target. This is the one appearance of Raskolnikov's deceased father in the entire novel, and his role is hardly neutral. Although he condemns the crowd's drunken rowdiness ("they are drunk, they are playing the fool"), he fails to intervene or even explicitly condemn Mikolka's violence. His terse response (especially marked in the original Russian) betrays his desire to quit the scene as soon as possible—in other words, it suggests his own sense of disempowerment and moral cowardice.[30]

Despite his elders' injunctions and his own morbid solipsism, Raskolnikov cannot "not look." Thus, he joins the ranks of gloomy monsters, along with Rakhmetov and all the Russian heirs of Radishchev who "see things that are not happy." The reader's sympathetic identification with Raskolnikov stems not from his quest to prove himself an extraordinary man when he isn't (or is) but from his Radishchevian/Dobroliubovian civic grief (grazhdanskaia skorb'), his spontaneous acts of compassion, and his acute desire to be a force for justice in the world, something that Dostoevsky makes clear in his *Notebooks* when he has Raskolnikov say: "I understand my calling to be life itself. I am not the kind of man who will permit some scoundrel to destroy the defenselessly weak. I want to take their part [and to do that] I need power. To do that I want to become a man."[31] He ends by killing an old woman and her simple-minded (and in the notebooks, pregnant) younger sister—precisely the defenselessly weak whom the Raskolnikov of the notebooks aspired to defend. What went wrong and can he endure it?

6

Spoiling One Idea to Save Another

There is only one explicit mention of Dmitry Karakozov's attempted regicide in Dostoevsky's correspondence in the months following April 4, 1866. It would be expected that with M. N. Murav'ev, the notorious "hangman of Warsaw" and head of the investigative commission, unleashing what Herzen's *The Bell* referred to as the "White Terror" on St. Petersburg and all of Russia, Dostoevsky would exercise extreme discretion in his writing. In point of fact, Dostoevsky knew that as a former Petrashevets he was under constant police surveillance, and that government permission for his proposed trip to Germany had been denied due to Karakozov's attempt.[1] Nonetheless, Dostoevsky did something characteristically contrary: rather than mute the political implications of Raskolnikov's crime, he amplified them and went "further" even than Pisarev. As Dostoevsky confessed in a letter dated June 17, 1866, to his former sweetheart, Anna Korvin-Krukovskaia, he was not one to shy away from the eccentric, the audacious, or the extraordinary: "I want to do an unprecedented, an eccentric thing: write *30* signatures in four months, in two different novels, of which I'll work on one in the morning, and the other in the evening and finish on time. Do you know, my dear Anna Vasilievna, that *even now I even like these sorts of eccentric and extraordinary things. I'm not fit for the ranks of people who live respectably* [italics mine]. I'm convinced that not one of our writers, past or living, wrote under the conditions in which I constantly write. Turgenev would die from the very thought. But if you only knew how hard it is to spoil an idea that has been born in you, made you enthusiastic, of which you know that it's good—and to be forced to spoil it consciously!"[2]

Turgenev would have indeed died at the thought of what Dostoevsky proceeded to do. Not only did he procrastinate in writing the second novel promised to his publisher, Stellovsky, until the eleventh hour, but he tactfully challenged his other publisher, Katkov's blackening of the nihilists. Katkov, whom Dostoevsky had described to Vrangel as "such a vain, conceited and vengeful person," held Dostoevsky's livelihood in his hands, so it was no small act of courage to take on this most ticklish of points.[3] In unmistakable but diplomatic counterpoint to Katkov's invective, Dostoevsky rushed to the defense of the maligned nihilist "Russian boys and girls" in a letter written only three weeks after Karakozov's attempt. "Our poor, defenseless Russian boys and girls have their own additional, eternally present basic point on which socialism will long be based, namely enthusiasm for goodness and the purity of their hearts. There is an abyss of swindlers and rogues among them. But all of these little gymnasium students, university students, of whom I have seen so many, have turned to nihilism so purely, so selflessly, in the name of honor, truth, and true usefulness!"[4]

Shortly thereafter, he entered into an editorial scuffle with Katkov and his assistant, Liubimov, who "saw evidence of nihilism" (where there was "even quite the contrary") in the scene where the prostitute Sonya Marmeladova reads the raising of Lazarus at Raskolnikov's request.[5] Finally, at a time when the findings of the Investigative Commission attributed Karakozov's crime to the pernicious influence of Chernyshevsky and his novel *What Is to Be Done?*,[6] Dostoevsky rendered the most sympathetic portrait of the muddle-headed but good-hearted Chernyshevskyite, Lebeziatnikov, who exposes Luzhin's slander of Sonya.[7] As he had done at the height of the 1862 fires, Dostoevsky also deflates the anti-nihilist hysteria spread by the likes of Katkov by satirizing Luzhin's exaggerated fear of the nihilists' power and their ability to destroy him by "unmasking" him as a fraud.[8] The degree to which Dostoevsky was conspicuously swimming against dangerous political currents is even more apparent when it is recalled that he wrote these chapters, 1-3 of Part V, during the trial, sentencing, and execution of Karakozov and the Ishutintsy in August-September 1866.[9]

What Dostoevsky didn't do was what he feared he would: "spoil a good idea consciously." Instead, he saved it unconsciously. His plan for the novel, as he originally pitched it to Katkov, had consisted precisely in spoiling Raskolnikov's ideas, those "strange, 'unfinished' ideas floating in the air."[10] His prospectus to Katkov emphasized the consequences of the murder for Raskolnikov: "Insoluble questions arise before the murderer; unsuspected and unexpected feelings torment his heart. God's justice, earthly law, comes into its own, and he finishes by being compelled to denounce himself. Compelled, so as to become linked to the people again, even at the price of perishing at penal servitude; the feeling of separation and alienation from humanity that came over him immediately after committing the crime has worn him out with torment."[11]

Critics have been almost united in lamenting the ending of *Crime and Punishment* as "manifestly the weakest section of the novel, and the regeneration of Raskolnikov under the influence of the Christian humility and love of Sonya is neither artistically palatable nor psychologically sound."[12] Indeed, Dostoevsky speeds up and makes the final parts far shorter than he had originally planned, citing the fear that his congenital verbosity would "ruin the concluding effect."[13] It would not be amiss to say that Dostoevsky skimps on those things that he seemed to promise Katkov: his hero's pangs of remorse, repentance, and redemption. These are squeezed—some would say implausibly—into the Epilogue. Instead, what explicitly galls and galvanizes Raskolnikov in the second half of *Crime and Punishment* is as much a sense of shame and regret at his own failure as a sense of guilt for his crime. Far from realizing the error of his ways, Raskolnikov realizes the *error of his crime* and forges ahead undaunted to develop his "by no means stupid" idea. In conceptualizing the crime that he *should have* committed, Raskolnikov progresses from ordinary murder, to outmoded tyrannicide, to "something a hundred million times more hideous"—modern terrorism.

We may recall from the novel that at the time of its commission, the aspect of the crime that most absorbs Raskolnikov's attention and emotional energy is its stealth. Raskolnikov is scared to death that he/it will be detected, seen. The only person who sees the crime, aside from his second victim, Lizaveta, is Raskolnikov himself, who is overwhelmed by the visceral emotions of fear and disgust. Once the danger of being caught *in flagrante delicto* is past, he wants to see and be seen: to read the newspaper reports, to revisit the scene of the crime, to taunt the foppish young investigator Zamyotov with his self-exposure, to engage in a cat-and-mouse game with the police investigator Porfiry Petrovich. While Raskolnikov is undoubtedly driven by guilt for his crime, and with it the desire to be caught, he is equally driven by pride in the "success" of the murder and the desire to be as boldly audacious as he wishes he had, in fact, been.[14]

In fact, Raskolnikov is torn by two conflicting impulses, the opposite imperatives of murder and terrorism: to be unseen (undetected) and to be seen, and the symbol in which these impulses meet and clash is the pyramid. This is a moment to admire Dostoevsky's multivalent symbolism. Immediately after Raskolnikov's visit to Porfiry Petrovich at which he unveils his Napoleonic idea while still concealing his identity as murderer, an unknown tradesman pops up from "under the ground" convincing Raskolnikov that he must have left tell-tale evidence or been seen. "Here's evidence as big as an Egyptian pyramid!"[15] The Egyptian pyramids as evidence too colossal to deny leads to Egyptian pyramids as an aesthetic ideal too mighty to overcome, as Raskolnikov slips into a stream of consciousness review of Napoleon's "beautiful and monumental" successes *and failures* contrasted with his own sordid ones: "Napoleon, pyramids, Waterloo—and a scrawny, vile registrar's widow, a little old crone, a moneylender with a red trunk under her bed—well how is Porfiry Petrovich, for instance, going to digest that! It's not for them to digest! . . . Aesthetics will prevent them [Estetika pomeshaet]: would Napoleon say, be found crawling under some 'little old crone's' bed! Eh, but what rot! . . ."[16]

What is perhaps even more shocking than the murder itself is the fact Raskolnikov should consider it from an aesthetic point of view, but this was inevitable in 1865–66, for reasons that will be discussed shortly.[17] In Raskolnikov's mind there are two elements that contribute to bad optics: "the little old crone" and the ignominious "crawling under the bed." Raskolnikov's concern with aesthetics is by no means for aesthetics sake, but rather because they interfere at a fundamental level with the act's meaning as apprehended by its imagined audience ("how is Porfiry Petrovich, for instance, going to digest that!").

This critique represents yet another "schism," an argument with Raskolnikov's internalized opponents, Porfiry Petrovich and Zamyotov. It was Zamyotov, after all, who "from the corner" insinuated the idea that the murder of an old woman was unbecoming of a Napoleon.[18]

This schism produces another that follows so abruptly in Raskolnikov's fracturing stream of consciousness that the reader may at first fail to notice Raskolnikov's exclamation "Eh, but what rot!..." signals that he has in fact moved on. The problem is no longer aesthetic considerations, but the consideration of aesthetics. Raskolnikov berates himself as an "aesthetic louse and nothing more" (esteticheskaia ia vosh', i bol'she nichego) whose concern with aesthetics is both the cause and a sign of his inability "to step over" and be an extraordinary man.[19]

The passages at the end of Part Three in which these ideas are expressed are striking for their compression and ellipses, which serve to both disguise and emblematize the radical nature of this lightning speed progression. It is no longer a matter of justifying the extraordinary man's right to kill in good conscience. After all the utilitarian justifications and self-justifications, aesthetics constitute the final frontier, the final set of norms to be transgressed. Once aesthetics have been relegated to the dustbin, Raskolnikov has an epiphany that takes the form of a cryptic non sequitur. "Oh, how well I understand the 'prophet' with his sabre, on his steed. Allah commands—obey, 'trembling' creature! He's right, the 'prophet' is right when he sets up a first-rate battery across a street somewhere and blasts away at the innocent and the guilty, without even stooping to explain himself!"[20]

Raskolnikov's reference to the "prophet's" unquestioning readiness to kill in the name of Allah stunningly conflates holy war (jihad) with Napoleon's ruthless use of artillery to quash a Royalist uprising in Paris. In imagining such total and indiscriminate violence, Raskolnikov has outstripped, or at least come neck and neck with, the thinker whom historians have recognized as the first theorist of modern terrorism, the German revolutionary exile Karl Heinzen.[21] Heinzen's incendiary pamphlet *Murder*, written after the crushing defeats of the 1848 Revolution and the onset of political reaction in Germany, was a pivotal moment "in the transition from traditional notions of tyrannicide to the larger violence of modern terrorism."[22] It is possible, but unlikely, that Dostoevsky was acquainted with Heinzen's pamphlet, which was first published as *Der Mord* (January 1849) in the Geneva newspaper *Die Evolution* before Dostoevsky's arrest in conjunction with the Petrashevsky affair. The pamphlet was republished as *Mord und Freiheit* in 1853 while Dostoevsky was in Siberian penal servitude and published again in 1881 with significant omissions and ameliorations.[23] Among these versions, none of which is definitive, there is significant variation. The spirit and message, however, are the same. Heinzen's point of departure is that legitimate violence is a fiction: murder is murder. "No clear-thinking, rational person can accept the hair-splitting distinctions by which certain methods of obliterating the enemy are justified and others condemned. Such distinctions rest on theological and legal fictions and do not in any way alter the facts of the matter, which are that in each case it is purely and simply a question of obliterating one's enemy."[24] Heinzen lavishes vitriol on the monarchs of Europe and exposes the ostensibly lawful violence of the Holy Alliance as butchery. The only rational course for the freedom fighter (Heinzen coined the term) is to match and surpass the butchery of governments: "Even if we have to blow up half a continent or spill a sea of blood in order to finish off the barbarian party, we should have no scruples about doing it.... The path to Humanity will pass through the zenith of Barbarity."[25] Statements such as these have led historians of terrorism to see Heinzen as advocating modern terrorism's quintessential form: random, mass civilian murder. But this is Heinzen's end point; he begins his pamphlet by presenting the criteria according to which "history" (not Heinzen) deems murder legitimate.

1. It seems that what is decisive in the way history judges a murder is the motive. History does not appear to condemn murder itself.
2. It seems that moral reactions to a murder are closely linked to the self-interest of those reacting for that which is esteemed a virtue among the ancients would be considered a crime in our age of police rule....
3. The courageous bearing of the murderer seems to be of equal weight in the scale of judgment as the success of the attempt.
4. It seems that murder is only justified when it selects a victim whose elimination also signifies the removal of a representative or upholder of a pernicious principle.
5. It seems that it is not just the "petty thieves" but also the petty murderers who are "hanged," while the "big" ones get off scot-free.
6. It seems that only the party of freedom has martyrs, the reactionary party having nothing but tools.[26]

Heinzen derives his first four points from justifications of tyrannicide, a form of violence strictly circumscribed by the ancients as an elite action taken to eliminate a morally vicious or illegitimate ruler. Its rationale was elaborated by ancient and early modern political theorists and revived with great fanfare by the Jacobins. Likewise, the representational vocabulary of tyrannicide was deeply conventional and reflected the assumed classicism of the practice. We need only compare the famous sculptures of Harmodious and Aristogeiton, who were venerated as the founders of Athenian democracy for their murder of the "tyrant" Hipparchus, and Donatello's sculpture of Judith and Holofernes (commissioned by the Medicis) to Raskolnikov's mortified visualization of his own act. *Crawling* under the old woman's bed is not only in violation of Heinzen's third point, but spatially aligns Raskolnikov with the slain tyrant, who from Cicero to André Chenier is troped as vile and subhuman. Meanwhile, Raskolnikov's victim, though undeniably a "representative of a pernicious principle," is *too insignificant* a representative, "unmonumental" . . . as he explains in his confession to Sonya, who completely fails to understand.[27]

Heinzen, perhaps, would not either, since aesthetics did not play a role in his theory of violence, but the literary critic Dmitry Pisarev and his ideological opponents would have. From the dungeon of the Peter and Paul fortress where he had been incarcerated since the summer of 1862, Pisarev participated in the intensification of the debate on aesthetics by launching a renewed assault. In case there was any doubt, in the 1864 article "Realists" Pisarev declared his antipathy toward aesthetics and earmarked it for destruction. "The reader will no doubt decide that aesthetics is my nightmare. Aesthetics and realism are indeed in a state of irreconcilable hostility, and realism must destroy aesthetics at the root, for at present it is poisoning and making nonsense of all branches of our scientific activity, starting with the highest spheres of scientific work and ending with the most ordinary relationships between men and women."[28] Pisarev and his allies at *The Russian Word* considered aesthetic apperception and aesthetic theory more generally pernicious and heralded its dissolution into the more scientifically grounded and useful disciplines of "physiology and hygiene."[29] Raskolnikov's derisive interjection "Eh, but what rot," in response to his own aesthetic musings, is a clear indication that he is in accord with the nihilist destruction of aesthetics.

Most readings of *Crime and Punishment* assume that in the second half of the novel, the question that torments Raskolnikov the most is whether to turn himself in or commit suicide, but the unregenerate Raskolnikov, the theorist of murder, by his own account suffers most keenly over the "aesthetic" question because the aesthetics of the act are intimately tied to his own identity, suspended between an extraordinary man and a louse. He belabors the point again in his confession to Sonya. "Wouldn't he [Napoleon] have shrunk from [this murder] because it was so unmonumental [eto uzh slishkom ne monumental'no] and . . . and sinful? Well, I tell you, I suffered a terribly long time over this 'question,' so that I was terribly ashamed when I finally realized (somehow all at once) not only that he would not shrink, but that it wouldn't even occur to him that it was unmonumental . . . and he wouldn't understand at all what there was to shrink from."[30] Clearly, Raskolnikov remains torn between the nihilists' destruction of aesthetics and the classical ideals of his creator, Dostoevsky, as described by Robert Louis Jackson. "Beauty to Dostoevsky is the beauty of what may be called ideal form—form that is the incarnation of harmony, measure, and repose. Dostoevsky's formal conception of beauty is the same as that found in Greek aesthetics."[31] In fact, Karakozov's attempt to assassinate Alexander II came closer to manifesting the "Greek ideal" of tyrannicide: he committed his crime in broad daylight and was unfazed at the time of his arrest. But most importantly of all, his victim was the man to whom monuments are raised—the sovereign, Alexander II. In its formal features, Karakozov's crime conformed to tyrannicide and at least had the potential to activate those moral meanings, regardless of whether or not Alexander II could be considered a "tyrant" in any real sense (not to mention whether Karakozov in fact considered him to be one).[32]

While Raskolnikov states that he "suffered a terribly long time . . . and finally realized somehow all at once," there is no hint of the "aesthetic question" in Parts I and II comparable to the foreshadowing of the Napoleonic idea.[33] The "aesthetic question" consumes Raskolnikov only in the second half of the novel, when he has "seen" the murder and has moved on to vacillate between two models of political murder: the traditionally aestheticized and legitimized form of tyrannicide and the "ugly" or "formless" (bezobraznyi) slaughter of civilians. Ultimately, Raskolnikov grasps a point on which Dostoevsky had long since insisted: that morality and aesthetics were inseparable, and that "stepping over" moral limits necessarily entailed stepping over aesthetic ones and embracing "the ugly."[34]

Raskolnikov stubbornly continues to develop his theory to the very end of the novel, and the connection between aesthetics and legitimate violence crystalizes in his parting conversation with his sister Dunya as he flares up once again to justify his "crime." "Ah, the wrong form, not so good aesthetically! Well, I decidedly do not understand why hurling bombs at people, according to all the rules of siege warfare, is a more respectable form. Fear of aesthetics is the first sign of powerlessness! . . . Never, never have I been more clearly aware of it than now, and now more than ever I fail to understand my crime! Never, never have I been stronger or more certain than now."³⁵ Raskolnikov's final insight—the most radical by far—echoes Karl Heinzen's exposure of legitimate violence as a fiction grounded in a purely conventional bias toward certain "forms." On the contrary, for Raskolnikov the undeterred theorist of murder, power and the "right to kill" proceed from the *destruction* of aesthetics, from actively embracing the "ugly" and "blast[ing] away at the innocent and the guilty, without stooping to explain himself." The extraordinary man, by definition, is one who has "stepped over" the distinction between innocence and guilt, beauty and hideousness, legitimate violence and merciless slaughter.

In his notebooks for *Crime and Punishment* Dostoevsky emphasized that Raskolnikov's "moral development begins from the crime itself; the possibility of such questions arises which would not have existed previously."³⁶ In the course of this moral development, Raskolnikov's internal division intensifies as he proceeds down an even more radical path, from a theory of the extraordinary man that "came out too unoriginally" in the form of an ordinary murder to a theory of modern terrorism. As Porfiry Petrovich concludes, "It's good that you only killed a little old woman. If you'd come up with a different theory, you might have done something a hundred million times more hideous [bezobraznee]!"³⁷ The point is that Raskolnikov *does* come up with a different, emphatically "more hideous" theory, but thankfully too late in the novel or too early historically to act upon it.

But is Raskolnikov really not an extraordinary man? Somewhat unexpectedly, Raskolnikov appears *more* rather than less extraordinary by the end of the novel, both because testimony to his extraordinariness comes in from all sides (at his trial, sundry witnesses testify to his altruism and heroic deeds) and because a new criterion of extraordinariness appears: suffering. It is Porfiry Petrovich who brings this new criterion to light, as he implicitly compares Raskolnikov to his namesake, another "raskolnik" (schismatic): "Do you know Rodion Romanych, what 'suffering' means for some of them? Not for the sake of someone, but simply 'the need for suffering'; to embrace suffering, that is, and if it comes from the authorities—so much the better. In my time there was a most humble convict in the prison; for a year he sat on the stove at night reading the Bible; so he kept reading it and read himself up so much that, you know, out of the blue, he grabbed a brick and threw it at the warden, without any wrong on the warden's part. And how did he throw it? He aimed it on purpose to miss by a yard, so as not to cause any harm! Well, everyone knows what's in store for a convict who throws himself armed at the authorities: so he 'embraced suffering.'"[38]

Porfiry Petrovich then opines that both Raskolnikov's idea and his execution of it show that he is not only "not such a scoundrel," but a martyr in the making. "I regard you as one of those men who could have their guts cut out and would stand and look at his torturers with a smile—provided he's found faith, or God," with the clear implication that faith may be in something other than God. Apparently, this capacity for suffering and martyrdom is in the family, as a completely different character, the lascivious a-moralist Svidrigailov, observes the same qualities in Raskolnikov's sister, Dunya: "She would undoubtedly have been among those who suffered martyrdom, and would have smiled, of course, while her breast was burned with red hot tongs. . . . She's thirsting for just that, and demands to endure some torment for someone without delay, and if she doesn't get this torment, she may perhaps jump out of the window."[39]

The ideas of martyrdom and "embracing suffering" are present from the beginning of the novel. Of all of the things that Raskolnikov has been thinking about, this is what he's been thinking about the longest: his sister's self-sacrifice and "martyrdom." "Mother writes that 'Dunechka can endure much.' I know she can! I knew it two and a half years ago, and for two and a half years I've been thinking about that, precisely that, that 'Dunechka can endure much.'"[40] In the Raskolnikov family, a strange sort of sibling rivalry revolves around martyrdom and who can endure more for whom, and Dostoevsky alludes to a theme that would receive further development in future novels: self-sacrifice as a form of self-assertion and a power play, a means of tyrannizing others. From Razumikhin's point of view, brother and sister are so alike that he suspects a conspiracy of siblings. "He's a political conspirator, he is, for sure! . . . And he's drawn his sister into it; that's very, very likely, given Avdotya Romanova's character."[41] In other words, both Raskolnikov siblings are equally disposed to "throw themselves armed at the authorities" and miss, as Dunya's faulty aim amply attests.[42]

Needless to say, it was not Porfiry Petrovich or his creator who added suffering to the equation of the extraordinary man. The perceptive Pisarev had spelled this out in his reflections on Rakhmetov in his belated review of *What Is to Be Done?* that appeared in *The Russian Word* in December 1865. In his sensitively psychological interpretation of Rakhmetov, Pisarev accounts for Rakhmetov's self-torture (sleeping on a bed of nails, etc.), which Chernyshevsky himself put down as a test of will, as self-punishment for his powerlessness to end suffering. "The active man's heart bursts because he can do almost nothing to relieve the general suffering and he wreaks his legitimate ire upon himself. 'So,' he says to himself, 'you can't help them, can you? Well take that! [Tak vot zhe tebe!] If you don't help others, suffer with them, suffer more than they!' And in fact he directs useless violence and constraint against himself.... There is one reason—the need common to such natures to take upon themselves the sins of the world, to scourge and crucify themselves for all the stupidities and villainies of mankind."[43]

In Raskolnikov's case, the "useless violence" that he commits against himself is an "ugly" ordinary murder that he knew he would not be able to endure. The key difference between Pisarev's Rakhmetov and Dostoevsky's Raskolnikov would seem to be that Rakhmetov suffers for the crimes of the world that he is unable to "help," whereas Raskolnikov suffers for his own crimes. Yet Raskolnikov suffers not only from guilt for his crime; as he clearly realizes at several points, he commits the crime in order to suffer. Compare Pisarev's ventriloquization of Rakhmetov to Raskolnikov's bitter musings on his helplessness after receiving his mother's letter projecting Dunya's unhappy fate. "It won't happen? How are you going to keep it from happening? Forbid it? ... How are you going to protect them from the Svidrigailovs, ... Go on, think of what may happen to your sister after those ten years, or during those ten years. Have you guessed?"[44]

At the very end of *Crime and Punishment* Raskolnikov submits, however unconvincingly, to the law's judgment and ultimately exchanges his own theoretical apparatus for Sonya's belief system ("Can her convictions not be my convictions now? Her feelings, her aspirations, at least..."). As the "murderer and the harlot" who had together read the raising of Lazarus contemplate the seven-year sentence stretching before them, the narrator foreshadows a possible future. "He did not even know that a new life would not be given him for nothing, that it still had to be dearly bought, to be paid for with a great future deed [velikii, budushchii podvig]."[45] The novel has looped stealthily back to Raskolnikov's original plan and sacrificial economy, in which a "new life" will be bought with a "great deed." In the end, in his inability to "step over" conscience and aesthetics and willingness to "embrace suffering," Rodion Romanovich Raskolnikov emerges as the first exemplar of those who would determine to "smash what needs to be smashed... and take the suffering upon ourselves!"[46]

7

A Gloomier Catechism

In 1868, the extraordinary man according to Raskolnikov's specifications still had not appeared, but the young radical writer Peter Tkachev had not lost hope. On the contrary, in the newspaper *The Deed* (Delo) Tkachev insisted on the imminent appearance of those he rebranded as "People of the Future" (in his article "Liudi budushchego i geroi meshchanstva"). These people, like Turgenev's Don Quixotes, appear perennially to fire the engines of human progress. "Among all peoples and in all centuries there appear individuals from time to time who sacrifice their personal interests for the sake of the common good and who—in the name of the common good, in the name of a great idea—are capable of heroic deeds and able to make their fellow men happy."[1] Whether or not Tkachev's "People of the Future" are a contingent of long-awaited "Oblomovs of the future," they are without question a more upbeat hybrid of Rakhmetov and Raskolnikov, combining the sacrifice of personal interests with heroic deeds "for the common good, in the name of a great idea" but with the express mission to make ordinary people "happy," rather than merely obedient or dead.

As the White Terror abated in 1867-68 to allow some semblance of radical activity, the cardinal problem remained that of revolutionary actions and actors. The first production of Tkachev's circle, which referred to itself as the "Central Committee" or "Action Committee," was appropriately enough "A Program of Revolutionary Actions." "The Program" affirmed political revolution as the only possible means to achieve the desired goal of social revolution, expressing confidence that the methods of political revolution had already been "worked out by the history of other revolutions" and therefore enjoyed the incontrovertible status of "historical law," albeit a law that needed to be kicked into gear.[2] This, in turn, was to be done by creating revolutionary types according to the method prescribed by the Program's authors. "To create the greatest possible number of revolutionary types," the authors wrote, "we must distribute certain types of proclamations in a certain spirit, arrange *skhodki* [meetings] and personal protests as preliminary probes, as a practical method for developing revolutionary types and separating from the masses the types which are already developed."[3] Whereas in literary naturalism the evocation of types depended on the writers' perceptiveness and prescience, in life the process was more questionable and involved "personal protests" and "preliminary probes," euphemisms that referred to the intentional incrimination of prospective recruits in order to radicalize them through the experience of arrest and imprisonment.[4]

As with so many revolutionary productions, historians have not conclusively established the identity of the authors of "A Program of Revolutionary Actions," but it has been consistently linked to Tkachev and Sergei Nechaev. Tkachev would emigrate in 1873 to Western Europe, where, as theoretician of Russian Jacobinism, his thinking would ultimately have a great influence on Vladimir Lenin. Sergei Nechaev, at the time a twenty-one-year-old auditor, was a self-made autodidact from the gritty industrial town of Ivanovo in central Russia. Nechaev made his way to Moscow for a brief sojourn in 1865–66 and then to St. Petersburg in the eventful spring of 1866. Nechaev's arrival in the capital in April 1866 coincided with Karakozov's "unheard of" attempt, and although there is no direct evidence, it's possible that Nechaev read the season's literary sensation, *Crime and Punishment*—or at least his idol Pisarev's review of it—the next year.[5] Nechaev is most often associated with Dostoevsky's 1870 novel *Demons*, but his rightful place both literarily and historically is precisely between Raskolnikov and Peter Verkhovensky.[6] This much is clear: had Nechaev been as perspicacious a reader of Dostoevsky as Dostoevsky was of Nechaev, the historical appearance of the terrorist might have occurred ten years earlier than it did. Instead, Nechaev failed to learn from Raskolnikov's mistakes and made a notorious blunder, the commission of an act of violence that could not be distinguished from an ordinary murder. His greater success lay in the realm of words and consisted in producing an even gloomier catechism than Raskolnikov's.

Above all else, Nechaev was an author—above all else—of himself. Nechaevshchina—the epithet later used to designate the Nechaev affair and the damage it did to the radical movement—was founded upon Nechaev's ability and willingness to "merge" life and art, revolution and text, fact and fantasy. What in literature is referred to as fictionalization in politics is referred to as "mystification," and Nechaev, as master mystifier, employed carefully staged ruse, dramatic self-presentation, and the written word to bring himself and the recalcitrant revolution, together, into being. The grandson of a serf, Nechaev was able to fashion himself as "one of the people" who had clawed his way out of the swamp to channel his populist rage into student protests. Regarded primarily as a revolutionary "agitator" by his contemporaries, Nechaev's success among the radical youth, as well as among more seasoned revolutionaries in emigration, Mikhail Bakunin and Nikolai Ogarev, was due to his unique ability to provoke strong emotion. With this inside track on emotions and how to transmute feelings into deeds, Nechaev's greatest success was somewhat paradoxical: he was able to project the image of the revolutionist as completely emotion*less*, and therefore without the shadow of a doubt extra-ordinary.

The role of emotion in the genesis of terrorism was already clarified in one of the first writings attributed to Nechaev, "Principles of Revolution" (Nachala revoliutsii—also "Beginnings of Revolution"). "Principles" reiterates Dobroliubov's thesis that the builders of "the paradise of future life" could not come from the current generation "bound by the concepts of filth of the present": the current generation was capable only of destruction, not creation. But even in this generation of destroyers, passion, thought, and action would become progressively unified. "The closer one approaches the time for a genuine popular movement, the less one finds a split between thought and action. More deeply infused with revolutionary ideas, the generations preceding the revolution contain individuals who cannot restrain their passion for destruction until the outset of the general struggle, who quickly seek enemies and do not hesitate to destroy them. At first appearing as exceptional events, called acts of fanaticism or frenzy by contemporaries, they must recur more and more frequently in various forms, and then become transformed into something like a general passion in the youth, and finally into a general insurrection. The annihilation of high-placed persons who personify the governmental forms or forms of economic exploitation must begin with isolated deeds."[7]

Individuals who for whatever reason could not restrain their passion commit "acts of fanaticism or frenzy"—or so they appear to contemporaries—but these are exceptional events. As the unity of thought, passion, and action becomes more routine, the acts of Karakozov, Berezovsky et al. serve as inspiration and give way to a general passion that manifests itself in collective action characteristic of the "comrades of Schiller's Karl Moor," with the stipulation, however, that "severe, cold, and merciless consistency will take the place of the idealism that kept them from doing what was necessary."[8]

The untitled document that became Nechaev's pièce de résistance, the so-called "Catechism of a Revolutionary" (Katekhizis revoliutsionera) depicts this "severe, cold, and merciless consistency" by prescribing the revolutionist's "attitudes/relationships" (otnosheniia)— his appraisals and feelings about people and the world. Everything is premised upon the revolutionist's status as "doomed" or "condemned" (obrechennyi) or more literally, "cut off." In *Crime and Punishment*, Raskolnikov's self-isolation preceding the murder is so extreme that it astonishes even Porfiry Petrovich: "Your life is so solitary that you don't even know things that concern you directly. It's a fact, sir",[9] and on his way to commit the crime, he imagines himself a "condemned" man: "It must be the same for men being led out to execution."[10] Raskolnikov has progressed beyond the renunciation (otrechenie) envisioned by Dobroliubov to its logical extreme—obrechennost'. After the murder, however, this sense of exclusion or ban (obrechennost') is a manifestation of Raskolnikov's moral guilt. For Nechaev, by contrast, the revolutionary's self-exclusion from society is necessary in order to wage war on it. "The revolutionary knows that in the very depths of his being, not only in words but also in deeds, he has broken all the bonds which tie him to the social order and the civilized world with all its laws, moralities, and customs, and with all its generally accepted conventions. He is their implacable enemy, and if he continues to live with them it is only in order to destroy them more speedily."[11]

The greatest hazard for the would-be extraordinary man would be ordinary human connection and feeling. Raskolnikov remains bound to the human community and to its moral/legal norms through his emotional connections to others—namely, to his sister, Dunya, and to Sonya. The expressions on their faces and looks in their eyes impel Raskolnikov, during the last flares of rebellion, to accept condemnation according to the law. "His eyes suddenly met Dunya's, and so great, so great was the anguish for him in those eyes that he came involuntarily to his senses. He felt, after all, that he had made these two poor women unhappy."[12] Nechaev's "Catechism" seeks to forestall such backsliding. Point Six specifies: "All the gentle and enervating sentiments of kinship, love, friendship, gratitude, and even honor, must be suppressed in him and give place to the cold and single-minded passion for revolution. He is not a revolutionary if he has any sympathy for this world. *He should not hesitate to destroy any position, any place, or any man in this world.* He must hate everyone and everything in it with an equal hatred. All the worse for him if he has any relations with parents, friends, or lovers; *he is no longer a revolutionary if he is swayed by these relationships.*"[13]

The emotional discipline that Nechaev dictates is more severe than even Rakhmetov's. It consists of a monstrously monomaniacal idea-feeling, "revolutionary passion," that is inculcated by means of an unsparing regimen: "it must be practiced every moment of the day until it becomes habit." Revolutionary passion is a dispositional monochrome, the one and only color on the revolutionist's emotional palette. Cold, impersonal, and egalitarian hatred, which hates all and everything equally, is not only the end but the *means* by which the revolutionary achieves his state of exclusion. By fusing this "passion" to a utilitarian calculus that guides all action toward the only admissible goal (revolution), Nechaev effectively rationalizes the "frenzy" and "fanaticism" associated with political crime and expunges the stigma of madness.

In keeping with his rationalizing project, Nechaev provides a systematic program of action, based on the revolutionist's prescribed attitudes, which divides society into five categories (rather than just two) and deals with them accordingly. The first category, containing the worst offenders, is earmarked for systematic destruction—in other words, terrorism. "Above all, those who are especially inimical to the revolutionary organization must be destroyed; their violent and sudden deaths will produce the utmost panic in the government, depriving it of its will to action by removing the cleverest and most energetic supporters."[14] While the destruction of the revolution's enemies is certainly instrumental in achieving its aims, the objective "to produce the utmost panic" specifies terroristic means to achieve revolutionary ends. The second category, while only slightly less pernicious, was to be left untouched, so that their own outrageous acts would naturally and consequently drive the people to revolt. Nechaev's plans vis-à-vis the third, fourth, and fifth categories involved the deception, manipulation, and exploitation that are the hallmarks of Peter Verkhovensky's modus operandi in Dostoevsky's 1871 novel *Demons*.

Nechaev wrote the *Catechism* while wooing his émigré patrons, Mikhail Bakunin foremost among them, in Switzerland sometime in the summer of 1869. Unlike Alexander Herzen, Bakunin was untroubled by doubts concerning Nechaev's sincerity when he provisioned him with credentials identifying him as the secret emissary of the Russian Section of the World Revolutionary Alliance—a fantasy organization—prior to Nechaev's return to revolutionary trenches in Russia. Upon his return, Nechaev commenced building his own conspiratorial organization, The People's Vengeance (Narodnaia rasprava), with ostensible ties to Bakunin's fictional World Revolutionary Alliance. In November 1869, one of the group's members, Ivan Ivanovich Ivanov, began to challenge Nechaev's decisions and authority; according to some accounts, Ivanov even threatened to establish his own autonomous circle.[15]

At Nechaev's instigation, the group presented Ivanov with an ultimatum: either submit or get out. When Ivanov opted for the latter, he aroused the suspicions of his comrades that he would inform to the police. In the course of a short three days, Nechaev and his most devoted follower, Peter Uspensky, convinced their co-conspirators that Ivanov posed an immediate threat and had to be eliminated. On November 21 Ivanov was lured to a pond on the grounds of the Agricultural Academy on the pretext that Ishutin's printing press had been located there. Once in the grotto, the conspirators fell upon Ivanov and a macabre slap-stick ensued in which Nechaev took the lead in the violence and first strangled Ivanov with a hood before finishing him off with a bullet through the back of the head.[16]

As usual, the police cast a broad net, and Nechaev's accomplices were swiftly rounded up along with other associates and acquaintances, for a total of 152 arrested in conjunction with the affair. Meanwhile, Nechaev slipped deftly through the police dragnet and out of the country sometime between December 15 and 17.[17] Despite this light-footedness after the fact, Nechaev's ineptitude in performing the deed allowed Alexander II's government to pursue a dual strategy, which was conceived as early as December 16: to try Nechaev's co-conspirators as political criminals and revolutionary conspirators while claiming that Nechaev, their leader, was himself just a common murderer. Tsarist officials in fact harbored no illusion about the specifically political danger that Nechaev presented, as K. F. Filippeus's report dated January 19, 1872, apprises his Third Section chiefs: "The interests of justice, extremely important in themselves, demand that the chief perpetrator of the crime not escape punishment. But aside from that, from the perspective of public safety and the personal security of the Emperor, Nechaev's agitational activity warrants extremely serious attention and it is necessary to end it, since it is capable of inspiring fantasies in young people, and it is impossible to remain confident that from among these fantasy ridden youths another Karakozov will not come forth."[18] Nechaev himself was presumed to be that "other Karakozov." During the years he remained at large, from 1869-72, police reports (based largely on rumors) and the testimony of his followers led the government to suppose that Nechaev was plotting an attack on the Winter Palace and on "the sacred personage of the Tsar himself."[19]

In July 1871, at the trial of Nechaev's so-called followers, the Nechaevtsy, one of the counsels for the defense, the ingenious V. D. Spasovich, offered what would become the standard interpretation of Nechaev's motivation for Ivanov's murder. By implicating them in the murder, Spasovich's story went, Nechaev had intended to bind his followers to him with the blood of their common victim. If this was indeed Nechaev's motivation, his miscalculation was profound. None of his accomplices felt particularly "bound"—they confessed their crime immediately and held Nechaev alone responsible—and the spilled blood failed to serve the function that Nechaev had envisioned.[20] Spasovich's interpretation is almost certainly too literary, as is evidenced by the fact that Dostoevsky readily appropriated it for his novel *Demons*. Another, slightly less literary interpretation can be found in *Crime and Punishment* in Raskolnikov's confession to Sonya. "I wanted to have the courage, and I killed.... I only wanted to dare, Sonya, that was the only reason!" This raises the question of whether Nechaev was a victim of his own agitation and propaganda, and of the long literary tradition of valorizing the deed. In the proclamation campaign (what the historian Philip Pomper referred to as "Nechaev's attempt to make a revolution with words") conducted from Western Europe in the summer of 1869, Nechaev sustained the insistent drumbeat of the deed (fakt), first in the proclamation "To the Students of St. Petersburg University." "Believe in deeds [fakty], my friends, and declare yourselves with deeds [fakty] and not with verbiage in order to gain the trust of those upon whose bread you were raised, whose hands put together the walls of your auditoria and printed your little books.... But take note friends, they are not awaiting chatterers [govoruny] nor preachers in evening dress, but men of action who will know how to show them their devotion with deeds [kotorye by sumeli katicheski dokazat' im svoiu predannost']."[21] The "fact" (fakt) to which Nechaev refers does not concern truth and falsehood, but the real and the unreal(ized). Nechaev's idiosyncratic usage echoes that of Karakozov, who referred to his prospective deed of tsaricide as a "decisive fact." In "Principles of Revolution," Nechaev goes on to specify the nature of the "practical deeds" he has in mind. "The activists [deiateli] of a true popular revolution, as soon as life has forged them, will declare themselves with deeds [zaiavliaut o sebe fakticheski].... We can believe only those persons who declare their devotion to the cause of the revolution with deeds [kto fakticheski zaiavlaiut o svoei predannosti k delu revoliutsii], fearing neither torture nor prison and we therefore reject all words which are not immediately followed by action.... We turn now for the first and last time to all oppositional elements of Russian life and call them to immediate practical deeds.... Revolution consecrates everything equally in this struggle.... They call this terrorism!... They have a loud epithet for it! Let them, we don't care."[22] Without himself daring to do the deed, Nechaev was nothing: a "babbler," "a mental masturbator," a pretender. Assez causé!—the deed would make him and the revolution.

Back on Russian soil after the longest manhunt in Russian revolutionary history and extradited as a common criminal by the Swiss, Nechaev, unlike Raskolnikov, relentlessly insisted that the murder had been exclusively political. At his civil execution on January 25, 1873, Nechaev's shouts "Down with the Tsar, down with despotism! Long live freedom! They've made me, a political criminal, a simple murderer!" were still heard by the assembled crowd, despite the convoy drummers' attempts to drown them out.[23]

Nechaev was sentenced to twenty years' Siberian penal servitude as a common murderer. As far as his family, his fellow radicals, and the Russian public were concerned, the murderer Sergei Nechaev met a fate similar to (if somewhat harsher than) that of the murderer Rodion Raskolnikov. However, the government was well aware that he was by no means an ordinary criminal, but an extraordinary one. Accordingly, by secret order of the tsar, Nechaev's police transport was diverted to

St. Petersburg, to the notorious dungeons of the Alexei Ravelin of the Peter and Paul Fortress. He was admitted there as "Prisoner Number 5," whose true identity was known only to the Fortress Commandant. And for a time, in his dungeon cell, when the authorities refused to provide him with any but religious reading, like Raskolnikov he underwent something resembling repentance and a spiritual conversion . . . but only as a ruse, in order to use formidable powers of psychological domination and emotional manipulation to convert the Ravelin's guards to his cause.[24] Seven years after his incarceration, Nechaev was able to send word through his guards to his ideological heirs, the astonished members of the Executive Committee of the People's Will, that he was alive and in St. Petersburg!

Part Two

Apparitional Terrorism in *Demons*

I

"Again, Like Before"

On November 25, 1869, a casual reader of *The Moscow Gazette* (Moskovskie vedomosti) might have easily overlooked the following notice: two peasants, walking through the park of the Petrov Agricultural Academy, spied a trail of blood leading to the frozen pond in the grotto. There, a corpse had floated to the surface and was visible beneath the ice.[1] The brevity of the report testifies to the incident's obscurity: the unidentified corpse was a silent cipher, discovered but as yet inscrutable. Two days later, an equally laconic notice established the identity of the victim as the auditor Ivan Ivanovich Ivanov.[2] Thanks to a surfeit of forensic evidence at the crime scene, a lucky coincidence (Uspensky's apartment was searched on the same day as the corpse's discovery) and hasty confessions, the murderers were quickly rounded up. While the *Moscow Gazette* provided periodic updates on the case as new evidence became available, nearly a month-and-a-half would elapse before the full import of the conspiracy was drawn out by the paper's editor-in-chief, Mikhail Katkov, and Russia's true enemies finally exposed.

For Dostoevsky's novel-to-be, *Demons*, Katkov's editorials would be foundational, as well as the impetus for subtle push-back (Dostoevsky, himself a former and hitherto undiscovered conspirator, was the arch anti-conspiracy theorist), but Dostoevsky's intention in writing the novel went beyond reportage, editorializing, or even history. His goal, as he explained upon the completion of *Demons* in 1873, was to "clarify its [the Nechaev affair's] possibility in our society, and precisely as a social event, not as an anecdote, not as a description of a particular occurrence in Moscow."[3] What interested Dostoevsky was not the "brute fact," but the "social fact"; in other words, he wanted to explore the social preconditions for the event's possibility and the as yet unrealized possibilities implicit in those same social preconditions. "Clarifying possibility" is the province not of history (which allows the realization of only one possibility) but of literature. It is not the prerogative of the historical actor (who makes his mark only with "real deeds" and "factual manifestations"); instead it is the privilege of the writer. Through the written *word*, Dostoevsky was able to surpass Nechaev's *deed* in order to transform the murder of Ivanov into something that it was not, an act of revolutionary terrorism.

For *Demons*, Dostoevsky drew unabashedly on the published details of Ivanov's murder, so that in their particulars, the murders of Ivanov and Dostoevsky's fictionalization, Ivan Shatov, are virtually identical.[4] In his novel, however, Dostoevsky supplied a dimension that the murder did not historically possess: its reception as terrorism. "One can imagine what a hubbub arose all over town. A new 'story,' again [opiat'] a killing! But there was something else here now: it was becoming clear that there indeed existed a secret society of killers, of arsonist-revolutionists, of rebels.... One can hardly imagine what conclusions and what mental anarchy our society, frightened to the point of panic, might have reached, if everything had not suddenly been explained all at once, the very next day, thanks to Lyamshin."[5]

In Shatov's murder there is clearly something in excess of Ivanov's, and that excess is provided by Dostoevsky's narrative arc, which stages Shatov's murder very near the long and architecturally complex novel's end. The reader is well prepared for the murder, privy not only to foreshadowing on the level of the implied author, but to the planning, execution, and immediate aftermath that Dostoevsky's first-person narrator, Lavrenty Antonovich G___v (who is not a member of the conspiracy), has presumably reconstructed. If from the point of view of the reader Shatov's murder is a *fait accompli*, from the point of view of the town's "society" it has an entirely different, oxymoronic aspect: that of a shocking repetition. It follows as the last of a series, is a "new story" that is "again a killing." In contrast to the blank presented to the police and to the *Moscow Gazette*'s readership by Ivanov's corpse, Shatov's already constitutes a "story" for the townsfolk, one that is simultaneously

"Again, Like Before"

"new" and old ("again"). Whereas Ivanov's murder is initially a meaningless anomaly, Shatov's corpse has meaning—and then some—already inscribed upon it.

"But there was something else here now" marks, by contrast, the advent of something actually new. Mishap and catastrophe had always evoked wild speculation regarding a malign agency, whether witches or revolutionary arsonists, as in the case of the 1862 fires; "now," however, that malign agency was proven verifiably to exist, even if there was as yet no designation specific to it, only a list of imprecise labels ("a secret society of killers, of arsonist-revolutionists, of rebels"). The capstone of Dostoevsky's achievement is the representation of the public's apprehension or understanding ("mental anarchy") of events as inseparable from its apprehension or emotional response ("frightened to the point of panic"). To sum up, it is in literature, in Dostoevsky's portrayal of the public's reception of Shatov's murder, that revolutionary terrorism becomes fully visible, despite the fact that it had not yet been historically actualized.

The hermeneutic hysteria and just plain hysteria that Shatov's murder brings to a pitch has its origin in earlier scenes of much more spectacular violence, even if that violence is on a completely figurative plane. As Yulia von Lembke's charitable fête for needy governesses descends into chaos, mercilessly sabotaged by the local nihilists and ruthlessly satirized by the narrator, G__v resorts to hyperbole to describe the crowd's reaction. "To calm them was impossible, at least for the moment, and—suddenly the final catastrophe crashed down like a bomb on the gathering, and exploded in its midst: the third reader, that maniac who kept waving his fist backstage, suddenly ran out on the platform."[6] A short while later, with the public's nerves strained to the utmost by the outrageous oratory, all hell breaks loose.

> The scene went very quickly. But I decidedly remember that part of the public rushed from the hall at the same moment, as if in a fright, precisely after these words of Yulia Mikhailovna's. I even remember one hysterical woman's tearful cry:
>
> "Ah, again like before!" [Akh opiat' kak davecha!]
>
> And suddenly, into what was already the beginnings of a crush, a bomb struck, precisely, "again like before."
>
> "Fire! All of Zarechye's in flames!"
>
> I only do not remember where this terrible cry first arose—but it was followed by such alarm as I cannot even begin to describe. . . . True, the

fire was still just beginning, but it was blazing in three completely different places—and that was what was frightening.
"Arson! The Shpigulin men!" came screams from the crowd.[7]

Two scenes are simultaneously enacted before the reader's eyes. In one, the crowd is perturbed to the point of panic by incendiary words of one sort or another (the "maniac's" oratory, Yulia Mikhailovna's gaffe, the alarm raised); in the other, the already panicked crowd is incinerated in sequential explosions. In 1871, there was no historical precedent for such butchery, but a literal reading of Dostoevsky's tropes insinuates this monstrous new "possibility," just barely alluded to by Raskolnikov (see Part One), into the social imaginary.[8] While it is likely that Ishutin's circle, inspired by Orsini's "infernal machine," had experimented with explosives, bombs featured nowhere in the programs, rhetoric, or the arsenals of revolutionaries until the People's Will embraced the technology later in the decade.[9] As bloodthirsty as Nechaev was, he never entertained the bombing of "soft targets," a tactic pioneered by the Fenians in the 1880s and taken up by the French anarchists in the early 1890s.[10] Yet the narrator's evocation from within the frenzied crowd captures every salient element of random, mass terrorism from the victim's point of view: the swiftness and suddenness, the repetition ("ah, again like before!"), the indescribability. Most notably, the "bombs" and the reaction to them are indivisible: the words are bombs precisely because the crowd reacts to them as if they were. Given the narrator's insistent repetition of the bomb metaphor, it is as if Dostoevsky were torn between the choice of devastating real violence at the fête or violence that was largely symbolic and by his canny use of tropes, split the difference.

Nevertheless, we must take great care in claiming that *Demons* is "about terrorism." In the first place, to speak of terrorism and *Demons* is to indulge in anachronism.[11] As we have seen, neither the tactic nor the concept was readily available when Dostoevsky began the novel in 1870 or when he finished it in 1872. Far from self-consciously constituting a terrorist organization and embracing the terrorist identity as the members of the People's Will would do, Peter Verkhovensky's motley fivesome—Virginsky, Liputin, Lyamshin, Tolkachenko, and Erkel—are mostly ignorant of his schemes and unwilling participants in the violence. The only viable contender for the label "terrorist," Peter Verkhovensky, thrice self-identifies as a "swindler" (moshennik), not even a revolutionary or a socialist.[12] Nikolai Stavrogin, the supposed chief and figurehead of the movement, is the most vexingly inert and non-committal of all. If anything, Dostoevsky's notebooks as well as the finished novel testify to a gap, both hermeneutic and practical, that appears between Karakozov's seminal act in April 1866 and the full-blown emergence of terrorism. This gap provides the opportune moment for Dostoevsky's project of preemption, a project that proceeds by the multi-pronged strategy of debunking, division, and diminution. First, however, even allowing for the notional existence of terrorism in 1870–72, Dostoevsky would reject it as inadequate to *Demons*, and here's why.

2

"The Only Possible Explanation of All These Wonders"

If Dostoevsky's aspiration, as author, is to "clarify possibility," his narrator G__v's much more modest ambition is "to describe the recent and very strange events that took place in our town."[1] Between these two purposes lies a hazard that *Demons* repeatedly exposes: explanation. Particularly in those cases where there is "only one possible" explanation or where "everything" is explained, we can be sure that there isn't *only* and not everything is.[2] As a typical feature of his poetics and a practical means of prepping his reader to read him, Dostoevsky often presents in microcosm (or as metaphor) what he dramatizes through the broadest level of the novel's plot. At the beginning of the novel we are confronted with an enigma: Nikolai Stavrogin, the unnaturally handsome aristocratic scion of General Stavrogin and his indomitable widow, Varvara Stavrogin, causes consternation with a *series* of outrageous antics. He pulls the elder Gaganov humiliatingly by the nose, he smooches the pretty and very married Madame Liputin, and he bites the ear of "dear, mild Ivan Osipovich."[3]

From the outset, the narrator and his fellow townspeople are at a loss, not only to *explain*, but even to find words for Stavrogin's "impossibly brazen acts." "The main thing lay in their being so unheard-of, so utterly unlike anything else, so different from what is usually done."[4] Since Stavrogin's behavior falls completely outside the bounds, the townspeople latch onto comically quaint epithets for Stavrogin ("pernicious ruffian" [vrednyi buian], "big-city swashbuckler" [stolichnyi breter]) that inevitably miss the mark. Just as society has no ready label, it has no ready recourse against behavior that it perceives as a menace and an affront: "perhaps some law may perhaps be found even for Mr. Stavrogin," huffs public opinion, but that law is lacking, among other reasons, for lack of words.[5] After his most grievous outrage, Stavrogin is arrested, only to conveniently manifest the unmistakable signs of brain fever. Within a single paragraph the narrator thrice effuses that "finally everything was explained!" and that the actions of a sick man constituted "the only possible explanation of all these wonders."[6] This explanation, according to the narrator, was "the elephant that everyone had failed to notice" largely because "they were inclined to expect such acts from Nikolai Vsevolodovich even when sane."[7] This explanation, in fact, directly contradicts the conclusion that it seeks to justify. "The only possible explanation" is in fact a cover for the utter lack of such. Stavrogin may have been 1) sane but capable of outrageous acts; 2) sick with brain fever; 3) both (in succession); or 4) something else altogether. The novel ends by reopening the question upon Stavrogin's suicide and then closing it just as definitively upon reaching the opposite conclusion: "Our medical men, after the autopsy, completely and emphatically ruled out insanity."[8]

One historical analogy and one homology within the novel present themselves. Stavrogin's "unheard of" acts take place three years prior to the contemporary events of the novel set in 1869, so that they coincide with Dmitry Karakozov's equally "unheard of" attempted regicide in 1866. As Verhoeven has shown, Russian society struggled to make sense of Karakozov's act, and Karakozov's legal defense (as well as his unsuccessful bid for the tsar's clemency) was that the cause of his unprecedented crime lay in his morbid condition (i.e., temporary insanity). The court, however, rejected Karakozov's insanity plea and deemed that "the determination and consistency with which his criminal plan was conceived ... exclude all possibility of ascribing his activities to an abnormal state of mental capacities."[9] In 1866 Raskolnikov and, as a revisitation, Stavrogin circa 1866 (and ultimately Ivan Karamazov circa 1866) literally *embodied* Raskolnikov's unresolved question: what is the relationship between psychic illness and moral illness, between madness and an idea?

Dostoevsky's notebooks also reveal that as of 1870-71, he had no overarching term for the tactics that he imagined Nechaev embracing (the closest would be "pokushenie," "attempt"), and tsaricide—whether singular or serial—was still conceived only in terms of Karakozov. In other words, "terrorism" was not yet available to designate the practice that Dostoevsky had in mind. So for example, under the heading "What Nechaev Wanted (from the author)" in his notebooks, Dostoevsky lists Nechaev's/Peter's tactics in ascending order, including: "a plague on livestock"; "the murder of governors somewhere, etc."; and "finally, if even possible, then Karakozov ~~sometimes~~ (Karakozov ~~inogda~~)."[10] Here, Dostoevsky seems to be anticipating the People's Will's tactic of systematic regicide, designating it by the name of its first practitioner: "Karakozov sometimes." Nechaev, if we recall, likewise had no stock term but defiantly embraced his opponents' pejorative "terrorism." However, in *The Principles of Revolution* he had described acts "at first appearing as exceptional events, called acts of fanaticism or frenzy by contemporaries [that] recur more and more frequently in various forms."[11] In the course of making his notes and writing the first parts of his novel, Dostoevsky had no access to these incriminating documents, which later became part of the public record during the trial of the Nechaevtsy in summer 1871.

In their formal features (unexpectedness, outrageousness, repetition) and reception, Stavrogin's acts correspond to "such exceptional acts," but nose-pulling—whoever's nose—is not assassination.[12] Within the Russian literary tradition Stavrogin's acts are misdemeanors with a Gogolian pedigree.[13] Within the revolutionary tradition, they are analogous to, but should by no means be mistaken for, acts of political terrorism. Nonetheless Stavrogin's acts, taken as a piece with their reception, are paradigmatic. They augur the far more lethal outrages that cause such distress, outrage, and confusion by the end of the novel. So when the narrator declares, "One can hardly imagine what conclusions and what mental anarchy our society, frightened to the point of panic, might have reached, if everything had not suddenly been explained all at once, the very next day, thanks to Lyamshin," the reader is primed and ready.[14] Dostoevsky, the consummate satirist, hands the "definitive explanation" over to Lyamshin, the most disreputable member of the quintet—a none-too-bright but inveterate parodist who produces an inadvertent parody, leaving out Dostoevsky's plot ("the tragedy of Shatov and Kirillov, the fire, the death of the Lebyadkins, etc., were all put in the background") but foregrounding Peter Verkhovensky's.

> To the question of why so many murders, scandals, and abominations had been perpetrated, he replied with burning haste that it was all "for the systematic shaking of the foundations, for the systematic corrupting of society and all principles; in order to dishearten everyone and make a hash of everything, and society being thus loosened, ailing and limp, cynical and unbelieving, but with an infinite yearning for some guiding idea and for self-preservation—to take it suddenly into their hands, raising the banner of rebellion and supported by the whole network of fivesomes, which would have been active all the while, recruiting and searching for practically all the means and all the weak spots that could be seized upon." . . . To the outright question: are there many fivesomes?—he answered that there was an endless network, and though he did not present any proofs, I think his answer was completely sincere. He presented only the printed program of the society, printed abroad, and a plan for developing a system of further actions, which though only a rough draft, was written by Pyotr Stepanovich's own hand. It turned out that with regard to "shaking the foundations," Lyamshin had quoted the paper verbatim, not omitting even periods and commas, though he had insisted it was merely his own understanding.[15]

This is the second time that Dostoevsky has presented Peter/Nechaev's program in the novel. The first time, Peter reveals his schemes in a tête-à-tête with Stavrogin, in almost delirious ravings that deeply unsettle the typically unfazed Stavrogin. This time we are given what amounts to a parody of the program, thanks to the none-too-bright Lyamshin's plagiarism ("not omitting periods and commas") of what was illiterate style to begin with. The tragedy of the novel itself notwithstanding, Dostoevsky makes Peter/Nechaev's tactics of destruction first lunatic, and then funny. By means of techniques such as these, Dostoevsky not only denigrates revolutionary terrorism by making it seem sordid, silly, derivative, and illiterate, but encourages the reader to assume a skeptical stance toward "explanations" that are taken as definitive and actionable but upon closer inspection merit skepticism.

This would redound upon the real-world explanations of the Nechaev affair, two of the most authoritative of which were the government's and that of Dostoevsky's own editor, Mikhail Katkov. Alexander II's government steadfastly maintained that Nechaev was a common criminal and successfully convinced the Swiss government to extradite him to Russia on this basis. His murder of Ivanov, as the Ministry of Justice claimed,

> did not issue exclusively from the demands of a secret political society founded by Nechaev, but rather the former was sooner guided by personal motives, enmity to Ivanov, in whom he saw a rival whose intellect and character were a threat to his personal position. As a pretext for the murder, Nechaev presented to his accomplices the suspicion that Ivanov intended to inform the government about the secret society; but this suspicion is not borne out either by the depositions of the accused and witnesses or by the actions of Ivanov himself, who although disagreeing with Nechaev in many areas, did not separate himself from the secret society, and to the contrary, continued until the end to consider himself one of the chief members of the society, which is proven by the pretext by means of which Ivanov was lured to the fatal grotto, a pretext which he would not have yielded to if he had before this moment left the secret society.[16]

In any case, the government's argument rests upon a disqualification made logically possible only by the insertion of an adverb. "The necessity of this murder did not issue *exclusively* [italics mine] from the demands of a secret political society founded by Nechaev." Not only does the Ministry of Justice claim for itself the ability to see into Nechaev's soul, but it effectively insists that the political must exclude the personal. By this standard, as long as human beings commit crimes, there can be no crime that is unequivocally political, and the category of political crime is therefore obviated. Dostoevsky, in his notebooks, finds neither classification satisfactory. "Nechaev is not a socialist, but a rebel. His ideals are insurrection and destruction, after which 'let happen what will' on the basis of the social principle according to which whatever might come would still be better than the present, and that the time has come to act, rather than to preach."[17]

Oddly enough, Mikhail Katkov's diametrically opposed explanation has this in common with the government's: that it sees the human and the political as mutually exclusive.[18] In his January 6, 1871, front-page editorial, Katkov outlined a vast and sinister conspiracy capable of turning any Russian, almost unwittingly, into an enemy of Russia. The centerpiece of Katkov's exposé of the Russian revolutionary movement is the scurrilous portrait of its émigré leader, Mikhail Bakunin, based in part on Katkov's own reminiscences. While the Soviet literary scholar Leonid Grossman's provocative argument that Bakunin served as one of Stavrogin's primary prototypes has been largely dismissed, Stavrogin undeniably resembles, if not the historical Bakunin, then *Katkov's* Bakunin.[19] "In his youth this was a person not lacking some sort of brilliance, capable of perplexing especially weak or nervous individuals and confusing and derailing those who were immature. His was a dry and callous temperament, an empty and fruitlessly aroused intellect. He snatched at a lot but did not achieve anything, didn't feel a calling for anything, didn't genuinely participate in anything."[20]

Katkov's plot has almost as many twists and turns as *Demons* does. At first Katkov asserts that Bakunin and the Poles have nothing to do with one another. ("Between the doctrines of savage destruction and coldly passionate annihilation that Bakunin addresses to his 'Young Brothers' and the Polish case [delo] there is indeed nothing in common. The Polish patriots are not little boys. They can't take the proclamations of Bakunin and Nechaev seriously.") Yet he also argues that "[if] Russia has enemies . . . any abomination [merzost'] works to the enemies' advantage, and if there weren't Nechaev, Bakunin *e tutti quanti*, then Russia's enemies would have to create them. And Russia's enemies did create them; our so-called revolutionaries are weapons in the enemies' hands."[21] Katkov ends by effectively denying that Russia has revolutionaries or an internal politics at all; rather, Russia has only "enemies of the Fatherland, the friends and collaborators of its enemies, their weapons and creatures" whom Russian society tolerates at its own peril.

Given these two competing explanations, one bent on complete depoliticization (albeit for political reasons) and the other tending toward the most extreme politicization by making all revolutionaries enemies in the most absolute sense, it is no wonder that *Demons* teaches its readers to be wary of explanations. In Dostoevsky's novels, no explanation or argument ever receives the rubber stamp of "truth"; characters' explanations and arguments are a mélange of truth and falsehood through which the readers must discerningly pick their way, attentive to the fact that "truth" in one mouth, with one nuance, in one context . . . will be falsehood in another. Explanations—whether "brain fever" or unimpeachable sanity; personal motivation or a conspiracy of dehumanized enemies—allow too much to fall between the cracks, which the novel makes it its business to catch. With that in mind, I would argue that the term "terrorism" as applied to the "recent and strange events" provides analytical purchase primarily with regard to the town's reception of them (described in the previous section) but serves only to obscure the fact that what is "again a killing" is in each case a very different story.

At the end of the novel, the town is still discussing Peter Verkhovensky's status, with some few astounded by his "organizational genius," although his talent lay not in organizing (his plan, in the end, goes bust), but in signifying. His forked tongue conditions first the governor's, then the public's apprehension of events as he uses words to take control of the meaning of others' deeds. The most striking example is the engineer Kirillov's suicide.[22] In one of the darkly ironic scenes of the novel, Kirillov (fanatical *believer* in God's nonexistence) and Peter Verkhovensky (who truly believes in nothing) go head to head over who will own the meaning of Kirillov's suicide before he commits it. "It is my *duty* to proclaim self-will," declares Kirillov, but like Raskolnikov, he has not properly theorized his "proclamation" as a communicative act that requires an audience, as Verkhovensky, the consummate communicator, maliciously points out. "'Who is there to know? He [Peter] kept prodding. 'There is you and me, and who—Liputin?' 'Everyone is to know; everyone will know. There is nothing hid that shall not be revealed. *He* said that.'"[23] Kirillov's intention was to commit an act of existential rebellion proving man's divinity by overcoming the fear of death—to dethrone God. "I kill myself to show my insubordination and my new fearsome freedom."[24] Verkhovensky uses his agitational skills to whip the otherwise low-key Kirillov into a lather of pride and megalomania, in the midst of which he purloins the meaning of Kirillov's act to use for his purposes.[25]

That said, Dostoevsky did not entirely eschew explanation and had a talking points version of the novel ready to present, along with a dedicated copy of the novel, to heir to the throne Alexander Romanov in February 1873. "These phenomena," Dostoevsky obligingly explained to his royal addressee, "are the direct consequence of the age old divorce of all Russian enlightenment from the native and distinct principles of Russian life."[26] "All Russian enlightenment" refers in particular to Dostoevsky's own generation's infatuation with Western ideas and a Western ethos, which he by the late 1860s had realized were at odds with and had dangerously corrupted the "native and distinct principles of Russian life." Russian nihilism, aka socialism, aka the Nechaev movement (nechaevskoe dvizhenie) represented a "continuity of thought which has evolved from the fathers to the children" and is hence responsible for "one of the most dangerous ulcers of our present civilization." This, we could say, is the "authorized" explanation of a novel that both ironizes and satirizes explanation, and the literary scholarship has tended to follow it closely. It is all the more crucial, then, to recall Dostoevsky's original artistic intentions as captured (and capitalized) in his *Notebooks*—"THE MAIN THING: that in the course of the novel it is never completely explained why Nechaev came."[27]

3

Tarantulas with a Heart?

> If it wasn't for the persecution, I'm not at all certain that I would have become a socialist at that time.
>
> VERA FIGNER, *Student Years*

The lack of a final conclusive explanation is not only the consequence of Dostoevsky's choice as an artist, but a consequence of the fact that he knew *he really did not know*. When it came to Nechaev, Dostoevsky's notes go only so far in penetrating the mystery before trailing off into a series of unanswered questions. His point of departure, however, is telling: "it ['it' is unspecified] began with Nechaev making a blunder, for he was acting in part from the heart—if such a tarantula has a heart."[1]

There is scarcely a more astonishing assertion, despite its qualification, in the *Notebooks*, and it is one that seems to contradict the entire tendency of *Demons*, which arguably boasts the largest cast of despicable characters in all of Dostoevsky's oeuvre (hence the title). The members of the younger generation and especially its central characters, Stavrogin, Peter Verkhovensky, and Liza Tushin, are to all appearances heart*less*. But Stepan Verkhovensky and his son Peter converge, as their only point of agreement, upon the opposite conclusion. This point of agreement is, incidentally, one of the few indicative statements in the novel that speaks to causality, that attempts to explain the phenomenon that Dostoevsky intends to dissect: Russian radicalism of the late 1860s.

Tarantulas with a Heart?

At the beginning of the novel, when word reaches their provincial town that Peter had been involved in the composition of seditious tracts and had fled to Geneva (the hub of Russian revolutionary émigrés), Stepan Trofimovich, representing the liberal "men of the '40s," is characteristically philosophical about his son's political shenanigans: "And you know, it all comes from that same half-bakedness, from sentimentality [vse ot toi zhe nedosizhennosti, sentimental'nosti]. They're fascinated not by realism, but by the sensitive, ideal aspect of socialism, its religious tinge, so to speak, its poetry . . . to someone else's tune, of course."[2]

Much later in the novel and quite independently of his father, Peter makes the same assertion when he describes the "forces" that he taps in order to draw people into revolutionary conspiracy. After uniforms ("there's nothing stronger than a uniform") the next force, naturally, is sentimentality. "You know, with us, socialism spreads mostly through sentimentality. But the trouble is with these biting lieutenants; you get burned every so often."[3] In other words, once inflamed, those volatile emotions may be difficult for even (someone who fancies himself) a master manipulator like Peter to predict or control. Peter's assessment is born out when G__v ultimately confirms that "sentimental, tender, and kindly Erkel was perhaps the most unfeeling of the murderers who gathered against Shatov, and having no personal hatred, could be present at his murder without batting an eye."[4]

First, we must grant that Dostoevsky presents both Stepan and Peter Verkhovensky as (uncharacteristically) completely sincere in their conclusions. Second, we must note the difference in perspectives of father and son. Stepan Trofimovich is a *chaise-longue* philosopher whose characterization of the radical generation applies most readily to his own. Peter, on the other hand, speaks from the perspective of a revolutionary agitator and organizer whose business is to get people to do things. Lastly, we must account for the particularity of the word "sentimentality" (sentimental'nost'), as opposed to sensitivity (chuvstvitel'nost') or sympathy (sochuvstvie) and its ideological connotations in 1860s Russia. Sentimentality is without doubt a pillar in the characterization of the older generation, and sentimentalizing (sentimental'nichan'e) is what they do. Peter Verkhovensky's accusation that his father is Varvara Petrovna's "sentimental clown" (ty pri nei sentimental'nyim shutom) rings true as a pithy distillation of Dostoevsky's own characterization.[5] Stepan Trofimovich and the other representative of the "Men of the Forties," the famous writer Karmazinov (named after the Father of Russian Sentimentalism, Nikolai Karamzin, and modeled on Ivan Turgenev) are notorious for high-flown expressions of sentiment undercut by base (in)action. Affected feeling without effective love and sympathy, most vividly illustrated by Stepan Trofimovich's virtual abandonment of his son, is a central component of both men's characterization, as is feeling as a form of egoistic indulgence and self-display. As Carol Apollonio perceptively observed, it was the older generation's (i.e., Stepan Trofimovich's) "retreat from responsibility and real human connection that clears the way for evil action" in *Demons*.[6] In the context of the intergenerational polemics, "sentimentality" was code for the older generation's (and, more generally, liberals') inability to translate their lofty ideals and sublime feelings into politically efficacious action. In the *Notebooks*, Peter makes explicit the association between inaction and sentimentality by posing the opposition between deeds and words as one between doing and "crying": "But I know what is to be done right now and I'm doing it. You used to know, too, but you do nothing but cry. Whereas we aren't crying but simply doing."[7]

In his father's rendering, Peter's "doing" amounts to nothing more and nothing less than "chopping off heads." This figure of speech is eminently appropriate, because the violence that Peter and his associates advocate—like that of their Jacobin predecessors—is motivated by a shared sentimental fantasy of return to a Golden Age. This fantasy receives a number of parodic/demonic incarnations in *Demons*, from the communal (Shigalyov's frightening dystopia, in which "These [nine-tenths of mankind] must lose their person and turn into something like a herd, and in unlimited obedience, through a series of regenerations, attain to primeval innocence, something like the primeval paradise"[8]) to the purely personal (Stavrogin's attempts to efface the difference between good and evil, and to thereby revert to a primeval innocence).[9] Even Lyamshin's genocidal solution—"I'd take these nine tenths of mankind, since there's really nothing to do about them, and blow them sky high, and leave just a bunch of learned people who then start living happily in an educated way"—belongs to the same species of sentimental fantasy.[10] Quite possibly, then, the pernicious crux of sentimentality lies in the appalling divergence between beneficent end (happiness) and the vicious means (mass murder). A conversation between Stepan Trofimovich and Peter in the *Notebooks* puts a point on it. "Stepan Trofimovich: But if you don't know for sure whether your program is founded on truth, aren't you burdening your conscience with criminal destruction? Peter Verkhovensky: We believe that our program is founded on truth and that everyone accepting it will be happy. That's why we are willing to shed blood, because this blood will be the price of happiness."[11]

Yet "chopping off heads" is not as easy or automatic as Stepan Trofimovich makes it out to be: the road to the guillotine is paved with words. For this reason, Peter, like his historical counterpart, launches his revolutionary venture with a proclamation campaign. In *Demons*, the tracts appear everywhere and are mentioned repeatedly, yet scarcely a drop of ink spills from the tracts themselves onto the pages of the novel. Dostoevsky could assume his audience's familiarity with them, but not its consciousness of the sentimentality that informed their tropes. From Shelgunov and Mikhailov's "To the Young Generation" (K molodomu pokoleniiu, 1861) through Nechaev's proclamation campaign, radical tracts deployed four interrelated topoi in order to engage the emotions and activate the moral impulses of their readers: the *narod* as victim, the relationship between the revolutionary and the *narod*, the revolutionary (terrorist) as victim/martyr for the people, and the relationship between the revolutionary and his comrades. Dmitry Karakozov's proclamation "To my Friends-Workers!" (Druz'iam-Rabochim!), which was stowed in the pocket of his peasant overcoat, sentimentally invokes "my friends-workers" as its putative addressee, though it becomes clear that the educated classes are the true addressee and the "muzhichok" (the diminutive form of muzhik, or peasant/common man) Karakozov's sentimentalized object. "It became sad and oppressive for me that my dearest people [liubimyi narod] perishes," wrote Karakozov, "and I decided to destroy the tsar-villain and die myself for my most cherished [liubeznyi] people. If I am successful in my intention, I will die with the thought that my death has been of use to my dear friend—the Russian little guy [muzhichok]."[12] Karakozov's sadness, his tender feelings for his "most cherished people," expressed in sundry diminutives and endearments, stands in stark contrast to his feelings or lack thereof vis-à-vis the tsar. The fact that utilitarianism and sentimentality are strange but nonetheless eminently compatible bedfellows finds expression in Karakozov's hope that his death be "of use" to "his dear friend."[13]

If Nikolai Ogarev was convinced that Nechaev harbored a poet within his breast, it was thanks to Nechaev's florid proclamations rather than to his spare and bracing *Catechism*. Nechaev's first proclamation, "To the Students of the University, Academy, and the Technological

Institute in St. Petersburg," was written as if from the pen of an underprivileged student, a son of the people who had himself experienced life's hardships. "Dispersing to our closets [kamorka], we thought of bread—a main theme of reflection, with which our entire outlook on the world was closely tied. Neither luxury nor the tinsel decorating this life was visible to us; the rear view was placed before us—the dirty scaffolding of the theater of life, where we saw the emaciated, oppressed peasant, dragging the scenery, straining his breast and unconsciously producing those transformations which cause such pleasure among the glittering riff-raff, who have occupied the most expensive seats. Thousands of emaciated, ragged, wounded, plundered people come to mind and among them we recognize our fathers and near ones."[14]

Nechaev's elaborate metaphor of life as theater portrays two victims: the deprived students, who though themselves on the verge of starvation witness the general misery ("the rear view"); and the peasants, who perform grueling labor (dragging "scenery") for the idle amusement of the upper classes. These unfortunate ones are not pictured as faceless masses, but as intimates—"our fathers and near ones." (Nechaev's father was in fact a *meshchanin*, a member of the urban tax-paying class). One of the hallmarks of Nechaev's agitational style is his ability to switch in a heartbeat from expressions of outraged sympathy and filial solidarity to hate-filled denunciations of the enemy, whether Alexander II and his ministers, students of the nobility (*barichi*, dainty barons' sons), writers (*govoruny*, "babblers"), or those revolutionaries who concern themselves with the future organization of society ("mental masturbators")— all are put on notice. "He who has eyes and ears will see and hear the activists and if he does not join them it will not be our fault that he perishes, just as it is not our fault if everything hidden behind the scenery . . . will be shattered with indifference and without mercy together with the scenery."[15]

This last quote from a later proclamation, "Principles of Revolution" (*Nachala Revoliutsii*), again makes recourse to the metaphor of life as theater, testifying to the importance of theatricality in both Nechaev's conception of revolution and his self-presentation. Prior to his first flight abroad in March 1869, as student protests in St. Petersburg were met with intensifying government repression, Nechaev used two gullible women in his circle, Vera Zasulich and his own sister, Alexandra, as dupes in order to propagate among radical circles the fiction of his arrest, incarceration, and subsequent escape from the Peter and Paul Fortress. Nechaev's first proclamation, "To the Students," in fact begins by launching his pathos-drenched myth as a revolutionary hero-martyr. "Having escaped, through fortuitous success, from the freezing walls of Peter-Paul Fortress, to the vexation of those dark forces that threw me in there, I send you, my dear comrades, these lines from another country, where I have not ceased to labor in the name of the great cause which unites us."[16]

Nechaev's legend was an obvious rip-off of Bakunin's own, and in *Demons* Dostoevsky reproduces a poem called "The Student," which Nikolai Ogarev had written in 1867 and rededicated two years later at Bakunin's behest to Nechaev. Dostoevsky's parody (but only just barely) of this poem, called "The Shining Light," appears on the desk of Governor von Lembke, in one of the proclamations confiscated from the Shpigulin factory workers. The title, which is more literally translated as "The Bright Individual," stands for the revolutionary martyr and the new moral matrix that he defends (liberty, equality, fraternity) but in an old Russian context. In Russia "The Bright Individual" is hounded by tsars and boyars and tormented with medieval implements of torture, the rack and tongs—but no, he is not tormented. At the critical moment of revolutionary uprising, the "bright individual" in fact escapes abroad, leaving the tsars, boyars, rack, and tongs in the dust. In other words, "The Bright Individual" is no martyr at all, but a martyr *poseur* who skips the country, leaving the restive masses to await his return so that the pillage and destruction may begin in earnest.

Nechaev's biographer Philip Pomper has argued that Nechaev's desire for suffering and martyrdom was the driving force of his psyche and that this desire was ultimately fulfilled once Nechaev was extradited from Switzerland to Russia. While Dostoevsky was writing *Demons*, however, Nechaev remained at large, and so "The Shining Light" is clearly one tremendous send-up of the sentimentalized revolutionary martyr. But it is also something far more sinister—a poem that is the silken thread with which Peter fatally ensnares his intended victims. The "Shining Light" is also the hinge that allows Peter to flip his and Shatov's roles according to his designs: for the consumption of the Governor, Shatov is the eponymous hero—and a dangerous revolutionary—and Peter the informer who will do the Governor the service of "tying up all the conspirators in a knot." For the consumption of the fivesome, Peter is "The Shining Light" and Shatov the Judas about to deliver his former comrades into the hands of the authorities. In the end, the reversibility of their roles is as fictional as the poem: Shatov is the victim and Peter the murderer, and neither is a revolutionary martyr.

By the end of the novel twelve people have fallen directly or indirectly to the violence and mayhem unleashed by Peter Verkhovensky. That prodigious body count obscures the fact that nearly half of those, including the central characters from the younger generation (Nikolai Stavrogin, Liza Tushin, Kirillov) themselves seek the role of victim/martyr: this is the sentimental script that the young people, despite their conformity to the behavioral and expressive norms of "the Russian generation," have inherited from their fathers. Stepan Trofimovich fancies himself a paragon of civic reproach, an "exile" and a persecuted man; Varvara Petrovna assumes the role of a spurned, yet indefatigably devoted woman. In addition to her role as "ruined woman," Liza Tushin presents herself as a scapegoat for the Lebyadkins' murder; while Dasha Shatov offers herself as a "nursemaid" to a ruin of a man (Stavrogin). Kirillov, finally, hopes by his suicide/martyrdom to free man to be his own God, just as Karakozov had hoped that his suicide/tsaricide might "be of some use to the people." It is essential to note that even though Dostoevsky renders Kirillov's suicide scene as the darkest and most hideous scene of the novel (largely because Peter takes charge of the meaning of the act), Dostoevsky intended that a preface express his more exalted view. "In Kirillov is the people's idea to sacrifice oneself and everything for the truth—here is the national trait of the generation. Bless it, God, and send it an understanding of the truth!"[17] Only Peter, ironically, seems to be immune to this involuted form of sentimentality and yearning for martyrdom, and therefore able to manipulate it in others. Or is he?

4

Dostoevsky's Counterterrorism

"The First Step"

When Nechaev was eventually tried in January 1873, his trial attracted remarkably little attention, and a guilty verdict was handed down after less than an hour's deliberation. The trial itself had lasted only five hours. What need was there to try Nechaev again, contended the prosecutor, when the Swiss Canton Court had judged him guilty of a common rather than a political crime prior to rendering Nechaev to the tsarist police for deportation to Russia? But there was at least one other trial of Nechaev in absentia: the trial of the Nechaevtsy was already underway when Dostoevsky returned to Russia on July 8, 1871, after a hiatus (in flight from his creditors) abroad. As Joseph Frank notes, "Some of the essential documents, including the cold-bloodedly Machiavellian *Catechism of a Revolutionary* . . . were placed in evidence and made publicly available on the very day that Dostoevsky stepped off the train."[1]

Ironically, the most detailed and perhaps the most damning portrait of Nechaev emerged in the speech of the defense counsel, V. D. Spasovich, who defended three of Nechaev's associates, Alexei Kuznetsov, Peter Tkachev, and Elizaveta Tomilova. Not only did these speeches appear in the government bulletin, but Spasovich republished them in his memoir *Za mnogo let, 1859-1871* the next year, 1872, while Dostoevsky's novel was still being serialized. Since there was no possibility of exonerating Kuznetsov, who had confessed to participating in the murder of Ivanov, the brilliant and rhetorically gifted defense counsel's strategy was to stake a claim to the court's condescension by demonstrating "how difficult it was to resist fascination" with Nechaev.[2]

By that time, Part I of *Demons* and the first two chapters of Part II had already appeared in Katkov's *Russian Messenger*, and thus Dostoevsky's characterization of the principles, Nikolai Stavrogin and Peter Verkhovensky, was also part of the public record. Literary historians have extensively considered how closely Peter resembles his historical prototype, but the questions in reverse—To what extent did Dostoevsky's creation influence contemporary perceptions of the real Sergei Nechaev? And possibly have influenced the outcomes of his trials?—are likely unanswerable. What is certain is that while Dostoevsky claimed that he was not at all interested in portraying actual individuals, Spasovich purportedly was, and his Nechaev bears an uncanny resemblance to Dostoevsky's Peter, with the notable exception that Peter does not fascinate anyone, least of all his creator ("In my opinion, these pitiful freaks are not worthy of literature," Dostoevsky wrote to Katkov).[3]

The power of fascination is instead invested in Nikolai Stavrogin, while Peter "adopts the role of his own person" and is, in his own words, "the golden mean—neither stupid nor smart, rather giftless, and dropped from the moon."[4] This self-characterization proceeds from an inspiration that visited Dostoevsky in mid-August 1870 and is recorded in his notebook under the heading "Something New." The entry reads, "And Nechaev's appearance on the scene as Khlestakov."[5] Almost simultaneously, Dostoevsky adds this revelation: "Everything is contained in the character of Stavrogin. Stavrogin is everything."[6]

The implications of this shift in characterization and the novel's center of gravity cannot be overstated. "No longer Bazarov or Pechorin, Nechaev (Peter Verkhovensky) is here *reimagined* [my italics] as the ingratiating, fast-talking, and totally deceptive impostor in Gogol's *Inspector General*, who now, like everyone else, revolves around Stavrogin and becomes an insidiously dangerous and semicomic rogue. Once this change had been made, the structural problems that had been plaguing Dostoevsky resolved themselves."[7] This one change is pivotal not only to the novel's structure, but to the counterterrorism strategy that the novel employs. I use the term "counterterrorism" to suggest that in taking Nechaev apart and putting him back together ("The Prince and

Nechaev are tied to each other") Dostoevsky sought first to dismantle and thereby disarm, but in that very process discovered the symbolic center of what would become "the Russian Method."

The cardinal problem confronting revolutionaries at this juncture was how to start a revolution. In the 1868 *Principles of Revolution*, Nechaev, Tkachev, et al. professed to believe in inexorable historical laws; however, the principles and methods of previous revolutions might, due to different historical circumstances, need to be tweaked a bit. In *Demons*, Dostoevsky finds many occasions to belabor the Russians' imitation of or "translation from" the French and has Stepan Trofimovich deplore the nihilists' gleeful predilection, á la the Jacobins, for "cutting off heads." But in this case, his son Peter proves him wrong. Peter knows that revolutions don't start with the guillotine: they end there. His concern is more immediately practical, and he unveils his plan late in the novel. "But one man, only one man in Russia has invented the first step and knows how to do it. That man is me," rhapsodizes Peter.[8]

Actually, that man was Dostoevsky, and as in *Crime and Punishment*, Dostoevsky goes further in his theorizing than his historical prototype, Nechaev. When Peter reveals his plan to Stavrogin in the chapter entitled "Ivan the Tsarevich," it is in the fragmented and frenzied way that Raskolnikov charts his shocking progression from the aesthetic form of political murder (tyrannicide) to mass civilian murder. Peter's method is neither one nor the other, and though Dostoevsky adopts Nechaev's tactics, his emphasis is not on the political but on the social and the moral. In both its means and ends, Peter's method can best be summed up as a "wager on the weak and the drunk."[9] The point of the murders, abominations, etc., as Lyamshin explains, was "to dishearten everyone and make a hash of everything," and the agents of these acts would be "all the weak spots that could be seized upon." Gone is the monumental "extraordinary man" taking crime upon his conscience; gone, too, is the saber-wielding holy warrior riding riot through killing fields. In their place are sundry "weak spots," as Peter avers. "Listen, I've counted them up: the teacher who laughs with children at their God and at their cradle is already ours. The lawyer who defends an educated murderer by saying that he's more developed than his victims and couldn't help killing to get money, is already ours. Schoolboys who kill a peasant just to see how it feels, are ours. Jurors who acquit criminals right and left are ours. The prosecutor who trembles in court for fear of being insufficiently liberal, is ours, ours. Administrators, writers—oh a lot of them, an awful lot of them are ours, and they don't know it themselves!"[10]

These "weak spots" are not those of Nechaev and Bakunin, who imagine an alliance of revolutionaries with society's outcasts, "with those elements of popular life which, ever since the very foundation of the state power of Muscovy, have never ceased to protest, not only in words but in deeds [and who] unite with the valiant world of brigands, who are the only true revolutionaries in Russia."[11] Rather, Peter Verkhovensky and Dostoevsky's "weak spots" represent Russian society's thorough-going demoralization and corruption by Western ideas, by liberalism, atheism, nihilism, etc.[12] Non-state, insurgent terrorism flits through Peter's ravings as only one of many means of chaos and destruction, deserving no special elaboration besides "I'll find such zealots for you in these same 'crews' as would be ready for any kind of shooting and would even be grateful for the honor."[13] Rather, the *terror* to which Peter aspires is complete societal and moral disintegration, disorder, and collapse. The political theorist Oliver Marchart, referencing the social imaginary of the philosopher Thomas Hobbes, points out that "terror is but another name for the absence of order in the state of nature where every man is enemy to every man. It names the experience of utmost disorder (whose phenomenal aspect in Hobbes is fear)."[14]

Hobbes paints this originary and essentially default state, appropriately, in naturalistic colors whereas Peter paints the collapse of social and political order in apocalyptic ones. "Well, sir, so the trouble will start! Such a heaving will set in as the world has never seen. . . . Russia will be darkened with mist, the earth will weep for the old gods."[15] For Hobbes, the way out of the state of nature into political society was by means of moral reciprocity contractually formalized, but Peter is decidedly not interested in the contractual or political, nor is the terror of disorder Peter's ultimate goal, only a way station to another order that is not terror's obverse, but its *double*. As Ernesto Laclau has explained, "people need an order. The order of the ruler has to be accepted not because of any intrinsic value it can have, but just because it is *an* order."[16] At that point, the time will be ripe, as Peter explains to Stavrogin: "Well, sir, and then we'll bring out . . . whom?"

Peter has cast Stavrogin in the role that he had scripted originally for the Pope ("and the old codger will instantly agree") but immediately "drops" the Pope ("ia brosil papu") to mollify Stavrogin. Instead of the embodiment of Western theocracy, Peter parades a series of figures more congenial to a Russophile sensibility: Ivan the tsarevich (the fairytale hero with magical powers who defeats sundry monsters); the Imposter (of whom there were many in Russian history); and the leader of the heretical sect, the Castrate. Taken together, these figures possess the requisite qualities of the charismatic leader that Peter envisions Stavrogin to be: "beautiful, proud as a god, seeking nothing for yourself, with the halo of a victim, in hiding."[17] The figure that Peter delineates is a paradox of ultimate power and powerlessness, ego and selflessness, visibility (beauty) and invisibility ("in hiding"—driven underground by the authorities). Unlike the French who killed their king so that there would be no king, Peter envisions replacing the tsar with an alternate, replacing the sovereign with an idol, and he isolates the qualities required by a revolutionary usurper to establish sovereignty on a charismatic basis.

Although the personal may not be political, for Peter appearance certainly is. "Stavrogin, you are beautiful! . . . I love beauty. I am a nihilist, but I love beauty. Do nihilists not love beauty? They just don't love idols, but I love an idol. You are my idol!"[18] Not only is Peter a "swindler, not a socialist," but he is a bad nihilist and readily abandons nihilist "orthodoxy" on idols and aesthetics to serve his purposes. In important respects, Peter's "first step" in *Demons* is a step backward. Raskolnikov at least nominally had rejected "aesthetics." Peter, however, demonstrates no compunction whatsoever about being a "louse," aesthetic and otherwise.[19] Regarding Stavrogin's appearance, we have the G___v's fascinated description at the outset of the novel: "He was a very handsome young man, about twenty-five years old, and I confess I found him striking. . . . He was not very talkative, was elegant without exquisiteness, surprisingly modest, and at the same time bold and confident like no one else among us. Our dandies looked at him with envy and were totally eclipsed in his presence. I was also struck by his face: his hair was somehow too black, his light eyes were somehow too calm and clear, his complexion was somehow too bright and clean, his teeth like pearls, his lips like coral—the very image of beauty, it would seem, and at the same time, repulsive, as it were. People said his face resembled a mask; however, they said much else as well, about his great physical strength among other things."[20]

We have all the proof we need that Stavrogin is the extraordinary man that Raskolnikov wanted to be, and he doesn't even have to do anything: in the novel he does next to nothing and remains aloof from Peter's schemes. The townspeople and the reader are led to believe, however, that Stavrogin had committed all manner of heinous offenses prior to the action of the novel. As it turns out, like Raskolnikov, Stavrogin sought to prove his transcendence of ordinary norms through a deed; like Raskolnikov, he committed the wrong deed; and like Kirillov, he was oblivious to its communicative requirements. In the chapter "At Tikhon's," Stavrogin presents a written testimonial to the monk Tikhon confessing the crime that has weighed on his conscience, the seduction and rape of an eleven-year-old girl, and the passive witness of her eventual suicide. Stavrogin's intention is to make public his confession, but just as Dostoevsky's editor, Katkov, refused to publish the chapter, so Tikhon strenuously advises Stavrogin against it. For Tikhon, it is not only the ridiculousness of the confession's self-conscious style, but because the crime itself is ridiculous and unaesthetic—"uncomely." Dostoevsky has distilled Raskolnikov's hard-won insights and presented them as the *aesthetic critique* of a holy man to a "Great Sinner": "'So, in the form alone, in the style you find something ridiculous?' Stavrogin persisted. 'And in the essence. The uncomeliness [nekrasivost'] will kill it,' Tikhon whispered, lowering his eyes. 'What, sir? Uncomeliness? The uncomeliness of what?' 'Of the crime. There are crimes that are truly uncomely. With crimes, whatever they may be, the more blood, the more horror there is, the more imposing they are, the more picturesque, so to speak; but there are crimes that are shameful, disgraceful, all horror aside, so to speak, even far too ungracious.'"[21] Like Raskolnikov crawling under the pawnbroker's bed, Stavrogin realizes that he "made quite a ridiculous figure when I was kissing the dirty little girl's foot."[22] The irony, of course, is that Peter would never have made the same mistake. In Stavrogin's case, it is as if his own appearance blinded him to how he looked: unlike Dostoevsky's Underground Man or even Raskolnikov, Stavrogin is too good-looking and charismatic to be self-conscious *enough*. Tikhon also sees through Stavrogin's desire for dramatic "martyrdom and self-sacrifice" and tries to persuade him to embrace a quieter penance that would nonetheless entail a "great sacrifice." Stavrogin huffily refuses, and Tikhon foresees that Stavrogin will commit a "terrible crime" to avoid publishing his confession.

In his seminal work *Violence and the Sacred*, René Girard describes certain rituals of kingship among central African tribes in which the ascendant king must commit all sorts of transgressions and vile acts, from acts of violence to incest to eating certain forbidden foods. "In certain instances he is literally bathed in blood and fed concoctions whose ingredients (bloody offal and refuse of all kinds), indicate their evil character."[23] The purpose of these acts, of their "encyclopedic" and "eclectic" character, is to "betray who it is that the king is supposed to incarnate: the paragon of transgressors, the man who holds nothing sacred and who fearlessly assumes every form of hubris."[24] The king's crimes must be so grievous as to merit the severest punishment and unmitigated hostility so that he will play his intended role as sacrificial victim or scapegoat.[25] The purpose of the sacrificial victim according to Girard is to take upon himself all of community's divisiveness and corruption. "It is important to cultivate the future victim's supposed potential for evil to transform him into a monster of iniquity—not for esthetic reasons, but to enable him to polarize, to literally draw to himself all the infectious strains in the community and transform them into sources of peace and fecundity."[26]

The model that Dostoevsky had in mind for Stavrogin was that of regenerative sacrificial kingship, but in its demonic form. Thus the novel's epigraph "Then people went out to see what had happened and they came to Jesus, and found the man from whom the demons had gone, sitting at the feet of Jesus, clothed and in his right mind; and they were afraid." (Luke 8:34-36). Stavrogin is not the healed possessed man—the community and all of Russia are. Instead Stavrogin is "driven out," or to put it another way, Dostoevsky does what Peter repeatedly vows to do but cannot—he "kills" the extraordinary man-monster to whom he is so deeply attached ("I will feel very, very sad if I don't succeed with him. It will be sadder still if I hear the criticism that the character is stilted. I have taken him from my heart.")[27]

Yet Dostoevsky leaves Stavrogin the honorable way out, and more importantly, allows him to commit an inviolable act. Unlike the other graphically portrayed acts of violence (Kirillov's suicide, Shatov's murder, Liza's "lynching") Stavrogin's suicide takes place offstage, behind closed doors and high above everyone's heads (in the attic). The act is sudden and unexpected, and the horror completely psychological, as the women who love him most, their alarm mounting as their suspicions grow, finally discover his body hanging behind the attic door. Stavrogin's suicide note is so definitively and impenetrably laconic that it constitutes an interpretative brick wall. "Blame no one. It was I."

With the omission of the chapter "At Tikhon's," which was not published until 1922, the reader would not realize what a star pupil Stavrogin was, how brilliantly he assimilated Tikhon's lessons and went beyond them.[28] In an essay entitled "The Emptiness in the Centre of Terror," the German poet Hans Magnus Enzensberger differentiated between forms of terrorism that communicate their message via ritualized means and what he identified as forms of "absolute terror"—"an act of terror which does not explain anything, which declines to give any reason or justification, which does not legitimate itself. It does not aim at any propaganda effect: what it publicizes instead, by remaining silent, is its very own groundlessness [Grundlosigkeit]."[29] As Oliver Marchart explains, Enzensberger speaks about an empty attack (ein leeres Attentat). "In the case of an empty attack, no language game is available for us which would facilitate our understanding of this form of absolute terror."[30] Who but Stavrogin could bring off such an act? Who but Stavrogin could virtuosically perform "groundlessness"? A critical mass of scholarly opinion on *Demons* views Stavrogin in precisely this way, as W. J. Leatherbarrrow succinctly put it: "Stavrogin is essentially a non-character, an ever-shifting and indefinite composite, whose meaning is derived from the readings and misreadings of both the other characters in the novel and the reader himself. He has no belief in himself, or in anything outside himself, on which to base his existence. He is empty and inactive, a black hole at the center of the novel."[31] Apollonio builds upon the conclusion that Stavrogin "himself has no substance," but his "main function is to appear to and for others."[32] But appearance, as we have seen, is *not* "nothing." As Peter has realized, Stavrogin is the perfect "king" for a terroristic order that replaces the terror of disorder. Without being a terrorist himself, or even a committed co-conspirator, Stavrogin cuts the perfect figure (both as image and metaphor) for terror/ism. After all, "the terrorist" as a discursive construct is the ultimate scapegoat—replacing Satan—onto which we seculars project absolute enmity and evil.

In one of the first histories of the Russian revolutionary movement (*Underground Russia*, 1882), the assassin of the St. Petersburg chief of police Mezentsev and propagandist Sergei Kravchinsky describes the appearance of the revolutionary terrorist on the stage of history: "He is noble, terrible, irresistibly fascinating, for he combines in himself the two sublimities of human grandeur: the martyr and the hero.... Proud as Satan rebelling against God, he opposed his own will to that of the man who alone, amid a nation of slaves, claimed the right of having a will."[33] There can be no doubt that *Demons* is an anti-nihilist novel, but Dostoevsky's project of preemption entails what is essential to all preemption: being first. Dostoevsky was able to foresee this "first step," or the symbolic replacement of the sovereign (sacrificial king) by the terrorist because only he united in himself a sentimental attachment to monarchy, an antipathy for the abuses of autocracy and a love of beauty that are equally emotional.[34] Peter's "first step" is first Dostoevsky's, which he gives Peter without letting him take it. Stavrogin, Peter's cherished "other half" on whom he has pinned such hopes, repeatedly leaves Peter hanging, then absconds, then hangs himself. So ends the novel, so begins an original, and purely Russian (in its sentimentality) idea: the terrorist as (sacrificial) king.

5

Dostoevsky's Counterterrorism (Continued)

Laughter through Fear

> As for rioting, the old Roman way of dealing with that is always the right one; Flog the rank-and-file, and fling the ring-leaders from the Tarpeian Rock!
>
> MATTHEW ARNOLD, *Culture and Anarchy*[1]

Dostoevsky's tactic of division effectively renders Peter a "zero," who like all Gogolian zeroes (Khlestakov, Chichikov) slips the net and is buoyed out of town by his first-class *bons vivants*. Just so, Spasovich, in his *in absentia* trial of Nechaev, declared that "there was a lot of Khlestakov in him"—too much for him to be taken entirely seriously.[2] Although it is possible to see *Demons*, as Irving Howe did, as "mocking and lacerating everything within reach" and therefore "entirely subversive in effect,"[3] I would argue that there is one thing that Dostoevsky mocks without subversive intent: state terror and its relationship to revolutionary terrorism. Large sections from the early parts of his notebooks are devoted to conversations between Granovsky (who later becomes Stepan Trofimovich) and Nechaev (Peter) and effectively show that

Dostoevsky had no doubt about "who was to blame": the "punks," as he called them. In the notebooks, the first bout between father and son posits state terror as the necessary and inevitable reaction to revolutionary terrorism: "Granovsky: 'It's you who reject discussion and want simply to exterminate the opposition. But if this is so, you leave them with no other initiative but to exterminate you.' Nechaev: 'In doing so, we are addressing ourselves to the people, asking for their sympathy.' Granovsky: 'That is, they will decide which of us they should pity more.' Nechaev: 'Precisely.'"[4] Just two pages later, Dostoevsky experiments with another expression of the same thought: "Granovsky: 'Now, as for these punks—it is they and nobody else, who by virtue of their program of action, have created a state of war between themselves and society. Therefore, they must not act surprised, or complain, when society is going to exterminate them.'"[5] Only one conversation between father and son, of a purely personal nature, appears in direct speech in the novel, while traces of these draconian debates are reported by Stepan Trofimovich to G___v post factum.

> "They say that the French mind . . . ," he began babbling suddenly as if in a fever, "but that's a lie, it has always been so. Why slander the French mind? It's simply Russian laziness, our humiliating impotence to produce an idea, our disgusting parasitism among nations. *Ils sont tout simplement des paresseux*, and not the French mind. Oh, Russians ought to be exterminated for the good of mankind, like harmful parasites! It was not for that, it was not at all for that that we strove; I don't understand any of it. But do you understand, I cry to him, do you understand that if you have the guillotine in the forefront, and with such glee, it's for the sole reason that cutting off heads is the easiest thing and having an idea is difficult!"[6]

However, rather than call for the extermination of the radicals, as suggested in the *Notebooks*, Dostoevsky goes for ironic gold by having Stepan Trofimovich propose the extermination of *Russians* for their *parasitical imitation* of the French, an imitation that Stepan Trofimovich perceives as boding particular harm. The original sense of the notebook passages shines through, however, once one recalls that the Russians who are intellectually parasitical of the French (who cut off heads) are the *radicals*. Nevertheless, Dostoevsky has lightened it up and toned it down, and in the process the reciprocal relationship between revolutionary violence and state terror is almost completely elided, and with it the role played by public sympathy in adjudicating between them. Likewise, the blood-thirsty conclusion that "extermination" (istreblenie) is the exterminators' just desserts is retained only in the novel's epigraph from Luke 8:32–34: "Then the demons came out the man and entered the swine and the herd rushed down the steep bank into the lake and were drowned."

Revolutionary state terror is not absent from *Demons*, as we have seen in the dystopian fantasies of Shigalyov and Peter. But the terror of the autocratic state is present in the novel only as slapstick administrative terror, bumblingly executed by the hapless Governor von Lembke and the blustery Filibusterov (and provoked anyway by Peter) or a ridiculous "fable" of state terror conjured by Stepan Trofimovich's overwrought imagination as the dark underbelly of his sentimental fantasy of martyrdom. As tensions escalate between the authorities and the "rioters," Stepan Trofimovich is undone by anxiety over the fate that awaits him as a "persecuted" intellectual. "'In our country they can take you, put you in a kibitka, and march you off to Siberia for good, or else forget you in some dungeon. . . .' And he suddenly burst into hot, hot tears. Tears simply poured out of him. I felt terribly sorry for him. He obviously believed as much in the 'kibitka' as in the fact that I was sitting beside him. . . . Such full, total ignorance of everyday reality was both moving and somehow disgusting."[7]

"Total ignorance of reality" is something that Dostoevsky repeatedly attributes in his notebooks to Nechaev/Peter Verkhovensky (whose efficiency is "based on stupidity, total ignorance, and on his being unfamiliar with reality"), and this is clearly a characteristic Dostoevsky intended father and son to share.[8] Ironically, this passage and the one below point to a willed ignorance of reality—and a selective forgetting of his personal past and strongest animadversions—on Dostoevsky's part as Stepan continues to pour out his anxieties.

"But . . . I'm afraid of something else" (again in a whisper, a frightened look, and mysteriousness).

"But of what?"

"Flogging" he muttered with a helpless look.

"Who's going to flog you? Where? Why?" I cried out, afraid he was losing his mind.

"Where? Why, there . . . where it's done."

"And where is it done?"

"Eh, *cher*," he whispered almost into my ear, "the floor suddenly opens under you, and you're lowered in up to the middle . . . Everybody knows that."

"Fables!" I cried, once I understood. "Old fables! And can it be that you've believed them all along?" I burst out laughing.

"Fables! But they must have started somewhere, these fables; a flogged man doesn't talk. I've pictured it ten thousand times in my imagination."

"But you, why you, if you haven't done anything?"

"So much the worse, they'll see I haven't done anything, and they'll flog me."[9]

"Fable" of course indicates a story that was never true except in an allegorical sense, and the added detail of the "floor suddenly opens up" adds to the absurdity of Stepan Trofimovich's fears, especially as he himself admits that the whole scene is basically a figment of his imagination (pictured ten thousand times), and that "they'll see I haven't done anything, and they'll flog me." Who gets flogged for nothing in tsarist Russia?

This is precisely what happens next—people get flogged for nothing—but Dostoevsky, using every Gogolian device in his arsenal, creates from this atrocity the most hilariously satirical scene in the novel. In contrast to *Crime and Punishment*, *Demons* entirely brackets social reality with the exception of the plight of the Shpigulin factory workers, who are ruthlessly exploited by their employers, who offer Peter a field for his agitational efforts, and whom Dostoevsky treats quite seriously until they serve their Machiavellian purpose as a Trojan horse whence Dostoevsky launches his most devastating attack on the nexus of sentimentality, public indignation, and radicalism.

This occurs in the chapter entitled "Filibusters. A Fatal Morning," when, in time-honored Russian fashion, the workers appeal to Governor von Lembke for redress. The governor, largely due to Peter's machinations, has become somewhat unhinged and induced to see not a "peaceful demonstration" but a "riot." As a result, he makes recourse to the traditional stock of devices for tsarist era crowd control: Cossacks, birch rods, water barrels. As the governor commands his troops to have birch rods at the ready, G__v stands poised to bear witness to the injustice that is about to unfold. But he doesn't stand poised for long; in fact, he doesn't come to a full stop, but instead moves briskly past any narration of what happens onto the minimalization of what did happen:

"However, only two men were punished in all, I think, not even three; I insist on that."[10]

Instead of a single eyewitness account that might focus sympathy and solidarity, the account of the "riot"—presumably, like the crowd itself—is effectively dispersed as the narrator instead serves up refutations of various other accounts, most centrally that concerning "a woman from the cemetery almshouse [bogadelenka], a certain Avdotya Petrovna Tarapygin, who, as she was crossing the square on her way back to the almshouse, supposedly pushed her way through the spectators, out of natural curiosity, and on seeing what was happening, exclaimed: 'Shame on 'em! [Ekoi stram!]'—and spat. For this she was supposedly picked up and 'attended to [otraportovali].'"[11]

Avdotya Petrovna Tarapygin has the makings of the ultimate sentimental victim: poor, aged, female, and (most importantly) acting, in her homespun way, out of the moral indignation that the scene ought to inspire. Avdotya is our and the narrator's surrogate: she sees what we don't and feels what he doesn't; she is also a diversion created by Dostoevsky and held up to distract us from the fact that he in fact doesn't allow us to see anything. But even the diversionary Avdotya doesn't exist: G__v's investigative efforts after the riot debunk her as a fabrication of the town rumor mill (the water barrels are debunked, too) who went on to acquire reality through the press. "And yet I later read about this lady myself in a report in one of the Petersburg newspapers.... Not only was this case printed, but a subscription for her benefit was set up here in town on the spur of the moment. I myself donated twenty kopecks. And what then? It turns out that there never was any such almshouse Tarapygin woman in our town at all!"[12] As the narrator reveals, the fiction of the Tarapygin woman owes itself to the appearance of Stefan Trofimovich on the scene, who because he was also almost flogged (but wasn't), presented himself as a sentimental template, a suitably effeminate paper doll who might be plausibly cross-dressed in *bogodelenka*'s clothes.

Dostoevsky's artistic achievement is staggering. His most hilariously satirical chapter features a flogging that wasn't, while the two (and a half?) floggings that *were* are hustled off stage. The target of his satire is, of course, not the floggings themselves (he is not *such* a reactionary ogre) but the public imaginaire, not just its sentimentalization of victims, but its outright fabrication of sentimental victims... and its sentimental susceptibility to its own fabrications (a subscription, no less!). The message is clear: no harm, no foul; no victims, no sentimentality; no agitation, no revolution.

To give Dostoevsky the benefit of the doubt, we will say that the satire of "Filibusters: A Fatal Morning" functions to defuse the nasty dynamic of mutual extermination by showing that the whole business has no basis in reality and is instead the unfortunate result of fear, fantasy, vanity, and "sleds shooting off down hill." That terror is, at base, an unholy figment of the disordered imagination is driven home when the narrator remarks: "The riot was as evident to him [Governor von Lembke] as the kibitkas had been earlier to Stepan Trofimovich."[13]

Here we arrive at the sentimental fantasy that Dostoevsky, as implied author, has slipped in, the fantasy that what amounts to a terrible misunderstanding (odno lish' nedorazumenie) may be cleared up by amends and a reconciliation. This moment of reconciliation occurs when the old liberal Verkhovensky finally confronts the governor with his violated rights (his papers were perquisitioned), upon which the intimidating façade of state authority, such as it was, crumbles as Von Lembke plaintively protests, "'but . . . but don't you see how unhappy I am myself?' he almost cried out and . . . and it seemed, wanted to hide his face in his hands. This unexpected, painful outcry, almost a sob, was unbearable. It was probably his first moment since the previous day of full and vivid awareness of all that had been happening—and then at once despair, full, humiliating, surrendering; who knows, another minute and he might have begun sobbing for the whole room to hear. Stepan Trofimovich first gazed wildly at him, then suddenly inclined his head and in a deeply moved voice said: 'Your Excellency, trouble yourself no more over my peevish complaint, and simply order my books and letters returned.'"[14]

On the one hand, the masks fall, the intertwining smoke of reciprocally constructing fantasies clears momentarily, and we witness one of the few moments of true empathy, if not human connection, in the novel. The Liberal, Stepan Trofimovich, rises to the apex of his magnanimity when he acknowledges that his is after all just a "peevish complaint" and requests only the most basic form of redress, the return of the Russian Liberal's most precious property: his words. This is the turning point for Stepan Trofimovich. Henceforward he ceases to be (for the most part) the butt of Dostoevsky's satire and becomes the rickety vehicle for Russia's redemption.

On the other hand, we may object that there is still too much Gogol here—Governor von Lembke as Akaky Akakievich—for us not to realize how unabashedly Dostoevsky is manipulating our sentiments. Our sympathy flutters nervously between its habitual solidarity with the victimized little man and the entirely novel spectacle of crushed and demoralized state power in the form of Von Lembke. Through Dostoevsky's offices it rests in the end with the man who ordered the flogging of innocents, who have since been entirely forgotten. Finally, we are left to wonder where everything actually stands: by having G⎯⎯v, an unreliable narrator (but the most reliable we have) dismiss the kibitkas, the water barrels, Avdotya Tarapygin, and the extraneous flogged Shpigulin men without in fact denying that two men were brutally flogged with birch rods for no reason, or by mistake, we are left to concede Stepan Trofimovich's point that fables, in fact, must start somewhere.

6

The Unity of All Terrorism(s)

In their exhaustive reference work *Political Terrorism* (revised in 2005), the social scientists Alex P. Schmid and Albert J. Jongman accord some worth to *belles lettres* and list Fyodor Dostoevsky's novel *Demons* in their bibliography on the etiology of terrorism.[1] This presents the student of terrorism, history, or Dostoevsky with a curious difficulty. Given that Schmid and Jongman acknowledge the absence of a consensus definition of terrorism—they devote the first chapter to the definitional problem—and given that by their best shot at a definition, "terrorism" had not come into historical existence as of *Demons*' writing,[2] what *exactly* do we find the etiology of in *Demons*?

The short answer is that a typology, such as J. Bowyer Bell's, may be of more use in describing and analyzing phenomena on the ground in *Demons* than a blanket definition that presumes to know in advance what a thing is based on what the word means.[3] And as *Demons* has long been viewed as portraying a menagerie of (often fantastical) revolutionary types, it only makes sense that it would also present a menagerie of types of political violence. Yet why any of these species of political violence should be seen as belonging to the same genus, terrorism, is not immediately obvious, either from the typologies of social scientists or from Dostoevsky's novel. I will argue here that in *Demons* Dostoevsky identifies the missing link—what it is that makes seemingly disparate types of violence by different social actors both political and terrorism—and draws this as a major thematic thread through the novel.

As we have seen, terror/ism in the novel is both actualized on the level of plot and presented purely discursively, through characters in conversation or by the narrator in his tropes. With the caveat that no act of violence in the novel is unambiguously political and each act is performed by agents acting according to their own intentions, the most obvious act of "terrorism" (and I use the word in quotes to signal the tentativeness, as well as the anachronism, of the designation) is Ivan Shatov's murder by Peter Verkhovensky and Co. The murder of Peter's own hired gun, Fedya, by Peter or on Peter's orders, may certainly also be counted as organizational terror, but also as simple personal vengeance. However, the murders of the Lebyadkins, which Peter instigates and Fedya executes (with tacit encouragement from Stavrogin), have no obvious place in Bell's typology.[4] This alerts us to the fact that categorization by typology must rely on a fair amount, and flexibility, of interpretation. We may conjecture that the Lebyadkins' murder had more than one purpose: to reel in the aloof Stavrogin and in conjunction with the fires in Zarechye, to create chaos and panic and therewith the general sense of "shaking foundations." Bell's typology offers only "allegiance terror"—"a less restrained variant of organizational terror ... in order to create mass support"—as an uneasy fit. In the jargon of Dostoevsky's time, "agitational terrorism" might better express the notion that acts of violence could unleash or galvanize hitherto dormant revolutionary forces.

On the level of plot, we also find state terror, although Dostoevsky uses Gogolian satire with great effect to take the sting out of the violent repression, at the orders of Governor von Lembke, of the Shpigulin factory workers. By contrast, the terror of the revolution in power, which exists only on the novel's discursive plane in Shigalyov's notorious dystopia and Lyamshin's even more horrifying travesty of it, is so ruthlessly total that it anticipates the scourges of the twentieth century: totalitarianism and genocide. Back on the non-state side of the ledger, we find the scourge of the twenty-first century—insurgent mass casualty terrorism. This, too, exists only on the discursive plane, in the hyperbolic tropes that the narrator uses to describe the crowd's reaction to events as they unfolded at Yulia von Lembke's ill-fated fête.

This catalogue of violence, sorted so far as possible with the help of Bell's typology, immediately casts into relief the diversity of the phenomena in question and the range in scale, means, perpetrators, victims, and purposes. The question then becomes: what allows us, other than the anachronistic application of linguistic convention, to lump all of these things together as "terror/ism?" How does Dostoevsky, who must do without the *Begriff* "terrorism" and so uses the somewhat comical "chopping off heads" as a synecdoche both for non-state revolutionary terrorism and revolutionary state terror, convey what terrorism in essence is, besides violence?

A common denominator can be found in a theme introduced at the very outset of the novel. Because it is sounded in a lighthearted and satirical key, its relationship to terrorism may go at first completely unnoticed. The narrator G__v, in introducing Stepan Trofimovich Verkhovensky, the man whom he had served as a close confidant and bosom companion, reveals that he had been utterly mistaken in his identity. "Just the other day, I learned, to my great surprise, but now with perfect certainty, that Stepan Trofimovich had lived among us, in our province, not only not in exile, as we used to think, but that he had never even been under surveillance."[5] Surveillance is the ultimate guarantor of identity; here, however, the surveillance was completely imaginary and so was the identity as an "exile"—and all that that entails. This revelation serves to satirically skewer Stepan Trofimovich's personal vanity, but the theme of mistaken and ultimate indeterminate identity takes on additional, more sinister significance as the novel progresses. As the plot of political intrigue thickens, two very similar scenes are enacted between close associates. The first scene is a dialogue, one significantly without dialogue tags between Stavrogin and Peter.

> [Stavrogin:] "Listen, Verkhovensky, you're not from the higher police, eh?"
> [Peter Verkhovensky:] "Whoever has such questions in his mind doesn't voice them."
> [Stavrogin:] "I understand, but after all we're among ourselves [u sebia]."
> [Peter Verkhovensky:] "No, so far I'm not from the higher police."[6]

The second scene, shortly thereafter, is between Stepan Trofimovich and the narrator.

> "Stepan Trofimovich, tell me as a friend, as a true friend," I screamed, "I won't betray you: do you belong to some secret society, or

do you not?" And now, to my surprise, even here he was not certain whether he was or was not a participant in some secret society.

"But that depends, voyez vous."

"How does it 'depend'?"

"When one belongs wholeheartedly to progress, and . . . who can vouch for it; you think you don't belong, and then, lo and behold, it turns out you do belong to something."[7]

The first scene between Stavrogin and Peter is striking because Stavrogin is rarely disadvantaged vis-à-vis Peter, but here his curiosity, uncertainty, and naïveté (!) get the better of him. Peter's reply to Stavrogin does not dispel, but intensifies the uncertainty ("No, so far I'm not") but not before issuing a stern warning regarding the perils of inquiry, even for one such as Stavrogin.[8]

Peter's father, too, intensifies the uncertainty, but only as an expression of his own, for in Stepan Trofimovich's hazy (or perhaps crystalline) understanding, the individual's belief about his own identity is hardly relevant. Stepan Trofimovich's reply also brushes aside the pedestrian issue of factual membership in any organization in favor of the broader and more diffuse question of philosophical orientation. If belonging (or not) to "progress" is what matters, actual membership in any organization is incidental. Compared to Verkhovensky junior and senior, G___v and Stavrogin are babes in their facile assumption of identity and what follows logically from it—solidarity and confidentiality. This is just what *Demons* belies: in a society cleaved by the mirror-symmetries of *secret societies* and *secret police*, the fundamental distinction between friend and enemy cannot be distinguished, least of all by the subject himself.

The implications of this indeterminacy play out in the hilariously satirical chapter entitled "With Our People" (in Russian, simply "U nashikh") when it becomes apparent that "our people" do not know whether they, in fact, are. "I should like to know whether we here and now constitute some sort of meeting, or are a gathering of mortals who have come as guests?"[9] The character known only as "the lame teacher" demands clarification of their status, which the assembled company strives to achieve by means of a procedurally democratic vote that must first settle such preliminary questions as what "yes" means ("da, chto *da*-to znachit?") and what "a meeting" is, a sign that the destabilization of identity is co-morbid with the destabilization of language.[10]

Yet procedural democracy does not survive for long among "our people." Why not? One answer would be to lay the blame on Peter's megalomania, but Dostoevsky clearly wants us to reach beyond this obvious conclusion. Both Bell in his description of organizational terrorism and Dostoevsky converge on another possibility: "every revolutionary organization, perhaps without exception, must face the problem of maintaining internal discipline"—every revolutionary organization must therefore practice some form of terror. This mechanism of terror takes the breathtakingly simple form of a question, an adaptation of the "Mandarin dilemma" from Balzac's *Le Père Goriot*.[11] Dostoevsky begins to pose it in various forms from the time of writing *Crime and Punishment*, which coincided with Karakozov's attempt to assassinate Alexander II in 1866, until, seemingly, the very end of his life. The dilemma can be characterized as one of means and ends and utilitarian versus deontological concepts of morality. Would you commit a crime to achieve some perceived good, whether personal (in Balzac) or communal (Dostoevsky)?[12] As the components are variable (the decrepit mandarin becomes a greedy pawnbroker in *Crime and Punishment* and later the tears of a child in *The Brothers Karamazov*), the dilemma varies in implication and intensity. The dilemma takes explicit political shape in the notebooks for *Demons* and involves merely knowing in advance about the commission of a crime.

> "Taking the case of Karakozov and knowing about his intentions two hours ahead of time, would you have informed the police?" (a question addressed to Shaposhnikov)
> Granovsky says "no" but keeps hedging on his answer, trying to qualify it.
> "Even if you weren't yourself involved in the conspiracy but having somehow learned about the intentions of the conspirators?"
> "No, I would not have informed the police"
> Shaposhnikov: "For my part, I'm going to inform the police. Why this is unnatural. You are not using your own emotions, or following your own rules."[13]
> The Student: "Shaposhnikov at least has the courage of his convictions, while you are a windbag even in this respect."[14]

In *Demons* when Peter whips out the dilemma among "our people," the hypothetical situation is more generic—a "planned political murder" rather than tsaricide—and the conflict between Granovsky and the Student entirely omitted in order to illustrate how terror pivots upon a single question.[15] In the scholarly literature, the Mandarin dilemma is characterized as a moral dilemma or a path to self-knowledge; here it becomes an identification badge.[16] Everyone is forced to declare himself; Peter's assurance that "you're all entirely free" to answer or not ironically reveals a trap. As Shatov's case makes clear, to not answer is to answer. "'Shatov, this is not to your advantage,' Verkhovensky shouted after him mysteriously." Stavrogin likewise does not declare himself, but confirms only for the dismayed group that "our people" don't know who they are.

In *The Concept of the Political,* Carl Schmitt posits the "friend/enemy" distinction as constituting the political. Schmitt does not refer explicitly to any constituting agency, or if he does, it is the individual, for whom the enemy is integral to the construction and assertion of his own identity.[17] In *Demons* the opposite is true. In its political variant, the Mandarin dilemma has been twisted into a tool of terror rather than one of moral clarification or self-knowledge, for it plainly states (or rather, coerces): "Tell me who your enemy is [the tsar or his would-be assassin], and I will tell you who you are."[18] The individual's subjective conception of his own identity is moot, paving the way for his political and physical annihilation.[19] Unbeknownst to Shatov and regardless of his own self-knowledge, he is marked as an enemy, an informer, and dealt with accordingly. To "shake the foundations," Peter shakes the unstable pillars of identity, already crumbling to dust on the bipolar field of revolution.

It is possible that Dostoevsky himself failed to appreciate the extent to which he was hoisted by this very petard.[20] According to the memoirs of Dostoevsky's close friend, A. A. Suvorin, in the last year of his life Dostoevsky put the fatal dilemma to the both of them in a different, considerably more elaborated scenario: "Imagine that we both were standing at a window of [a store] and looking at some paintings. Near us stood a person, who was pretending to look. He was waiting for someone and kept looking around. Suddenly another person hastened to him and said, 'The Winter Palace will soon be blown up. I have placed the machine.' Imagine that we hear this, and that the men were so agitated that they did not take account of the circumstances or their voices. Would we go to the Winter Palace to warn of the explosion, or would we turn to the police, or to a policeman on the beat to arrest them? Would you go?' 'No [replied Suvorin], I would not go.' 'Nor would I, [said Dostoevsky].'"[21]

Fifteen days earlier, just such an explosion had occurred at the Winter Palace, courtesy of the People's Will, killing eleven and wounding fifty-six. The tsar himself was spared thanks to the fortuitous tardiness of his guest-of-honor. "After turning over all the reasons that would cause me to do it [inform]," Dostoevsky concluded that there was only one reason that held him back: "Simply the *fear* [italics mine] of being reputed to be an informer." Peter Verkhovensky/Nechaev's terrorism had struck deep roots not only in "our people" but in those who considered themselves loyal to the regime, like Dostoevsky. Coincidentally, just the day before Alexander II had arrived at his own conclusion concerning Dostoevsky's true affiliation after carefully reading a draft of Dostoevsky's jubilee address on behalf of the Slavic Benevolent Society. "I never suspected the Slavic Benevolent society of solidarity with the nihilists."[22]

Part Three

"The Little Devil Sitting in Your Heart"

I

A Change of Heart

In 1880, Dostoevsky was at the pinnacle of his career, and, as the honor of writing the jubilee address from the Slavic Benevolent Society attests, in good graces with the monarchy. Nonetheless, it was not for him to say whether he was in solidarity with the nihilists. In the seven years since *Demons'* completion in 1873 the political ground had undergone seismic shifts. Sympathy for the young radicals caught up in the *Nechaevshchina* was accompanied by equal antipathy for Nechaev's methods and inclined a new generation of radicals to embrace peaceful and patient propaganda, first among St. Petersburg workers and then among the peasants in the countryside. At the vanguard of this movement "To the People" (khozhdenie v narod) was a group of young people who had gathered around Nikolai Chaikovsky in St. Petersburg, and who fused the communal ideals of Chernyshevsky with the populist views of the historian Peter Lavrov to inspire their own activist outreach and socialist vision of Russia's future.

Unsurprisingly, the government responded to these activities with the full weight of its repressive authority, arresting and imprisoning without charges hundreds of young people in the summers of 1873-74. As a result, educated society (whose children languished in pretrial detention) became increasingly estranged, while oppositional groups had no other choice than to go "underground" and become illegal. The first formally organized revolutionary party, Land and Freedom (Zemlia i Volia), came into existence in St. Petersburg in 1876, and the radicals took advantage of the modern urban environment to create an indispensable base of operations: the revolutionary Underground.[1] Meanwhile, the southerners in Kiev were more restive and formed a group called the Southern Rebels (Iuzhnye buntari), which orchestrated daring prison breaks, grisly acts of revolutionary vengeance, and a (failed) peasant uprising in the Chigirin district that was right out of the Nechaev/Peter Verkhovensky playbook. In the summer of 1879, in a series of meetings in Lipetsk, Voronezh, and St. Petersburg some of the northern and southern movements' most seasoned members founded a rigidly hierarchical, centralized organization, the People's Will, which embraced terrorism and committed itself to the destruction of the emperor.[2] In the very first number of the party's organ, *Narodnaia volia*, a programmatic article by Lev Tikhomirov announced that the tactics of peaceful propaganda in the village were based on illusions and were no longer realistic: "A party aspiring to some kind of future should establish itself above all on a strictly realistic relationship to life." This realistic relationship to life precluded anything but active political struggle with the government—in other words, terrorism.[3]

The bombing of the Winter Palace was the People's Will's third attempt at tsaricide.[4] Though it had failed to achieve its goal, by striking at the tsar in the very sanctum of absolutism the People's Will demonstrated its power to "shake the foundations," and the vision of Peter Verkhovensky and Dostoevsky was realized. "We are experiencing a time of terror like that of the French Revolution," wrote Grand Duke Konstantin Nikolaevich in his diary on February 7, 1880. "The only difference is that we do not see, do not know, do not have the slightest idea of their numbers.... Universal panic."[5] And General A. A. Kireev, Adjutant to Grand Duke Konstantin Nikolaevich, seconded his distress, writing on February 15, "The nihilists have started a general panic among all classes. Many have left the city. The most fantastic rumors about bombings circulate."[6]

That the foundations had been shaking already for quite some time is attested to by one of Alexander II's most independent-minded ministers, P. A. Valuev, who confided to his diary a month before the explosion, "Everything is going to pieces, everything is going to the dogs. One feels the earth shaking, the building is threatening to collapse, but people do not seem to be aware of this. Perhaps" he speculated, "in order to move to a different order of ideas and events, it is necessary that the earth should tremble even more beneath our feet."⁷ Naturally, he was unaware that the terrorist plot currently in the works would do precisely this, but the expression of such a desire by one of the tsar's most trusted ministers illustrates how bitterly alienated educated society, with its consistently thwarted hopes for participation in the political process, had become.⁸ Thus it was not Dostoevsky alone who could be suspected of "solidarity with the nihilists."

The jubilee speech that smacked of such solidarity was very much a recapitulation of things that Dostoevsky already had written in *Demons* and elsewhere. It reviewed the course of Russian history and deplored "the Fall" when, in the wake of Peter the Great's reforms, a Westernized elite emerged, separated from the people, its truth, and its God, and consequently spawned "impatient destroyers, ignorant even in their convictions . . . sincere evildoers, proclaiming the idea of total destruction."⁹ As in *Demons*, it framed the conflict in filial terms and declared that the Slavic Benevolent Society stands firmly opposed "both to the faintheartedness of so many fathers, and the wild madness of their children, who believe in villainy and sincerely bow down before it" and instead quickens to "the ancient truth, which from time immemorial has penetrated into the soul of the Russian people: that their Tsar is also their father, and that children always will come to their father without fear so that he hears them, with love, of their needs and wishes; that the children love their father and the father trusts their love; and that the relations of the Russian people to their Tsar-Father is lovingly free and without fear, not lifelessly formal and contractual."¹⁰

The conception of the relationship of sovereign and subject in filial terms goes beyond that of a trope and is one of the central legitimizing pillars of Russian monarchy. In keeping with Slavophile ideas, Dostoevsky imposes certain conditions on this relationship—and specifically, on the tsar—but in emotional as opposed to rational "contractual" (i.e., Western) terms. Though the relationship is by no means one of equals, it entails the father's responsiveness to "their [the children's] needs and wishes," and most importantly, freedom. Mutual, freely given love—love that is not commanded—is integral to the relationship of subject and sovereign in Dostoevsky's sentimental political theory.¹¹

From the point of view of Alexander II, what was likely most suspect about this declaration of fealty was that it was a glaring counterfactual, not only in light of recent events, but in light of Dostoevsky's novel, *The Brothers Karamazov*, which was then being serialized in Katkov's *Russian Messenger*. That novel, in which the debauched and despised *pater familias* is murdered by his son(s), was so transparently allegorical that as Joseph Frank remarks, "No wonder that every installment of *The Brothers Karamazov* was snapped up and read with such passionate intensity, as if the literate classes were hoping the novel would help them find some answer to their quandary."[12] Indeed, the timing of the novel was remarkable, with chapters recounting Fyodor Karamazov's murder (Book 8) appearing on November 1, 1879—just weeks before the first attempts by the People's Will on the tsar's life. The quandary, then, was precisely the extent of society's own sympathy and responsibility for the attacks. Given the censorship, reports of these attacks—much less open discussion of the causes of and solutions to *kramola*—were severely circumscribed. The most fraught questions, such as the moral and religious upbringing of Russian youth, economic inequality in the wake of the reforms, the revolutionaries' ideology and goals, and constitutional limits to autocratic power were prohibited topics.[13] Members of society, however, addressed their thoughts and concerns about these questions privately, in personal or collective letters to high officials, and often under cover of anonymity.[14]

The Brothers Karamazov has not been read as "about terrorism" in the same way as *Demons* has been, for the obvious reason that *Demons*' plot overtly features an (ambiguously) political crime committed by *faux* revolutionary conspirators, whereas *The Brothers Karamazov* centers on the unfolding tragedy of an unhappy family with a subplot involving wayward children. Parricide was, however, an all-too-transparent allegory for tsaricide (in the Church's interpretation, tsaricide was one of the most grievous sins and was equated with patri/matricide), and wayward youths and dropouts were considered to be the terrorists of the future.[15]

Dostoevsky's novel became a public forum for the "discussion" of the causes and solutions of the revolutionary crisis, which makes it all the more ironic that he gave private readings of his work-in-progress to his royal admirers at the Winter Palace. It is in *The Brothers Karamazov* that Dostoevsky expresses his most profound understanding of Russian revolutionary terrorism and undertakes a final reckoning. As of 1878, when he suspended publication of his wildly successful one-man periodical, *Diary of a Writer*, to devote himself exclusively to the novel that had been germinating, he found himself playing catch-up. It was no longer a matter of conjuring and then preempting an apparitional terrorism, but countering a full-fledged terrorism and its emotionally compelling claims to moral legitimacy.

2

An Original Plan

On January 24, 1878, two young women, Vera Zasulich and Maria Kolenkina, undertook the simultaneous assassinations of the notorious governor general of St. Petersburg, Fyodor Trepov, and the public prosecutor in the recent mass trial of the populist propagandists ("The Trial of the 193"), Vladislav Zhelekhovsky.[1] While Kolenkina aroused suspicion and was barred access to Zhelekhovsky, Zasulich fired at her victim from point blank range and inflicted a serious, though not fatal, wound. For this reason, Zasulich alone became renowned as the first revolutionary terrorist, although the women's innovation is better appreciated as it was conceived, rather than as it was realized. On the surface, Zasulich's attempt—like Dmitry Karakozov's attempted regicide in 1866—failed. Yet unlike Karakozov's failure, Zasulich's was the key to her ultimate success. Her act, and not Karakozov's, marked the inception of terrorism as a systematic method of political struggle.

Zasulich's attempt may legitimately be considered the first act of terrorism thanks to the coalescence of elements previously absent, the most important of which was only marginally within Zasulich's personal control: the public reception of her deed. What distinguished Zasulich's and Kolenkina's plan from the actions of the Southern Rebels or even a parallel plot hatched by their male comrades in Land and Freedom to assassinate Trepov was their acute consciousness of the public impact of their act as a "double blow" that would be subsequently broadcast by the media.² Zasulich's media-consciousness is reflected in the meticulous preparations she made prior to the assassination attempt with the realization that "tomorrow" her act "would be in all the papers."³ And unlike Karakozov, who when questioned regarding his motive by his intended victim (the tsar), gave a reply so cryptic that no one is sure what he actually said,⁴ Zasulich had an unambiguous message to broadcast: "For Bogoliubov."⁵

Arkhip Bogoliubov was the revolutionary pseudonym of Alexei Stepanovich Emilianov, a member of Land and Freedom who had been arrested and imprisoned in the House of Preliminary Detention (Prelim) for his participation in the demonstrations outside of Kazan Cathedral on December 6, 1876. Bogoliubov joined 395 fellow political prisoners in the Prelim, many of whom had been awaiting formal charges and trial by the government for more than two years.⁶ On July 13, 1877, Bogoliubov precipitated a public scandal when in the course of his daily walk in the prison yard he encountered the visiting governor general and reportedly failed to doff his prisoner's cap. The outraged Trepov, aware that the windows facing the courtyard made it something of a theater-in-the-round for the prisoners who had observed the incident, ordered an exemplary (though illegal) flogging of Bogoliubov, with preparations carried out in full view of the women prisoners.⁷ News of Bogoliubov's flogging and the "prison riot" that supposedly ensued was smuggled out of prison and reported in liberal newspapers in the capital as well as in provincial centers, but a brief public outcry and calls to account faded swiftly in light of more pressing political and economic issues, namely the war in the Balkans and the economic recession.⁸

Zasulich and Kolenkina essentially adapted the model of political terrorism pioneered by the Southern Rebels, in which an act of revolutionary violence was linked to a specific government abuse.⁹ This had the effect of conferring instantaneous legibility, and in the process staking a claim to moral and political legitimacy. Yet it remained for this instantaneous legibility to be further fleshed out by the word, in the first place, through the radicals' own publications, but also ideally through the official law courts and the mass media. In recalling earlier acts of revolutionary violence in the countryside, the veteran revolutionary Vera Figner cited the lack of publicity and resonance as an impediment not only to revolutionary morale, but more specifically to the consolidation of the terrorist struggle.¹⁰

Zasulich and Kolenkina's innovation consisted in transporting these tactics of the periphery to St. Petersburg, the hub of the law courts, media, and public opinion. Zasulich was not incorrect in her "wager on the media." After the initial shock and horror had subsided, the press was enthralled with the drama of the attack, the details of Trepov's condition (although he himself won little sympathy), and the person and motivation of the "villainess." Minister of Justice Pahlen, believing that the execrable nature of Zasulich's act was clear to all, did not foresee the necessity of restricting the press's presence at the trial scheduled for March 31, 1878.

Historians have unanimously accorded Zasulich's trial more importance than the attempt itself, with Richard Pipes characterizing it as "the most important judiciary event in the history of Imperial Russia with profound repercussions on both the tsarist regime and public opinion."[11] The trial was notorious, in the first place, because Zasulich was found not guilty of a crime to which she had freely confessed. This shocking acquittal and the unseemly public jubilation in response opened the way for rapprochement between liberal public opinion and the radicals, something that had not existed since 1862. The radicals interpreted this rapprochement as sanction for an escalation of warfare, which the government likewise intensified after Zasulich's acquittal.

The trial was no less a watershed for Dostoevsky, who as luck would have it, was in the courtroom audience as a member of the press. Given that he left only a few rather cryptic and belated notes in his notebook for *The Brothers Karamazov* regarding the Zasulich trial, we can only guess what Dostoevsky experienced as he watched while his inner demons did battle in the St. Petersburg courtroom that day. He did not devote any pages of the *Diary of a Writer* to Zasulich, as he had done for celebrated civil and criminal cases for the simple reason that he had suspended publication in order to devote himself entirely to his work-in-progress. In his insightful examination of Dostoevsky's relationship to the legal culture of the time, Gary Rosenshield has underscored the importance of the Zasulich trial for Dostoevsky and *The Brothers Karamazov*, going so far as to argue that "the vitriol that Dostoevsky displays toward the jury trial in *The Brothers Karamazov* almost certainly derives from his outrage at the result of the Zasulich case," and that "the Zasulich affair probably gave Dostoevsky the idea of incorporating a jury trial in *The Brothers Karamazov*."[12] Historians, for their part, duly acknowledge Dostoevsky's presence at the trial as a celebrity author and relay his words exemplifying public sympathy for Zasulich and his anticipation of the "heroic narrative" of revolutionary terrorism. "She should not be convicted, and punishment is inappropriate, superfluous; but one wishes one could say to her 'go and do not do that again.' It seems we do not have such a judicial formula, and for all I know she will now become a heroine."[13] As for the trial itself, while its drama has often been recounted in the historiography, no scholar has analyzed it as a laboratory for the invention of a new type of act and a new actor, as well as a testing ground for their reception by public opinion. And while acknowledging the undeniable influence of the trial on Dostoevsky's last masterpiece, no literary scholar has peered into the proceedings in order to glean what Dostoevsky experienced that fateful day and how it profoundly shaped his last masterpiece and his own "new word." The following chapters will attempt to do so.

3

Emotions on Trial

Witness Testimony and the Prosecution

Before the presiding judge, the erudite and well-respected A. A. Koni, dismissed the jury of the St. Petersburg Municipal Court to deliberate on the verdict in the Zasulich case, he instructed them to answer three questions: "1) Was Zasulich guilty so that, wanting to wreak vengeance on Commandant Trepov for his punishment of Bogoliubov and having acquired for this purpose a revolver, on January 24, with deliberate intent, she inflicted on the General-Adjutant a wound in the region of the pelvis with a bullet of large caliber? 2) If Zasulich carried out this act, did she intend to deprive Commander Trepov of life? and, 3) If Zasulich did intend to deprive Commander Trepov of life, did she do everything in her power to attain this objective, given that death did not ensue for reasons that did not depend on her?"[1] If found guilty of the first count, a negative answer to either or both of the two remaining questions would have resulted in a mitigation of Zasulich's sentence. The jury deliberated for a shockingly short time (anywhere between ten and thirty minutes) before returning to a courtroom audience that awaited her inevitable conviction with breathless tension. When the jury elder read the first question and the response "No, not guil—" the courtroom erupted. "Whoever was not present, cannot imagine either the outburst of sounds, which drowned out the voice of the jury elder, or the commotion that spread across the entire hall like an electric current. The shouts of unconcealed joy, hysterical sobs, impassioned applause, the stomping of feet, the shouts 'Bravo, Hurrah! Well done! Vera! Verochka! Verochka!'—all fused into a single din, groan, and howl. Many crossed themselves. In the upper floors, the more democratic section set aside for the public, people embraced one another."[2]

This evocative description from Koni's memoir has been frequently quoted by historians to illustrate the courtroom's—and more broadly, the Russian public's—reaction to Zasulich's acquittal. A strong emotionality irradiated the Zasulich case from the earliest newspaper reports and was carried into the courtroom, packed with six hundred spectators, and the restive crowd of more than a thousand clogging the streets outside the courthouse.[3] But feeling was made the central issue of the trial largely by default—because the substantive issues of politics and Zasulich's revolutionary background and activities were barred, first by the Minister of Justice, Count Pahlen, and then, with entirely different motives, by Zasulich's defense attorney, P. A. Alexandrov. In violation of Russian law, Pahlen had suppressed police information regarding Zasulich's radical connections in order to send her trial to a criminal court, rather than risk the debacle of the most recent political trials that had been tried in the Senate.[4] By Pahlen's reasoning, because Zasulich had confessed her guilt a jury would have no choice but to convict her, as Pahlen assured the tsar that "the jurors would deliver a guilty verdict and thereby teach a sobering lesson to the insane, small coterie of revolutionaries; they would show all of the Russian and foreign admirers of Vera Zasulich's 'heroic exploit' that the Russian people bow before the tsar, revere him, and are always ready to defend his faithful servants."[5] The defense attorney, Alexandrov, on the other hand, bracketed Zasulich's revolutionary past and convictions in order to transmute her act of violence into a communicative act: a cry of the heart.

Alexandrov was helped in this endeavor by the indictment itself, read at the beginning of the trial. This indictment presented as motivation for her act the foundational moral sentiments: empathy and sympathy. When Zasulich herself testified, her emphasis was not on Bogoliubov or his punishment, but on its effect on the inmates of the House of Preliminary Detention (Prelim).

> I heard about the events of July 13 and the motives for it from various individuals in Petersburg. They talked about how the soldiers tore into the cells [of the Prelim], how those making noise were thrown in the

punishment cells [kartser]; then I heard that Bogoliubov was not given 25 lashes, but was punished until he stopped screaming. From my own experience I know to what extremes of nervous tension long solitary confinement leads.... I could vividly imagine what a hellish impression the flogging would have made on all the political prisoners, not to mention those who had already been subjected to whipping, beatings, punishment cells and what cruelty you had to have in order to force them to endure all of that, on the pretext [po povodu] of a hat that wasn't doffed upon a second meeting.[6]

Zasulich, therefore, does not emphasize her identification with or sympathy for the victim of the flogging himself, Bogoliubov, so much as with those like herself who were political prisoners and "forced to endure" not the mere spectacle of the flogging, but its hellish "impression" on its intended audience. It is possible that this emphasis may have in part resulted from the questioning of witnesses that directly preceded it. While the first line of questioning, pursued both by the presiding judge and the public prosecutor, Kessel, sought to establish the forensic aspects of the case through questions such as "At what distance did she stand?" "Was her shawl wide?"[7] Alexandrov veered off in a different, emotionally charged direction, one designed to lay the groundwork for the arguments of his summation.

"Inconsequential and ephemeral details"

The first witness, Major Fyodor Kurneev, Trepov's assistant and acting warden of the House of Preliminary Detention, was a critical link between July 13 and January 24, having been present both at the Prelim on July 13 as director and, in his capacity as guard, at the shooting of General Trepov. With relative ease, Alexandrov secured two significant victories during this first round of questioning, the first in favor of his client, the second to the detriment of her victim. Kurneev, who immediately following Zasulich's attack, whether from zeal or in panic, had grabbed Zasulich by the throat, confirmed that Zasulich had immediately thrown down her revolver—not, as Trepov had claimed in his statement, persisted in her attack or resisted arrest. When Alexandrov abruptly switched to the events of July 13 and seemed bent on unearthing all the details of the illegal flogging, Koni intervened to request that he "keep only to the circumstances of the case," to which Alexandrov ingenuously begged "indulgence, because perhaps some questions may seem irrelevant, but in advance it is difficult to decide, which question is necessary for the defense or not. I always go by the rule: better to ask more than to not ask enough [doprosit']"—a philosophy in full accord with Koni's instruction to the jurors that they "regard the case with the fullest attention, without missing the slightest, apparently inconsequential and ephemeral details, but which in their totality to a significant degree draw [risuiut] the case and illuminate its true meaning."[8]

These inconsequential and ephemeral details quickly led ineluctably to a staggering conclusion: that the flogging of Bogoliubov was completely arbitrary. The written order for the flogging was given on the pretext that Bogoliubov had incited the prisoners to riot. Alexandrov's questioning quickly exposed that as a lie.

>   Q. As a consequence of what followed the order for the punishment of Bogoliubov?
>   A. As a consequence of the fact that the inmates began to riot [buntovat'].
>   Q. What was the connection between the riot of the inmates and the punishment of Bogoliubov?
>   A. That I don't know.

It is Koni who puts a point on it.

>   Q. Was Bogoliubov punished for the noise that the inmates made, or for the act of rudeness, that he himself committed?
>   A. As a result of the noise that the prisoners made.[9]

It is a case, then, of being at the wrong place at the wrong time (twice, as the historian Ana Siljak observed), as Bogoliubov was subjected to a fate that Stepan Trofimovich narrowly escaped in *Demons*, but which his imaginary avatar, Avdotya Tarapygin, didn't.[10] Bogoliubov's fate was a latter-day confirmation of the "old fable," roundly ridiculed by *Demons'* narrator, that in Russia people are flogged for nothing.

Terror by Any Other Name

The remaining witnesses for the defense were inmates who had been present during the disturbances at the Prelim. None had witnessed the actual punishment of Bogoliubov, which had been conducted in the

Emotions on Trial

prison corridor. Instead, they were called not in the capacity of witnesses, but as became clear over the course of testimony, as themselves victims of terror. The first two witnesses, Nikolai Petropavlovsky and Sergei Goloushev, described the confrontation between Trepov and Bogoliubov, and the inmates' outrage at what they perceived to be Trepov's abuse of Bogoliubov.

> Goloushev: When Bogoliubov again approached the Governor, then the Governor yelled "To the punishment cells! To the punishment cells! Hat off!" And he waved his hand at Bogoliubov. Whether he knocked the hat from Bogoliubov's head, I don't know, but I saw the wave that should have landed on Bogoliubov, and the hat fell. Then the noise began, it couldn't have been otherwise.[11]

But that was not the worst of it.

> Goloushev: I remember that after a time, as the noise began to quiet, Kurneev came out into the courtyard and explained that Bogoliubov would be flogged—probably in order to calm the prisoners. Perhaps, I'm bringing a certain amount of agitation into the story....
> Koni: Don't worry, calm yourself a bit.
> Goloushev: I was too close a witness of that event and I can't forget it and it's difficult for me to overcome my agitation.[12]

The particular dynamic of events should be familiar, even though their presentation and its effect are radically different. The disorder prevailing at the Prelim caused the governor to overreact. The prisoners saw the enraged governor strike Bogoliubov—whether he did or not—and reacted, almost independently of their will ("it couldn't have been otherwise"), with indignation to that perceived abuse. Just as the furor was dying down, the administration intervened, in the person of Major Kurneev, to "calm" the rioters by announcing a completely arbitrary flogging, "after which arose a general clamor" followed by the administration's "revenge" (*rasprava*). Prisoners were flung into punishment cells, a hundred troops were called to quell the disturbance, fire hoses—rather than water barrels—were contemplated.

The situation degenerated into a vicious cycle of imaginary *kibitkas* and "sleds shooting off down hill," to use G___v's euphemistic metaphors. But the tragedy is that, as Stepan Trofimovich points out by circuitous way of a gentleman's anecdote, there are "mistakes" that cannot be undone and affronts too grievous for any apology to make good, much less erase from memory. The testimony of Goloushev and a female inmate, the witness Anna Charushina, demonstrated the indelible imprint on memory, the lasting trauma. Charushina's account eliminates any doubt as to the true intent behind Bogoliubov's flogging: to terrorize the inmates. From the women's wing, she recounted, unusual activity was clearly visible:

> Charushina: Across from our windows, in the passageway there were two barns; suddenly the doors were opened and from there gigantic bunches of birch branches were pulled out and from them they began to make small bundles: it became clear what was being prepared, something serious [tiazheloe], everyone began to guess—a flogging [eksekutsiia]... I can't help but become agitated by these memories [ia ne mogu ne volnovat'sia pri etom vospominanii].
> Koni: Calm yourself, don't worry. Talk only about that which concerns Bogoliubov.
> Charushina: When they bundled the birch branches, the bundlers made threatening gestures, looking at our windows and in the direction of the men's wing.[13]

A tense moment followed this deeply emotional testimony when the prosecutor asked Kurneev whether he had been investigated for his not insignificant role in the July 13 disturbances. He had, but not, as defense attorney Alexandrov quickly underscored in a deft save, in conjunction with Bogoliubov's flogging. Thus the ground was laid for Zasulich's own testimony: "I could vividly imagine, what a hellish impression the flogging would make on political prisoners.... All of this made the impression on me not of a punishment, but of ridicule, provoked by some kind of personal malice. It seemed to me that such an act could not, should not occur without consequences. I waited, wouldn't it elicit some kind of response, but everything was silent, and in the press not another word appeared.... Then, not seeing any other way in this case, I decided, even at the cost of my own destruction, to prove that one shouldn't be confident in getting off scot free [v beznakazannosti], having so trampled upon an individual personality."[14] The transcript notes here in parentheses: "V. I. Zasulich was agitated to such an extent, that she couldn't continue." The judge invited her to rest and to calm herself. Shortly thereafter she resumed, "I didn't find, I couldn't find another method to direct attention to this incident.... It's terrible to lift a hand against a human being, but I had to do it."[15]

Emotions on Trial

These words of Zasulich evidently made a particular impression on Dostoevsky, as he recalled them in his notebook almost verbatim fully two years later in conjunction with the dilemma facing the second Karamazov brother, Ivan. "Zasulich: 'It is hard to raise a hand to shed blood'—this vacillation is more moral than the shedding of blood itself."[16] The idea that the shedding of blood is moral and vacillation over the shedding of blood is still more moral sends us ricocheting backward to the unresolved role of conscience for Raskolnikov in *Crime and Punishment*. Zasulich—and with her "terrorism"—had not "crossed over," but resolutely remained on the side of conscience.

Psychological Generalizations and Their Discontents

It was left to Prosecutor Kessel, whose junior status made it impossible for him to refuse Pahlen's unenviable assignment of serving as prosecutor in the case, to dispel the charged atmosphere and defuse the emotional testimony of the witnesses for the defense.[17] As Gary Rosenshield has noted, summations were the narrative crown of the trial in post-reform 1864 Russia and often clinched the jury's verdict.[18] The summation depended on the rhetorical prowess of the attorneys, who crafted them with scrupulous attention to their literary quality, often drawing upon famous works of Russian literature (as seen in Spasovich's comparison of Nechaev to Gogol's Khlestakov and Goncharov's Mark Volokhov) for their tropes. Kessel's speech is an exception in this regard: it relies exclusively upon psychological, moral, and legal reasoning and is largely devoid of rhetorical or literary devices. For this reason, or because Kessel's faint voice was almost inaudible, the emotional charge of the foregoing testimony was indeed dispelled—by boredom, as fatal to an attorney as to any performer.

Kessel offered no story, no account of the crime based on the unique circumstances and individuality of the accused, but an argument patched together from one-size-fits-all generalizations about human psychology, which he marshaled in order to refute Zasulich's contention that she was indifferent to whether she killed or merely wounded Trepov because her motivation was to attract attention to the incident involving Bogoliubov. All of Kessel's generalizations are easily falsifiable and demonstrate the absence of even the most elementary understanding of psychology as *individual* psychology. In *The Brothers Karamazov*,

Dostoevsky will satirize and undercut (with what the reader already knows to be the truth of the crime) the prosecutor Ippolit Kirillovich's narrative, which stands upon the pillars of precisely such psychological assumptions and commonplaces about Dmitry or crimes and criminals in general. Kessel's intention was to prove that Zasulich intended to kill, rather than merely wound, Trepov and chose the surest means available to see that she did. But the success of his case hinged upon his ability to cast aspersions upon her stated motivation and to put emotion back in the Pandora's box whence it came. "I completely believe Zasulich, that those facts which she presents as the motive for her act, appear to her as she explained them here; I believe also in those feelings, about which she spoke here. With that I don't wish to say that I acknowledge the raison d'être, the correctness or incorrectness of those feelings. I simply acknowledge them as facts, departing from the general supposition, that every person is free to have whatever feelings, whatever sympathies and antipathies, they like.... But when those feelings are translated into action, when sympathies or antipathies from the individual's inner life cross over into the outer world, populated by other people—then the matter changes.... Everyone is free to love or hate whom they like, but no one can violate the rights of others."[19]

Despite the fact that Kessel's stilted discussion of feelings as "facts" resembles a parody of 1860s positivism, his reasoning is sound and echoes liberalism's most fundamental precepts regarding individual liberty: an individual's freedom stops where it impinges upon the rights and freedom of another individual. Kessel was not an enemy of feeling: he argued that the good of society depends upon the mutual enhancement of feeling by reason and vice versa, for "reasonable feelings and the wisdom of the heart."[20] Nevertheless, he needed to decisively discredit feeling as a legitimate motivation for Zasulich's act: "the court is required to demand an accounting from an individual who expresses her feelings, as Zasulich did hers," in particular by underscoring the "chasm" (propast') between her ostensible feelings of empathy and her act of attempted murder. "That is why Zasulich is trying to build a bridge to cross that chasm."[21] Kessel would have to evoke the chasm in Zasulich's terms and in the tried-and-true tactic of literary polemics, turn his opponent's weapons against him. Yet his failure to engage with the particular and the concrete (most especially the particular feelings in question, rather than "feelings" as such) opens the way for his adversary to do precisely that, and in the process, to "build a bridge to cross that chasm."

4

Emotions on Trial II

The Defense

Dostoevsky was profoundly disturbed by the fact that lawyers served not their consciences, but their clients and their own agendas, and therefore were bound to use any means to achieve a verdict favorable to them.[1] The most notorious example was the Kroneberg case, a case of horrific child abuse, in which the father was accused—and exonerated—of torture. Kroneberg's defense attorney, the celebrated V. D. Spasovich, who had defended the Nechaevtsy, insisted on a very legalistic understanding of torture, and, what was worse, impugned the moral character of the seven-year-old victim, and the well-intentioned witnesses who had come to her aid. Dostoevsky was so incensed by the acquittal of Kroneberg that he devoted one of his most impassioned entries in *Diary of a Writer* to the pillory of Spasovich, the evisceration of the law courts, and the harrowing of readers' sensibilities with the torture of an innocent child. For this he drew liberally on his special expertise in corporal punishment and his own well-established authority as a former political convict in Siberia.

> I would like to inform Mr. Spasovich that in Siberia, in the convicts' wards in the hospital, I chanced to see the backs of prison inmates

immediately after they had been subjected to flogging with spitzrutens (driven through the ranks after five hundred, one thousand and two thousand blows inflicted at a time). This I saw several dozens of times. Would you believe me, Mr. Spasovich, that some backs literally swelled almost two inches thick, and yet think how little flesh there is on the back! These backs were of a dark purple color, with a few gashes from which blood would still be oozing.... Now I ask you, Mr. Defense-Lawyer, I will ask you this question: even though these sticks did not threaten her life and caused her not the slightest injury, isn't such a punishment cruel and doesn't it constitute torture? For heaven's sake, didn't the little girl suffer for a quarter of an hour under the dreadful rods, which lay on the table in court as an exhibit, screaming: "Papa! Papa!" Why then are you denying her her suffering, her torture?[2]

P. A. Alexandrov, however, served his conscience. Initially a rising star in the public prosecutor's office, Alexandrov's political sympathies led him to cross over to the defense, most recently of some of the accused in the Trial of the 193. Zasulich's co-conspirator, Maria Kolenkina, was able to raise a subscription among St. Petersburg students in order to engage the brilliant attorney in the defense of Zasulich, and the unprepossessing Alexandrov undertook the mission with zest and what seemed like unfounded confidence in an acquittal for his obviously guilty client.[3] As opposed to Kessel's uninspired fifty minutes, Alexandrov's summation lasted two hours, was rehearsed to perfection, and was delivered in his customary off-the-cuff and intimate manner. While initially graciously conceding his agreement with his adversary on many points, he quickly and deftly made his client's "feelings" the legitimate key to the case.

"In order to completely judge the motives of our deeds, one needs to know how they were reflected in our understanding. In the same way, in my judgment about the events of July 13 there won't be discussion about the actions of the officials, but only the illumination of how those events were reflected in the mind and convictions of Vera Zasulich."[4] With this move, Alexandrov frees himself to graphically portray the action of officials without, in fact, "discussing" them and to relocate the debate about Zasulich's guilt from the territory of objective guilt and universally valid moral principles to the completely subjective realm of Zasulich's inner life, as told by her lawyer, Alexandrov.

Poor Vera

Just as historical narratives may display the unmistakable features of literary genres, so too legal summations—especially where literature played such a prominent and authoritative role—may be consciously or unconsciously crafted according to literary conventions.[5] In Zasulich's case, Alexandrov chose sentimentalism as best suited to Zasulich and her crime. While he claimed to dwell only on some of "the biographical data," Alexandrov was intent on casting Zasulich as a modern-day "Poor Liza," the heroine of Nikolai Karamzin's iconic sentimental tale.[6] He began by sketching the portrait of a seventeen-year-old maiden, a diligent student who passes her governess exam with distinction, returns to St. Petersburg to live with her "old mother" (*starukha mat'* suggests a vulnerable old mother in need of care), and is promptly ensnared by the unscrupulous Sergei Nechaev. If Nechaev is Erast, Karamzin's aristocratic seducer, then the Litovskii and Peter and Paul fortresses are the "pond" in which Liza/Zasulich is drowned—for one-and-a-half years.[7]

Not the physical deprivations, emphasized Alexandrov, but the emotional deprivations of prison life were the most onerous, and Alexandrov's sentimental tropes form the discursive weave for his moving portrayal of these emotional deprivations and their consequences. Cut off from human community and the sympathy that it offered, Zasulich, he contended, constructed an imagined community, a Prison Nation of unfortunates like herself, and invested her affective energies in the unseen comrades behind the prison walls. Alexandrov had already dipped unreservedly into the language of sentimentalism for his reverie on youth; now with even greater pathos he evoked the only emotional fulfillment and consolation that solitary confinement offered: "In these years of growing sympathy, Zasulich in fact created and strengthened in her soul one sympathy forever—a sacred love for anyone, who, like her, is forced to drag out an unfortunate life suspected of a political crime. A political prisoner, whoever he might be, became for her a dear friend, a comrade of youth, a comrade in upbringing. Prison was her alma mater, which strengthened this friendship, this comradeship."[8] Solidarity with those who share one's fate is almost a matter of course, but what Zasulich experiences, according to Alexandrov, was far more intense and profound—a feeling that transcended the prosaic and profane to achieve the transcendent heights of "sacred love," by which, of course, he implies the ideal love of Christian agape, rather than eros. The experience of arrest, one-and-a-half year's imprisonment without charges, sudden, arbitrary re-arrest, exile to Krestsy, and unremitting police surveillance, all combined to shape Zasulich's subjectivity, her emotional (pre)disposition, not to resentment against the government and to revenge, but to sympathy and love for political prisoners. As Rosenshield has noted, it was common practice in the post-reform courts for lawyers to artfully use and abuse empathetic narratives to sway the jury.[9] Alexandrov, however, goes even further and makes empathy the motive for Zasulich's terrorist act.

"A small digression"

It is this tale that Alexandrov unfolds for his audience, stopping only for a "small digression on the subject of the birch rod." The birch rod, of course stands in rather conveniently for the villain (Trepov) and is a synecdoche not only for him, but for all of Russian history prior to the 1864 legal reforms.[10] In this sense, the digression, small as it is, constitutes a walloping condemnation of almost perpetual Russian barbarism and brutality. "The birch rod reigned almost everywhere," Alexandrov declares of pre-reform Russia, "at school, at civil assemblies, it was an indispensable possession of the landowner, then in the barracks, at the police station. . . . No sooner did the glorious day April 17, 1863, dawn, than it receded into history, to become a mere souvenir."[11]

In his *Diary of a Writer*, this is what Dostoevsky had to say about the putative obsolescence of the birch rod in June–July 1877, as he commented on the case of the Dzhunkovsky family, the parents of which were accused and acquitted of mistreating their three children. "They [the children] were beaten with birch rods. . . . Well, who doesn't beat children with birch rods? Nine-tenths of Russia does."[12] Whether it is Dostoevsky or Alexandrov who is exaggerating, for Alexandrov it is critically important to establish that the sensibilities of both Zasulich and Bogoliubov, members of the post-reform generation, had been formed after the ubiquitous reign of the birch rod had come to an end. Not only had Zasulich and Bogoliubov been weaned on the ideals of individual dignity and bodily integrity, but their sensitivity to human suffering, and particularly to suffering inflicted not on the flesh, but on the human personality, had intensified as a result. "A person, who by birth, upbringing and education was foreign to the birch rods; a person feeling and understanding all of its shameful and humiliating significance, a person, who by his intellectual make-up, by his convictions and feelings would not be able without heartfelt shuddering [sodroganiia] to see and hear the execution of such a shameful punishment on others,—that person should himself endure on his own skin the overpowering action of the humiliating punishment."[13]

At the fore of Alexandrov's theory and rhetoric is feeling; Alexandrov embeds his discussion even of abstract ideals (human dignity) in a discussion of particular feelings (as opposed to feelings in general), for to paraphrase the historian Lynn Hunt, the concept of human dignity means nothing without the *feeling* of human dignity—and horror at its violation.[14] With the language of feeling, Alexandrov relentlessly kneads the already tenderized sensibilities of his audience. Alexandrov intends, ultimately, not to bridge a chasm but to collapse it entirely.

Another Small Digression in the Form of a Poem

For the sake of dispelling rumors that Zasulich and Bogoliubov had been romantically involved, and that Zasulich sought to avenge her lover, it was equally important for Alexandrov to stress the distance between Zasulich and Bogoliubov. The two were in fact complete strangers. "What was Bogoliubov to her? He wasn't a relative, a friend, he wasn't an acquaintance, she had never seen him and didn't know him. But really in order to become disturbed at the sight of a morally oppressed person, in order to become indignant about the shameful mockery against a defenseless creature [bezzashchitnyi], is it necessary to be a sister, a wife, a lover?"[15]

Not only is sympathy at the plight of "a morally oppressed person" understandable, but the opposite, he suggests, would be reprehensible. Just over half a year later, an untitled lyric by the liberal poet Yakov Polonsky appeared in *The Messenger of Europe* (Vestnik Evropy) expressing precisely the same sentiment in almost exactly the same words. The title, "The Female Prisoner" (Uznitsa) had been "destroyed" at the request of M. M. Stasiulevich, the journal's cautious editor, before publishing the poem in November 1878.[16]

Что мне она, не жена, не любовница
И не родная мне дочь!
Так отчего-же ея доля проклятая

Спать не дает мне всю ночь?
Спать не дает оттого, что мне грезится
Молодость в душной тюрьме
Вижу я своды . . . окно за решеткою,
Койку в сырой полутьме . . .
С койки глядят лихорадочно-знойные
Очи без мысли и слез,
С койки висят чуть не до полу темные
Космы тяжелых волос.
Не шевелятся ни губы, ни бледные
Руки на бледной груди,
Слабо прижатые к сердцу без трепета
и без надежд впереди.
Что мне она!—не жена, не любовница,
И не родная мне дочь!
Так отчего-же ее образ страдальческий
Спать не дает мне всю ночь?[17]

> What is she to me, not wife, not lover and not my own daughter!
> Then why in the world does her accursed fate keep me awake all through the night?
> Keeps me awake, because I am tormented by youth in the damp prison.
> I see arches . . . a window behind bars, a cot in the gray half-light . . .
> From the cot eyes look feverishly burning without thoughts and tears,
> From the cot tresses of heavy hair hang almost to the floor.
> Neither the lips nor the pale hands on the pale breast stir,
> Weakly pressed to the heart without trembling and without hope for the future.
> What is she to me!—not wife, not lover and not my own daughter!
> Then why in the world does her suffering image keep me awake all night long?

The title was no loss, as it was eminently clear to Polonsky's readers that the young woman in the poem was imprisoned for political crimes. What has been less clear, at least to posterity, is the identity of the young woman. Because the lyric was published shortly after Zasulich's acquittal, contemporary readers and subsequent scholars have usually assumed that the female prisoner in question was Vera Zasulich (or later, Vera Figner). The prominent Soviet historian N. A. Troitsky has presented evidence that the woman in question was in fact the lovely Lydia Figner, who was tried in the Trial of the 50 in 1877.[18] If Troitsky is correct, then it is more than possible that the lyric circulated by manuscript or by word of mouth (Polonsky's poem immediately enjoyed tremendous popularity in "democratic circles," and, like Chénier's *Jeune Captive* before it, was set to more than one musical arrangement, most famously by A. G. Rubinshtein in 1881)[19] prior to its publication and that Alexandrov borrowed freely for his summation.

Regardless of who borrowed from whom, the change of gender—in Alexandrov's summation it is Zasulich, the female, who is the sympathizing subject and Bogoliubov, the male, who is the pathetic object of sympathy—allows Polonsky to employ what is essentially the cliché of "virtue in distress" as the equivalent of Alexandrov's sentimental narrative of Zasulich as the perpetual victim of government repression, the oppressed "female prisoner." Polonsky's lyric, however, reinforces the boundary between the male subject and his gaze and the female object. Polonsky's lyric persona sees—it could be said that he sees obsessively—the female prisoner of his imagining, but he feels only his own feelings, not hers, which are left completely undescribed. The boundary between the two subjectivities is as impervious as the prison walls. This is not the case with Zasulich: Alexandrov consistently creates an ambiguity based on the intensity of her feeling and her identification with the fate of the political prisoner. "For Zasulich Bogoliubov was a political prisoner, and in that word was everything for her: a political prisoner wasn't for Zasulich an isolated image from books, known from rumors, from court trials—an image awakening in the honest soul the feeling of pity [sozhalenie], compassion [sostradanie], heartfelt sympathy [serdechnaia simpatiia]. A political prisoner was for Zasulich— she herself, her bitter past, her own history. . . . A political prisoner was her own heart and every crude touch on that heart was reflected in her agitated nature."[20] Zasulich's self is painfully permeable; she (or rather her heart) is and is not also Bogoliubov's.

Zasulich, it must be recalled, was not a direct witness of Bogoliubov's punishment, but like Polonsky's insomniac persona becomes obsessed with Bogoliubov's image. In the depths of the provinces, in the loneliness of her isolation, in the official and media silence that reigned following initial reports, Bogoliubov's punishment becomes a fantasy that she relives in its emotional dimensions. "Once again in the exalted female mind arose Bogoliubov's image, subjected to a shameful punishment, and the imagination tried to divine, to feel [perechuvstvovat'] everything that the unfortunate felt. A picture that agitated the soul was drawn, but it was still just a picture of her own imagining, not checked against any facts, unembellished by rumors, stories of eye-witnesses, the witnesses of the punishment; soon there appeared both of these [i to i drugoi]."[21]

Did there? None of the prisoners called as witnesses at Zasulich's trial had actually seen Bogoliubov's punishment, or even the blows Bogoliubov received from Trepov in the courtyard, but Alexandrov references this testimony, dwelling in particular on the emotional agitation that accompanied it as the basis for the "real picture" of Bogoliubov's flogging, which he presents as the climax of his summation to the courtroom audience:

> Now, from fragmented stories, from guesses, from hints, it was not difficult to imagine the real picture of the flogging [ekzekutsiia]. The pale, frightened figure of Bogoliubov rose up, ignorant of what he had done, what they wanted to do to him. There arose in thoughts his afflicted image. There he is, led to the place of flogging and shocked by the news of the shame being prepared for him . . . there he is, falling beneath the massive weight of human bodies, carrying him by the shoulders, spread-eagled on the floor, shamefully, several pairs of arms, like iron, pinning him down, deprived of any opportunity to resist, and above this whole picture, the measured whistle of the birch branches and the equally measured count of blows by the auspicious executor of the punishment. Everything froze in alarmed expectation of a moan; that moan was emitted—but it wasn't the moan of physical pain—that wasn't expected;—it was the torturous moan of a suffocated, humiliated, cursed, oppressed individual. The sacred deed was done, the shameful sacrifice was made! (. . . Applause, loud shouts: bravo!)[22]

We can only speculate as to why members of the audience burst out in shouts of approval precisely at this moment. Was it at Alexandrov's daring, the virtuosity of his vivid and moving depiction of Bogoliubov's flogging, his insistence that Bogoliubov's moan expressed not physical pain, but the emotional pain of human dignity shamefully violated? Or Alexandrov's ironic characterization of Bogoliubov's arbitrary punishment as a "shameful sacrifice"—presumably made at the altar of the powers that be? Or was it the clear analogy between the punishment of Bogoliubov (whose pseudonym means "lover of god") and Christ's crucifixion? Or was it because Alexandrov had attentively studied at

Emotions on Trial II

the feet of the master, Dostoevsky, who had powerfully rendered both the physical and moral torture of Kroneberg's seven-year-old daughter in his *Diary of a Writer*? Whatever the reason, the uproar in the courtroom and particularly the shouts of "Bravo!" seem to indicate that Alexandrov had not simply given an account of the flogging, but that he had in some sense performed it, thereby creating of the courtroom audience those "eyewitnesses" who were in fact conspicuously lacking.

5

Whose Rebellion?

As has been frequently noted by literary scholars, Dostoevsky used some of the arguments—and some of the techniques—from the Zasulich trial in the penultimate book of *The Brothers Karamazov*, devoted to Dmitry's trial. Or rather, it is more accurate to say that he exposed the arguments and techniques even as he used them. But the more momentous trial occurs before the "crime" of the novel, Fyodor Karamazov's murder by one of his sons, even takes place. This is Ivan Karamazov's trial of God, in Ivan's first genuine conversation with his younger brother Alyosha, a gentle and virtuous novice at the local monastery. Dostoevsky entitled this chapter "Rebellion" (Bunt), and scholars have identified many sources for Ivan's arguments and the examples he uses to support them, including the previously mentioned Kroneberg case and Dostoevsky's own commentary on it in *Diary of a Writer*. But Ivan's "rebellion" is far more than an argument (words): it is a reenactment (deed), and a key source for it (at times used almost verbatim) is the Zasulich trial.

The conversation between the two brothers begins when Ivan baits Alyosha by cynically denying the existence of true empathy. "Let's say that I, for example, am capable of profound suffering, but another man will never be able to know the degree of my suffering, because he is another and not me, and besides, a man is rarely willing to acknowledge

Whose Rebellion?

someone else as a sufferer (as if it were a kind of distinction). And why won't he acknowledge it, do you think? Because I, for example, have a bad smell, or a foolish face, or once stepped on his foot?"[1]

What better testifies to this fundamental lack of empathy than the intentional cruelty of human beings who inflict suffering on their fellows, and worse, on defenseless innocents, on children? "In order to reduce the scope of my argument about ten times," says Ivan, he proceeds to focus exclusively on children and unfurls before Alyosha a catalogue of atrocities, crimes, villainy, and abuse committed against them—what he refers to at first as "certain little facts," "certain little anecdotes" that he claims to have taken from newspapers and historical chronicles. From the narrator's introduction of him at the beginning of the novel, the reader knows that Ivan made a living and a pseudonymous name for himself as "Eyewitness" (ochevidets) with his piquant articles on street incidents.[2] It is not, ultimately, as a teller of anecdotes but as an "eyewitness" that Ivan harrows Alyosha with what he characterizes as primarily visual "lovely pictures" and "little pictures," each one more graphically portraying "the defenselessness and angelic trustfulness of the child, who has nowhere to turn and no one to turn to."[3]

When Ivan reaches the climax of his exposition, he refers to it, just as Alexandrov did, "as one more picture, just one more" supposedly a typical one. Like the picture of Bogoliubov and General Trepov, this one also features a general, a very wealthy landowner with two thousand souls who also kept hundreds of dogs. Upon noticing that one of his dogs was limping, the general discovered that an eight-year-old serf boy had thrown a rock and wounded its paw. The general's retribution was immediate: he took the boy from his mother, and the next day:

> The house-serfs are gathered for their edification, the guilty boy's mother in front of them all. The boy is led out of the lockup. A gloomy, cold misty autumn day, a great day for hunting. The general orders them to undress the boy; the child is stripped naked, he shivers, he's crazy with fear, he doesn't dare make a peep.... "Drive him!" the general commands. The huntsmen shout, "Run, run!" The boy runs.... "Sic him!" screams the general and looses the whole pack of wolfhounds on him. He hunted him down before his mother's eyes, and the dogs tore the child to pieces...! I believe the general was later declared incompetent to administer his estates. Well... what to do with him? Shoot him? Shoot him for our moral satisfaction? Speak Alyoshka!

"Shoot him!" Alyosha said softly, looking up at his brother with a sort of pale, twisted smile.

"Bravo!" Ivan yelled in a sort of rapture. "If even you say so, then.... A fine monk you are! See what a little devil is sitting in your heart, Alyoshka Karamazov!"⁴

Dostoevsky's serf boy, torn to pieces by hounds, is Bogoliubov to the tenth power. What unites the episode with (Alexandrov's rendering of) Bogoliubov's punishment is the orchestration of the spectacle: the spectacle of the boy's terror, torture, and horrific death that is meant to "edify"—in other words, to terrorize those present. What unites this episode with Bogoliubov's punishment is that it takes place before the mother's [Zasulich's] eyes, as she is forced to witness the atrocity inflicted on her own flesh and blood, "her own heart." What unites this episode with Zasulich's crime is Alyosha's deeply ambivalent assent to "shoot the General." And finally, what unites this scene with Alexandrov's courtroom performance is Ivan's outburst "Bravo!" which reveals that the conversation was in fact a theater, and that Ivan's performance in turn elicited the desired performance from his unsuspecting brother, Alyosha.

Contemporary readers who previewed these chapters, foremost among them Dostoevsky's friend and unofficial "censor," Konstantin Pobedonostsev, were disturbed by Ivan's rhetoric and protested its "superfluous" details and the *"distressing colors."*⁵ Pobedonostsev, the conservative tutor to the tsarevich and soon-to-be procurator of the Holy Synod, opined to Dostoevsky: "This is a very strong chapter—but why did you paint the torture of children in this way?"⁶ Dostoevsky defended himself by insisting that he "invented nothing" and holding Ivan accountable for the rhetorical excesses of this chapter: "perhaps [the details] could be superfluous if it came from me as an author.... But those details, how necessary they are to the artistic task!"⁷ Dostoevsky thus diverts attention from the effect of Ivan's rhetoric to the exigencies of his characterization: Ivan's mastery of the "details" demonstrates his sincere love of children. Since the novel provides scant evidence of such love (as opposed to Alyosha's active and demonstrable love), we might assume that Dostoevsky quite purposely obfuscates the true function, which Pobedonostsev certainly intuited, of the "details": to embellish Ivan's terrible "little pictures" and thereby arouse the auditor within the text (Alyosha) and the reader "outside" of the text to cross the border from sympathy to shooting.

In his famous analysis of Dostoevsky's novels, Mikhail Bakhtin for the most part limits his discussion to the world of Dostoevsky's novel. He gives minimal consideration to the effect—physiological and ideological—of what he lauds as the hero's "free and unfettered word" and the novel's dialogicity on the reader. In the case of "Ivan's confession," that effect is at this point mediated only by the feeble protestations of the mesmerized Alyosha. Bakhtin says only: "This interaction provides no support for the viewer who would objectify an entire event according to some ordinary monologic category (thematically, lyrically or cognitively), and as a consequence makes the viewer also a participant."[8] While Bakhtin minimizes the issue in order to preserve his utopian view of Dostoevsky's dialogism, Robert Belknap extends his analysis to reader reception, arguing that Dostoevsky departed from the general European trend of "developing narrators whose consistency and integrity of identity . . . would guarantee the verisimilitude of the account; but the Russians, with Gogol, Tolstoi, and Dostoevsky at their head, were exploring a new kind of novel, the manipulative novel, which may tell and show, but which gains its power by carrying the reader through the same experiences that the characters are having."[9]

For this, Belknap continues, they were "inventing a whole range of new narrative techniques" and remarks that "it was painfully difficult for Dostoevsky because no tradition and no body of critical understanding existed to give names to the enterprise in which he was engaged."[10] While there can be no doubt about Dostoevsky's innovations, he clearly availed himself of traditional rhetorical genres and devices for that purpose. If Ivan's oratory is subject to rhetorical criticism, it becomes clear that it may be classified as the rhetorical genre of exhortation, a genre that uses words to generate emotion, and ultimately, action. As Edwin Black asserts in his *Rhetorical Criticism*, exhortation is "not merely suasory, but didactic": it seeks to alter the worldview of its auditors "from top to bottom," to achieve, in effect, a "conversion."[11] In exhortation, the evident excitation, together with the words of the orator, arrests the attention of the listeners and holds them captive. At the same time, exhortation uses concrete and vivid description (ekphrasis) to evoke pictures that "replace the auditor's own life experience" (the basis of his or her previous judgments about the world) and to generate emotional excitation which in fact produces belief rather than accompanies or proceeds from it. In his study of terrorist rhetoric, Richard Leeman identified exhortation as the rhetorical genre most frequently employed by terrorists to justify their recourse to violence and to incite others to act.[12] Exhortation, therefore, is the rhetorical genre on which rebellion, if not terrorism, is forged. Ivan's exhortation has the desired effect—for him and for Dostoevsky ("*If even you say so* . . .") The point here is less Alyosha's or Ivan's characterization than reader participation and implication in retributive violence—or the shooting of "generals"—something that by 1879, when "Rebellion" was published, had become common terroristic practice.[13]

6

False Christs and Little Devils

Alexandrov, however, was certainly not exhorting his courtroom audience of Petersburg ladies and luminaries, to say nothing of representatives of the legal profession, to commit acts of terrorism; he was merely seeking acquittal for his client. Yet after the presiding judge Koni had restored order in the court, Alexandrov continued to speak from his client's point of view, to express her thoughts upon receiving reports of Bogoliubov's punishment: "The fateful question arose with all of its agitated insistence. Who will intervene for the offended honor of the helpless political prisoner [katorzhnik]? Who will wash away, who will redeem and how will the shame be redeemed that the unfortunate will remember about himself forever with inconsolable pain. . . . But who and how will the memory of the shame, of his insulted dignity, be smoothed out of his heart, who [will wash it away] and how will the stain be washed away?"[1]

Alexandrov's shift to religious metaphors, the ground for which was prepared by the passion of Bogoliubov, is nonetheless abrupt. Bogoliubov, the Christ, is himself in need of a self-sacrificial savior "to redeem" and "wash away the stain." In Alexandrov's rendering, the redeemer is also an avenger. The new Christ, in other words, Christ's own savior-to-be, must be both. But Alexandrov attributes these thoughts and words to Zasulich herself. "So thought, and not so much thought, but instinctively felt V. Zasulich. I am speaking her thoughts. I am speaking *almost* [italics mine] her words,"[2] insists Alexandrov, but if that is so, then Ivan Karamazov is also speaking *almost* her words (or Alexandrov's). Transmuting Bogoliubov's "inconsolable pain" and the "memory of the shame" into the tears of tormented children, Ivan demands this of Alyosha: "This is the question I can't solve. They [the tears] must be redeemed, otherwise there can be no harmony. But how, how will you redeem them? Is it possible? Can they be redeemed by being avenged? But what do I care if they are avenged, what do I care if the tormentors are in hell, what can hell set right here, if these ones have already been tormented?"[3]

Dostoevsky has taken up the offer implicit in Alexandrov's tropes to broach the question of abuse, suffering, and revenge in its metaphysical aspect. Ivan is the quintessential spokesperson for the atheist nihilist (terrorist) who, lacking belief in immortality, demands revenge "right here and now so I can see it myself, or I will destroy myself."[4] But Ivan is sufficiently insightful to recognize that revenge—whether here or in the afterlife—would impede the harmony that he craves: "I want to forgive, and I want to embrace, I don't want more suffering."[5] At the same time, Ivan stresses the role and responsibility of the eyewitness not to forgive under any circumstances. In her capacity as "mother" the mother may forgive for herself, for her "immeasurable maternal suffering," but as a witness and therefore the embodied principle of memory, without which there can be no justice on earth or in heaven, "she has no right to forgive the suffering of her child who was torn to pieces, she dare not forgive the tormentor, even if the child himself were to forgive him!"[6]

Alexandrov considers for a moment that the punishment of Bogoliubov, however seemingly outrageous, might be proven to be just (or at least legal) according to some principle of order of which Zasulich is unaware. "It could be that some experienced observer of order would prove that to proceed otherwise than was done with Bogoliubov is impossible, that otherwise order could not exist. Perhaps, not an observer of order, but just some practical person would say, in the full certainty of the reasonableness of his advice 'Give it up, Vera Ivanovich: after all it wasn't you who was torn up.'"[7]

Likewise, Ivan considers the possibility that there is some higher order that he fails to grasp: "Some joker will say, perhaps, that in any

False Christs and Little Devils

case the child will grow up and have time enough to sin, but there's this boy who didn't grow up but was torn apart by dogs at the age of eight. Oh, Alyosha, I'm not blaspheming! I do understand how the universe will tremble when all in heaven and under the earth merge in one voice of praise and all that lives and has lived cries out 'Just art thou, O Lord, for thy ways are revealed!' ... Then of course the crown of knowledge will have come and everything will be explained."[8] Even if this were to be the case, Ivan vows to "remain with my unrequited suffering and my unquenched indignation, even if I am wrong," which, in addition to suggesting that he loves suffering and indignation for their own sakes, also indicates that he (like Polonsky's persona) will not himself go beyond words to action. Zasulich, however, steadily comes to the realization that she herself must fulfill the role of savior, and this revelation bursts forth in Alexandrov's defense address almost as a poem, albeit not in verse, around two lines that Alexandrov quotes from the poet-revolutionary M. L. Mikhailov's poem. When Alexandrov's summation is given stanzaic form, the many affinities of his "prose poem" with Polonsky's "Female Prisoner" are unmistakable.

> [From Alexandrov's defense summation]
> And expectations remained expectations
> But heavy thoughts and spiritual disquiet were not soothed
> And once more and once more and again and again
> Arose the image of Bogoliubov and all his circumstances
> Not the sound of chains disturbed the soul
> But the melancholy arches of the dead house froze the imagination
> Scars—shameful scars—cut the heart
> And a sepulchral voice buried alive rang out:
> "Why do you keep silent about evil [zloba], brothers"
> "Why does love keep silent?"[9]

The obsession with the image of the unfortunate prisoner, the Gothic paraphernalia of melancholy arches, chains, and sepulchral voices, and the theme of inaction all strongly recall Polonsky's "Female Prisoner." Alexandrov's, however, was a defense summation, not a poem; only the last lines were taken from Mikhailov, who had been arrested in 1861 in conjunction with one of the first proclamations, "To the Young Generation."[10] While the lines that Alexandrov quotes speak of love, he wisely omits the battle cry at the end of Mikhailov's poem ("Brothers, let love move you into a friendly martial formation/Let evil lead you into an honest and open battle!") and instead inserts his own strategic metaphor:

> And suddenly a sudden thought, like lightning
> Flashed through Zasulich's mind: "Oh, I myself!
> Everything about Bogoliubov was silenced, hushed up
> A shout is needed; in my breast I will find the air for that shout
> I'll shout out and force it to be heard!"[11]

In notable contrast to Polonsky's poem, an agent is found to do something, or rather, consonant with the dichotomy of silence/speech that is the dominant trope, to say something. By poetic means, Alexandrov converts the damning deed into a redeeming word, transforms Zasulich's shot into a "shout." How can she be legally or morally condemned for a sho[u]t? "Love doesn't keep silent."

Alexandrov delineates a new form of political action, absolutely distinct from "revenge" as it is commonly conceived and also distinct from Mikhailov's tropes of traditional military formations and battle. If the word "revenge" was used by Zasulich herself in her testimony and subsequently in the indictment, Alexandrov explains, then only as a term "simpler, shorter, and somewhat suitable for designating the impulse guiding Zasulich."[12] Revenge is personal; it is accomplished obscurely, without publicity; it seeks to inflict the most harm possible upon its victim because it is motivated by malice. On none of these counts does Zasulich's act qualify as revenge (mest'). Rather, out of love, she sought to "resurrect [the question of the justice and legality of Bogoliubov's punishment] and pose it loudly and clearly."[13] To do this, "Zasulich decided to seek out a trial for her own crime, in order to raise and call forth a discussion about the forgotten case of Bogoliubov's punishment."[14]

In this new form of action, opposites unite to achieve an extreme paradox. The deed is indistinguishable from the word, a communicative act; the crime of (attempted) murder is transformed into a sacrifice of both the victim (in this case, Trepov) of the crime and the perpetrator (Zasulich), the latter being a self-sacrifice that "may prevent the repetition of the case, which called forth her act."[15] In other words, vengeance accompanied by self-sacrifice may act as social prophylaxis and bring about harmony, despite Ivan Karamazov's skepticism. Finally, all the feelings that motivated Zasulich condense at the very end of the summation into a hitherto unmentioned "idea": the idea that motivated Zasulich was "to stand up for the idea of the moral honor and dignity of the political criminal." Alexandrov now required a bridge between his emphasis on the emotional motivation for Zasulich's crime and the prosecution's demonstration of the carefully premeditated nature of the crime; he needed, in other words, to show how an idea is inseparable from the feelings that give rise to it, and how rational thought serves feelings. In arguing that Zasulich's meticulous planning was not at odds with, but served, her deeply emotional inspiration, Alexandrov offers this comparison: "in the same way the inspired thought of the poet remains inspired, not contrived, even though she may reflect upon the choice of words and rhyme for its realization." Zasulich, in other words, is a poet of the deed.

This new form of action requires an actor, a self-elected self to pronounce "I, myself" (Ia sama!) will be the Christ who *saves* Christ. This scenario of the most egregious egoism/self-sacrifice brings the paradox to its very pitch. When decades later Zasulich wrote her memoirs, she recalled the deep spiritual and imaginative impact of her first reading of the Gospels, and her subsequent fantasies of herself in the role of Christ's savior: "I didn't want His intercession, I wanted to serve him, to save Him" to save him from his death on the Cross at the behest of the traitorous crowd. "What bothered me most was that everyone, absolutely everyone had fled and abandoned Him, even the children who had greeted Him with palm branches and hosannas."[16]

Zasulich echoes the most compelling embodiment of state terror in world literature, Dostoevsky's Grand Inquisitor. In the chapter following Ivan's rebellion, with its exhortation to terrorism, Ivan recites to Alyosha his mystery play poema, set in Seville at the time of the Inquisition, in which Christ returns to earth at the height of the Inquisition. He is immediately recognized and "the children throw down flowers before him, sing and cry 'Hosana,'" but upon his arrest, the Grand Inquisitor grimly predicts that "at my first gesture they will rush to heap hot coals around your stake."[17] Yet according to the Grand Inquisitor, this is all in the service of doing Christ's true work and "correcting his deed."

Though cast as a medieval mystery play, Ivan's poema is in fact a long monologue that is a species of judicial rhetoric. While the criminal court tried—and acquitted—Zasulich (de facto condemning Trepov instead), and Ivan tried, convicted, and sentenced the General/God, the Grand Inquisitor "tries" Christ with the intention of convicting him and vindicating himself. Dostoevsky, of course, engineers it so that he does the opposite. The Grand Inquisitor's indictment reads as follows: Christ committed the ultimate injustice in his "wager on the strong"— those strong enough to freely choose spiritual bread over earthly bread and freely given faith in Christ over faith compelled by "mystery, miracle, and authority." In the Grand Inquisitor we recognize Peter Verkhovensky's "pope" or sacrificial king, but by *The Brothers Karamazov* he is no longer like Stavrogin, an empty figure. Dostoevsky has discovered the moral, religious, and emotional justification for terror(ism) and given it in the Grand Inquisitor's *apologia pro vita sua*, an apologia befitting a figure of such gravitas. If there is any connection between Zasulich and the Grand Inquisitor it is this: that she, or rather Alexandrov, justified her violence and violation of conscience with her compassion for Bogoliubov and indignation over the mockery of his human dignity. The Grand Inquisitor justifies his reign, founded on deceit and despotism, with his greater compassion for weak, contemptible mankind, whose freedom leads only to misery. "With us everyone will be happy, and they will no longer rebel or destroy each other, as in your freedom, everywhere," he tells Christ.[18]

Nonetheless, there is considerable distance between Zasulich, a young female "avenger" armed with a Bulldog, and the Grand Inquisitor, commanding armies of Jesuits. The same can be said of any insurgent or revolutionary terrorism versus hegemonic state terror. This distance is mediated by a third figure: Christ. In Hannah Arendt's highly suggestive reading, Christ and the Grand Inquisitor relate very differently to humankind: whereas Christ manifests the ultimate compassion, the Grand Inquisitor displays pity.[19] For Arendt, compassion is contagious, physiologically experienced, and "abolishes the in-between," whereas pity is purely cognitive and limits itself to language. Because compassion abolishes the "in-between," it has no use for politics as such, for "predicative and argumentative speech": it has use only for wordless communion, the gesture, or the act.[20] Compassion, Arendt observes, "rarely enters the world with the objective of changing it," but when it does it shuns politics and its processes of persuasion, negotiation, and compromise to "lend its voice to the suffering itself, which must claim for swift and direct action, that is for acts with the means of violence." Zasulich's "shout" that is in reality a *shot* is the perfect illustration of Arendt's point.[21]

Arendt does not turn her distinction between compassion and pity and her political-linguistic theory of compassion back onto the text that inspired it to speculate that this may be the link between Christ and the Grand Inquisitor, that Christs who enter the world with the objective of changing it "come to bring not peace, but the sword" and that Christ's wordless gesture of compassion—"kissing the old man on his bloodless lips"—acknowledges that False Christs begin as real ones. However, an anonymous poem that appeared in the first number of *Narodnaia volia*

(October 1, 1879), entitled "The Last Confession" (Posledniaia ispoved'), certainly did. The poem was written by an aspiring young writer with radical sympathies, Nikolai Minsky (1855-1937), who had only recently graduated with a law degree from St. Petersburg University and had undoubtedly read the latest installment of *The Brothers Karamazov*, featuring the chapter "The Grand Inquisitor."[22] The poem's setting—more minimally described than in Ivan's poema—is a dank prison cell in which a holy father enters to offer a prisoner condemned for political crimes the opportunity to repent of his sins before execution.

In Minsky's poem, the roles (and arguments) in Dostoevsky's Grand Inquisitor are reversed, and the old priest is deferentially silent while the condemned prisoner charges him with hypocrisy and offers his *apologia pro vita sua* in the form of a mock confession for his revolutionary predilections:

> Forgive me, Lord, that I loved
> the poor and the hungry like brothers.
> Forgive me, Lord, that I didn't consider
> eternal harmony an unrealizable fairytale.
> Forgive me Lord, that I served the good
> Not only with my mellifluous words
> But wholly: with my mind, heart and hands . . .
> That I confused the gluttonous feast of hypocrites
> for the mad cry of revenge,
> That I executed [kaznil] the killers for their murders.[23]

The condemned prisoner (Christ) of "The Last Confession" is a far truer expression of Ivan's professed beliefs (rather than his unconscious faith), and in this respect the young poet Minsky could be said to be "correcting Dostoevsky's word." But the most overt act of "literary theft"[24] comes at the end of Minsky's poem, when the priest, thoroughly shaken by the prisoner's powerful sermon, acknowledges his defeat and prepares to leave. Moved to compassion by the evidence of the old man's compassion for him ("In your eyes I glimpsed tears/and your voiced breathed concern for me//in prison yours is the first/face without malice"),[25] the prisoner expresses his gratitude and forgiveness with a gesture—in this case a bow.

> As a priest—you are an enemy to me, but as a human being
> It may be,
> That you are a friend to me . . . Accept with gratitude

My bow and warm thanks!
(He bows to the priest, and the executioner binds his hands).[26]

There can be very little doubt about whom and what the Grand Inquisitor represents, since Dostoevsky spelled this out for his editors who, he believed, were eminently capable of misunderstanding. "A contemporary negator [otritsatel']," he hastened to clarify, "our Russian Socialists (and they are not all just underground nihilist scum—you know that) are conscious Jesuits and liars who do not admit that their idol is violence to man's conscience and the leveling of mankind to a herd of cattle."[27] Dostoevsky's caution was born of long experience, as well as of his own awareness that "until the conclusion of the novel it is really possible to misapprehend these ideas and positions";[28] in other words, *ambiguity and ambivalence were conscious compositional principles of the novel*. In this regard, it is necessary to note that another, more immediately dangerous "misinterpretation" was certainly possible. In Dostoevsky's novel, the Grand Inquisitor is safely located in Western Europe's Roman Catholic past, and readers like Arendt have also identified him with revolutionary state terror, either Jacobin or Soviet. But one needn't look so far for embodiments of hegemonic state terror.[29] Following the explosion at the Winter Palace on February 5, 1880, Alexander II convened an emergency meeting of his advisers, at which the tsarevich (the future Alexander III) "proposed an impossible supreme investigative commission with dictatorial powers over the whole of Russia."[30] The plan, as the historian Peter Zaionchkovsky has deduced, originated not with the tsarevich, but with Dostoevsky's own editor, Mikhail Katkov (and was transmitted through Pobedonostsev), who had published an editorial on February 7, 1880, declaring "the fight against organized sedition . . . must be waged by a single strong arm. It is essential that one government agency, possessing the full confidence of the tsar, should exercise dictatorial power in the struggle against evil. On it should rest all responsibility and it should be granted all available weapons to carry on the fight. . . . The agency must enjoy complete freedom of action in political affairs. It should direct and coordinate the Governors-General; no procedural formality should hinder the use of its power."[31] It is the irony of history and of counterterrorism that Katkov, Peter Verkhovensky, and the Grand Inquisitor all shared essentially the same vision of sovereign power. Although the tsar initially rejected the proposal for the creation

False Christs and Little Devils

of a "single . . . dictatorial power in the struggle against evil," on February 9 he announced the formation of a Supreme Administrative Commission headed by Count Loris-Melikov, an illustrious commander of the Caucasus theater and the uniquely effective Governor of Kharkov Province, who would be empowered "to control and direct investigations of political cases." Unlike Katkov, Loris-Melikov favored rapprochement between oppositional elements and the government, and he attempted to enlist the cooperation of society in general so that his tenure as supreme commissioner earned the moniker "Dictatorship of the Heart." While Dostoevsky had written "The Grand Inquisitor" in June 1879—that is, more than half a year earlier—he would have been gratified, as always, by the predictive powers of his literary fiction. Such "fantastic people" as supreme commissioners (i.e., grand inquisitors) with hearts did, in fact, exist.

Society, Dostoevsky insisted, could not survive without compassion/pity, and he claimed for the Russian nation a special capacity for it. In *The Brothers Karamazov*, Dostoevsky leaves us our pity for the "wee ones" and devotes a substantial part of the novel to children, despite the fact that they are one and all "little devils," members of the youngest generation to be infected by nihilist ideas. Dostoevsky had learned to avoid the implausible "excess" of Raskolnikov in his characterizations and divided Raskolnikov's contradictory qualities between two of the boys, Ilyusha Snegirov and Kolya Krasotkin. The "noble" and "morbidly sensitive" Ilyusha, who viciously attacks (throwing stones and biting) Alyosha as an acceptable surrogate for his brother, Dmitry, is the most direct reflection of Zasulich in the novel.[32] Ilyusha's father, Captain Snegirov, acts the improbable part of the boy's attorney when he relates to Alyosha (who he believes has come to demand Ilyusha's punishment) the circumstances that prompted the attack: "Well, and so, sir your good brother, Dmitry Fyodorovich, dragged me by my beard that day, he dragged me out of the tavern to the square, and just then the schoolboys were getting out of school, and Ilyusha with them. When he saw me in such a state sir, he rushed up to me: 'Papa,' he cried, 'papa!' He caught hold of me, hugged me, tried to pull me away, crying to the offender: 'Let go, let go, it's my papa, my papa, forgive him'—that was what he cried: 'Forgive him!' And he took hold of him, too with his little hands, and kissed his hand, that very hand, sir."[33] Here it is not a question of physical abuse, but of humiliation and mockery that cannot be "redeemed"—the Captain cannot possibly accept Dmitry's challenge to a duel—that sets Ilya against his peers, the Karamazovs, and the whole world. The truth that there is no justice for the poor and powerless "crushes" Ilyusha and inflames the child's own fantasies of revenge against Dmitry on behalf of his father, even if it must be revenge delayed. "I'll grow up, I'll challenge him myself, and I'll kill him."[34] When his papa dutifully explains that it "is sinful to kill," Ilyusha cleverly revises his scenario. "'Papa,' he said, 'papa, I'll throw him down when I'm big, I'll knock the sword out of his hand with my sword, I'll rush at him, throw him down, hold my sword over him and say: I could kill you now, but I forgive you, so there!'"[35] Ilyusha imaginatively choreographs an act in which the violence is completely symbolic (a mock execution) and in which forgiveness, too, is a form of revenge.

The precocious Kolya Krasotkin is Ilyusha's other half, the half with a will to power and domination, but who has surpassed his predecessors and their fetishes (he refers derisively to Raskolnikov's idol, Napoleon, as a "pseudo great man"). Unlike Ilyusha and Zasulich, Kolya is outwardly "insensitive" and evinces a cultivated coldness and disdain of "sentimental slop" (vrag vsiakikh teliach'ikh nezhnostei).[36] Despite his denigration of "feelings," Kolya, at the tender age of almost fourteen, is a virtuosic manipulator and agitator who takes pride in "stirring up fools in all strata of society."[37] Although Kolya regurgitates barely digested radical ideas in the words of others, he is more action-oriented and battle-ready than the previous generation and has steeled himself with death-defying feats: "I've become notorious with everybody; they say I'm a 'desperado' [otchaiannyi]."[38] Not only has he mastered the art of mixing explosive powder to fire his toy cannon "to amuse the kids," but he knows how to stage a spectacle for the maximum effect (oblivious to its "killing" impact on its audience), when he performs the "miracle" of resurrecting the dog that Ilyusha believed he had killed, Zhuchka/Perezvon.[39] Kolya, like Raskolnikov, is self-conscious enough to see through his own motives ("it was vanity that kept me from coming, egoistic vanity, and base despotism"),[40] and his drive to dominate is firmly welded to a rebellious outrage against unjust powers-that-be. When the haughty Moscow doctor prescribes a cure for Ilyusha, oblivious to the family's poverty, Kolya, sensing his opponent's vulnerabilities, launches an attack with impeccable aim. "'Don't worry, leech, my dog won't bite you,' Kolya cut in abruptly, having noticed the doctor's somewhat anxious look at Perezvon, who was standing in the doorway.

False Christs and Little Devils

An angry note rang in Kolya's voice. And he used the word 'leech' on purpose, as he declared it afterwards, and 'meant it as an insult.'"⁴¹ The confrontation intensifies as Kolya persists in his barrage of insults, until the doctor furiously demands his punishment: "'Whip-ped, he ought to be whip-ped!' the doctor, who for some reason was utterly infuriated, began stamping his feet." To which Kolya responds with an outright threat: "'On the other hand, leech, my Perezvon may just bite!' Kolya said in a trembling voice, turning pale, his eyes flashing. 'Ici, Perezvon!'"⁴²

The scene ingeniously reprises and distills Bogoliubov's ("Whip-ped, he ought to be whip-ped!" for not doffing his hat) and the serf boy's punishments. This time, though, the tables are turned, and Kolya, armed with the resurrected Perezvon, is ready to "sic" (shoot), were it not for Alyosha's desperate and extremely uncharacteristic intervention, which amounts to a threat of "ex-communication": "Kolya, if you say another word, I'll break with you forever!"⁴³ Is this, in the end, Dostoevsky's solution?

7

"That Is the Whole Answer"

Perhaps the riskiest move of Dostoevsky's literary career, and the one he "trembled" most over, was the use of the conventions of faith-based hagiography for the purposes of refuting the powerfully rendered "nihilist" arguments of "Rebellion" and "The Grand Inquisitor" in Book V and pronouncing his own "new word." Dostoevsky's anxiety about the form, themes, "realism," and ultimate success of his refutation pervades his correspondence at the time. If the critical consensus is correct, then Dostoevsky, the inveterate gambler, lost the riskiest artistic gamble of his literary career, in Part VI "The Russian Monk."

The reasons for this failure are multiple, and first among them is certainly the fact that Dostoevsky does not attempt a direct refutation of Ivan's arguments or a conversion from his view: the persuasiveness of Zosima's answer depends to a large extent on a preexisting faith. Instead, Ivan's horrifying "little pictures" as well as the Grand Inquisitor's monumental canvas of a depraved and weak humanity are countered only by the very personal epiphany of Zosima's dying brother, Markel, who attests that "life is paradise, and we are all in paradise, but we do not want to know it, and if we did want to know it, tomorrow there would be paradise the world over."[1]

This vision of "life as paradise" does not entail the dawning of a new and universal Golden Age, but may only be realized and transmitted from one individual to another by the example of word and deed. Dostoevsky's most striking departure in Book VI from the traditional Orthodox saint's life (zhitie) is its lack of focus on the single saint and his holy works. Nowhere, in fact, does Dostoevsky realize his intention to portray "a pure ideal Christian . . . as a tangible and real possibility appearing before our own eyes";[2] no such image of Zosima materializes in Book VI.[3] Instead of the traditional saint's life, or even the prosaic life of a saint (such as Victor Hugo's portrayal of Bishop Myriel in *Les Misérables*), Dostoevsky gives us a series of imitative acts performed by different, decidedly unsaintly, individuals.[4] First it is Markel, who relates to his bewildered mother his epiphany "that each of us is guilty in everything before everyone, and I more than everyone."[5] Later, after the passage of many rowdy and dissipated years, Markel's teachings reverberate in his brother, the officer Zinovyi (the young Zosima), who throws down his weapon in the middle of a duel that he had provoked and declares to his opponent "for it is my own fault that I offended you and have now made you shoot at me. I am ten times worse than you, if not more."[6] Finally, the stern and righteous "mysterious stranger," Mikhail, is captivated by talk of Zinovyi's deed and himself impelled to commit a similarly daring act of public confession for a long-ago crime.

The prototype for these acts can be traced to *Crime and Punishment*, where Sonya demands that Raskolnikov bow down to the earth in the middle of Haymarket square to confess his guilt before God, Man, and all the earth—or even further, to Dostoevsky's deranged clerk who confesses before his highness to "being Garibaldi." It is also developed in the suppressed chapter containing Stavrogin's written confession in *Demons* and the monk Tikhon's request that Stavrogin forgive him "for my sins both voluntary and involuntary." Yet the act evolves so that the emphasis falls on its aesthetic form and public rather than private and interpersonal nature.[7] These are deeds performed before an involuntary audience in public places (in the square, at the dueling ground, at large social gatherings) and addressed to the community as a whole. The initial reception of the act is unfailingly negative—uncomprehending or mocking—and its repercussions are unpredictable and sometimes devastating. In *The Brothers Karamazov*, the first such act occurs at the beginning of the novel in the elder's cell, before the assembled Karamazov family and assorted witnesses. "The elder stepped towards Dmitry Fyodorovich and, having come close to him, knelt before him. Alyosha thought for a moment that he had fallen from weakness, but it wasn't that. Kneeling in front of Dmitry Fyodorovich, the elder bowed down at his feet with a full, distinct, conscious bow, and even touched the floor with his forehead. Alyosha was so amazed that he failed to support him as he got to his feet. A weak smile barely glimmered on his lips 'Forgive me! Forgive me, all of you!' he said, bowing on all sides to his guests."[8]

At first, even Alyosha mistakes the elder's act as unintentional, an accident, but then realizes "it wasn't that [eto bylo ne to]." Courtesy of Fyodor Karamazov's correct surmise ("What's that—bowing at his feet? Is it some sort of emblem?"),[9] I will refer to this "something else" as an emblematic act. The emblematic act gives aesthetic form and, in so doing, crystallizes meaning in a ritualized gesture. It unifies word and image and sets them in motion while seemingly arresting time. The public performance and ritualized form differentiate it from a spontaneous interpersonal gesture, such as Christ's kiss of the Grand Inquisitor, which has no other addressee and changes nothing ("the kiss burned in his heart, but he clung to his former views").[10] In the affect and effect it produces, the emblematic act is similar to another type of disruptive action—scandal—in which community and consensus collapse under the strain of violated norms. But unlike scandal in which many participate, the emblematic act is performed by a lone actor, and its form or image (*obraz*) distinguishes it from the ugly formlessness (*bezobrazie*) of scandal. It is precisely by means of the emblematic act that the elder halts the unfolding scandal in his cell. "But the whole scene, which had turned so ugly, was stopped in a most unexpected manner. The elder suddenly rose from his place."[11]

The emblematic act stands at the intersection of the two critical approaches to Dostoevsky—the Bakhtinian, which takes the word and dialogue as the cornerstone of Dostoevsky's art, and Robert Louis Jackson's emphasis on image and aesthetic form. Dostoevsky valued the gesture precisely for its ability to convey an idea through its very form and believed that an idea might be spoiled by taking not only the *wrong* but the *opposite* form.[12] The emblematic act is proof against such slip-ups, and its existence betrays a strong undertow in Dostoevsky's poetics and ethos. As Gary Saul Morson has argued in his sonorous essay "The God of Onions," in *The Brothers Karamazov* Dostoevsky finally arrives at a mode of action that poses an alternative to the heroic exploits that Dostoevsky always planned for his characters but never realized. Morson explains that this anti-poetic or "prosaic" mode of action consists of small acts of kindness and compassion, such as giving an onion to a beggar or propping a pillow under a sleeping head. Such actions constitute Dostoevsky's response to "the thirst for the immediate exploit," which "links Alyosha first of all to terrorists, who are also prepared to sacrifice life to make a sudden change. . . . Exploits are performed in folktales, in epics, and in saints' lives, but the term cannot be used without irony in a realistic novel, where it necessarily comes under the shadow of the quixotic." [13] Without question, the emblematic act has affinities with the quixotic or with holy foolishness, but it differs from both in that it is a "break-out" or anomalous act (not a pattern of behavior) that is both uncharacteristic for the actor and unassociated with a culturally inscribed identity. Suddenly, a seemingly ordinary individual breaks out to perform an extraordinary act, an act that disrupts the flow of events and subverts social, moral, and judicial norms. The act is communicative, but as communication it is completely unidirectional (monologic rather than dialogic), and although it is ostensibly addressed to an imminent community, its ultimate addressee is transcendent.

The emblematic act is structurally parallel to the immediate exploit of revolutionary terrorism modeled on tyrannicide that Raskolnikov had rejected on (anti)aesthetic grounds. In Dostoevsky's schema, the purpose of its poetry (unexpectedness, form, symbolism) is precisely to disrupt the social and symbolic order without deploying physical violence—in other words, to end the cycle of violence by directing the purely symbolic violence toward oneself, effectively crowning oneself scapegoat or "sacrificial king." The core of Zosima's prescription for nonviolence is the rerouting of the symbolic violence of judgment and punishment. "Remember especially that you cannot be the judge of anyone. For there can be no judge of a criminal on earth until the judge knows that he, too, is a criminal, exactly the same as the one who stands before him, and that he is perhaps most guilty of all for the crime of the one standing before me now. If you are able to take upon yourself the crime of the criminal who stands before you and whom you are judging in your heart, do so at once, and suffer for him yourself, and let him go without reproach."[14]

Zosima's contradictory formula "we are all guilty but I most of all" with its distinction of "most guilty" retains a residue of the elitism—albeit inverted—of Raskolnikov's extraordinary man. Zosima's ethos of mutual responsibility, in which we are all responsible for one another, is a prosaic ethos that is most clearly realized in the reciprocal and symmetrical interaction between Grushenka and Alyosha, when by acknowledging their responsibility for one another, they "save" each other. The ethos that is preached and modeled in Book VI as Dostoevsky's answer to Ivan and the Grand Inquisitor is semantically and structurally different. It does not belong to the mythic prosaic, but partakes of a mythic poetic that is common to it and revolutionary terrorism.

8

The Khokhlakov Principle

Russian Society in the Mirror of Revolutionary Terrorism

Dostoevsky's evocation of this mutual responsibility is most successful in the novel-as-allegory: the brothers' collective guilt for their father's murder as Russian society's collective guilt for (attempted) tsaricide.[1] In this regard, each of the brothers clearly stands for an estate or social group: Dmitry, for the feckless gentry outraged at being cheated of their inheritance; Alyosha, for the clergy who failed as the nation's spiritual guides in time of crisis; Ivan, for the Westernized intelligentsia, the primary agent of moral and intellectual corruption; and Smerdyakov, for the resentful dispossessed. The path to redemption, to the salvation of the individual and the community, lies in the assumption of one's own responsibility for collective guilt. Smerdyakov, the despised illegitimate brother, is the only one who refuses to assume his considerable share of the guilt: he is the brother who actually killed Fyodor Karamazov. Instead, in accusing Ivan of wanting to shift all the blame onto him, he shifts all the blame onto Ivan, contending "You killed him, you are the main killer and I was just your minion, your faithful servant Licharda, and I performed the deed according to your word."[2] Rather than acknowledge even his own guilt, much less his guilt for others,

Smerdyakov opts out and takes his final revenge against the Karamazov family by committing, like Stavrogin, a perfectly opaque suicide that defies any attempt to make it signify.

Each of the groups represented by the brothers bore some measure of direct responsibility, but Dostoevsky was also acutely aware of the complicity that followed from merely being a spectator or bystander, like the loyal subjects who stood breathlessly by during the February 19, 1880 jubilee, wondering if and when the tsar would be blown to pieces. Educated society (obshchestvo) was largely passive, ambivalent, and fickle, and both the regime and the revolutionaries vied for its support. After the assassination of Chief of Police Mezenstsev in August 1878 and again in February 1880, when Loris-Melikov assumed the role of supreme commissioner, the government took the unusual step of actively appealing for the support of *obshchestvo* in the struggle against sedition. Although these appeals generated an outpouring of letters and projects to combat "the criminal gang of nihilists," society would remain noncommittal until its longstanding demands for active participation in government, an easing of censorship, and the inviolability of the individual were met.[3]

In *The Brothers Karamazov*, Dostoevsky lavishes satiric attention on obshchestvo in the person of Madame Khokhlakov. The vain, frivolous, and muddle-headed Khokhlakov is the mirror that Dostoevsky holds up to Russian society so that it can clearly see its own role and responsibility in the crisis. Khokhlakov represents both provincial obshchestvo and Russian obshchestvo's provinciality; nonetheless, in the chapter "An Ailing Little Foot," the government (in the person of the dapper official Perkhotin) and the radicals (in the person of the nihilist journalist Rakitin) vie for her "forty-year-old charms." Early in the novel she is introduced as "A Lady of Little Faith" whose superstitious religiosity has survived the corrosive effects of fashionable atheism, but her most characteristic and fatal shortcoming is her attention deficit and her tendency to forget or neglect "the main thing." "The main thing is not to forget the main thing,"[4] she reminds herself repeatedly, but thanks to her solipsism and the ideological muddle that is her mind, she inevitably does. The tragedy of the novel results directly from her fatal misunderstanding of Dmitry, when he turns to her as his last hope before "killing and robbing someone for the three thousand."[5] Madame Khokhlakov's salvific plot for Dmitry shows her to be a Grand Inquisitress in her own right ("I will save you, Dmitry Fyodorovich, but you must do as I say!").[6] Dmitry's frustration understandably grows as Khokhlakov, in raptures over her own beneficence, rather than giving him the three thousand categorically declares (this time in a parody of Christ):[7] "But to you, to you especially I would not give anything, out of love for you I would not give anything, in order to save you I would not give anything, because you need only one thing: mines, mines, mines . . . !"[8]

Madame Khokhlakov's plan for Mitya's salvation "out of love" was of course the same as the government's plan for revolutionaries' perdition. In nineteenth century Russia, the mines were less likely to figure in a "get-rich-quick" scheme than as the destination of hapless convicts and political prisoners. Mitya's real-life prototype, the convict Il'insky, whom Dostoevsky had profiled in the *House of the Dead*, was initially sentenced to the mines as a wrongfully convicted parricide, and being sent to the mines (should he kill and rob the three thousand) is exactly the fate Dmitry is seeking to avoid.[9] It is little wonder that he erupts with rage and indignation, terrifying his would-be benefactress, who later avows that he intended to murder her along with the others. The trajectory of Russian society's attitude to the nihilists since 1865 and *Crime and Punishment* becomes clear when we compare Madame Khokhlakov's insistence on "mines, mines, mines!" to the advice Raskolnikov receives from the enlightened police investigator Porfiry Petrovich: "All you need is air now—air, air!"[10]

Whereas in the mid-1860s society and the censorship were willing to tolerate the limited airing of nihilist ideas, by the late 1870s the only "salvation" lay in driving them and their adherents underground, whether that meant the revolutionary underground or penal servitude in the mines. Madame Khokhlakov's exaggerated perception of her own personal jeopardy is the issue here. "How often, how often have I looked at that terrible man and thought: here is a man who will end up by murdering me. And now it's happened. . . . That is, if he hasn't killed me now but only his father, it is most likely because the hand of God is obviously protecting me."[11]

Especially when the tsar's life was "miraculously" spared in one of the People's Will's failed attempts, the official government and Church line was that the "hand of God was protecting" the divinely anointed one.[12] But whose hand would protect society? As the historian Yuliia Safronova has recently demonstrated, although the People's Will did not target civilians, its adoption of dynamite as its weapon of choice and the casualties resulting from the explosion at the Winter Palace had created a sense of widespread jeopardy. Wild rumors and mystical predictions concerning an impending catastrophe on par with St. Bartholomew's Eve circulated in anticipation of the twenty-fifth anniversary of Alexander II's ascension on February 19, 1880.[13] The anniversary was celebrated without incident, but the public remained anxiously aware that the terrorists did not eschew collateral damage.

And finally, Dostoevsky uses Madame Khokhlakov to once and for all lay to rest his perennial bugbear: the question of crime and the fashionable theory of "temporary insanity." In Khokhlakov's rendering as a "fit of passion" (affekt) the theory is pushed to the height of absurdity. "So, look: a man sits there and he's not crazy at all, only suddenly he has a fit of passion [affekt]. He may be fully conscious and know what he's doing, but at the same time he's in a fit of passion [v affekte]."[14] According to Khokhlakov, who had just received a visit from the cosmopolitan Moscow doctor, it was in just such a fit of passion that Dmitry committed murder. In response to Alyosha's objection that Dmitry *did not* kill their father, Madame Khokhlakov explains to her stunned interlocutor that of course it was the devoted servant Grigory who killed Fyodor Karamazov. "After Dmitry Fyodorovich hit him [Grigorii] on the head, he came to, had a fit of passion and went and killed him. And if he says he didn't kill him, then maybe he just doesn't remember."[15]

Should there remain any question about the theory of temporary insanity, the etiology of [political] crime, and the relationship of an idea to disease, Khokhlakov clarifies it by finally remembering the "main thing," her daughter Lise. Lise, whom her mother claims is "v affekte," is the most extreme and disturbing manifestation of the ability of "ideas floating in the air" to engender pathology. What in Raskolnikov's case was new and unresolved is in Lise's case old and vulgarized. Lise wants to destroy ("Ah, I want disorder. I keep wanting to set fire to the house"),[16] and she wants to suffer and to inflict suffering ("I want someone to torment me, to marry me and then torment me").[17] All the scenarios of nihilist (self-)destruction unite in this "little demon" (besënok), but as with Kolya's precocity, Lise's grants her profound insight into our relationship to violence and terror(ism). When Alyosha reflects that "there are moments when people love crime," Lise effusively concurs "Yes, yes! You've spoken my own thought, they love it, they all love it, and love it always, not just at 'moments.' You know, it's as if at some point they all agreed to lie about it, and have been lying about it ever since."[18]

In *Demons*, as in *Crime and Punishment*, Dostoevsky makes certain concessions to an aesthetic apprehension of the act of violence. In *The Brothers Karamazov*, however, when Lise asserts that "they all love it that he [Dmitry] killed his father," it is an unequivocal reproach directed at Russian society for its *delectation* of violence. Lise's horrifying fantasy

The Khokhlakov Principle

of the crucified boy takes the nihilist destruction of aesthetics—the contention that aesthetic appreciation is completely subjective and a matter of taste—to its logical conclusion. "Sometimes I imagine that it was I who crucified him. He hangs there moaning, and I sit down facing him, eating pineapple compote. I like pineapple compote very much. Do you?"[19]

It is therefore surprising that the buffet to which the courtroom adjourned after the lawyers' summations at Dmitry's trial was not serving pineapple compote. The courtroom audience relishes the spectacle of the trial, the humiliation and scandal of witness testimony, the theatrical performances of the prosecuting and defense attorneys, and most of all the violation of the taboo of parricide that stands for tsaricide. The prosecutor, Ippolit Kirillovich, uses psychological and emotional arguments to skewer Dmitry, whereas the defense attorney, Fetyukovich, brilliantly demolishes both witness testimony and circumstantial evidence to arrive by rational means at the truth of the crime, but without faith in that truth. Where Fetyukovich goes catastrophically wrong, however, and insures his client's doom is in his political theory, which is an allegorically veiled updating of tyrannicide theory. If the father cannot give proof that he is deserving of a son's love, argues Fetyukovich, then his "rule" is illegitimate: "the family is finished then and there: he is not a father to his son, and the son is free and has the right henceforth to look upon his father as a stranger and even as his enemy."[20] In other words, a bad father, like a bad ruler, is a *hostis humani generis* who by natural right may be killed with impunity. Fetyukovich combines natural right with the fashionable theory of "a fit of passion" to argue that in Dmitry's case, it was in fact a *"natural* [italics mine] *fit of passion . . . avenging its eternal laws unrestrainably and unconsciously, like all things in nature."*[21]

Unfortunately for Dmitry and Fetyukovich, Dostoevsky's jury is as atavistic and unyielding as a totem. It is impervious to and unconcerned with empathetic narrative, with "beyond reasonable doubt" and with liberal political theory. In other words, it is unmoved by words, and its only function is to staunchly uphold patriarchy and reassert the taboo of parricide. The jury's verdict is as categorical and devastating as a bomb, and as such, it "reverses" the verdict of the Zasulich trial and finishes Dmitry off.

9

Again, Like Before (Again)

Quite possibly the two most important speeches of Dostoevsky's career were delivered in 1880: Alyosha's momentous "speech at the stone," which concludes *The Brothers Karamazov*, and Dostoevsky's own remarkable speech at the Pushkin Days on June 8, 1880. Unsurprisingly, much has been written about both, since Dostoevsky's often vague and seemingly contradictory pronouncements have necessarily given rise to conflicting interpretations. These speeches, however, are less important for what they say than for what they do.

As many commentators have noted, Dostoevsky's Pushkin speech was inseparable from the reaction to it; in fact, it seemed to be not at all the same speech when removed from the rarefied atmosphere of its delivery. Dostoevsky's description of his own performance in his letter to his wife, Anna, bears faint yet distinct echoes of Stepan Trofimovich's self-aggrandizement, but Dostoevsky's "complete, absolutely complete victory" (as he put it) was undeniable. "The hall was packed. No Ania, no you will never be able to imagine and envision the effect it produced. What are my Petersburg successes! Nothing, zero compared to this! When I went to read the hall began to thunder with applause, which kept me from starting for a long, a very long time. I took a bow, made gestures asking that they let me read—nothing helped: rapture, enthusiasm (all because of Karamazov)."[1]

As of June 1880, the novel was suspended just prior to Dmitry's dramatic trial for the murder of his father, the trial that, according to Dostoevsky scholars, was based on Dostoevsky's experience at Zasulich's trial. At this point, the Elder Zosima had left his mystical utopian prescriptions as his legacy, and it was in the context of Zosima's homilies—and the charismatic vacancy left by his death—that Dostoevsky's words had their effect.

In Dostoevsky's account, his speech, in an atmosphere of intense, unbounded emotion, achieved instantaneous social transformation: "When I proclaimed about *universal unity* at the end the hall was in hysterics, and when I finished, I can't describe the roar, the wail of rapture. People, strangers to each other in the audience, cried, wept, hugged one another, and *vowed to each other to be better, not to hate but to love one another from now on.*"[2] As Dostoevsky describes it, the scene recalls that of two years previously, when the St. Petersburg Municipal Court erupted upon hearing the verdict in the Zasulich case. What stands out is not only public expressions of excessive emotion, but the fact that only in the crucible of such feverish emotion is the desired transformation possible. The violent effect of the emotions is captured most evocatively in the reporter Vasilevsky's account, which recalls nothing so much as G__v's description of the chaos and hysteria at the end of Yulia von Lembke's fête, in that it "exceeded all usual limits. It was a fever, an intoxication, an explosion. . . . The exalted gathering did not have the means to express its ecstasy, and people simply flung themselves over the hall. [Dostoevsky's] fanatical, bottomless faith in the truth, beauty, and grandeur of his ideals reigned supreme. . . . Its gleam and glitter burned and blinded."[3] Together, the reception of the Pushkin speech and Dostoevsky's patent jubilation make clear that the "new word" Dostoevsky had been seeking was the word that transcended words. (Aksakov, who spoke next, declared, "I consider Fyodor Mikhailovich's speech an event in our literature," while Vasilevsky averred, "Human words cannot aspire to greater effect.")[4]

Written only a few months after Dostoevsky's Pushkin speech to conclude his last novel, Alyosha's speech at the stone reprises Dostoevsky's coup de grâce on a smaller, less hysterical scale. Alyosha is breathlessly awaited by his twelve preteen apostles, and his speech ends with the youngest brother of a convict (Dmitry), a madman (Ivan), and a murderer (Smerdyakov) celebrated amidst mutual embraces and cries of "Hurrah for Karamazov!" Whoever expected that Karamazov, forming a near rhyme with that name of infamy, Karakozov, would be hurrahed? In Alyosha's speech and by the very fact of the speech, the two tendencies that have contended for Dostoevsky's soul have one final showdown. For the duration of the novel, Alyosha, whom Dostoevsky characterizes in his author's mock apologetic preface as an "indistinct actor" (deiatel'), has spoken little and acted with circumspection; he has been the embodiment of Zosima's prescription of active, nonjudgmental love. Robert Louis Jackson has contrasted the quiet authenticity of Alyosha's speech with the theatricality of Ivan's exhortation in "Rebellion," and although the speeches are without doubt delivered in different keys, the fact that Alyosha gives a speech at all (when, as we recall, he barely spoke at all during Ivan's harangue) is a striking departure for him.[5] Not only is the speech radically different than anything Alyosha has ever done, but it is quite different from what he has only just recently said.

For our purposes, though, it is most important to note that Alyosha's speech has been read as the key passage foreshadowing the path of the children in Dostoevsky's projected sequel. These children, with Kolya Krasotkin at their head, were clearly destined to become revolutionary terrorists, and as proof of their future terrorist vocation, the eminent Dostoevsky scholar James Rice pointed to the "following rhetorical series [from Alyosha's speech] ominously evoking their collective destiny": "Even if we were to fall into great misfortune.... Maybe we shall even become evil later on, and won't even be strong enough to avoid a wicked deed.... But in any case no matter how evil we may be, which God forbid.... The most cruel and cynical among us, if that is what we become, still won't dare laugh at how kind and good he was at this present moment... maybe just this memory alone will keep him from great evil.... I say this in case we become wicked people (continued Alyosha). But why should we become wicked, right, gentlemen?"[6]

Why indeed? The absolute strangeness of this passage must not be overlooked. Why, in parting from the boys for many years, would Alyosha suggest repeatedly that they may become "wicked"—unless he recalls how ruthlessly they tormented Ilyusha? That aside, what "wicked" means is decipherable from the context and from the fact that the impetus for his speech is a wrenching memory of "Ilyushechka, crying and embracing his father, exclaiming, 'Papa, papa, how he humiliated you!' Something shook, as it were, in his [Alyosha's] soul." Alyosha has something very specific in mind that Rice's ellipses have surgically excised. The restored passage reads: "Perhaps we will even become wicked later on, will even be unable to resist a bad action, *will laugh at people's tears and at those who say, as Kolya exclaimed today: 'I want to suffer for all people'* —*perhaps we will scoff wickedly at such people."*⁷

These words transport us immediately to Ivan's rebellion, to the tears of children, and to Alyosha's feeble murmur "I want to suffer, too"—and remind us that Ivan's rebellion is and remains also Alyosha's. Rice, in other words, was not wrong in seeing this passage as perhaps foreshadowing future involvement in revolutionary terrorism for the boys and even for Alyosha, but not because they would "become wicked people."⁸ They would become wicked *only* if they laughed at those who want to suffer for all people, for the "suffocated, humiliated, cursed, oppressed individual." Even as recently as the beginning of the chapter, Alyosha seemed steadfastly to hold the line against such poetic self-sacrifice by reacting with dismay to Kolya's misguided envy of Dmitry and his wish to emulate him ("Oh, if only I, too could some day offer myself as a sacrifice for truth!" exclaims Kolya).⁹ In the Speech at the Stone, Alyosha changes his tune and repeatedly insists that to laugh at such people would be evil, for to laugh at such people would be to laugh, by association, at Ilyusha and the feelings that his suffering and death inspired in them, feelings that made them also "good."

In fact, the sentimental memory that Alyosha contrives does not remotely resemble the real, raw, and powerful memory that caused something to shake in his own soul; it sanitizes the angry and agonized boy ("a small creature, but great wrath") whose actions and motivations were considerably more complex and morally questionable than "to suffer for all people." Alyosha, in fact, takes control of the meaning of Ilyusha's death in the same way that Peter Verkhovensky takes control of the meaning of the violence and mayhem in *Demons* (or wants to take control of his "idol," Stavrogin) but to opposite ends. In Jackson's words, "what Alyosha seeks is for the boys, figuratively speaking, to create an icon out of the deceased Ilyusha, that is, a fully formed ethical and spiritual memory associated with Ilyusha" in order to encourage and unite, rather than demoralize and destroy.¹⁰ Whereas in *Crime and Punishment* and *Demons* the reader is prompted to resist the highly selective "truths" offered in the novels' epilogues, in *The Brothers Karamazov* Alyosha's "icon" of Ilyusha requires forgetting the novel that Dostoevsky wrote. Dostoevsky asks us to forget that Ilyusha was "crushed once and for all" not only by the injustice of the world, but by his own, ultimately false assumption of guilt *for all*. It is Ilyusha who quite literally "suffers for all people"—for his father, for Dmitry, for his schoolmates, for Smerdyakov—and his death devastates his family. In short, the reader is confronted with a choice that is not a choice: to accept the hymn and the icon, and the sacrificial mechanism that comes with it, or to reject a harmony that cannot be justified by the facts. It has been the business of the novel to make the consequences of the latter choice abundantly clear. As Ivan recognizes, "One cannot live by rebellion."[11]

The crowd's ecstasy in the wake of Dostoevsky's Pushkin speech was fueled by the conviction that "He has the solution!" not simply to the immediate question—Pushkin's place in Russian literature—but to Russia's internal division and its role in the world. In fact, Dostoevsky's solutions are driven by the same ideals as those of the revolutionary terrorists and deploy the same mechanisms. Dostoevsky was by no means an enemy of autocracy or a closet socialist, nor did he have some "vital score" to settle for the "joke" of his mock execution in 1849 and the indelible stigma of a political criminal.[12] Instead, Dostoevsky shared with his radical colleagues the yearning for a "new, regenerated man," upheld the human dignity of the individual made in the image of his creator, and expressed a sentimental longing for universal reconciliation (a return to the Golden Age), in which Russia would be the exemplar and prime mover. In Dostoevsky's case, all of these ideals had their origins in his Christian faith, although in his early manhood they were certainly given further impetus by his exposure to "all of European Enlightenment," as well as its heirs within his own literary tradition. His method for realizing these ideals also drew upon the same cultural repertoire: the instantaneously transformative word/deed (the emblematic act) that enacted the individual's self-sacrifice for communal guilt.[13]

Endings make certain demands that Dostoevsky attempted always somewhat awkwardly to meet. In *The Brothers Karamazov* Dostoevsky gives us a sad ending with a happy feeling, but more importantly, he upends the prose of the novel to give us the poetry of a speech that is a deed. The novel has been a long and prodigious labor of digging up and exposing the moral/emotional root system of revolutionary terrorism: its moral justification grounded in the emotions of outraged compassion, its desire to be Christ and sacrifice oneself for all people. He digs these up and exposes the pride and vanity, the manipulation of feelings, and the despotism that lie beneath. But Dostoevsky can't help himself: with the speech at the stone, he throws this prodigious labor to the wind and has his modest hero Alyosha, give a speech that is not merely a speech, but the replanting of this same seed of heroic self-sacrifice in the fertile ground of the next generation, thereby enacting the novel's epigraph: "Verily, verily I say unto you, Except a corn of wheat fall into the ground and die, it abideth alone, but if it die, it bringeth forth much fruit" (John 12:24).

Part Four

The Beautiful Dead (Deed)

But there is no such substratum; there is no "being" behind doing, effecting, becoming; "the doer" is merely a fiction added to the deed—the deed is everything.

FRIEDRICH NIETZSCHE, *The Genealogy of Morals*

I

Writing in Blood

On March 1, 1881, the Russian public could not have been surprised when a bomb thrown by a member of the People's Will fatally wounded the emperor. As the seventh attempt on his life in less than two years, the only astonishing thing about it was its success. As the police closed in on the People's Will's most elaborate conspiracy to date and arrested key members of the Executive Committee (Alexander Barannikov, Nikolai Kletochnikov, Alexander Mikhailov, and Andrei Zhelyabov) in late January and February 1881, the conspirators who remained at large feverishly finalized their preparations.[1] Zhelyabov's second-in-command, Sophia Perovskaya, took charge of the operation and deployed four "throwers" armed with bombs that were effective only when thrown at close range. As the tsar's convoy sped past along the Ekaterinsky Canal, the first thrower, Rysakov, threw his bomb beneath the horses' hooves. The resultant explosion did not meet its mark but destroyed the back of the tsar's carriage and the lives of a Cossack guard and a young boy.[2] The tsar, stunned but miraculously uninjured, had stopped to question his assailant and examine the crime scene when a second explosion at close quarters accomplished its deadly goal. A member of the tsar's retinue, Colonel Dvorzhitsky, recalled the unprecedented scene: "I was deafened by the new explosion, burned, wounded and thrown to the ground. Suddenly, amid the smoke and snowy fog, I heard his majesty's weak voice cry 'Help!' . . . Twenty people with wounds of varying degree lay on the sidewalk or on the street. Some managed to stand, others to crawl, still others tried to get out from the bodies that had fallen on top of them. Through the snow, debris, and the blood you could see fragments of clothing, epaulets, sabers, and the bloody chunks of human flesh."[3]

Illustrations of terrorist attacks featuring the tsar or explosions had been prohibited by the censor, and following March 1, a number of requests to print lithographs of the attack were rejected by the Minister of the Imperial Court.[4] Nonetheless, a few images did slip through, and descriptions of Alexander II's mortal injuries (shattered legs, a crushed abdomen) published in daily mass circulation papers such as the *St. Petersburg Gazette* conveyed the horror of the carnage, and in doing so, constituted a radical re-imagining of the king's body and the tsar's inviolability.[5] When the tsar died in the Winter Palace only a few hours after suffering his fatal wounds, the government, the conservative Russian press, and the Church joined forces to portray Alexander II as a martyr (muchennik) who had perished on the First Sunday of Lent (the Feast of Orthodoxy) at 3 p.m.—precisely the hour when Christ died on the cross.[6]

Scarcely a month later, over the personal appeals of Leo Tolstoy and the philosopher Vladimir Solovyev, the convicted tsaricides were hanged on Semyonovsky Square before a massed crowd of more than 100,000 spectators and an international press corps. Whether the executioners were drunk (as was rumored) and/or merely incompetent, the regime squandered both public support and international prestige as a consequence of the bungled and barbarous spectacle of the scaffold.[7] In a diary entry for April 3, Minister of War Count Miliutin noted with evident disgust: "They did not even know how to hang them properly. Mikhailov twice fell from the gallows. During the transportation of the criminals there were some disturbances along the street: the crowd almost tore apart several madmen [bezumtsy] who got it in their head to express sympathy for the tsaricides."[8] The challenge for the remaining *narodovol'tsy* during the intensified manhunt that followed was to capitalize upon the illusion of power that their unprecedented success had conferred and project an image befitting such an illusion.[9]

The revolutionaries' hopes for a popular revolt upon the successful regicide proved unrealistic, at best, and the public was aghast at the atrocity and deeply unnerved by the uncertainty of the situation, as were the revolutionaries themselves, who found themselves both unprepared for a seizure of power and in mortal danger. The instantaneously transformative act, so long awaited, failed to transform, and the party rushed in to fill the gap with words.[10] On March 10, 1881, the People's Will published *A Letter from the Executive Committee to Alexander III*, written by Lev Tikhomirov and edited by the literary and social critic Nikolai Mikhailovsky.[11] The letter presented its view of the revolutionary struggle and its ultimate denouement (the murder of Alexander II) as necessitated by the government's harsh repression and its ultimate illegitimacy. Most critically, the letter laid out the conditions for the cessation of terrorist activities: a general amnesty of political prisoners, the institution of fully representative government, and the entire panoply of civil liberties (full freedom of the press and freedom of speech, assembly, and electoral programs). In what is certainly one of the more tragic ironies of history, Alexander II had finally signed a decree sanctioning Loris-Melikov's constitutional proposals, which represented the first steps toward fulfilling the People's Will's demands to his heir, on the morning of his death. The assassination effectively scuttled Loris-Melikov's plans for gradual political reform and left the reactionaries, Pobedonostsev and Alexander III, masters of the field.[12]

At this point, as oblivion and immortality hung in the balance, the terrorist party was forced to confront the dilemma that Raskolnikov in *Crime and Punishment* realizes early in his self-recriminations: the disjunction between the horror of the act and the heroic image to which he aspired. Since its inception, the People's Will had made use of the word to paper over the infelicities of the deed. The party had no less than three publications to its credit, *The People's Will*, *The Bulletin of the People's Will*, and *The Laborer's Newspaper*, all of which continued to thrive despite the intensification of repression after the regicide.[13] *Narodnaia volia*, edited by Lev Tikhomirov and Nikolai Morozov, appeared in the fall of 1879 and began the longest and most voluminous print run of any underground publication (between two and three thousand copies per printing from 1879 to 1886).[14] Among its readership, it counted both radically inclined youth and upstanding citizens who were keen to satisfy their curiosity about the notorious underground organization.[15] *Narodnaia volia* painted a grand canvas of the revolutionary struggle as it was waged from the center to the peripheries and exposed the regime's countless abuses, from draconian prison regimes to statistical breakdowns of political criminals by ethnicity and religion. Aside from its programmatic articles, *Narodnaia volia* had a strong literary bent and published poems, propagandistic exposés written as short stories (the regular series "From the Village"), and even satirical feuilletons.[16]

As the struggle with the state took its toll, revolutionary biographies or "martyrologies" became one of the journal's centerpieces, and in the first number the following notice appeared: "The editors of *Narodnaia volia* request that all who know any facts or circumstances from the lives of those executed in the current year send this information as soon as possible for the composition of the biography. To collect and furnish this information, however insignificant it may seem, constitutes a moral duty of everyone for whom the memory of the first martyrs for the people and freedom are dear."[17] Biographical observations and notes (zametki, or sketches) of Valerian Osinsky (executed May 1879), Alexander Kviatkovsky (executed November 1880), and Dmitry Lizogub (executed in August 1879) followed in short order. As early exemplars of revolutionary hagiography, the biographies are largely devoid of sacralization and romantic idealizations and instead rich with the prosaic detail that *Narodnaia volia*'s editors had requested. The revolutionaries' childhood and early family life; their parents' careers and influence; their education and reading; their revolutionary curriculum vitae; and finally, their imprisonment, trial testimony, and execution—no aspect of their activity was left unrepresented.

On the pages of *Narodnaia volia*, the "men of the future" had arrived and were on full display, although they themselves had no future but that of immortality. In the meantime, writers aiming for a broader audience and legal publication continued to refine strategies for representing the impermissible. Less than a month after the Zasulich trial, the staunchly liberal writer Ivan Turgenev would be the first to mint the image of the revolutionary avenger, an image more powerful (and versatile) for being entirely imageless.

2

An Icon with Death

In concluding his summation in defense of Vera Zasulich, Peter Alexandrov had emphasized that all of the preceding arguments were made not for the benefit of his client, but rather only for the purpose of helping the jury resolve "the questions standing before it." As for Zasulich, the ultimate proof of her selflessness was her complete indifference to the outcome of the trial: "for her it is all the same to be buried according to this or that law." He continued: "When she crossed the threshold of the governor's house with the determined intention to allow the thought that was tormenting her, she knew and understood, that she was sacrificing everything—her freedom, the remains of her broken life, all of that small portion given her by stepmother fate."[1]

Ivan Turgenev, the renowned author of *Notes of a Hunter* (Zapiski okhotnika) and *Fathers and Children* (Otsi i deti), regarded the furor surrounding the Zasulich affair from France.[2] An avowed liberal and devoted champion of reform, Turgenev recoiled from acts of revolutionary violence and terror.[3] Nevertheless, he, like Dostoevsky, was swift to temper his condemnation of the revolutionaries by implicating the government's mishandling of sedition as well as general misrule in the escalation of anti-state violence. Turgenev regarded the "Vera Mania" that swept Western Europe (especially France) in spring 1878 with ironic bemusement and cannily refused requests to serve as the resident expert on nihilists. On April 30 he reported to Stasiulevich: "From Germany I have received a pressing request to write an article on the trial [of Zasulich] because all the newspapers see a close link between Zasulich and Marianne in *Virgin Soil* (Nov′, 1877). I have even been nicknamed *der Prophet*. I naturally refused."[4] As natural as his refusal might have been, Turgenev did not entirely let slip the opportunity to immortalize his prophetic vision in a prose poem that embraced Trepov's threshold as a metaphor for the double-edged "moral choice" to sacrifice the self and another.

Порог

Я вижу громадное здание.

В передней стене узкая дверь раскрыта настежь, за дверью—угрюмая мгла.

Перед высоким порогом стоит девушка . . . Русская девушка.

Морозом дышит та непроглядная мгла; и вместе с леденящей струей выносится из глубины здания медлительный, глухой голос.

—О ты, что желаешь переступить этот порог,—знаешь ли ты, что тебя ожидает?

—Знаю,—отвечает девушка.

—Холод, голод, ненависть, насмешка, презрение, обида, тюрьма, болезнь, и самая смерть?

—Знаю.

—Отчуждение полное, одиночество?

—Знаю. Я готова. Я перенесу все страдания, все удары.

—Не только от врагов—но и от родных, от друзей?

—Да . . . и от них.

—Хорошо. Ты готова на жертву?

—Да.

—На безымянную жертву? Ты погибнешь—и никто . . . никто не будет даже знать, чью память почтить!

—Мне не нужно ни благодарности, не сожаления. Мне не нужно имени.

—Готова ли ты на преступление?

Девушка потупила голову . . .

—И на преступление готова.

Голос не тотчас возобновил свои вопросы.

—Знаешь ли ты,—заговорил он наконец,—что ты можешь разувериться в том, чему веришь теперь, можешь понять, что обманулась и даром погубила свою молодую жизнь?

—Знаю и это. И все-таки я хочу войти.

—Войди!

Девушка перешагнула порог—и тяжелая завеса упала за нею.
—Дура!—проскрежетал кто-то сзади.
—Святая!—принеслось откуда-то в ответ.⁵

The Threshold

I see an enormous building.
At the front a narrow door is flung open: behind the door—forbidding gloom.
A girl stands before the high threshold . . . A Russian girl.
The impenetrable doom breathes frost; and with icy streams a deliberate hollow voice resounds from the depths of the building.
"O you who wish to cross this threshold, do you know what awaits you?"
"I know,"—the girl answers.
"Cold, hunger, hate, ridicule, contempt, humiliation, prison, disease, and death itself?"
"I know."
"Total isolation, loneliness?"
"I know . . . I'm prepared. I will tolerate all the suffering, all the blows."
"Not only from enemies—but also from family, from friends."
"Yes, from them as well."
"Good. Are you prepared for sacrifice?"
"Yes."
"For anonymous sacrifice? You will die—and no one . . . no one will even know, whom to commemorate."
"I need neither gratitude nor pity. I do not need a name."
"Are you prepared to commit a crime?"
The girl lowered her head . . .
"And I'm prepared to commit a crime."
The voice did not immediately resume its questions.
"Do you know," the voice began at last, "that you may lose faith in what you believe now, that you may come to understand that you deceived yourself and that you destroyed your young life in vain?"
"I know that also. And nevertheless I want to enter."
"Enter!"
The girl crossed the threshold and a heavy curtain fell behind her.
"Fool!" screeched someone behind.
"Saint!" came from somewhere in answer.⁶

In the last years of his life, Turgenev was accumulating what he referred to as "prose poems" under a working title, which alternated between the doleful *Posthuma* and *Senilia*. "The Threshold," written a month-and-a-half after Zasulich's acquittal, was prudently consigned to the desk drawer, but then submitted to Stasiulevich for publication at an equally inauspicious time—just a year after the assassination of Alexander II. As in the case of Polonsky's "Female Prisoner," the cautious Stasiulevich made a number of changes. In order to disclaim any possible historic reference, Stasiulevich added the subtitle "dream" (son). To give the impression of impartiality and create balance between the two contesting voices at the end of the poem, he replaced "screeched" with the neutral "said" (govoril), and the "came from somewhere in answer" with "came from the other side" (razdalos' c drugoi storony).[7] The most profound change, however, was Stasiulevich's elimination of the lines "Are you prepared to commit a crime? The girl lowered her head. And I'm prepared to commit a crime."

These lines are in fact the lynchpin of Turgenev's poem. They indicate that the "Russian girl" stood not merely on the threshold of Underground Russia, but on the threshold of an act of violence, of revolutionary terrorism. The lowering of the head is a gesture that iconically represents the critical conflict between moral conscience and political commitment expressed by Zasulich at her trial. "It is a terrible thing to raise one's hand against a fellow man . . . but I decided that this is what I had to do."[8] Dostoevsky was so impressed by this remark that he referred to it two years later in his diary, noting this parallel between Ivan Karamazov and Zasulich: "What is moral is not completely decided by the simple concept of consistency with one's convictions, and the convinced personality himself, keeping his own convictions intact, stops because of some feeling and does not complete the act . . . he recognized that stopping and not following his conviction was an act more moral than if he had followed it. . . . Zasulich: 'It is hard to raise a hand to shed blood'—this vacillation is more moral than the shedding of blood could have been."[9] Zasulich, of course, did not "stop," but rather acted in accordance with her convictions despite the vacillation that Dostoevsky deemed "more moral."

Turgenev rejected Stasiulevich's changes, preferring instead to withdraw the poem rather than alter it in any way. It was only after other readers from among Turgenev's circle of literary intimates (which consisted of some of Russia's foremost men of letters, among them the presiding judge of the Zasulich trial, A. F. Koni) expressed serious reservations that Turgenev urgently requested that "The Threshold" be withdrawn. On the very eve of publication, Turgenev finally recognized the danger and wrote to Stasiulevich: "My first order of business—is to ask you to throw out 'The Threshold.' ... Over that 'threshold' you may trip ... especially if it is allowed to pass [by the censorship]. And for that reason, it's better to wait."[10] Nonetheless, Turgenev had succeeded in publicizing, if not publishing, his poem. When Pavel Annenkov, for example, noted the absence of "The Threshold" in *The Messenger of Europe*, he queried Stasiulevich about the whereabouts of "the lady who is declared a criminal and a saint at the same time"—summing up the Zasulich trial in a nutshell. In the final analysis, Annenkov agreed with the editorial decision to "throw" her out: "Yes, the removal of the poem is understandable—it's more peaceful this way."[11]

When read in the context of the *Poems in Prose* manuscript in the order stipulated by Turgenev, the "Threshold" reveals an aspect that is obscured when it is read independently of its original literary context. Like many of the poems that precede it in the collection ("The Old Woman," "The Opponent," "The End of the World"), it is a frightening poem about death, albeit in the culturally valorized form of heroic self-sacrifice. "The Threshold" is by far the most ambivalent of Turgenev's poems on the theme of self-sacrifice, first and foremost because it refers to the commission of a "crime" by the girl. We are not allowed to forget that the girl has conceded to sacrifice not only her own life, but another's. Had Turgenev concluded the poem with the disappearance of the girl behind the curtain, her death would have been unredeemed, and "The Threshold" would have been a poem of foreboding and condemnation. However, by eavesdropping on "public opinion" at the end of the poem, Turgenev gainsays the guardian's dire prophecy. Publicity, if not glory, greets the Russian girl's sacrifice. Moreover, the voice of sanctification has the parting shot, thereby reaffirming the sacred content of the poem (the crossing of the threshold as a rite of religious initiation).

Once extracted from its original literary context, the artistic features signaling Turgenev's ambivalence could be easily overlooked or even entirely omitted. And this is exactly what happened: Peter Yakubovich, a *narodovolets* and aspiring litterateur,[12] acquired a copy of Turgenev's "The Threshold" through unknown channels (there appear to have been a sufficient number of copies in circulation). Upon Turgenev's death in 1883, Yakubovich printed on fine paper a pamphlet entitled simply "I. S. Turgenev," which was later published in *Narodnaia volia* (October 1883). Yakubovich zestfully joined in the "mêlée" among political tendencies (conservative, liberal, radical) to claim Turgenev for their own, insisting that although Turgenev was undeniably a "gradualist," "The Threshold" constituted proof that "he [Turgenev] served the

Russian revolution with the heartfelt meaning [serdechnyi smysl'] of his work, that he loved the revolutionary youth, recognizing it to be "saintly" (or "holy," sviatoi) and "self-abnegating."[13] Not only did he serve the Russian revolution, but he had in some sense created it. "The images of Rudin, Insarov, Elena, Bazarov, Nezhdanov, and Markilova are not only live images and taken from life, but as strange as it may seem at first glance—these are types that the youth imitated and that themselves created life."[14] Despite the presence of hundreds of undercover secret police officers at Turgenev's funeral at the Volkhov Cemetery in St. Petersburg, members of the tattered Narodnaia volia organization achieved a veritable propaganda coup when they managed to distribute Yakubovich's fliers among the crowd of mourners, thereby propagating "their Turgenev" as the charismatic moral authority who had sanctified the terrorist struggle.

A broader public was now privy to the underground version of "The Threshold," which by word of mouth trickled down to members of the liberal and radical intelligentsia far removed from the capital. Thus, in Tula *oblast'* the pedagogue and bibliographer Nikolai Mikhailovich Gorbov preserved what is essentially a second hand account of Turgenev's funeral, one that remarks upon the "underground flier" and includes the following paraphrase of "The Threshold."

A young girl stands on the threshold, from which two paths lead, one—the path of pleasure, the other—the path of deprivation and hardship, ending in the gallows [viselitsa].
Some voice whispers, that all manner of suffering and deprivation etc. await her along that path.
—I'm going.
—Your loved ones, mother, father, relations, will turn away from you.
—I'm going.
—You will be greeted by ridicule, insult.
—I'm going.
—You will be persecuted by those, for whom you sacrifice yourself.
—Over there are the gallows . . .
—I'm going.
—Fool! rang out from above.
—Saint! [a voice] pronounced in the air.[15]

Gorbov's version suppresses the two moments of the dialogue that suggest Turgenev's ambivalence: the girl's assent to crime (along with the moral compunction that was so important to both Dostoevsky and Turgenev) and the voice's warning concerning future disillusionment. These loci of tension are replaced by explicit mention of the girl's ultimate destination—the gallows—entirely absent from Turgenev's poem, since Zasulich, of course, was acquitted. Gorbov's insertion of the "gallows," or more specifically, the "gibbet," owes itself most probably to the hanging of Sophia Perovskaya, the "ringleader" of Alexander II's assassination on March 1, 1881.[16]

Gorbov (or his source) introduces a few significant additions: the "Russian girl" is clearly a member of the upper classes, since her sacrifice consists of forfeiting pleasures while Turgenev's poem makes no such allusion. Further, she is distilled to the principle of action, to conviction in motion. "I'm going" (idu) replaces her words of assent "I know" (znaiu) in Turgenev's poem. How had Turgenev's poem lent itself so well to this refurbishment as a (revolutionary) icon, not in this case, by revolutionaries but by liberal pedagogues who were at best revolutionary sympathizers? First of all, it was conceived as a discrete and detachable entity. Both Baudelaire and Turgenev emphasize this as a primary virtue of their prose poems in the prefatory letters to their collections. In the case of "The Threshold," however, this autonomy facilitated the elision of the context that signaled Turgenev's ambivalence toward self-sacrifice. Second, it must not be forgotten that it was the agnostic Turgenev who had chosen a religious rite of initiation as the metaphor for passing from a legal existence in autocratic Russia to an underground existence, and accepting murder as a necessary means. Finally, Turgenev emphasizes not the girl's active participation in revolutionary conspiracy, but (like Polonsky) her *stradal'cheskii obraz*—her suffering image. Compositionally, Turgenev's prose poem may be likened to the iconic genre known as the "icon with saint's life" (ikona s zhitiem), "which combines the principle of the icon in the strict sense (one central image, strictly subordinated to iconographic tradition), and, at the same time, the principle of fresco décor (viz. the individual scenes [kleima, or stamp] along the border) which, being subordinated to a single composition and a single content, form a general ensemble which narrates the story of the saint's life."[17]

The central figure, of course, is the Russian girl, and it is by means of the dialogue between the initiate and the guardian of the threshold that "scenes along the border" are depicted. Each question is the equivalent of a "stamp" that foretells a scene from her future ordeal should she choose to cross the threshold. Whether in Turgenev's or Gorbov's version, the ability of "The Threshold" to function as an icon lies paradoxically in its imagelessness, the visual emptiness of the "Russian girl." Her image is constituted by her acts—and how she is acted upon. The visual austerity of the poem is itself congruent with the girl's asceticism, as well as with the poetic persona's claim to prophetic vocation. Note well, however, that in no version of the poem is the Russian girl doing anything *now*. The threshold, in space-time, is a liminal place prior to action that will inevitably come once the threshold has been crossed. Turgenev's prophesy, with its visual minimalism and dialogue structure, is less foreseen than fore*heard*.

In the year and a half between Zasulich's acquittal (March 1878) and the Trial of the 16 (October 1880), terrorism evolved with lightning speed. The threshold was irrevocably crossed, and Turgenev would have been aghast at what lay on the other side. An anonymous poem published in *Narodnaia volia* (No. 4 1880), entitled simply "After the Execution of November 4," provides an instructive contrast to "The Threshold."

And once again scaffolds! . . . Be quiet, cry of the heart!
Once again corpses sway in nooses,
While the lifelessly dumb masses watch the valiant martyrdom of our best sons.
No! It's high time after all to stop; to the end of ages we can expect no good
From the Tsar with his pack of hounds.
And we are forced anew to battle with the horde of enemies,
For freedom, for human rights . . .
I will sharpen the axe, I will teach myself to fire heavy artillery,
I will kill pity in my heart so that my hand will become a terrifying and unfeeling judge.
Don't forgive anyone, don't spare anything!
A death for a death, blood for blood, vengeance for execution![18]

By the time of the Trial of the 16 and the executions of Alexander Kviatkovsky and Alexander Presniakov, any moral hesitation with reference to some vaguely alluded-to crime had been replaced by explicit reference to the means and urgency of vengeance. The People's Will had finally "stepped over"—at least in verse—where Raskolnikov had feared to tread. In important respects, however, the poem lagged behind advances in party theory: government atrocities as incitement to terrorist acts were already somewhat passé. The Trial of the 16 was the first time that the terrorist program was aired in public, that revolutionaries used the word "terrorist" to describe themselves, and that the various attacks on Alexander II were identified with a single, conspiratorial organization, the People's Will. In their trial testimony, excerpted in *Narodnaia volia*, Kviatkovsky and Shiraev had described terrorism (*terror*) as a reluctantly embraced defensive strategy against the state's repressive juggernaut of arrest, imprisonment, exile, and execution. Recourse to terrorism was a case in which the "lamb," through force of circumstance, became a "lion"—when "individuals, who by disposition were the most benevolent and humane, were forced to engage in such activities which were intrinsically revolting to human nature."[19] The editors of *Narodnaia volia* were in the awkward position of declaring the revolutionary martyrs' conception outdated, explaining that while in prison the defendants could not keep abreast of the latest developments. By autumn 1880, terrorism occupied a central place in the party's program as an offensive strategy of disorganization and agitation. "Who of them would now deny, that terror helps organizational work, awakens the mind and feelings of the people and of the intelligentsia, targeting the strongest enemy and proving the possibility of a battle with him?"[20]

What "The Threshold" celebrates, as Yakubovich clearly realized, is the Russian girl's/ revolutionary terrorism's self-abnegation, not her self-asserting violence. When Yakubovich distributed his flier in October 1883, it was already an anachronism, a monument to a transitional moment. Yet by means of Turgenev's aesthetic asceticism, the selflessness of the Russian girl translated into facelessness, and the facelessness translated into timelessness. "The Threshold" was first published legally in *Russian Wealth* (Russkoe bogatstvo) in 1906, when the journal's editor, SemyonVengerov, paired it with Polonsky's "The Female Prisoner" just in time to salute several female terrorists who participated in the violence of the 1905 revolution. (Re)citing "The Threshold" to members of the newly elected State Duma, the Kadet deputy Nikolai Ognyov made a plea for clemency for six young women (known as the *Shesterka*) who were implicated in prominent political assassinations. Referring to Turgenev's "The Threshold," Ognev declared, "Gentlemen, I see familiar traits . . . in this young woman. I recognize in the face of this girl the traits of Zasulich, Volkenshtein, Izmailovich, Spiridonova and others."[21] Given that the Russian girl, as noted above, has no face, what is it that Ognyov (who was, incidentally, a priest) recognized?

3

Celebrity Icons

The year 1878 earned the distinction of "The Year of Assassinations" as across the European continent malcontents lashed out against emperors and heads of state,[1] but it could just as well have been designated "The Year of the Threshold." Not only did Russian revolutionary terrorism stand poised to emerge, but so did the *attentat* (attempt) of anarchist terrorism on the continent, followed by Fenian dynamite outrages. In Russia, 1878 was the year when revolutionary terrorism as a practice of serial assassinations came into being, inspired in part by Zasulich's acquittal (applauded by public opinion) and in part by the increasing militancy of revolutionaries in the south, who founded the precursor to the People's Will, Liberty or Death. While Zasulich's attempt served as the inspiration, the act that heralded the new strategy of political violence occurred six months later, when assassins struck down the St. Petersburg chief of police, General Nikolai Mezentsev, in broad daylight. Two days later, an anonymous declaration entitled "A Death for a Death" (published in the party organ of Land and Freedom) claimed responsibility for Mezentsev's murder—on behalf of "us," "socialist-revolutionaries," and trumpeted "we are embarking on a whole series of killings and are transforming it into a system" (My reshaemsia na tselyi riad ubiistv i vozvodim ikh v sistemu).[2] As the title "A Death for a Death" implies, the author(s) of the pamphlet took the logic of Zasulich's

Celebrity Icons

trial to its ultimate conclusion: if government abuses remain unpunished, the revolutionaries would take it upon themselves to answer in kind.

In his long tenure as chief of police, Mezentsev had quite a tally to his credit, but he had only one life to give, and this life was taken, explained the author of "A Death for A Death," for the execution on August 2 in Odessa of Ivan Kovalsky. The timeline drawn is as unambiguous as the equivalences established: a death will follow — invariably and in short order — a death. Revolutionary terrorism had articulated a narrative of reciprocity as instantaneously legible and mathematically precise as two points connected by a line.

What Franco Venturi has called "the most perfect act of terrorism of the time" was conceived and carefully planned long before Kovalsky's execution.[3] At 9 a.m. on August 4, two gentlemen collided with General Mezentsev while walking in the Mikhailovsky gardens in the city's center. One fatally wounded the General with an Italian stiletto, while the other fired at his adjutant in order to forestall apprehension. A coach, with a dark mustachioed coachman on the box, whisked the assailants away from the scene without leaving a trace. A sharper contrast with Nechaev's amateurish murder of Ivanov is hardly imaginable. The police launched a futile manhunt, but the perpetrators had disappeared seemingly into thin air, but in fact into the interstices of legal Russia that came to constitute another dimension, soon to be known as "Underground Russia." *Sans* perpetrator, the only thing left to do was to "create by imagination" — to quote Dostoevsky — "the person, the type, that really corresponds to the crime."[4]

The person to accomplish this task was in fact the assassin himself, Sergei Stepniak-Kravchinsky.[5] Wanted for Mezentsev's murder, Kravchinsky fled abroad, where he undertook a series profiling the most notorious figures of the Russian revolutionary movement for the Milanese newspaper *il Pungolo*. The series enjoyed tremendous success, so much so that at the invitation of his Italian publisher, Kravchinsky compiled the profiles into a book titled *La Rossia Sotteranea* (Underground Russia), which was published in all the European languages, as well as in Japan and North America. Meanwhile, Kravchinsky's co-conspirator, Alexander Barannikov, as a member of the Executive Committee of the People's Will, participated in all but one attempt of the fatal Emperor Hunt while living inconspicuously as Dostoevsky's neighbor.[6]

Kravchinsky has proved as elusive a biographical subject as he was an outlaw, and scholars have had great difficulty in establishing even the most fundamental facts of his childhood and youth. In the introduction to *Underground Russia*, the revolutionary historian Peter Lavrov confidently presented Kravchinsky as a man at the hub of the revolutionary movement through its formative phases in the 1870s and therefore able to impart to "European readers a sufficiently truthful idea of [its] form and substance."[7] Without doubt, Kravchinsky was everywhere: a member of the Chaikovsky circle (the utopian commune inspired by Nikolai Chernyshevsky), he was also a propagandist on Vyborg Island, one of the first to "go to the People" in 1873, and a volunteer in the struggles for national liberation in Italy and Herzegovina. No sooner did a general amnesty of political prisoners secure for Kravchinsky a well-timed release from prison in Benevento, Italy, than he hailed Vera Zasulich's shooting in the newspaper *Obshchina* (published in Geneva), taking a uniquely personal approach to the heroine of the day: "What is her face like and her eyes and her voice, how does she dress, how does she speak, what does she love?"[8] Kravchinsky openly pined for the doer behind Zasulich's deed, and upon his return to Russia in May 1878 he hastened to make Zasulich's acquaintance; he also hastened to commit an act that would surpass Zasulich's in its impact and audacity.

That act, the murder of Mezentsev, has already been described in its particulars. The composition of the act, with the dagger (immortalized in Alexander Pushkin's 1821 poem *The Dagger*) as the weapon of choice, was meant to recall the venerated tradition of tyrannicide. In *Underground Russia*, Kravchinsky (writing under the pseudonym Stepniak) foregoes literal realism and resorts entirely to tropes, that is to say—to poetry. Mezentsev's murder is the doing of a new, unprecedented entity, "the Terrorism," rendered a proper noun in English and preceded by a definite article. This usage alternated with "terrorism" in Anglophone media and would persist until the 1917 Revolution, with "Nihilist" and "anarchist" used interchangeably. In contrast to Zasulich, whom Kravchinsky characterizes as "an angel of vengeance, not of terror," this entity wages not a new form of warfare, but an old form of social rectification: the duel of honor. "The Terrorism," recounts Kravchinsky, "by putting to death General Mezentzeff [sic] the head of the police and the entire camarilla, boldly threw down its glove in the face of autocracy. From that day forth it advanced with giant strides, acquiring strength and position, and culminating in the tremendous duel with the man who was the personification of despotism."⁹

Kravchinsky and his co-conspirators are nowhere to be seen. On the one hand, there is "the Terrorism," a collective within which the individual terrorist is subsumed but which nevertheless may be personified, and on the other hand, "the Terrorist." "He is noble, terrible, irresistibly fascinating, for he combines in himself the two sublimities of human grandeur: the martyr and the hero." With these words of introduction, Kravchinsky unveils a new type: A martyr, without religion. A warrior, captivated by "the beauty of his dreams, the grandeur of his mission, ... the strong passions which this marvelous, intoxicating, vertiginous struggle arouses in his heart." Whatever the specific type of contest, Kravchinsky is sufficiently detached to marvel at the spectacle. "Proud as Satan rebelling against God, he opposed his own will to that of the man who alone, amid a nation of slaves, claimed the right of having a will. But how different is this terrestrial god from the old Jehovah of Moses! How he hides his trembling head under the daring blows of the Terrorist! True, he still stands erect, and the thunderbolts launched by his trembling hand often fail; but when they strike, they kill. But the Terrorist is immortal. His limbs may fail him, but as if by magic they regain their vigour, and he stands erect, ready for battle after battle until he has laid low his enemy and liberated the country."¹⁰

This is Kravchinsky's most overt attempt to stake a claim to the sovereign's legitimacy, as he stages a contest of doubles, of gods facing off against one another. The contest is necessarily marked by ambiguity, as the syntax makes it impossible to say for certain who the "he" who still stands erect is, and whose the thunderbolts—traditionally the weapon of the gods—properly are. The contestants are interchangeable. Like the gods, and like the king who enjoys immortality by means of a second body, the Terrorist is immortal, thanks to magically revitalized limbs. Insofar as the Terrorist is an embodied individual, his emphatically masculine body is the epitome of hardness that corresponds to an equally inflexible will. "He is a wrestler, all bone and muscle." "If he is a man of generous impulses, he will become a hero, if he is of stronger fibre, it will harden into iron; if of iron, it will become adamant."¹¹ But, unexpectedly, he has a soft heart. As Kravchinsky shifts from a mythic into a realist mode, the Terrorist he describes draws recognizably on earlier extraordinary types—Rakhmetov and Nechaev's Revolutionary—with one important difference. Kravchinsky's Terrorist does not eschew personal interests or emotional ties: these are precisely what motivate him to his extraordinary feats. "He fights not only for the people, to render them the arbiters of their own destinies, not only for the whole nation stifling in this pestiferous atmosphere, but also for himself; for the dear ones whom he loves, whom he adores with all the enthusiasm which animates his soul; for his friends who languish in the horrid cells of the central prisons, and who stretch forth to him their skinny hands imploring aid. He fights for himself. He has sworn to be free and he will be free, in defiance of everything."[12] On the one hand, Kravchinsky's masculinist characterization of the Terrorist may be interpreted as a reaction against Zasulich, whose deed was so inordinately feminized by Alexandrov's defense. At the same time, having passed through the movement To the People and through Zasulich, the Terrorist has clearly absorbed and now openly proclaims the force of love and personal attachment. Yet he does so in almost the same clichéd terms, relying on the same sentimental *topoi* as Nechaev in his proclamations (parodied by Dostoevsky in *Demons*). In contrast to Nechaev's *Catechism*, however, Kravchinsky insists on the Terrorist's self. "He has a powerful and distinctive individuality. He is no longer, like his predecessor, all abnegation." Instead, in his profiles Kravchinsky concerns himself precisely with rendering, preserving, and immortalizing that distinctive individuality, all the while concealing his own.[13]

As a terrorist and a writer, Kravchinsky was uniquely aware of the formal means (rhetorical and aesthetic) used to produce certain effects, and of his diverse audiences. For his innovative choices of media (major European dailies rather than the radical press), form (profiles) and content (highly personal), Kravchinsky was called to account by his revolutionary comrades, Vera Zasulich and Lev Deich. His defense emphasized the commemorative intentions of his project and pointed to contemporary precedents—the corpus of literature that had arisen around prominent leaders of French Republicanism and the Italian national movements, such as Giuseppe Garibaldi and Léon Gambetta. By the time of his writing (November 1881) the majority of Kravchinsky's youthful friends and associates had been executed or immured in the Peter and Paul Fortress, the island penitentiary of Schlisselburg, or Siberian *katorga*. Thus, *Underground Russia* was the first Russian revolutionary martyrology directed to a broader public written by a "sole survivor," while at the same time offering, as martyrologies do, contemporary templates for the heroic life and death, a *Stepniak's Lives*. Indeed, when the 1905 Revolution finally enabled the legal publication of *Underground Russia* in Russia, a new generation of revolutionaries embraced it as inspirational literature and a manual for revolutionary self-fashioning—in other words, for imitating.[14]

Zasulich did not take offense at the commemorative features and function of Kravchinsky's profiles; rather, she was discomposed to find herself the victim, at his hands, of that invasion of privacy which has become unremarkable in the twenty-first century. Kravchinsky's profiles were early exemplars of a new generic offshoot, the celebrity profile, and Zasulich was an international celebrity. Alone among his comrades, Kravchinsky understood the means and ends of celebrity, and the benefits to the Russian revolutionary movement that celebrity would confer. In a letter to Zasulich from the winter of 1881-82, Kravchinsky offered Zasulich a tutorial in celebrity, explaining that the old ways of doing business by securing *rekomendatsii* (or *rekomendatel'nye pis'ma*, letters of introduction) to exclusive circles were passé: "If you want to do business [sdelat' delo], you need to appeal to the entire public, and not to some faction. Well, and who but your name can give you a letter of introduction to the whole public?"[15] Kravchinsky's advice reveals that he had in fact set his sights on "the whole public."

Kravchinsky's keen grasp of celebrity suggests an affinity between it and "the Terrorism." In its archaic English usage, "celebrity" denoted the visual and symbolic display of power and prestige by the aristocracy and the king.[16] By the nineteenth century, "celebrity" was notoriety that could be achieved by anyone, for anything, just as anyone could kill the king. (William Hazlitt, one of the first cultural critics to analyze the phenomenon, identified Napoleon and Byron as celebrities).[17] This progression—from early modern Europe's ideology of kingship to the nineteenth century's worship of heroes and great men and twentieth-century mass culture's celebrity fetish—suggests that celebrity is the modern instantiation/appropriation of the king's irrational, nonroutinized, charismatic authority.

By the late nineteenth century, discourses of celebrity vied with notions of heroes and great men, and in his profiles Kravchinsky draws on both. What makes celebrity distinctively modern, however, is that a mass public participates in the elevation and co-creation of said celebrity. While the distinctive individuality of the celebrity is ostensibly what is celebrated, in fact this individuality—simulated through infinitely variable constellations of features—is grafted onto cultural types.[18] Kravchinsky understood this, and so his profiles embrace the devices of the celebrity profile that highlight the uniqueness of his individual subjects while clearly delineating the type to which they belong. At the end of his profile of Dmitry Lizogub, Kravchinsky even does the public the favor of explicitly designating his subjects according to type.

Celebrity gained ground with the visuality of modern media. D. W. Griffith's cinematic innovation of the close-up focused audience attention on the actor's face. As the literary precursor of the cinematic close-up, the celebrity profile proliferated in the mass circulation press beginning in the early 1880s. It featured individuals who had come to the public's attention and whom editors believed their readers wanted to know more about. The celebrity profiler claimed to render an intimate portrait of his subject; in other words, to peel back the façade, to penetrate the mask and offer the reader privileged access to the subject's ostensibly authentic self.

Kravchinsky therefore assumes a completely unprecedented role: he is simultaneously one of Underground Russia's notorious denizens and a celebrity profiler. With regard to the latter role, he demonstrates his bona fides by hitting all the right notes. So, for example, Kravchinsky's melodramatic announcement chimes perfectly with the revelatory purposes of the celebrity profile: "I will now introduce my readers to the inner life of Underground Russia, and of those terrible men, who have so many times made him tremble, before whom all tremble. I will show them as they are, without exaggeration and without false modesty."[19] In fact, it is in Zasulich's profile that Kravchinsky makes unabashed, almost garish use of the genre's devices. He begins by hyping Zasulich's celebrity ("In the whole range of history it would be difficult, and perhaps, impossible to find a name which, at a bound, has risen into such universal and undisputed celebrity") and inflaming the reader's desire to know more about "this dazzling and mysterious being."[20] Like a dogged paparazzo, in fact, Kravchinsky harries the reclusive Zasulich even in her thoughts and exhibits her as typical of that species of morbidly introspective Russian familiar to foreign readers, subject to "gloomy moods," "probing her own mind, sounding its depths, pitilessly dissecting it, searching for defects, often imaginary and always exaggerated."[21]

It was this psychological portrait, which despite or because of its Romantic flourishes suggested melancholia and mental instability, that most incensed Zasulich. The cultivation of authenticity and intimacy so central to Kravchinsky's representative strategy came at a price for those of his subjects who were not already dead. Yet even Zasulich's dogged aversion to celebrity served his project, by enabling Kravchinsky to tout the reclusive would-be assassin as a new type of celebrity—the anti-celebrity—who intensifies public interest by rejecting celebrity trappings, publicity in particular. The nexus of qualities that constitute Zasulich's anti-celebrity are exactly those that indicate her selflessness—the moral precondition, in the ethos of populist political terrorism, of the right to take another life. Ironically, Kravchinsky's celebrity profile of Zasulich implicitly poses celebrity itself as a problem of means and ends: his reader, after all, is aware that it is by means of an act of terrorist violence that Zasulich attained instantaneous "universal celebrity."

Of all of Kravchinsky's subjects, Zasulich was the only genuine celebrity "who had captured world attention for 48 hours." The others ranged from the well-known (Sophia Perovskaya, Peter Kropotkin) to completely obscure (Valerian Osinsky, Dmitry Lizogub). Of them, only Valerian Osinsky and Sophia Perovskaya qualify as terrorists, and Valerian Osinsky, about whom so little is known, deserves special notice as the first "terrorist." As a member of the Southern Rebels based in Kiev, Osinsky was the first to advocate terrorism, to practice terrorism, to call himself a "terrorist," and to die a terrorist's death on the scaffold. His influence, innovations, and arguments would propel the faction of Land and Freedom that became the People's Will down the road to terrorism. While the devices of the celebrity profile remain subtly in play in Osinsky's and Perovskaya's profiles, they yield to the more stately features of literary type and cultural archetype. Vis-à-vis Osinsky, though, Kravchinsky himself models the role of avid fan and is starstruck upon his first, avidly sought meeting:

> I advanced towards him. I shook him by the hand, and held it for a time in my own, being unable to take my eyes off him. He was as beautiful as the sun. Lithe, well-proportioned, strong and flexible as a blade of steel. His head, with its flaxen hair somewhat thrown back, was gracefully poised upon his delicate and sinewy neck. His high and fair forehead was furrowed, upon his somewhat narrow temple, by some blue veins. A straight nose, which in profile seemed as though it had been carved by an artistic chisel, gave to his countenance that character of classical beauty so rare in Russia. Small whiskers, and an elegant flaxen beard, concealed a very delicate, expressive, eager mouth, and all this Apollo-like face was lighted up by two very fine eyes, large, intelligent, full of fire, and of youthful daring.[22]

In Osinsky, divine kingship shines through the husk of celebrity. The Apollonian imagery of sun and fire radiate from his unblemished, more classical than typically Russian, beauty. With his striking good looks, glamorous air and panache, Osinsky is "the Terrorism" charged with sexual magnetism, its swashbuckling Rudolph Valentino ("He was a warrior strong of heart and arm. He loved danger, for he was at home in it, as in his natural element.... He loved women—and was loved in return.")[23] In flourishes such as these, Kravchinsky departs most sharply from the biographical notes published in *Narodnaia volia* that engaged in neither prudery nor whitewash. While Kravchinsky counts on the double standard of the English bourgeoisie to wink indulgently at Osinsky's amores, he is careful to avoid mentioning that Osinsky's common-law marriage to Sophia Leshern figured prominently in Osinsky's courtroom defense, in which he angrily charged the prosecutor with "throwing dirt at us." Nor does he mention that Osinsky left behind as widow a different woman, Maria Gerasimovna Nikol'skaia, whom he had married in St. Petersburg in 1877.[24]

Nothing is more indicative of Osinsky's personal charisma than his ability to acquire that without which there would be no terrorism: money. Not only does he captivate his comrades—all of their memoirs testify to that—but "this irresistible young man" induced tightfisted old ladies and miserly gentlemen to open their wallets for the Terrorism. It is difficult to believe in Osinsky; as he stoically mounts the scaffold while the military band mocks his death with an indecent *komarinskaia*, he steps off the pages of Dumas and Hugo and into a literary type, the Romantic outlaw, who translates terrorism for its foreign audience into something familiar yet fascinating and deeply alluring.

The last and widely considered the most masterful of the profiles was that of Sophia Perovskaya, well-known to the international public for her prominent role in the March 1 regicide. Here Kravchinsky seeks to capitalize upon the fascination provoked by a woman in such a formidable capacity while dislodging the negative image created by chauvinistic press coverage. The same London *Times* that opened its pages to Kravchinsky had, for example, consistently referred to her as Andrei Zhelyabov's "concubine" and reported that in the course of the trial, Perovskaya was "analysed and found wanting in everything that was womanly and attractive in her sex."[25] Kravchinsky sets out to demonstrate the opposite: that Perovskaya possessed feminine (but not sexual) charms with her "small, slender, graceful figure, and a voice as charming, silvery, and sympathetic as could be"[26] and was in fact the picture of the dutiful, demure Victorian girl who fulfilled the duties of schoolmistress or nurse in exemplary fashion.

Once established, however, this image serves only to heighten the piquancy of the contradiction between it and Perovskaya's identity as "one of the most dreaded members of the Terrorist party." As in Zasulich's profile, Kravchinsky promises to penetrate the façade—"What titanic force was concealed under this serene appearance?"—but despite his long acquaintance with Perovskaya, no penetrating psychological sketch is forthcoming. Instead, Perovskaya coincides so entirely with the movement that her story is told largely through it, as Kravchinsky admits "The story of her early days is that of all the young in Russia. To relate it would be to present in a concrete form, what I have narrated in an abstract form in my preface."[27] In this sense, Perovskaya is the feminine incarnation of an abstraction. Not only is she the embodiment of the movement, but of Movement, of the ceaselessly doing Deed ("she was always endeavoring, therefore to enlarge [her activity] by finding fresh channels and means of activity, and consequently became even an initiator of fresh undertakings"[28]).

Finally, of course, Perovskaya is not only a saint, but like Osinsky, a deity—this time in the Christian tradition. Perovskaya's apotheosis comes unexpectedly by the back door, in a homely fashion that serves simultaneously as the celebrity profiler's eleventh-hour peep-hole into an almost inaccessible interior. For the hanging of the regicides, Kravchinsky becomes a strict documentarian and cites the account published in the *Kölnische Zeitung* of April 16, 1881. "Kibalcic [sic] and Geliaboff [sic] were very calm, Timothy Micailoff [sic] was pale, but firm, Rissakoff [sic] was liver-colored. Sophia Perovskaya displayed extraordinary moral strength. Her cheeks preserved their rosy colour, while her face, always serious, without the slightest trace of parade, was full of true courage and endless abnegation. Her look was calm and peaceful; not the slightest sign of ostentation could be discerned in it."[29] The close reading of the condemned's physiognomy just prior to execution is a long tradition, as is the apotheosis on the scaffold. Kravchinsky foregoes the latter in order to broadcast Perovskaya's voice from beyond the grave, by means of a personal letter written by Perovskaya to her mother a few days before her death, but conveyed to Kravchinsky by her friends "after [the profile] had already gone to press."

The letter therefore has the whiff of a scoop, but instead of revealing a scandalous love affair (the bread and butter of celebrity lives), it declares Perovskaya's most intimate feelings of love and devotion toward her mother. At the same time, it enables Kravchinsky to use the relationship of mother and daughter to inscribe Perovskaya in Christianity's master plot. By indignantly chronicling Madame Perovskaya's thwarted attempts to see her daughter prior to her execution, and telling the intervening story through documents, Kravchinsky composes a passion narrative grounded in the emotional connection between mother and daughter, but especially in their mutual witness of and compassion for each other's suffering. Perovskaya, whose "stoicism and apparent coldness" Kravchinsky could not help remarking upon, expresses profound tenderness, solicitude, and guilt for the pain she has caused her mother. "I await my fate, therefore, with a tranquil conscience, whatever it may be. The only thing which oppresses me is the thought of your grief, oh, my adored mother! It is that which rends my heart; and what would I not give to be able to alleviate it?"[30]

Kravchinsky's profile of Perovskaya, the Deed incarnate, ends on some of the very few words of hers preserved for posterity. Without these words, Perovskaya's death on the scaffold, witnessed by her grieving mother, would have been strictly *in imitatio*—with Perovskaya as Christ and her mother as Mary. Instead, the self-transcendence evinced in Perovskaya's letter allows Kravchinsky to merge the Christ with the Marian figure, as had Alexandrov in Zasulich's case, so that the suffering Perovskaya experiences is not her own ("My fate is not such a sad one after all") but is wholly identified with the mother who must bear witness to the suffering.

In a vaguely self-congratulatory vein, Kravchinsky subsequently described the approach that had ensured the success of his *Profiles* in achieving their purpose. "Therefore in my first book [*Underground Russia*] I completely avoided apologetics on anything or anybody.... I even tried to show my own sympathy with them as little as possible in order to give the book the character of impartiality. When I read it in English—I myself was astonished. I simply tell the reader: look, and see and judge for yourself—I don't want to force any conclusion on you. This is the best way—in fact the only way of making someone believe what you want him to.... The reviews of the reactionary *Saturday Review* and several German journals testify to the fact that I have achieved my aims to a significant degree."[31] It is, I think, no coincidence that Kravchinsky rendered "look and see" according to the ecclesiastical formulation *"smotri i vizhd."* Among the primary justifications for the use of icons by the iconodules was the Aristotelian epistemology in which knowledge is dependent upon and indeed founded in sense perception, with sight awarded pride of place. As he had described it to his wife, his intention from the beginning had been "to give the characteristics of the movement in faces and images."[32] While his comrades in fact spotted and criticized his iconodule tendencies, his profiles succeeded so splendidly with an international public because he catered to more modern sensibilities by employing devices from the celebrity profile that offered the semblance of authenticity, intimacy, and aura. Most importantly, the profile, with the intense focus on the Doer, managed to side-step the Deed, so that in the end, the most salient Deed was *to appear*—beautifully—and to die.

4

Terror in Search of a Face

"You are queer people, Messrs. Russian artists. Charlotte Corday! Don't you have enough of your own? What do you have to do with Charlotte?"[1] In Vsevolod Garshin's 1885 novella *Nadezhda Nikolaevna*, the writer Bezsonov uses this purely rhetorical question to vent his pique at his artist friend Lopatin. In fact, it was absolutely clear to Bezsonov, as it was to Garshin's contemporary readers, what "Charlotte" had to do with it.

In 1884, three years after members of the People's Will hunted down Tsar Alexander II and were themselves publicly executed, Garshin sought to render terror's most obscure aspect: its face. This obscurity was no accident, for both sides—the government and the revolutionaries—had a vested interest in keeping terror's face veiled. The paradoxical hallmark of modern terrorism was its invisibility. Invisibility was terrorism's primary tactical advantage, as well as its affective mechanism for creating fear. Arm-in-arm with invisibility, anonymity likewise served tactical aims (concealment of identity protected comrades still at large). The government, by contrast, was keen to publicize the name, age, place of residence, and estate of all apprehended terrorism suspects, but otherwise assiduously repressed all information, personal effects, contact with, and images. A long tradition dating back at least to the Decembrists testifies to the tsarist government's clear understanding that one man's portrait of a terrorist is another man's icon of a freedom fighter.[2]

This being the case, revolutionary portraiture in Russia was strictly verboten. Unlike Charlotte Corday, the five condemned regicides of the People's Will did not have the luxury of sitting for their portraits in the interval between their trial and execution.[3] In fact, the haste and secrecy with which the trial was conducted and the strict sequester of the prisoners until their public execution served the government's aim of invisibility, even while it spawned rumors that the prisoners spent their last days under torture.[4] On the scaffold at Semyonovsky Square, the individual identities of the regicides were amalgamated in their collective branding as "regicides," and the identical black cowls they were made to wear. After the debacle of their hanging, the bodies were placed in coffins and transported to the prisoners' burial ground in Preobrazhensky Cemetery. Whether they were buried individually or in a collective grave remains unknown.[5]

Revolutionary publicists were therefore charged with countering this erasure, but Kravchinsky's profiles were not published legally in Russia until 1905. Meanwhile, visual artists and writers had to proceed almost exclusively through the circumlocution of allegory. From fall 1883 to winter 1884, for example, the artist Ilya Repin worked on three paintings: *Ivan the Terrible and his Son Ivan, November 16, 1581*; *They did Not Expect Him* (Ne zhdali), and his second portrait of Vsevolod Garshin.[6] The first two presented difficulties throughout their execution and exhibition, while the portrait came easily, because its sitter's face, with its "dove-like purity," was so congenial to the artist.

The experience of sitting for Repin and their conversations together served Garshin as the inspiration for his story long since underway, but stalled: a tragic love triangle.[7] But the story would now add a layer about the painting of a historical portrait. The dilemma that sets the story in motion came directly from Repin's artistic practice: he required a model who embodied his vision, or else he could not realize it. A key instance involved Garshin himself: Repin's preliminary sketches of *Ivan the Terrible* emphasized violence and mayhem, but Garshin altered the picture in a fundamental way. His beatific face as the face of the murdered tsarevich made it possible for contemporary (re)viewers to interpret the painting as portraying "forgiveness and reconciliation."[8] In response to public outcry and critical attacks, Alexei Suvorin waxed rhapsodic over the picture's expressiveness, praising its ability to "terrify and evoke pity—the murderer terrifies us, while the victim evokes pity, touching us to the point of pain."[9] Clearly, a face can and must change a picture, as an element of that picture, but is a face alone itself a picture, an image, with the intrinsic symbolic efficacy? More specifically, can a face launch, rather than a thousand ships, a terroristic revolution? The procurator of the Holy Synod, Konstantin Pobedonostsev, apparently thought so, for he banned the exhibition of *Ivan the Terrible* in Moscow for its obscenity as well as its ostensible irrelevance, and anticipating Bezsonov's objection peevishly queried, "What's the point of Ivan the Terrible here? . . . One can't call this historical painting, since this moment and the entire setting is entirely fantastical, rather than historical."[10]

Pobedonostsev was correct in perceiving that the painting was not strictly historical, but it was only as "fantastical" as present day reality. To its contemporary viewers, *Ivan the Terrible* was too clearly an allegory for state and revolutionary terrorism, for the murder of restive sons by repressive fathers.[11] In the same way, in Garshin's novella *Nadezhda Nikolaevna* the artist Lopatin envisions his Charlotte Corday through a lens tinted by contemporary Russian political violence as "standing directly in front of the viewer, with her eyes directed in front of her; she has already decided on her heroic deed-crime [podvig-prestuplenie], and it's written only on her face; the arm that will inflict the fatal wound for the time being hangs inertly and is tenderly distinguished by its whiteness against the dark-blue cloth dress; a lace shawl, tied across, sets off her tender neck, along which a bloody line will pass tomorrow."[12] The image, he claims, "was created in his soul" when he read Corday's story in "one sentimental and perhaps deceitful history by Lamartine; from the lying pathos of the babbling and grandiloquent Frenchman, there emerged for me clearly and starkly the figure of a girl—a fanatic for good."[13] For the artist, the process of creation is one in which the affected and artificial language of Lamartine is purified in the crucible of his soul, so that the true image is revealed. Lopatin dwells obsessively on this image, observing that "the first painting, like the first love, completely possesses the soul."[14]

All the more bitter is his disappointment when Lopatin finds at his disposal only the wrong face: his model's ordinary Russian face described as "a plump young face, with a slightly upturned nose, good-natured grey eyes, trusting and quite pathetically looking from beneath completely round brows." The wrong face, through no fault of its own, "smashes his dream" and forces an attempt to render the image from his head.[15] Even while Lopatin sees Corday as "if alive," his creative efforts produce "instead of a living face, some kind of scheme. The idea was not realized in flesh and blood."[16]

By contrast, Sergei Vasilevich Bezsonov, Lopatin's writer-friend, is delighted that the project has failed. Not only is he delighted, but he knew it would fail because Lopatin, he avers, is constitutionally unsuited to his subject matter. Bezsonov invokes some sort of biological determinism and insists that Lopatin would have to be a French revolutionary or at the very least, French or a revolutionary ("an inhabitant of those times, a descendant of those people"), but instead he is "the softest Russian intellectual, sluggish and weak." No matter what the provocation, he could not "throw down the paint brush and take up the dagger."[17] Bezsonov's certainty on this point is grounded in the same epistemology as Lopatin's futile quest for Charlotte's face in the flesh and blood. Despite his denial "I don't believe in Lavater," Bezsonov and Lopatin both operate on principles espoused by the mystical Swiss physiognomist Johann Kaspar Lavater (1741–1801). Lavater, of course, *was* a contemporary of Marat and Charlotte Corday, though his physiognomic thought continued to hold sway over visual arts and writers alike into the late nineteenth century even as it was being updated in the researches of Charles Darwin and Cesare Lombroso. His ultimate goal was to crack the moral code of mankind by claiming a correspondence between the material world and the spiritual, according to which facial features were an infallible indicator of moral constitution—material signs of an immaterial, or spiritual, reality. As a pastor, Lavater intended his physiognomy to provide knowledge of one's fellow men, the better to love them. For the purposes of my argument, however, Christopher Rivers's analysis of Lavater's project is most relevant: "Lavater has a very specific reason for believing in the necessity of physiognomy: he believes the corporeal, 'natural' (i.e., God-given) signs must be interpreted so as to transcend the less trustworthy man-made verbal signs. His goal is to create a method of interpreting bodies which will supercede the necessity of interpreting language itself."[18] The physiognomic reading of the face would therefore constitute the gold standard in a world of otherwise ambiguous verbal signs.

His rejection of Lavater notwithstanding, Bezsonov positions Lopatin next to him before a mirror, the better to draw an opposition that is at the forefront of both characters' consciousness. Quoting Shakespeare's *Hamlet*, Bezsonov characterizes the contrast between the two men as "'Hyperion to the goat-legged Satyr.' The goat-legged satyr—that's me. . . . And compare: do you see this here? (he lightly touched his receding hairline). Yes, old fellow, all of that is 'the heat of the soul wasted in the desert!' Yes, and what kind of heat of the soul! Just beastliness."[19] Clearly, Lavater lives. The physiognomic juxtaposition of the two characters completely corresponds to the moral juxtaposition. We, as readers, have also seemingly been given a fool-proof code for deciphering the increasingly convoluted relationships of the novella. Unsurprisingly, such an overt moral juxtaposition must be a source of tension and conflict, as it immediately becomes when Bezsonov lets slip that he knows a dead-ringer for Lopatin's Charlotte Corday, but then willfully refuses to produce her. "I can give her to you or not. I'll act in accordance with my wishes. I don't want to give her to you. I won't give [her]. Dixi."[20]

It's Alive!

Bezsonov does not give "Charlotte" to him, but Lopatin gets her nonetheless, through the intervention of his artist-friend, Gel'freikh, who spots her with Bezsonov in a music hall frequented by the demimonde. The inevitable question—how do both Bezsonov and Gel'freikh know that this is *Lopatin's* Charlotte Corday when they have never seen her?—is explained by the novella's Lavaterian premises. To find your face, you must begin with an interpretation and locate the features that correspond to this interpretation. This tautological procedure is what we might call "profiling."[21] Lopatin of course immediately recognizes *his* Charlotte, but as it turns out, her face belongs to a fallen woman, a prostitute—and not just any prostitute, but rather one with a back-story that Lopatin will spend most of the rest of the novella trying to tease out, but which Garshin's contemporary reader was privileged to know. Nadezhda Nikolaevna was the first-person narrator and protagonist of Garshin's 1878 story "An Incident" (Proisshestvie), which his biographer Peter Henry characterized as Garshin's curious response to the Zasulich affair. Withdrawing from the furor surrounding Zasulich's trial and acquittal, Garshin chose instead to write a "'sentimental and pessimistic story about a fallen woman' hoping thereby to draw attention to the social evil of prostitution."[22] In "An Incident" Nadezhda Nikolaevna, a middle-class, well-educated and proud young woman, refuses out of principle to leave her life of prostitution. She rejects the proposal of a besotted young intellectual who had taken the topos of "the rescue of a fallen woman" too much to heart, realizing that her would-be savior,

Ivan Ivanovich, hadn't the moral strength for the task. Rather than drag them both down, Nadezhda Nikolaevna lets Ivan go and returns to the brothel. In response to her rejection, Ivan Ivanovich shoots himself, and Nadezhda Nikolaevna holds herself responsible for his death: "I killed him."[23]

But was "An Incident" so completely tangential to the Zasulich affair after all, or is the connection between the two only finally drawn out in the story's belated sequel, which bears the name of its eponymous heroine? In the first place, Vera Zasulich, whose shooting of General Fyodor Trepov for the illegal flogging of a political prisoner launched the first wave of systematic terrorism (see Part Three), was frequently compared to Charlotte Corday, and Corday, according to Walter Laqueur, was the first modern terrorist.[24] The resemblance that Garshin wishes to point out between Corday, Zasulich, and Nadezhda Nikolaevna is certainly not one of vocation, but of crime and conscience. Their crimes are precisely crimes of conscience, motivated by conscience, and they are likewise subject to conscience, to the torments of guilt and self-recriminations. "It is hard to raise your hand against your fellow man, but that's what I had to do," testified Zasulich at her trial.

In the second place, Nadezhda Nikolaevna's face is essentially just an *obrazets* (model), not the final product. Over Bezsonov's vociferous objections, Nadezhda Nikolaevna agrees to serve as Lopatin's model (*naturshchitsa*), and as she models for him, he re-forms her. This occurs not through any explicit didactic-moral influence or "sermons read," but through art itself. The moment she dons Charlotte's costume and assumes her pose (both creations of Lopatin), the transformation begins. "She quickly stood at her place, raised her head, dropped her pale arms, and on her face everything was expressed that I had dreamt of for my picture. Decisiveness and longing, pride and terror, love and hate."[25] Lopatin's dichotomous vision is doubly realized: on the canvas and in the flesh. If he is Pygmalion, who is rewarded by Venus when the adored product of his fancy comes to life, he is also Dr. Frankenstein, who must reckon with the monster of his creation. Bringing Charlotte Corday to life in the Russia of Alexander III can only have fatal consequences.

Fatal Triangles

Garshin's earliest conception of his novella was as a "personal story with love affairs and a very bloody dénouement."[26] The personal story with love affairs is that of two men, artists in different media, who fall in love with the living image of Charlotte Corday in Alexander III's Russia. The bloody denouement must necessarily follow as a consequence of bitter sexual rivalry, as an allegory for the fatal political rivalry of reactionary forces (represented by Bezsonov) versus progressive forces (Lopatin and the regenerated Nadezhda Nikolaevna). The most combustible rivalry, however, is not sexual or mimetic in the Girardian sense, but political-artistic. The question of art's responsibility for violence is at the forefront of the novella. Is it the duty of art to raise the question of (political) violence, or does art, by its mimetic power, itself contribute to that very violence in the process?

Although Garshin himself was poised on the cusp of a turn in the literary arts away from social-utilitarian concerns to "art for art's sake" and away from the voluminous forms of the great realist novels to more compact forms such as the prose poem and short story, he remained throughout his career under the sway of "accursed questions" and the authors who asked them. In 1877 Garshin became an instantaneous literary sensation for his anti-war story "Four Days," based on Garshin's own experiences in the Russo-Turkish war. As was true of many radical young men, Garshin's opposition to the regime had been overcome by patriotic appeals and tales of Turkish atrocities. However, battlefield experiences served to quickly disillusion him, and he realized that war induced men to kill each other "blinded by an idea"—in this case, by the nationalist idea.[27]

That an "idea" was likewise at issue in the revolutionary struggle was clear to Garshin, but at the same time he was himself in thrall to this idea, unequivocally supported the cause of social justice, fraternized with radicals, and was duly suspected by the secret police of being a member of the People's Will.[28] On the other hand, Garshin's almost hysterical aversion to bloodshed lent him unusual courage and clarity in attempting to stop the cycle of violence. In February 1879, when the young Polish Jewish student I. O. Mlodetsky attempted to assassinate the newly appointed chairman of the Supreme Administrative Commission, Loris-Melikov, Garshin paid a nighttime visit to Russia's "Dictator with a Heart" and pleaded with him in the following terms to stay Mlodetsky's execution. "Pardon the man who tried to kill You! Thereby You will put to death or rather, I should say, commence the task of putting to death *the idea* that sent him to death and assassination, thereby You will completely kill the moral force of the *men* who put the gun in his hand, the gun that was aimed at your honorable breast yesterday."[29]

As Garshin was convinced that his pleas had saved the life of the would-be assassin, his devastation upon learning that the hanging would proceed contributed to the rapid deterioration of his mental health. March 1, 1881, found him an inmate of the mental institution near his family's estate in Ukraine. After further recuperating on the Black Sea and during a summer idyll in the company of the Polonsky family at Turgenev's estate, Garshin returned to St. Petersburg to resume his place at the center of literary and artistic life.

The point of Lopatin's painting is clear to his artist-friend Gel'freikh, who had exchanged "the accursed questions" for more lucrative work catering to his bourgeois patrons. Despite this, Gel'freikh's view on the social role of art remains unequivocal: "The task of art is to put the question before the viewer."[30] Gel'freikh is effectively Nadezhda Nikolaevna's double: he had "sold out," prostituted his talent, and succumbed to the lures of a dissolute lifestyle. No sooner does Lopatin drag him out of the gutter than he is a convert and conceives of a work even more ambitious than Lopatin's Corday: the *bogatyr* Ilya Muromets, in his underground dungeon, contemplating Christ's injunction to "turn the other cheek." The choice of Muromets as subject effectively Russifies the questions posed by Lopatin's Corday. Muromets is in fact the obrazets for the extraordinary man, the knight errant (Don Quixote) and veteran warrior who defeats the infidel and embraces the Gospels to become a holy man.[31] Gel'freikh imagines him confronted, after a life of retributive violence and an "eye for an eye," with the question of violence, and insists on art's *duty* to do precisely that: "One has to pose it every day, every hour, every moment, so that it doesn't leave people in peace. And if I think that the picture will succeed in prompting one-tenth of its viewers to ask the question, then I should paint it."[32]

The question, then, of art's purpose is resolved unambiguously. But the question of the artist's responsibility for his work's affect and effect is not. Garshin's novella presents itself as the memoir of the artist Lopatin as he lies on his deathbed, and at the beginning of the story, he justifies his change of medium as one prompted by "the familiar pictures and images" that pass before him when he wakes up at night, but most especially by "one pale image, his face flaming and hands clutched ... as on that day, when I stood face to face with my mortal enemy."[33] His mortal enemy, we learn, is Bezsonov, and writing is Bezsonov's medium. Thus the rivalries are thematized from the beginning. Lopatin the artist is an image-maker, and the face-as-image is immediately apprehensible, universally affective and infallible truth. Bezsonov, on the other hand, is a writer, and words are ambiguous, if not downright deceitful, beginning with Lamartine's French prose and ending with Bezsonov's diary entries, interpolated into the novella, which cannot tell the truth even when they try.

What Bezsonov envies most of all and what drives him to distraction is that Nadezhda Nikolaevna is not his regenerated creation, but Lopatin's. ("Oh, can it be that I want to be in Lopatin's place? . . . Step aside? Never! All of my pride rises up in the face of that one assumption. I found her. I could have saved her and didn't want to. Now I want to.") As Bakunin noted, the passion for destruction is a creative passion; thus, the creative outlet remaining to Bezsonov is the destruction of his rival's work.[34] When, in the midst of their mutual confessions of love, Nadezhda Nikolaevna expresses to Lopatin her concern over Bezsonov's strange and threatening behavior, Lopatin dismissively responds, "What does Bezsonov have to do with us?"—only moments before a deranged Bezsonov comes in by the back door.[35] The novella's bloody denouement consists in the violent stand-off between a successful artist who fatally wields a staff (*kop'e*—a handy prop from one of his pictures, and one that Garshin plagiarized from Repin's *Ivan the Terrible*) and a failed writer who has exchanged his pen for a revolver.

Terror in Search of a Face

That said, as a writer Garshin is able to do what a (realist) artist who works in a visual medium, like Repin, is not: to entirely omit the face. Nadezhda Nikolaevna's face is never described. In all the depictions of her, only her expression, her dress, her demeanor are detailed. Garshin withholds the details that Kravchinsky was so avid to obtain ("What is her face like and her eyes and her voice?"). Properly speaking, she has no face (neither is her face described in "An Incident"), nor does Lopatin, a clear heir to Dostoevsky's "perfectly beautiful man," Alyosha Karamazov: only the "wrong" faces are subjected to physiognomic analysis. By contrast, the face of Charlotte, a "fanatic for good," is left to the reader's imagination where presumably it cannot wreak havoc in the real world. Latter-day heirs to the physiognomic tradition, such as Cesare Lombroso, were not as cautious. In his 1892 study *The Political Criminal and the Revolution*, Lombroso produces a tally of "30 famous Nihilists [of whom] 18 present a beautiful face," and he proceeds to list them by name.[36] Lombroso owes his Nihilist profiles, which include physiognomic analysis keyed to a short character sketch, almost verbatim to Kravchinsky's *Underground Russia*. Among the copious materials included in Lombroso's appendix is the first assemblage of photographs of Russian Nihilists, along with other political criminals, published in school yearbook format. Twelve of the Nihilists, Lombroso concedes, possess certain anomalies, but only one has three and only two have "two each of such signs [anomalies which indicate degeneration]."[37]

In other words, the Nihilists, whom Lombroso classifies (along with Charlotte Corday) as "[Political] Criminals from Passion" (Verbrecher aus Leidenschaft) are to be distinguished above all from the depraved, degenerate, and mad. This leads him to cast aspersions on his own project, asserting that to "want to subject them [the Nihilists] to 'the Light of Psychiatry' is akin to wanting to fathom the beautiful lines of the Medici Venus with a compass, while ignoring the sublime purity of the whole art work," and he follows this statement with an apostrophe to said Nihilists: "Oh, you holy ones, you souls devoted to the Idea, forgive us; we feel that the sight of you alone is sufficient to teach humanity to strive for the ideal and to forget the majority of them, for whom crude enjoyment is the only goal; but the researcher has his duties, and after we have offered our wonder and admiration, we must return to the compass."[38]

So while Garshin and Lombroso might share the same epistemology and even join together in wonder and admiration, they do not share the comfort of facile moral categorizations. As an ideal-typical or exemplary face, Charlotte Corday's might serve Russian Nihilist terrorism as well as any. But Garshin himself will give us that face no more than Bezsonov will [give it to] Lopatin. Instead, Garshin insists that the face of terror may be imagined only ever in terms of its moral duality. Nadezhda Nikolaevna's face, we know, expresses this duality, while the characters Lopatin and Bezsonov each embody one aspect of it. In sum, the face of terror must be two-faced (deranged and righteous; reactionary and revolutionary), and its duality will necessarily find reflection in the ambivalence of the viewer. Nothing is more ironic, therefore, than the collector Pavel Mikhailovich Tretiakov's insistence after the purchase of Repin's *They Did Not Expect Him* that the artist repaint the somewhat deranged face of the returning political prisoner so that it resembled Garshin.[39] The face of revolution (terror)—at least for this most successful capitalist thespian—belonged to the writer, Garshin.

To forestall this or a similar eventuality, the image with which Garshin leaves the reader at the end of *Nadezhda Nikolaevna* is not an icon-portrait, but a tableau of devastation on par with Repin's *Ivan the Terrible*. The wounded Lopatin covers the face of his lifeless Corday with desperate kisses, while her murderer lies dead with a "severe and terrifying face" and a head wound gushing blood.[40] By this means, Garshin accomplishes what he had begged Loris-Melikov to do: put to death the idea that obsessed and possessed Russian radicalism, and haunted the artistic intelligentsia. *Contra* Bakunin, the passion for destruction is not creative, but entirely destructive. Violence, even if defensive, is annihilating rather than generative, and in the final days remaining to him on Earth, Lopatin effectively becomes his own vision, the morally righteous but conscience-stricken murderer. Although he is not charged for his crime, which was clearly committed in self-defense, Lopatin arrives at the same place as Dostoevsky's protagonists, accepts his guilt and metes out his own punishment. "For the individual conscience there are no written laws, no insanity pleas, and I will bear the punishment for my crime."

Nadezhda Nikolaevna puts to death one idea—the idea of righteous murder embodied by Corday—but another lives on more vitally than ever. This is the idea of the image as a more affective and therefore effective sign, one that through unmediated mimesis inspires the deed. Most ironically, then, Konstantin Pobedonostsev's sense of the public danger posed by Repin's painting and the government's temporary ban receives support from an unexpected quarter: from the writer Vsevolod Garshin, whose "angelic" face expanded the interpretative possibilities for Repin's painting in the first place. Lopatin's Corday, with her demonstrable ability to wreak havoc beyond the frame, is Pobedonostsev's nightmare. To compound the already compounded ironies, *Nadezhda Nikolaevna*, while valorizing the immediacy and efficacy of the artistic image, is nevertheless a work of literary art. Garshin affirms that the Russian writer has the same artistic responsibility, if not the same direct power, and while words may be implicated in ambiguity and outright duplicity, they also have the capability to render more complex and therefore fundamentally more ambiguous realities, with all their attendant ironies.

Epilogue

"All of Europe Thrills to the Horror"

As the year 1881 dawned, the outlook for Russia—at least to Western observers—was promising, and the London *Times* confidently referred to the country's "much brighter prospects [and] progress towards real liberal reform."[1] By contrast, in Ireland the prospects were increasingly bleak, as the *Pall Mall Gazette* reported "new developments of Fenian terrorism in Dublin" and lamented that "the Chief Secretary cannot walk through the streets of one of the important Irish towns without being accompanied by large armed bodies of police."[2]

The picture was suddenly and radically altered and the *Times*'s rosy optimism dashed on March 13, 1881 (March 1 by the Russian calendar) when, in dirge-like tones, the *Times* announced: "The desperate revolutionists who have so often attempted the life of the Emperor of Russia have at last succeeded in the perpetration of the atrocious crime," and it predicted: "All of Europe will be thrilled with horror at the intelligence of this tragic termination of a career that was full of promise at its commencement."[3] In this case, the *Times* proved correct, and the thrill of horror ran up and down the telegraph wires and was taken up by a Greek chorus of the international press.

"There is no civilized state in either hemisphere which this morning has not been thrilled with horror at the tidings telegraphed from St. Petersburg," echoed the *Pall Mall Gazette* (*PMG*).[4] "No words could be too strong to express the feeling of horror and detestation with which the perpetrators of this crime will be regarded the world over," *The Scotsman* chimed in.[5] It is of course the prerogative of the civilized to "thrill with horror," and this quaint and now necessarily obsolete turn of phrase testifies to a Victorian sensibility steeped in melodrama with its unmistakably Gothic excesses and journalistic sensationalism. In the late nineteenth century it was still possible and admissible—after the surfeit of twentieth-century horrors it no longer was—for the public to thrill to such a "terrible illustration" of the combined power of shadowy conspirators and modern technology to fell the most powerful sovereign on Earth. This was in fact a condition of terrorism's emergence: that it would send a powerful jolt through a restless and sensation-craving mass public.

Thrill aside, the first reports of Tsar Alexander II's assassination were steeped in categorical condemnations of the act and unsparing vilification of its perpetrators.[6] With the details of the assassination as yet unavailable, the press sketched the story of Alexander II's reign, emplotted as Shakespearean tragedy, which had "begun with such high hopes of beneficent reform" and culminated in "profound pathos."[7] The Tsar-Liberator was obviously the "Abraham Lincoln of Russia" but also Russia's "Prince of Denmark"—too soft and indecisive for "times out of joint" that his abolition of the feudal order had ushered in.[8]

The tragedy as evoked in the British press was not Russia's alone but one in which every Western nation and citizen shared. Not only was Alexander II admired as one of Europe's (and indeed, history's) most progressive, humanitarian monarchs, but in 1880–81 imperial rivalries had subsided and relations between nations were characterized by an almost unruffled calm and amicability.[9] Finally, of course, Alexander II was a relation of Queen Victoria: her own flesh and blood had been felled at the same time that the monarchical principle came under renewed and deadly assault. The British would recall the similarly heinous though luckily unsuccessful attempts on their own Queen. These were among the reasons that in the days following the assassination the Western press locked arms in solidarity to mourn the murdered sovereign. The details of lavish funeral and memorial services, with entire imperial families and diplomatic corps present, were reported from St. Petersburg and all the Western capitals; the British court promptly

Epilogue   249

went into one month's mourning; private and state festivities (in Dublin, the St. Patrick's Day Ball) were cancelled; and perhaps most indicative of the somber import of the occasion, the *Times* gave notice "that her Majesty's staghounds will not go out today."[10]

In this otherwise unified outpouring of grief and opprobrium, a few dissenting voices were heard, only to be unceremoniously shushed. Socialists in New York defiantly adopted resolutions "applauding" the assassination, and in Paris the radical papers the *Intransigeant* and the *Citoyen* openly celebrated the assassination as tyrannicide, with the *Intransigeant* declaring "the shell which killed the Czar would do for Russia what the arrow of William Tell did for Switzerland and the scaffold of Charles I and Louis XVI did for England and France."[11] Although France was a republic, four French editors were expeditiously tried on the charge of "approving assassination of the Czar" and sentenced to six months' imprisonment and a fine of 2,000 francs. Radical writers had already honed the art of portraying these acts in terms of something old and venerable—the heroic tradition of tyrannicide—but to observers from both sides of the political spectrum, the phenomenon appeared as something new, or at least as something "newish."

Five days after the tsaricide, on March 18, the *Times* reported an explosion at Mansion House, residence of the Lord Mayor of London, and confessed to a perplexing quandary. "It is hardly possible not to imagine a connexion [sic] between the crime which was perpetrated in St. Petersburg on Sunday and the mysterious explosion at the Mansion House Wednesday night. The connexion, however, if it exists at all must be a very remote one."[12] The explosion did remarkably little damage, and the origins of the explosives as well as the identity and motive of the perpetrator remained unknown, and yet a "connexion" had to exist and did in fact exist—and not merely a remote one. The "connexion" was in the mind of the commentator and in the birth of a new discourse—terrorism discourse—which inevitably and helplessly linked the two events while acknowledging that there was no actual basis (common identity or unity of purpose) for such a linkage. Yet the positing of such a "connexion" gave this commentator precocious insight into the phenomenon by allowing him to conclude that whoever the perpetrator and whatever the motive, the political effect "is to create the general feeling of terrorism." Whether terrorism may be a successful political tactic, either in Britain or in Russia, the author remained undecided, though he observed that "it cannot be doubted that the Fenian scare, though it never amounted to anything like a terror, indirectly produced important political results." What is certain, concludes the author of this highly contradictory but insightful commentary, is that "Science has lately put very powerful weapons into the hands of the secret foes of society and it is only common experience that such a crime as that of Sunday should find its clumsy imitators among the reckless conspirators and crazy fanatics always to be found in every large population."[13]

"The Fenian scare," like Nihilist plots in Russia, was duly reported in the British press, as noted above, just weeks prior to the assassination of Alexander II. But when "such a crime as that of Sunday" made its meteoric impact on international discourse, it provided the basis for a "connexion," to say nothing of inspiration for imitators, whether clumsy or adept. March 1/13, 1881, did not represent something entirely new but it did constitute a watershed in the international perception and reception of terrorism comparable to that of the September 11, 2001, attacks. While terrorism certainly existed before, both in word and deed, only now had terrorism discourse *begun* to coalesce in the West around its object. Now, regardless of the species (Fenian, anarchist, Nihilist) the genus was understood to be the same: terrorism. Contemporary observers detected this new *transnational* trend, conceding that terrorism and political assassination were "for the moment, in vogue, every country has its share"[14] and that it constituted a "peculiar peril of the age," one "to some extent new in form," though historically conscious authors found parallels even in the sixteenth and seventeenth centuries.[15]

Yet Russian Nihilism especially presented a striking case of the "new and the strange," and it was the "shock of the Czar's murder which ... has warned all civilized nations of the violent and destructive impulses that slumber" and thereby awakened the world to the reality of terrorism.[16] What was it about Russian Nihilist terrorism that made it stand out as new and strange, or was it merely that Russia itself was known to the Western reader principally in its role as a rival imperial power, but on its own terms was substantially "new and strange"—uncharted territory? For Nihilism to be comprehensible, Russia had to be explained, and before the era of degree-holding regional experts, foreign correspondents and retired diplomats did duty as area studies specialists.

For the month between the assassination of the tsar and the trial and execution of his murderers, the narrative of "tragedy," while embellished with forensic details, factual and fantastical (and equally fantastical rumors of further plots) held sway. Because the Russian government made it a point of pride to stage—"stage" being the operative word—fair and open proceedings, the defendants were allowed some limited opportunity to account for their actions. This gave the press and the reading public the chance to replace clichéd caricatures with more life-like portraits, as in the case of the workingman Timofei Mikhailoff [sic], whose testimony at trial appeared to the *Times* unimpeachable. "[He did] no more than allege the facts which have long been known to all who have observed the condition of the Russian people." The regicides so impressed with their dedication and courage, that on April 11, the *PMG* could no longer contain its admiration—"They evidently went into their enterprise with the intrepidity of soldiers who volunteer for a forlorn hope, and to judge from the reports of their demeanour during the trial, they show no signs of flinching before the penalty that awaits them"—evidently providing the source for Karl Marx's paean in his letter to Jenny of the same day (quoted in the introduction).[17]

Once the imperative to condemn and excoriate had passed, as it did when the assassins were tried and publicly executed, more nuanced narratives and ambivalent images made their appearance. Things went so far that on June 16 the *PMG* ran an article under the headline "Russian Revolutionary Heroines" that began with the claim that Slavic women's brains were larger than that of Slavic men's, a fact that explained the reversal of gender characteristics and roles among them. This accounted for the prominence of women in the Russian revolutionary movement and for the notorious "Russian Charlotte Cordays"—Sophie Bardin, Sophie Peroffski [sic], and Vera Sassulitch [sic]—who were heralded as "popular heroines" and "ruthless . . . destroying angels" whom they exhorted to "keep up the Red Terror in Russia."[18]

A core delusion of modernity is the belief at every juncture that the latest pestilence is something new and never seen before. Journalistic impulsiveness—the race to report before all facts are known—is often laid at the door of the 24-hour news cycle, the insomniac blogosphere, and manic tweetboards, when in fact the nineteenth-century press exhibited precisely the same market-driven compulsion to race to conclusions and explanations. Immediately following the assassination, in the absence of further detail, the European press sought to clarify Nihilism's nature and explain to its readers "whence come these unwearied plotters." With few other resources as rich in insight, they understandably turned to literature, first to exotic and rather poorly known Russian authors. "Nihilism is not one but many things: revolt against the weary monotonousness of Russian life—the revulsion against the ennui which an accurate novelist such as Jaroueneff [sic; badly mangled spelling of Turgenev?] and a true poet such as Pouchkine [sic] paint as characteristic of the countryman's lot."[19] And then to those comfortably within their own wheelhouse: "One might also term it Byronism or Wertherism applied to politics, for it often has its roots in sentimentalism, in egotistical discontent, and the vagaries of vanity."[20]

Two days after the assassination, the *Times* proffered literature as a complete and closed loop of an explanation: Russian life is boring and inspires revulsion (as the accurate novelist and true poet show)—hence Russians feel the necessity of escaping into European literature. According to the commentator, here is where the mistake lies: Nihilism derives from the application of imaginative literature (the sentimental Werther, the Romantic Byron)—instead of the sober political economy of Smith or Mill—to politics. This explanation comes within the broader context of Russia's delayed and uneven development, which begs the key question of Russia's imitativeness or originality and hence of terrorism's newness. That Russia's development was delayed was uncontroversial: "The people labor under the disadvantage of having come late into the race of civilization." So was the conclusion that this delay had caused an unbridgeable rift between the "conservatism of the moujik [sic]" and the radicalism of "a few" who ransack the bookstalls brimming with foreign translations. These sundry foreign translations inspire their untutored Russian readers to throw off all "prejudices" except one: "the belief that the Czar, so he is the nominal, so he is also the real head of the Government of the country, and that a blow struck at the Imperial person may redress some of the evils which this Government is the means of inflicting upon the people."[21] Thus European "theory" unites with an intransigent belief in the omnipotence of the tsar, and voilà—"The Russian Method."

Most contemporary commentators found themselves in agreement on this apparent paradox: that Nihilism was derivative and imitative of European ideas and theories, but original and distinctive in practice. Its originality, for the majority, derived from the purely negative features of Russian life and the national character. "Russian nihilistic terrorists have, it is true, grown up on Russian soil and distinguish themselves by an Asiatic barbarity and savage strength."[22] "Revolution in Russia means at once a great deal more and a great deal less than it does in other parts of Europe. Its destructive impulse is more determined, its constructive aptitude is less articulately developed."[23]

Aside from Russian and European literature, the French historian Anatole Leroy-Beaulieu's very timely publication *L'Empire des Tsars et les Russes*, the first volume of a multi-volume work, was one of the pioneering studies to offer indispensable insight into the phenomenon of Nihilism, which it loses no time in addressing. Russia found one of its most perceptive and sympathetic foreign observers in Beaulieu, for while he was both clear and far-sighted in his analysis of its shortcomings, he did not stint in portraying its charms. Less generous commentators denied Russia any originality whatsoever, but Beaulieu perceived that "this newcomer among nations already manifested an original genius in all branches of human activity—in arts, in science, in letters."[24] Far from the portrait of a servile imitator of the West, Beaulieu portrayed an ambitious and reckless upstart who "takes pride in overdoing things, and pride in overleaping the West, in revolutionary as in other matters."[25]

Nihilism was symptomatic of this paradoxical reaction *against* Western civilization and the desire to overleap it in one bound. In what sounds like a thumbnail sketch of Dostoevsky's Raskolnikov, Beaulieu describes Nihilism as a "disease of childhood" that combined avid questioning with daring speculation, and the "scorn of others' solutions with secret conceit."[26] Likewise, the individual Nihilist of both sexes combined contradictory and extreme qualities, "pledging to nefarious doctrines the loftiest, most generous capabilities of the heart."[27] For this reason, Russian Nihilism/terrorism was anything but an imitation. The undeniably awe-inspiring qualities of its adherents ("the power of logic as to intellect, a force of will as to character, a capacity for passion, for fanaticism, stubbornness and self-devotion") were "to Europe a veritable revelation."[28]

After March 1/13, 1881, "terrorism" began to take shape as a single unified concept that encompassed the Nihilists, the Fenians, the Land League, and later, the Continental anarchists. However, not all terrorists/terrorisms were created equal, and a double standard was applied to Nihilist terrorism and Fenian terrorism, so that Fenian terrorism, even at its most spectacular, was belittled as a mere "scare" or tarred with the brush of moral indignation as an "outrage." Following the incident at Mansion House in January that may or may not have been a case of "Fenian vindictiveness," an explosion in Liverpool on July 26 was characterized as a "rough reminder of the present state Ireland," and no less a reminder that a war, no matter how distant, could be brought home to roost.[29] The Fenians, however, were not seen as national liberation fighters à la Garibaldi and Mazzini, or as Nihilist terrorists arrayed in desperate courage against a despotic regime. They were portrayed as low-class, low-brow, mercenary ruffians and puppets of the Irish party in the United States. If the Nihilists were characterized by a restless and extreme intellect and an excess of imagination (fueled by literature), the Fenians were reduced to remote-controlled limbs ("the hands") while the heads in America were "the stringpullers of conspiracy."[30] By these lights, the blockheaded Fenians appealed to and attracted the support of their like, the English lower classes. The workman's clubs were regarded as dens of Fenian dynamitards, and the saying "every can of dynamite helps on the cause" was held to be popular with the workingmen.[31] The Land League, although opposed to the Fenians in its methods and goals, suffered the same stigma, if not worse. Land League protest in the Irish countryside was decried as government by lawlessness or mob rule through violence, while British soldier and constables were portrayed as the merely passive and helpless victims of violence.[32]

Nothing better illustrates this double standard than the most innovative terrorist attack of the decade. The orchestrated simultaneous explosions on January 25, 1885, at the Houses of Parliament, the Tower of London, and Westminster Abbey in London elicited the most ferocious invective from the *Times*, though the *PMG* drily regarded these events as nothing but "The Scare."[33] Indeed, despite the force of the explosions, no one was killed, only a dozen were slightly injured, and the material damage to such stalwart monuments as the Tower was negligible. When the *PMG* featured side-by-side "Interviews with a Nihilist and a Fenian" the day after the attack, the Nihilist, Sergei Stepniak-Kravchinsky (see Part Four), got top billing and simply scoffed at the attack. "Mere baby work... any child could do as much. Stupid, objectless, directed against no particular individual, furthering no great cause. Besides, what is the result?" Not only was this "mild attack of terrorism" scarcely worth the name, but Stepniak insisted, "the Russian Nihilist is quite a different person from the American-Irish dynamitard."[34]

The *Times* concurred with Stepniak on key points but refused to see the attacks as innocuous "baby work"; instead they were far more heinous than anything yet conceived or executed by Nihilists or anarchists, who, the *Times* averred

> compassed the assassination of a Sovereign or a Minister.... [B]ut such designs are at least intelligible; they go straight to their mark, and they

are subject to limits of their own. The Irish-American "dynamite fiend" chooses, by preference, for the scene of his operations the crowds of the labouring classes, of holiday makers, of ordinary travelers, and sweeps them at random into the meshes of his murderous plot with as little concern for their personal merits or demerits as the Thug feels for the victims of his deadly cult. In war the slaughter of non-combatants has always been looked upon as the blackest barbarism, but the worst acts of mediaeval tyrants and of savage tribes have now been surpassed by the blind, though calculating, malignity of men domiciled as citizens of the most progressive country of the modern world.[35]

Strong language that—considering that the upholstery on benches in the House of Commons was the chief casualty in the attack. But the *Times* saw beyond the damage that was done and pointed to the damage that might have been done under less fortuitous circumstances. Like Dostoevsky's Raskolnikov (see Part I), in the sorry spectacle of a crime that missed its mark the *Times* grasped the distinction between violence that observes certain norms and the unbridled slaughter of innocents.

The *Times* visions of apocalyptic destruction were not idle, but were strategically intended to goad the United States to take some action against "the murderous gang of Irish desperadoes who make their living in New York and elsewhere by a profession of terrorism."[36] An international discourse of counterterrorism was integral and in fact indispensable to the historical emergence of terrorism. In the wake of March 1/13, the Russian government spearheaded the effort to have the violence of secret societies of whatever stripe recognized as of the same stripe—in other words, as "terrorism." Nihilist violence was not merely a domestic problem—not age-old sedition (kramola) in a new bottle—but a new international menace. To that end, the Russian government sought to form a coalition of Western powers that would entail cooperative international police work and extradition treaties.[37] While Chancellor Bismarck of Germany welcomed the Russian initiatives, Great Britain and especially the United States regarded them with no little skepticism, if not downright suspicion, and condescension that is deeply ironic in light of twenty-first-century Russian-U.S. cooperation in the War on Terror. "When Russia has reached approximately our level of culture and progress, we may consider her offer of an alliance, offensive and defensive, against revolutionary forces such as Nihilism. . . . But when that period arrives, Russia, like England at present day, will not require such an alliance."[38]

While Russian overtures were consistently rebuffed, as Irish troubles mounted so did the parallels between the British struggle with Fenianism and the Russian struggle with Nihilism. Ten days prior to the "day of dynamite," the *PMG* hosted one of its most rapier-tongued commentators on Russian affairs, Madame Olga de Novikoff (Novikova), on its front pages, under the provocative headline "The Russianization of England." In this case the British were imitative of the Russians, but in the direction of autocracy rather than of revolution. Novikova, who was one of the most scintillating salon hostesses in London, a close correspondent of Prime Minister Gladstone himself, and also a contributor to Mikhail Katkov's conservative daily, *The Moscow Gazette,* exposed the recent hypocrisy of British public opinion and officialdom vis-à-vis Russia. "It was not long ago, however, that supreme disdain was displayed whenever Russian dynamitards were discussed. We Russians were dogmatically advised to listen to the voice of such men as Kropotkin and Stepniak. 'Only tyranny,' exclaimed some uninvited judges, 'could breed Nihilism.' . . . But now you almost all talk and write like sensible Russians. The moral efficacy of dynamite," observed de Novikoff with biting sarcasm, "must really be great."[39]

De Novikoff concluded by noting that "theoretically, England's policy in Ireland is Russian"—and England would be more successful in dealing with Ireland if it adopted Russia's policy in practice, as well. We should not mistake the liberal *PMG's* editorial line or the layers of irony in printing de Novikoff's editorial. While as a member of the court, a Pan-Slav, anti-Semite, and possible Okhrana agent, de Novikoff was a serious (though thoroughly sarcastic) apologist for the tsarist government. *PMG* used her commentary to show up England's repressive Irish policy, particularly the notorious Coercion Law. While the right of asylum was a pillar of British national pride and identity, the United States was consistently cited as the ultimate impediment to any type of international cooperation on the counterterrorism front. If terrorism was imitable, so in fact was counterterrorism, although it wasn't until the twenty-first century that the Western powers belatedly embraced Russia's suggestions (but needless to say without acknowledging the intellectual debt).

Nihilism did not lose its luster or fascination for the West any time soon. Before and more especially after Vera Zasulich's dramatic acquittal in March 1878, European writers and artists themselves took up the Nihilists, usually for the sensation and melodrama of the subject matter, but also out of political conviction. The precocious young Oscar Wilde made his debut as a playwright with the ill-fated *Vera; or the Nihilists*, which was inspired by Vera Zasulich's attempt, though it demonstrated complete unconcern with the facts. In Wilde's melodrama, the beautiful Vera's band of Nihilists succeeds in assassinating the tsar and plots an attempt on the heir-to-the throne (who was in fact an incognito member of their conspiracy and Vera's lover). This second attempt is foiled at the last minute by Vera herself, who sees in her beloved Russia's only hope for salvation and kills herself instead of him to appease the notorious Nihilist bloodlust. Nonetheless, because the New York premiere of *Vera* awkwardly coincided with the actual assassination of the tsar, propriety demanded that it be cancelled.[40]

The French were even more fascinated by and sympathetic to the Nihilists than the Anglo-Americans. If one were not content to simply read about Nihilists, as in the feminist travel writer Olympe Audouard's fictional tale of star-crossed lovers (a Nihilist and the daughter of the chief of the secret police),[41] then one could experience the sensation of almost being among them, at the latest Paris novelty, the newly opened Musée Grévin. According to the museum's founder, since "written reporting [had] not entirely satisfied the Parisians," the Grévin aspired to "create what we call a 'living newspaper'"—albeit in the medium of wax.[42] The Grévin was trumpeted as a "pantheon of the moment" with its exhibits changing as swiftly as the headlines, and when it opened in June 1882, its first big hit was "Histoire d'un crime" in seven tableaux, but also the critically acclaimed "Arrest of the Russian Nihilists."[43] The latter work bears an unmistakable resemblance to Ilya Repin's "Arrest of the Propagandist," and the mutual influence of painting and tableau certainly suggests itself (Repin worked on the painting from 1880–89, during which time he made multiple trips to Paris). The Grévin's striking "Arrest" was praised by reviewers for its genuine authenticity. "Not a detail is missing, the icons, papers, cartons, thick newspapers," all of which had been imported from Russia, and were not, as in the inferior tableau in the President's library, mere facsimiles or wax "doubles."[44] Needless to say, the Nihilists themselves were.

But if wax failed to satisfy, as it surely must, then the possibility of travel to Russia beckoned. An entire fleet of journalists and curiosity seekers set sail for Russia in the decade after the regicide and subsequently dedicated their impressions to paper and publisher. Perhaps counterintuitively, Nihilist terrorism proved something of a tourist attraction: there was always the rather remote possibility that a Nihilist bombing might occur somewhere en route (the People's Will had placed a mine beneath the tracks on the Odessa-Moscow line in 1879). Add to this the obligatory but necessarily discreet visit to a Nihilist "den," as well as the off chance that one was being shadowed by police detectives.... But this made travelling in Russia all the more piquant.[45] Less adventurous souls might prefer the role of armchair tourist and simply read avowals such as the one by William Eleroy Curtis of the *Chicago Daily News*, who travelled to Russia with his wife in June 1887 in order to portray "The Nihilist at Home." "When I went to Russia I supposed that Nihilism was something like political hysterics, the result of national indigestion, like the anarchist outbreaks in Chicago. The trouble in this country [the United States] is that we have swallowed too much uncooked food, admitted too many half-baked citizens to our body politic; but in Russia the conditions are different. Even the casual visitor feels like entering some sort of a protest against the despotic restrictions he feels there.... And when he gets out he invariably confesses that he would be a Nihilist himself if he were compelled to spend his life in such an atmosphere."[46] Curtis's comments reflect the universal conservative conviction, shared by Katkov, *The Times*, and (in his later years) Dostoevsky, that homegrown radicals must in fact be foreign-born or foreign influenced ("half-baked citizens"). From the Western point of view, however, an exception must be made in Russia's case: Russia would turn the most well-baked citizen into a murderous rebel. Disappointingly, but rather predictably, Curtis found no Nihilists "at home": they were either in Siberian exile, European emigration, or dead, so he and the reader had to rest content with the recycled "portraits and sketches" already familiar from Stepniak's *Underground Russia*, in addition to some very dubious illustrations, including one of a sumptuously coiffed Sophia Perovskaya (bearing absolutely no resemblance, but at least the transliteration is correct), and the illustration of a bearded and venerable old peasant bearing the caption "After Ten Years Exile," but resembling no one so much as the celebrated author, Turgenev.

In 1886 the French Orientalist Eugène-Melchior de Vogüé inaugurated Russian literary studies with the first volume in a Western language on *Le Roman Russse* (translated as *The Russian Novelists*) including the little-known Leo Tolstoy and Fyodor Dostoevsky. His entrée to his subject was of course through Russian Nihilism, which he considered partly the product of the Slavonic mind's hereditary disposition to the negative, and partly "a peculiar state of discouragement" to which all the accidents of Russian history had contributed.[47] While Turgenev was given credit for coining the term Nihilist and creating its first exemplar, Bazarov, to the then almost unknown (in the West) Dostoevsky went the honor of penetrating its most extreme manifestations.[48] De Vogüé praises *Crime and Punishment* as Dostoevsky's most perfectly realized novel and dubs Raskolnikov a Nihilist "in the true sense of the word," but he expresses misgivings about the novel's strong effect that echoes contemporaries' reactions. "The curious of a certain type will find in this book the entertaining mode of torture which is to their taste; but I think it will terrify the greater number of readers. . . . The writer's graphic scenes of terror are too much for a nervous organization."[49] The power of the novel to spawn real-life effects was clear, as de Vogüé attested: "Its appearance was the great literary event of the year 1866. All Russia was made ill by it, so to speak. When the book first appeared, a Moscow student murdered a pawn broker in almost precisely the way described by the novelist; and I firmly believe that many subsequent attempts, analogous to this, may have been attributable to the influence of this book. Dostoevsky's intention, of course was undoubtedly to dissuade men from such acts by representing their terrible consequences, but he did not foresee that the intensity of his portrayals might act in an opposite sense, and tempt the demon of imitation existing in a certain type of brain."[50] In the same way, *Demons* (Les Possédés) is a prophecy and an explanation. De Vogüé, who as secretary to the French embassy in St. Petersburg attended the Nihilist trials in 1871 of the Nechaevtsy, insists that many of the defendants and the conspiracies brought to trial were "exact reproductions" of those portrayed in Dostoevsky's novels. But more significantly, the novel provided an explanation of the problem "which is even to-day imperfectly understood, because its solution is sought only in politics."[51]

De Vogüé was a personal acquaintance of Dostoevsky in the last three years of the author's life and was no less fascinated with and ambivalent about the man than he was about his novels. His characterization of Dostoevsky as "a phenomenon of another world, an abnormal and mighty monster, quite unique as to originality and intensity" was an extremely backhanded compliment that recalls the Marquis de Custine's portrait of Russia itself.[52] De Vogüé does not explicitly draw parallels between Dostoevsky and the phenomenon (Nihilist terrorism) that his work so singularly elucidated. It is possible that when de Vogüé recalled Dostoevsky's "fiery indignation" at European society and at the city of Paris in particular that he failed to notice in the venerated author's tirade an alarmingly familiar note. "I remember the very words—'Some night a prophet will appear in the Café Anglais! He will write on the wall the three words of fire; that will be the signal for the end of the old world, and Paris will be destroyed in fire and blood, in all its pride, with its theaters and its 'Café Anglais.'" De Vogüé only wondered why this Russian "seer" had wrathfully called destruction down on the entirely inoffensive (in his opinion) "Café Anglais."[53] He needed only to ask Émile Henry, the anarchist terrorist who in Paris on February 12, 1893, lit a fuse with his cigar and threw a bomb into the door of the Café Terminus, or the members of ISIL who orchestrated the November 2015 attacks.[54]

His acquaintance with Russia was long and deep enough for de Vogüé to realize that Dostoevsky died just in time. Not only did he die barely a month shy of the regicide, but he died before the regime realized how "dangerous" this unimpeachable monarchist was, which became plainly evident only on the occasion of his death. In recounting the great author's wake and funeral, de Vogüé revisits the poles of Dostoevsky's vision of mass terror on the one hand and universal harmony on the other. The first scene, although under entirely different circumstances, reprises the governor's ill-fated ball in *Demons* (see Part II). At Dostoevsky's wake, which took place in the family's apartment, de Vogüé recalls, "the temperature of the room became suffocating," and "suddenly the air seemed to be exhausted, all the candles went out, and only the little flickering lamp before the holy images remained. Just in this moment, in the darkness, there was a terrible rush from the staircase, bringing a new influx of people . . . the first comers were hurled against the coffin, which tottered—the poor widow, crowded, with her two children, between the table and the wall, threw herself over the body of her husband, and held it, screaming with terror."[55] In this case, the "blast" is caused neither by fires nor bombs, but by an explosion of Dostoevsky's bereaved fans into the room. However traumatic the event for the mourners and especially for Dostoevsky's widow, de Vogüé speculates that the author himself would have "appreciated just such exaggerated homage."[56]

Even more so, the crowd of 100,000 that gathered from early morning on the day of Dostoevsky's funeral did not bode well for the authorities in a time of Loris-Melikov's precarious "Dictatorship of the Heart," when "the most trifling incident might produce an explosion."[57] Instead, the apprehension of mass disturbances or terrorist acts by the People's

Epilogue

Will turned out to be unfounded, and the scene of Dostoevsky's funeral was one of unprecedented social harmony, as members of all social classes and groups, or as it seemed to de Vogüé—all of Dostoevsky's creations—were united around the great author's dead body, just as they were around Ilyusha's at Alyosha's speech at the stone (see Part Three). "Through one of those unexpected combinations, of which Russia alone possesses the secret, all parties, all adversaries, all the disjointed fragments of the empire now came together, through the death of this man, in a general communion of grief and enthusiasm."[58] De Vogüé refused to pronounce definitively upon Dostoevsky's literary merit or his moral effect. While acknowledging that Dostoevsky was the soul of sympathy and sympathized with the common people as well as aroused sympathy in them, it was at an inordinately high price: "what excessive ideas and moral convulsions he engendered!"[59] Leroy-Beaulieu, by contrast, understood Russia's aspirations to greatness and the widely divergent means entertained to achieve this end. "Too many Russians await their country's grand future as a thing that *must* come on its appointed day as a fruit ripening on a tree. Too many others, scorning the possible, rail at the liberties which the West offers them as models... while the impatient, fancying that they can revolutionize the country with one wave of their magic wand, do not scruple to have recourse to the maddest, most odious machinations."[60] For Beaulieu the realization of Russian aspirations was no fantasy, but a very real possibility and even a certainty. "The Russian mind," he avowed, "does not shrink from daring initiatives, even risky ones. From that side, to which we do not much look for examples, we shall some day receive more than one lesson."[61]

Notes

Introduction

1. Fedor Dostoevskii, *Polnoe sobranie sochinenii v tridtsati tomakh* (henceforward *PSS*), 25:202; Fyodor Dostoevsky, *A Writer's Diary*, 2:1072.

2. Karl Marx, letter dated April 11, 1881. Quoted in David Footman, *Red Prelude: A Life of A. I. Zhelyabov*, 222. The full letter may be accessed at http://www.marxists.org/archive/marx/works/1881/letters/81_04_11.html.

3. Stephen G. Marks also sees terrorism as among Russia's foremost contributions to the modern world. Although terrorism does not figure in the alliterative list of his title, he devotes the first chapter of the book to it. See *How Russia Shaped the Modern World: From Art to Anti-Semitism, Ballet to Bolshevism*, 7–37.

4. "Western Eyes" refers to the title of Joseph Conrad's 1911 novel about revolutionary terrorism. Martin Malia took it for his historical study of the West's perceptions of Russia, *Russia Under Western Eyes: From the Bronze Horseman to the Lenin Mausoleum*. Malia claims that the apex of the West's perception of Russia as an "oriental despotism" preceded the Crimean War and that by the late nineteenth century Russia was perceived as a modernizing nation. However, the image of "oriental despotism" died hard, thanks to a pronounced desire on the part of the West to continue to orientalize Russia and the Russian state and to cast it as a cultural/ideological enemy of the West.

5. The Fenians developed the techniques of skirmishing, guerilla warfare, and dynamite campaigns just as terrorism in Russia took the shape of the "Russian Method." They also had their propaganda vehicles, such as the newspaper *The Irish World*, based in New York. The historian Niall Whelehan cites two

primary differences between the Russian Nihilists and the Fenians in order to account for the traditional recognition of the Russians as the first terrorists: 1) Russians consciously embraced the word "terrorist" whereas the Fenians rejected it as a pejorative; and 2) intellectuals (i.e., writers) predominated among Russia's revolutionary terrorists. See Whelehan, *The Dynamiters: Irish Nationalism and Political Violence in the Wider World, 1867-1900*. See also Owen McGee, *The IRB: The Irish Republican Brotherhood from The Land League to Sinn Féin*.

6. In his response to the Fenians' first salvo in December 1867, the demolition of the outer wall of Clerkenwell Prison using 458 pounds of gunpowder, Friedrich Engels expressed his opprobrium in terms precisely the opposite of Marx's praise for the People's Will. "The Clerkenwell folly was obviously the work of a few special fanatics; it is the misfortune of all conspiracies that they lead to folly 'because we really must do something, we really must get up to something.' Especially in America there has been a lot of bluster amongst this explosive and incendiary fraternity, and then along come some individual jackasses and instigate this kind of nonsense." Engels to Marx, Manchester, 19 December 1867. The full letter can be accessed at http://www.marxists.org /archive/marx/works/1867/letters/67_12_19.html.

7. David Chalmers was one of the first historians to identify Klan violence as "terrorism." See Chalmers, *Hooded Americanism*. Scholars such as Carola Dietze have explored the United States' very problematic relationship to its own history of terrorism. See Dietze, *Die Erfindung des Terrorismus in Europa, Russland, und den USA 1858-1866*, 31-33.

8. In his *The Age of Terrorism*, Walter Laqueur is explicit on this point. "The achievements of Irish terrorism have been much less striking, but it has continued on and off for a much longer period. There have been countless ups and downs ever since the emergence, partly due to agrarian unrest, of the United Irishmen in 1791." Laqueur, *The Age of Terrorism*, 17. One of the few historians to give "precedence" to the Irish American Fenians has been Michael Burleigh in his *Blood and Rage: A Cultural History of Terrorism*.

9. There were in fact seven attempts on Queen Victoria's life between 1840 and 1882, none of which have gone down in the annals of terrorism and none of which succeeded. For comparative chronologies of terrorism, consult two recent reference works on terrorism: Barry Rubin and Judith Colp Rubin, eds., *Chronologies of Modern Terrorism*, and Sean Anderson and Stephen Sloan, eds., *Historical Dictionary of Terrorism*. The latter omits both Karakozov's 1866 attempt on Alexander II and the attempt on Queen Victoria, but includes Nechaev's 1869 *Catechism of a Revolutionary*.

10. The influence of the *Catechism* on post-World War II anticolonial terrorism is particularly noteworthy, and Nechaev's literary influence on Frantz Fanon's "Concerning Violence" in *The Wretched of the Earth* is easily discernable. See Marks, *How Russia Shaped the Modern World*, 35-36.

11. "Gloomy monster" is the revolutionary Rakhmetov's own self-description and will be discussed in Part One. Dmitry Pisarev also uses "monster" [urod] to describe Turgenev's Bazarov, or "nihilists" more generally. We can add to this tally Stavrogin and Peter Verkhovensky, the latter vilified by his own father as a "monster" [izverg]. Dostoevskii, *PSS*, 10:240.

12. *Chronologies of Modern Terrorism* describes Nechaev's importance in the following terms: "[He] developed the first comprehensive plan for underground revolutionary groups focusing on a terrorist strategy. He also created the concept of a professional revolutionary, an individual deliberately shaped to be the pitiless deliverer of social justice in the form of murder." Rubin and Colp Rubin, *Chronologies of Modern Terrorism*, 12.

13. Laqueur, *The Age of Terrorism*, 193.

14. Dostoevsky supposedly made this remark to the French orientalist and literary scholar Eugène-Melchior de Vogüé, who undertook the first foreign study of Russian literature, *Le Roman Russe* (1886), at the height of French and Western European fascination with Russian Nihilism. Simon Karlinsky has traced the quote to de Vogüé. See Karlinsky, *The Sexual Labyrinth of Nikolai Gogol*, 135. The reception of Russian literature in the West coincided with the reception of "the Russian Method," as the Epilogue will show.

15. Stephen Marks has also identified nonviolence as one of Russia's contributions to the modern world, although he has in mind Leo Tolstoy's preachments of nonviolence. See Marks, *How Russia Shaped the World*, 102–39.

16. Visual technologies suitable for mass reproduction of the terrorist spectacle, such as block prints in illustrated magazines, were just beginning to appear. These, however, lacked the realism and naturalism that photography would achieve in the early twentieth century. I am grateful to Susan Morrissey for this insight.

17. Cited in Gregory Freidin, "By the Walls of Church and State: Literature's Authority in Russia's Modern Tradition," 149. Aleksandr Gertsen, *Sobranie sochinenii*, 8:158.

18. See Jurii Lotman and Boris A. Uspenskij, *The Semiotics of Russian Culture*. I have in mind especially Lotman's essays "The Decembrist in Everyday Life" and "The Poetics of Everyday Behavior in Russian Eighteenth-Century Culture."

19. Lydia Ginzburg, *On Psychological Prose*, 17. Ginzburg is interested primarily in "ideal images" that the individual chooses "at a certain moment in the process of his maturation" to orient himself to, the image that he creates for himself (as in Bakunin's case), or the image others create of/ for him (as in Stankevich's case).

20. Irina Paperno, *Chernyshevsky and the Age of Realism*, 9.

21. Susan Morrissey, *Heralds of Revolution*, 20.

22. Specifically, "After 1862 almost all the young Russians who came to see me [in London] were right out of Chernyshevskii's *What Is to Be Done?* with the admixture of a few Bazarovian traits." Quoted in Ginzburg, *On Psychological Prose*, 17.

23. Richard Jackson, ed., *Terrorism: A Critical Introduction*, 119.

24. Ibid.

25. Tsvetan Todorov, *The Fantastic: A Structural Approach to a Literary Genre*, 26–27.

26. Max Fasmer's etymological dictionary notes the Early Russian usage of *kramola* in the thirteenth century. Its probable origin is the German root "karm" [complaint, lamentation]. Fasmer, *Etimologicheskii slovar' russkogo iazyka*.

27. See Iuliia Safronova, *Russkoe obshchestvo v zerkale revoliutsionnogo terrora. 1879–1881 gody*, 227–29.

28. Richard Pipes, *Russia Under the Old Regime*, 109.

29. Lotman describes this disjuncture in meaning creation versus reception in the following way: "In the real substance of culture non-synchronicity does not appear as a sudden deviation but as a regular rule. At the apogee of its activity the transferring agent simultaneously produces innovative and dynamic features. The addressees as a rule are still experiencing a former cultural stage." Iurii Lotman, "On the Semiosphere," 217.

30. Joseba Zulaika and William Douglass, *Terror and Taboo: The Follies, Fables, and Faces of Terrorism*, 155–56.

31. Ibid., 152.

32. Ibid., 155.

33. Martin Miller, *The Foundations of Modern Terrorism: State, Society, and the Dynamics of Political Violence*, 3.

34. See, for example, Anthony Anemone's distinction between Russian revolutionary and Western European anarchist terrorism in the introduction to his edited volume, *Just Assassins: The Culture of Russian Terrorism*, 5.

35. Manfred Hildermeier, *The Russian Socialist Revolutionary Party before the First World War*, 56.

36. Cited in Derek Offord, "Alexander Herzen," 62.

37. Quoted in Alex P. Schmid and Albert J. Jongman, *Political Terrorism: A New Guide to Actors, Authors, Concepts, Data Bases, Theories, and Literature*, 23.

38. Laqueur, "The Futility of Terrorism," 103.

39. The historian Claudia Verhoeven has attempted to restore Dmitry Karakozov to his rightful place as the originator of Russian revolutionary terrorism. While a fascinating microhistory of the Karakozov affair, Verhoeven's book makes larger claims about Karakozov's place in the history of terrorism (Karakozov's complete originality in acting without precedent or model and independent of cultural influences) that warrant reconsideration. For Karakozov's failure to be considered the "first terrorist," see Verhoeven, *The Odd Man Karakozov: Imperial Russia, Modernity, and the Birth of Terrorism*, 5.

Prologue: "Just You Wait! (Uzho tebe!)"

1. Derrida, *Specters of Marx*, 2. As Derrida remarks, what is unusual about Marx's specter is its futurity. Specters usually pertain to beings that were once alive.

2. Karl Marx and Friedrich Engels, *The Communist Manifesto*, 33–34.

3. See Joseph Crawford, *Gothic Fiction and the Invention of Terrorism*, for a fascinating exposition of this argument. With his spectral metaphor Marx is, of course, lampooning the discourse of Communism's foes, as the "Nihilists" would by ironically using these same Gothic tropes. For a prime example, see Dmitry Pisarev's quote that serves as the epigraph for Part One.

4. Randall Law, *Terrorism: A History*, 66–72; Laqueur, *The Age of Terrorism*, 26, 28; Benjamin Grob-Fitzgibbon, "From the Dagger to the Bomb: Karl Heinzen and the Evolution of Political Terror," 97–115.

5. The name derives from the nickname of the Plot of the rue Saint-Nicaise, aka "the Machine infernale," which was an attempt on the life of the First Consul of France, Napoleon Bonaparte, on December 24, 1800. See Philip Dwyer, *Citizen Emperor: Napoleon in Power*, 60–61. Giuseppe Marco Fieschi also devised an infernal machine of his own invention for his attempt on King Louis-Philippe I in 1835. Fieschi, a fiery Corsican, was a veteran of Napoleon's campaign to Russia, had a bold and arrogant character, and was sentenced to death as a parricide. Jill Harsin, *Barricades: The War of Streets in Revolutionary Paris, 1830–1848*, 150–66.

6. In the late eighteenth and early nineteenth centuries, the Terror (1791–94) in France was by no means referred to as *terror* in Russian, but as the "vremia Uzhasa" [time of Horror]. See Pushkin, *Sobranie sochinenii*, 6:508.

7. Iuliia Safronova, *Russkoe obshchestvo v zerkale revoliutsionnogo terrora*, 127–30. Harmodius and Aristogeiton were the first to be referred to as "tyrannicides" for their murder of the tyrant Hipparchus in the sixth century BC. Many ancient authors, including Aristotle, Plutarch, and Herodotus, recounted their stories, and they were venerated by ancient Athenians as the saviors of democracy. See S. Sara Monoson, *Plato's Democratic Entanglements: Athenian Politics and the Practice of Philosophy*, and Michael W. Taylor, *The Tyrant Slayers: The Heroic Image in Fifth Century B.C. Athenian Art and Politics*.

8. The scholarship on the *Journey* is voluminous. As the historian Douglas Smith recently noted, "Perhaps no other work has been so exhaustively mined, particularly for its criticisms of the evils of tsarist Russia, for its harsh indictment of serfdom, for evidence of the corrupting influence of the ruler's court and the rapacious inhumanity of the noble landlords. It would seem that there is nothing more to be said about this most studied of texts." See Smith, "Alexander Radishchev's *Journey from St. Petersburg to Moscow* and the Limits of Freedom of Speech in the Reign of Catherine the Great," 61. To my knowledge, the specific reasons that the *Journey* belongs in a literary history of *terrorism* have not been addressed in the scholarship.

9. D. S. Babkin, *Protsess Radishcheva*, 157.

10. Diary of A. V. Krapovitsky, entry for July 7/18, 1790, quoted in Thaler, ed., *Journey*, 11.

11. David Marshall Lang, *The First Russian Radical*, 122. For additional biographical information based heavily on Babkin, see the eminently readable Allen McConnell, *A Russian Philosophe: Alexander Radishchev 1749–1802*.

12. Lang, *The First Russian Radical*, 122.

13. Babkin, *Protsess Radishcheva*, 157. For Catherine, who relied on the ancient humoral paradigm, melancholics were malcontents and therefore natural subversives, and Martinists were already suspect as political conspirators. For Catherine's well-known aversion to and suspicion of melancholics as seditious subjects, see Ilya Vinitsky, "A Cheerful Empress and Her Gloomy Critics," 25–45.

14. Babkin, *Protsess Radishcheva*, 160.

15. Ibid., 188–89.

16. A. S. Pushkin, *Sobranie sochinenie v desiati tomakh* (henceforward *SS*), 6:217. Pushkin's antipathy toward sentimentalism is well known. For a recent exploration of it, see Hilde Hoogenboom, "Sentimental Novels and Pushkin: European Literary Markets and Russian Readers," 553–74.

17. Andrew Kahn, "Self and Sensibility in Radishchev's *Journey from St. Petersburg to Moscow*: Dialogism, Relativism, and the Moral Spectator," 280–304.

18. As Kahn points out, "The demand that is found in Radishchev criticism for a three-dimensional portrait of a realistic, psychologically nuanced narrator ignores the prevalent literary models of the 1790s where authors created first-person narrators with little regard for psychological plausibility." Kahn, "Self and Sensibility in Radishchev's *Journey*," 284.

19. George A. Test, *Satire: Spirit and Art*, 12.

20. "That satire is an attack is probably the least debatable claim one can make about it." Ibid., 15.

21. Its origins, as Robert Elliot's classic work postulates, were in the ritual context of Hellenic fertility rites, in the magically potent language of iambs (invective) that could literally drive its victims to death or suicide. Elliot quotes Francis Cornford in recollecting that "the simplest of all methods of expelling . . . malign influences of any kind is to abuse them with the most violent language." Even as belief in its magical efficacy waned, through its practices ranging from ridicule to denunciation to dehumanization, satire retained its destructive capabilities. Elliott, *The Power of Satire: Magic, Ritual, Art*, 7–9.

22. The political scientist Artemy Magun also makes a similar argument, although he does so in political-philosophical rather than literary-historical terms. Radishchev's *Journey* is also central to his argument. See Magun, "The Birth of Terrorism Out of the Spirit of Enlightenment," http://www.academia.edu/4084600/THE_BIRTH_OF_TERRORISM_OUT_OF_THE_SPIRIT_OF_ENLIGHTENMENT._The_subject_of_Enlightenment_and_the_terrorist_sensorium (accessed October 1, 2015).

23. See, for example, David Denby, *Sentimental Narrative and the Social Order in France*, and Lynn Hunt, *Inventing Human Rights*. Following the thesis-antithesis of conservative vs. progressive sentimentalism, literary scholars such as Lynn Festa have made more ambivalent claims about how sentimentalism might function to arouse feelings of sympathy and compassion, but nonetheless provide moral justification for reactionary projects such as colonial patronage and Empire. See Lynn Festa, *Sentimental Figures of Empire in Eighteenth-Century Britain and France*.

24. William M. Reddy, "Sentimentalism and Its Erasure: The Role of Emotions in the Era of the French Revolution," 139.

25. This likewise remained a truism for Romantic historians of the French Revolution, such as Jules Michelet, who implicated this conceptual structure in the spontaneous acts of terrorism (i.e., non-state terrorism) during the early phases of the revolution. "A fact, too little noticed, but which enables us to understand a great many things, is that several of our terrorists were men of an exquisite feverish sensibility, who felt cruelly the sufferings of the people, and whose pity turned into fury." Michelet, *History of the French Revolution*, 204.

26. My interpretation concurs on many points with Radishchev's leading Soviet biographer, G. P. Makogonenko, who writes that the "book [was] written with the goal of multiplying the number of people with a 'clear-sighted' view of reality, with the goal of breeding a hero." See Makogonenko, *Radishchev i ego vremia*, 443.

27. There are countless ways of conceptualizing consciousness, and I have chosen the model offered by the neuroscientist Antonio Damasio. Damasio's approach is admittedly biological-materialist, rather than mentalist-metaphysical, but in this respect it has much in common with the sentimentalist science of Radishchev's time. The way we feel feelings, according to Damasio, is that they arise as biological responses to appraisals that are monitored and mapped by the brain, and effectively translated into a mental state that we interpret as a known quantity or "feeling." There is no priority in this inseparably interconnected cognitive, emotional, and bodily process. "The investigation of how thoughts trigger emotions and of how bodily emotions become the kind of thoughts we call feelings provides a privileged view into mind and body, the overtly disparate manifestations of a single and seamlessly interwoven human organism." Damasio, *Looking for Spinoza: Joy, Sorrow, and the Feeling Brain*, 7.

28. As Kahn notes, "In the Journey, Radishchev will repeatedly draw attention to the physiological basis of sensibility by anatomizing his own reactions." Kahn, "Self and Sensibility in Radishchev's *Journey*," 290.

29. Radishchev, *Journey from St. Petersburg to Moscow*, 48; Radishchev, *Puteshestvie iz Peterburga v Moskvu*, 24.

30. Radishchev, *Journey from St. Petersburg to Moscow*, 49; Radishchev, *Puteshestvie iz Peterburga v Moskvu*, 24.

31. Makogonenko also analyzes Radishchev's method of describing consciousness, but he notes only the cognitive rather than the emotional/biological components. Makogonenko, *Radishchev i ego vremia*, 441. Makogonenko's emphasis on the rational, self-controlled Enlightened aspects of consciousness is understandable given the Marxist-Leninist context in which he was writing.

32. Radishchev, *Journey from St. Petersburg to Moscow*, 49; Radishchev, *Puteshestvie iz Peterburga v Moskvu*, 25.

33. Radishchev, *Journey from St. Petersburg to Moscow*, 56; Radishchev, *Puteshestvie iz Peterburga v Moskvu*, 33–34.

34. Radishchev, *Journey from St. Petersburg to Moscow*, 56; Radishchev, *Puteshestvie iz Peterburga v Moskvu*, 34.

35. Radishchev, *Journey from St. Petersburg to Moscow*, 98; Radishchev, *Puteshestvie iz Peterburga v Moskvu*, 74.

36. Radishchev, *Journey from St. Petersburg to Moscow*, 99.

37. Radishchev, *Puteshestvie iz Peterburga v Moskvu*, 74.

38. Radishchev, *Puteshestvie iz Peterburga v Moskvu*, 80–81. If, for example, positive law should not function to adequately protect the citizen from harm, then "the citizen enjoys the protection of natural law [prirodnoe pravo]."

39. Babkin, *Protsess Radishcheva*, 159.

40. See Oszkár Jászi and John D. Lewis, *Against the Tyrant: The Tradition and Theory of Tyrannicide*; Franklin F. Ford, *Political Murder: From Tyrannicide to Terrorism*; and Dan Edelstein, *The Terror of Natural Right: Republicanism, the Cult of Nature, and the French Revolution*.

41. Radishchev, *Puteshestvie iz Peterburga v Moskvu*, 81. "And anyone, who has sufficient power, may exact vengeance for the insult done to him" [i vsiak, imeia dovol'no sil, da otmstit na nem obidu, im sodelannuiu].

42. Edelstein, *The Terror of Natural Right*, 16–17.

43. Ibid.
44. Radishchev, *Puteshestvie iz Peterburga v Moskvu*, 81.
45. Babkin, *Protsess Radishcheva*, 159.
46. See, for example, Marc Raeff, "Filling the Gap between Radishchev and the Decembrists," 395–413. Raeff is particularly interested in those who carried forward Radishchev's ideas in a more traditionally liberal, less radical vein.
47. Foreign diplomats interpreted the appearance of the *Journey* as another sign of discontent with the regime and Catherine and Potemkin's war policy, as well as with autocracy more generally. Among those who sent reports of the Radishchev affair were the Saxon diplomat and memoirist Helbig, the British Minister, Charles Whitworth, and the French chargé d'affaires, Genet. See Lang, *The First Russian Radical*, 191–95.
48. Among those who decidedly did not were Countess Vorontsova-Daskhkova, the sister of Radishchev's long-time friend and patron, Alexei Vorontsov, and Vorontsov himself, who was chagrined that Radishchev had dedicated the book to him. Lang, *The First Russian Radical*, 200.
49. "The outbursts of sensitivity, affected and inflated and sometimes extremely funny." Pushkin, *SS*, 6:217.
50. Thaler, ed., *A Journey from St. Petersburg to Moscow*, 11; Babkin, *Protsess Radishcheva*, 27.
51. See the "Death Sentence of A. N. Radishchev, Pronounced by the High Criminal Court [Smertnyi prigovor A. N. Radishcheva, vynesennyi palatoiu ugolovnogo suda]," in Babkin, *Protsess Radishcheva*, 260–68.
52. Lang, *The First Russian Radical*, 191.
53. Aleksandr Gertsen, ed., *O povrezhdenii nravov v Rossii kniazia M. Shcherbatova i Puteshestvie Radishcheva*, 106. Like Pushkin, Herzen also emphasized Radishchev's humor and irony and dismissed his "neo-romanticism."
54. Pushkin, *SS*, 6:507. Pavel Annenkov published the biography in a supplementary volume of *Sochinenii Pushkina*.
55. Thaler, *A Journey from St. Petersburg to Moscow*, 35.
56. Pushkin, *SS*, 6:507.
57. Ibid., 6:212.
58. Ibid., 6:213.
59. Ibid.
60. The flood occurred on November 7, 1824, while Pushkin was at his estate Mikhailovskoe, and, as was his wont, Pushkin did substantial research on it in preparation for writing his poema. See Andrew Kahn, *Pushkin's "The Bronze Horseman,"* 5.
61. "The householder, who sees the meaning of life in the rich joys of family love, in the concerns of providing and caring for wife and children, may feel that he is far from appreciating these joys at their full or from giving himself to these concerns unstintingly. But he senses that his ultimate allegiance is there.... He is deeply committed to building over time a web of relationships which gives fullness and meaning to human life." Charles Taylor, *Sources of the Self: The Making of Modern Identity*, 46.
62. A letter that Pushkin wrote to his brother shortly after the flood suggests that the opposing perspectives of Peter I's lofty indifference and Evgenii's

frustrated helplessness originated with Pushkin himself. "The flood would not leave my mind, it is not at all *as amusing as it seemed at first glance* [italics mine]. If it occurs to you to help any unfortunate person, do it from the proceeds of *Evgenii Onegin*." Quoted in Kahn, *Pushkin's "The Bronze Horseman,"* 5.

63. Pushkin, *SS*, 3:296.
64. Ibid., 6:298.
65. Ibid.
66. Kahn, *Pushkin's "The Bronze Horseman,"* 81.
67. Pushkin, *SS*, 6:298.
68. Platt, *Terror and Greatness: Ivan and Peter as Russian Myths*, 61.
69. With this I am by no means suggesting that the People's Will read Pushkin's poem in 1880 and consciously implemented Evgenii's "program" of revenge. Vasily Zhukovskii published the entire poem after the poet's death in 1837, but only by deferentially observing the tsar's changes. The challenge scene was restored in Maikov's 1880 version, but the poema was first published according to Pushkin's original 1833 version in 1924. See Kahn, *Pushkin's "The Bronze Horseman,"* 7.
70. In his magisterial *History of the French Revolution*, Jules Michelet noted Pushkin's "Hymn to the Dagger" as a manifestation of the "cult of the dagger . . . at the very extremity of Europe." *The History of the French Revolution*, 6:148.
71. For Pushkin's involvement with conspiratorial circles during his southern exile, see Iurii Lotman, *Pushkin*, 77.
72. Ibid., 112.
73. Verhoeven also reads "The Overcoat" in light of terrorism, but her focus is the paradox of terror and "the universalist ethics of fraternity" that Akaky Akakievich's spirit expresses. See Verhoeven, *The Odd Man Karakozov*, 105–6.
74. Nikolai Gogol', *Polnoe sobranie sochinenii* (henceforward *PSS*), 2:121; Nikolai Gogol, "The Overcoat" in Richard Pevear and Larissa Volokhonsky, trans., *The Collected Tales of Nikolai Gogol*, 417–18.
75. Gogol', *PSS*, 2:121.
76. Ibid., 2:123.
77. Ibid., 2:124.
78. Jackson, *Terrorism: A Critical Introduction*, 119.
79. https://www.marxists.org/reference/archive/bakunin/works/1842/reaction-germany.html.
80. Ibid.
81. Goethe, *Faust First Part*, 82.
82. Joseph Frank, *Dostoevsky: The Years of Ordeal*, 7.
83. In-depth investigations of the Petrashevsky affair are available in both English and Russian. See N. F. Bel'chikov, *Dostoevskii v protsesse Petrashevtsev*; I. L. Volgin, *Propavshchii zagovor: Dostoevskii i politicheskii protsess 1849 goda*; and Liza Knapp ed. and trans., *Dostoevsky as Reformer: The Petrashevsky Case*. Dostoevsky's biographers also provided relatively detailed accounts of the affair. See Joseph Frank, *Dostoevsky: The Years of Ordeal*; Leonid Grossman, *Dostoevsky: A Biography*; and Konstantin Mochulsky, *Dostoevsky: His Life and Work*.
84. Quoted in Frank, *Dostoevsky: The Years of Ordeal*, 8.

85. Knapp, *Dostoevsky as Reformer*, 96.
86. Dostoevskii, *PSS*, 18:126.
87. Belinskii, *Izbrannye sochineniia*, 889.
88. Ibid., 890.
89. Dostoevskii, *PSS*, 18:118.
90. Dostoevskii, *PSS*, 18:121; Knapp, *Dostoevsky as Reformer*, 32.
91. Dostoevskii, *PSS*, 18:125; Knapp, *Dostoevsky as Reformer*, 35.
92. Dostoevskii, *PSS*, 18:121; Knapp, *Dostoevsky as Reformer*, 32.
93. Dostoevskii, *PSS*, 18:120; Knapp, *Dostoevsky as Reformer*, 31.

Part One, Chapter 1. What Do Nihilists Do?

1. Venturi, *Roots of Revolution*, 208.
2. Dostoevskii, *PSS*, 19:72.
3. As in English, in Russian the word "flibust'er" was a calque of the Spanish *filibustero*, which derived from the Dutch vrijbiuter ["freebooter"], meaning privateer, pirate, or robber. Filibusters menaced the Spanish Main and the Florida coasts in the 1810s and Texas in the 1850s. As one of their first American historians relays "[Filibusters] had, it must be admitted, a technique all their own, derived from countless rebellious and revolutionary states set up elsewhere in Spanish America, a technique which made colorful almost any narrative of their exploits." See Rufus Kay Wyllys, "The Filibusters of Amelia Island," 298.
4. Dostoevskii, *PSS*, 19:72.
5. Ibid.
6. Frank, *Dostoevsky: The Stir of Liberation*, 146. The proclamation made its first appearance in St. Petersburg on May 14, 1862.
7. Peter Kropotkin, *Memoirs of a Revolutionist*, 158.
8. Ivan Turgenev, *Literary Reminiscences*, 194.
9. For the origins of the word and its virtually opposite meanings, see Venturi, *Roots of Revolution*, 326. The word "nihilist" was a pejorative of anti-nihilist discourse that first gained currency in official and police circles in the mid-1860s. As Peter C. Pozefsky points out in his study of the nihilist imagination, the "Ministry of Internal Affairs experienced considerable difficulty finding flesh and blood nihilists to investigate" and "for the most part were tilting at phantoms based on literary images of nihilists and their own anti-nihilist discourse." See Pozefsky, *The Nihilist Imagination: Dmitry Pisarev and the Cultural Origins of Russian Radicalism*, 101–2, 119.
10. Ivan Turgenev, *Polnoe sobranie sochinenii v dvenadtsati tomakh* (henceforward *PSS*) 3:193; Ivan Turgenev, *Fathers and Sons*, 47.
11. J. L. Austin, *How to Do Things with Words*, 8, 32.
12. Turgenev, *PSS*, 3:193; Turgenev, *Fathers and Sons*, 47.
13. Turgenev, *PSS*, 3:195; Turgenev, *Fathers and Sons*, 49–50.
14. D. I. Pisarev, *Polnoe sobranie sochinenii i pisem v dvenadtsati tomakh* (henceforward *PSS*), 2:84.
15. Quoted in Frank, *Dostoevsky: The Stir of Liberation*, 174.
16. "Molodaia Rossiia," reprinted in Rudnitskaia, ed., *Revoliutsionnyi radikalizm v Rossii: Vek deviatnadtsatyi*, 146.

17. Ibid., 149.
18. Cited in N. G. Rosenblium, "Petersburgskie pozhary 1862 g. i Dostoevskii," 24.
19. Ibid., 26, 43.
20. Cited in ibid., 48.
21. Ibid., 51.
22. Cited in ibid., 26.
23. Dostoevsky and Chernyshevsky's biographers have attempted to sort out conflicting stories that describe Dostoevsky's rare visit to Chernyshevsky as the fires raged. In Chernyshevsky's unflattering reminiscence, written more than twenty years later, Dostoevsky, in the grip of hysteria, appealed to Chernyshevsky to rein in his minions—i.e., the revolutionary arsonists. This would imply that Dostoevsky believed in the existence of such revolutionary arsonists when the textual evidence of his suppressed articles indicates that he did not. In Dostoevsky's version, he visited on literary business and calmly asked Chernyshevsky to use whatever influence he had to ease the situation. See Frank, *Dostoevsky: The Stir of Liberation*, 151–59.
24. Rosenblium, "Petersburgskie pozhary," 36. Dostoevsky's fellow writer Nikolai Leskov was not so lucky. His editorial was not suppressed and consequently appeared in *The Northern Bee* on May 30, 1862. Although he cautioned that the wild rumors endangered the life of innocent students, "he did not dismiss the notion that the fires had been caused by arsonists and specifically by revolutionary arsonists." See Hugh McLean, *Nikolai Leskov: The Man and His Art*, 81–82.
25. Gleason, *Young Russia*, 174–75.
26. Venturi, *Roots of Revolution*, 301.
27. *Kolokol*, No. 139, July 15, 1862, 1149. Cited also in Gleason, *Young Russia*, 175.

Part One, Chapter 2. "Very Dangerous!"

1. N. A. Dobroliubov, *Literaturnaia Kritika*, 344–45, 360.
2. Ibid., 348–49.
3. Ibid., 360.
4. Ibid., 373.
5. Ibid., 374.
6. Ibid.
7. Paperno, *Chernyshevsky and the Age of Realism*, 10.
8. Nikolai Chernyshevsky, "Esteticheskie otnosheniia isskustva k deistvitel'nosti," *Polnoe sobranie sochinenii v 15 tomakh* (henceforward *PSS*), 2:89.
9. Chernyshevsky, *PSS*, 2:84.
10. The urgent quest for the positive hero in Russian literature commenced with the new era inaugurated by Alexander II's new reign and continued into the Soviet period. See Rufus W. Mathewson Jr.'s classic work, *The Positive Hero in Russian Literature*.
11. Turgenev, *PSS*, 12:194.
12. Ibid., 12:195.

13. Ibid.
14. Ibid.
15. Ibid., 12:208.
16. Ibid., 12:203.
17. Ibid.
18. Ibid., 12:202.
19. Ibid., 12:203.
20. In the Prologue of *Don Quixote*, Cervantes cites the Spanish proverb "Al rey mando" ["I give orders to the king"], which has the same sense as the English proverb "a man's home is his castle," emphasizing a man's autonomy and sovereignty within his own domain. In his Prologue, Cervantes mock-belittles his own novel and hero and uses the proverb to grant his reader absolute autonomy of critical judgment: "you are neither relative nor friend but many call your soul your own and exercise your free judgment. You are in your own house where you are master as the king is of his taxes, for you are familiar with the saying, 'Under my cloak I kill the king.' All of which exempts and frees you from any kind of respect or obligation; you may say of this story whatever you choose without fear of being slandered for an ill opinion or rewarded for a good one." Cervantes, *Don Quixote*, 11. Dostoevsky uses this same device and tone in his letter "From the Author," which prefaces *The Brothers Karamazov* and defends his choice of quixotic hero, Alexei Karamazov.
21. Leonard Schapiro, *Turgenev: His Life and Times*, 161.
22. *Pervoe polnoe sobranie sochinenii N. A. Dobroliubova*, 4:50.
23. Shapiro, *Turgenev: His Life and Times*, 155.
24. *Pervoe polnoe sobranie sochinenii N. A. Dobroliubova*, 4:71.
25. Ibid., 4:88.
26. Ibid.
27. Ibid., 4:71.
28. Ibid., 4:73.
29. Ibid.
30. Ibid., 4:90.

Part One, Chapter 3. Extraordinary Men and Gloomy Monsters

1. Dmitry Pisarev, *Selected Philosophical, Social and Political Essays*, 147.
2. See Lampert, *Sons Against Fathers*, 126–27; Venturi, *Roots of Revolution*, 175–76.
3. Lampert, *Sons Against Fathers*, 128.
4. Quoted in Paperno, *Chernyshevsky and the Age of Realism*, 27.
5. Pisarev, *PSS*, 8:242.
6. As is always the case in the polemics of the 1860s, a very specific type was meant by the "perspicacious reader," and Pisarev gives an extensive gloss on this type in his review of *What Is to Be Done?* The "perspicacious reader" whom Chernyshevsky often mocks very severely "has nothing at all in common with the ordinary artless reader that every writer loves and respects. The ordinary reader takes up a book in order to spend the time pleasantly or to learn something, but the perspicacious reader does so to bully the author and critically inspect his ideas." The "perspicacious reader," in other words, is the polemical

reader, first and foremost literary critics from the opposing camp. See Pisarev, *PSS*, 8:208-9.

7. Both Andrew Drozd and Claudia Verhoeven offer boldly revisionist readings of Rakhmetov. Drozd takes Rakhmetov's absurdity at face value and reads him as an anti-model—"what is not to be done." Drozd, *Chernyshevskii's "What Is to Be Done?,"* 117-19, 140. Verhoeven also finds Rakhmetov "funny" and characterizes Chernyshevsky's contemporaries as "bad readers" for mistaking Rakhmetov as a self-sacrificial and suicidal terrorist prototype whom Karakozov supposedly imitated. Verhoeven, *The Odd Man Karakozov*, 41.

8. Nikolai Chernyshevskii, *Chto delat'?*, 308-9; Nikolai Chernyshevsky, *What Is to Be Done?*, 272.

9. Chernyshevskii, *Chto delat'?*, 342; Chernyshevsky, *What Is to Be Done?*, 300.

10. Chernyshevskii, *Chto delat'?*, 342. "Voobshche vidish' neveselye veshchi: kak zhe tut ne budesh' mrachnym chudovishchem?" Chernyshevsky, *What Is to Be Done?*, 300.

11. Chernyshevskii, *Chto delat'?*, 334-35; Chernyshevsky, *What Is to Be Done?*, 295.

12. Pisarev, *PSS*, 8:242.

13. Chernyshevskii, *Chto delat'?*, 342; Chernyshevsky, *What Is to Be Done?*, 301.

14. Chernyshevskii, *Chto delat'?*, 343; Chernyshevsky, *What Is to Be Done?*, 301.

15. Drozd, *Chernyshevskii's "What Is to Be Done?,"* 126-28. Pavel Alexandrovich Bakhmetev (b. 1828), from Chernyshevsky's native Saratov, has much in common with Rakhmetov, including the fact that he sold his considerable estates and handed over the proceeds to Herzen in London. Because of Chernyshevsky's apparent "condescension" toward Bakhmetev and other such repentant noblemen whom he termed "saintly babies," Drozd argues that Chernyshevsky's attitude toward Rakhmetov is in fact negative and that as a character he represents "what is not to be done." While certainly provocative, this interpretation is an overcorrection that ignores too much of Rakhmetov. Drozd's conclusion, in which he concedes that the final chapters of the novel represent "a call to action," strongly suggests that Rakhmetov *is* presented as "what is to be done."

16. Ibid., 6-9.

17. Ibid., 126-28.

18. Adam Bruno Ulam attributes this explanation to Vladimir Nabokov. See Ulam, *In the Name of the People*, 136.

19. For the initial impact of *What Is to Be Done?* on Dostoevsky, see Frank, *Dostoevsky: The Stir of Liberation*, 286-91.

20. Ibid., 324-31. Frank, however, does not note that "mansion" is not the same as "Crystal Palace" or "chicken coop." The latter two in *Notes from the Underground* refer to social systems, whereas "mansion" in Chernyshevsky is a metaphor for the extraordinary man, Rakhmetov. Dostoevsky makes it clear in his letter to Mikhail that for him the ideal (the "mansion") is the one embodied in Christ.

21. Quoted in Drozd, *Chernyshevskii's "What Is to Be Done?,"* 14.

22. Venturi, *Roots of Revolution*, 183.

23. Under George Habash, the Popular Front for the Liberation of Palestine (a faction of the PLO) perfected the highly dramatic and effective strategy of hijacking airliners and holding their passengers hostage to secure the release of captured comrades. See Randall Law, *Terrorism: A History*, 220-21.

Part One, Chapter 4. "Daring and Original Things" (Assez causé!)

1. "Enough talk!" These are the words with which Raskolnikov provocatively concludes his veiled confession to the greenhorn police investigator Zamyotov. According to Anna Dostoevskaia, this was one of her husband's favorite phrases, taken from Honoré de Balzac's *Le Père Goriot*. Svidrigailov repeats it. See Dostoevsky, *Crime and Punishment*, 482, 557n23.

2. Dostoevskii, *PSS*, 6:6; Dostoevsky, *Crime and Punishment*, 3-4.

3. Dostoevsky, *Complete Letters*, 2:155.

4. For the autobiographical reflection of Dostoevsky's financial struggles in *Crime and Punishment*, see Leonid Grossman, *Dostoevsky: A Biography*, 346-52.

5. Dostoevsky, *Complete Letters*, 2:152.

6. Ibid., 2:174.

7. Ibid., 2:155.

8. Ibid., 2:177.

9. Ibid., 2:190.

10. Cited in Frank, *Dostoevsky: The Miraculous Years*, 45. Some of the initial sensation had to do with the fact that a crime very similar to Raskolnikov's was committed by a student, A. M. Danilov, who killed a moneylender and his servant under very similar conditions, contemporaneously with the novel's appearance in Katkov's *Russian Messenger*. However, there were numerous crimes similar to Raskolnikov's that might have served as sources, first and foremost that of Pierre-François Lacenaire. Dostoevsky published riveting accounts of Lacenaire's trial in the inaugural volume of his periodical *Time* in 1861.

11. Konstantine Klioutchkine, "The Rise of *Crime and Punishment* from the Air of the Media," 88-89, 92-93.

12. Ibid., 89, 97.

13. Dostoevsky, *Complete Letters*, 2:212.

14. In her history of the reception of Karakozov's attempt, Verhoeven implies that Karakozov's act had some direct influence on Part III and specifically on Raskolnikov's Napoleonic idea as the theoretical-philosophical core of modern terrorism. While Dostoevsky's notebooks for *Crime and Punishment* indicate that many aspects of this idea were already worked out, it indeed took its final form only after Karakozov's attempt.

15. Gleason puts it best: "Neither Ishutin personally nor the members of Hell collectively were *directly* involved in Karakozov's decision to assassinate the Emperor. He arrived at the idea in an agonized, inward, personal way." Gleason, *Young Russia*, 325.

16. Verhoeven, *The Odd Man Karakozov*, 130-31. Karakozov's pockets also contained shooting paraphernalia, a letter incriminating his cousin, Nikolai

Ishutin, and others, and a scrap of paper bearing the initial "K." Verhoeven believes "K." to be the nihilist physician Alexander Kobylin, "who was not only the source of all three suspicious substances found in the pockets of his *armiak*, but also the spark that had ignited the idea of the crime in Karakozov's mind."

17. "The media are the terrorist's best friend. The terrorist's act by itself is nothing. Publicity is all." Walter Laqueur made this statement in "The Futility of Terrorism," 104. Since then, the study of terrorism and the media constitutes almost a subspecialty within the field. Joseba Zulaika and William Douglass foreground the media (and narrative's) role in their groundbreaking *Terror and Taboo*, as did Alex P. Schmid and Janny de Graaf in *Violence as Communication: Insurgent Terrorism and the Western News Media*. David Rapoport, who originated the idea of the "four waves" of terrorism, explicitly identified media technology as a necessary condition of the first wave. See David C. Rapoport, "The Four Waves of Rebel Terror and September 11."

18. For Verhoeven's witty and imaginative treatments of conspiracy/conspiracy theory in the reception of Karakozov's attempts, see *The Odd Man Karakozov*, 42–49; for her equally witty and imaginative treatment of O. I. Komissarov's stellar rise and fall as the celebrity savior, see 66–84.

19. Stephen T. Cochrane, *The Collaboration of Nečaev, Ogarev, and Bakunin in 1869, Nečaev's Early Years*, 23.

20. Despite the stifling atmosphere of the novel-in-progress, Dostoevsky spent a very pleasant summer in the resort village of Lublino outside of Moscow as guests of the Ivanovs while making far less pleasant weekly trips to the offices of Katkov's *Russian Messenger* to wrangle over the editors' changes to his novel. See Frank, *Dostoevsky: The Miraculous Years*, 55–58.

21. Philip Rahv, "Dostoevsky in Crime and Punishment," 559.

Part One, Chapter 5. "Vous trouvez que l'assassinat est grandeur d'âme?"

1. "Tut chto-to drugoe" Dostoevskii, *PSS*, 6:411; Dostoevsky, *Crime and Punishment*, 536.
2. Vladimir Nabokov, *Lectures in Russian Literature*, 113–14.
3. Dostoevsky, *Crime and Punishment*, 417.
4. Ibid., 416.
5. Ibid., 417.
6. "It is absolutely necessary to establish the course of things firmly and to destroy uncertainty, that is explain the whole murder one way or another and make its character and relations clear. Pride, personality and insolence." Dostoevskii, *PSS*, 7:141–42.
7. Bakhtin, *Problems of Dostoevsky's Poetics*, 238.
8. Dostoevskii, *PSS*, 6:39; Dostoevsky, *Crime and Punishment*, 45.
9. Ibid.
10. Dostoevsky, *Crime and Punishment*, 519.
11. Safronova, *Russkoe obshchestvo v zerkale revoliutsionnogo terrora*, 233.
12. In Russia, both madness and its causal ontology were ambiguous. Holy fools were regarded as blessed ones and had the privilege of behaving and

speaking provocatively, even of "telling the truth to Tsars." But other forms of madness, such as klikushestvo [shrieking], were variously attributed to punishment by God, witchcraft, or demonic possession. The fact that the mentally unbalanced were likely to express unorthodox and impolitic opinions meant that they were frequently subject to police surveillance. See Sergei Ivanov, *Holy Fools in Byzantium and Beyond*; Christine Worobec, *Possessed: Women, Witches, and Demons in Imperial Russia*; and Lia Iangoulova, "The *Osvidetel'stvovanie* and *Ispytanie* of Insanity: Psychiatry in Tsarist Russia."

13. Dostoevsky, *Crime and Punishment*, 71.
14. Ibid., 536.
15. Ibid., 413.
16. Pisarev, *PSS*, 4:176.
17. Tolstoi, *Sobranie sochinenii L. N. Tolstogo v dvadtsati dvukh tomakh*, 4:27–28; Tolstoy, *War and Peace*, 19–20.
18. Dostoevskii, *PSS*, 6:201; Dostoevsky, *Crime and Punishment*, 261.
19. Dostoevskii, *PSS*, 6:321; Dostoevsky, *Crime and Punishment*, 418.
20. Lotman, "The Decembrist in Everyday Life," 98.
21. Dostoevsky, *Crime and Punishment*, 418.
22. Strictly speaking, Pisarev had three categories. The intermediary category consists of "Rudins" (based on the eponymous hero of Turgenev's novel), who intellectually reject the norms and shibboleths of their society, but are unable to do so in deed. Dostoevskii, *PSS*, 6:200; Dostoevsky, *Crime and Punishment*, 260; Pisarev, *PSS*, 4:175–76.
23. Dostoevsky, *Crime and Punishment*, 259.
24. Ibid.
25. Ibid., 261.
26. Ibid., 264.
27. Ibid., 55.
28. Ibid., 58–59.
29. Ibid.
30. Ibid. In the original Russian, "p'ianye, shaliat, ne nashe delo, poidem!" Dostoevskii, *PSS*, 6:49.
31. Dostoevsky, *The Notebooks for "Crime and Punishment,"* 56.

Part One, Chapter 6. Spoiling One Idea to Save Another

1. Frank, *Dostoevsky: The Miraculous Years*, 50.
2. Dostoevskii, *PSS*, 28 b. 2:160. Dostoevsky's death-defying escapade was mandated by the "biggest gamble of his life." The rights to his future literary works were in hock to the ruthless publisher Stellovsky in exchange for the desperately needed advance of 3,000 rubles, and unless Dostoevsky produced the promised novella (eventually aptly entitled *The Gambler*) by November 1, 1866, he would lose all the proceeds from his future literary work for a period of nine years. Frank, *Dostoevsky: The Miraculous Years*, 32.
3. Dostoevskii, *PSS*, 28 b 2:140. Letter to Alexander Vrangel, September 16/28, 1865 Wiesbaden. For a more in-depth look at Dostoevsky's quite complex relationship with Katkov, see Susanne Fusso, "Dostoevsky and Mikhail Katkov: Their Literary Partnership (*Crime and Punishment* and *The Devils*)," 35–70.

4. Dostoevskii, *PSS*, 28 b. 2:154. Letter to Katkov, April 25, 1866.
5. Dostoevskii, *PSS*, 28 b. 2:166. Letter to Alexander Miliukov, July 10–15, 1866.
6. Paperno, *Chernyshevsky and the Age of Realism*, 30; Verhoeven, *The Odd Man Karakozov*, 40. The verdict of the supreme criminal court concluded, "The novel of that criminal had the most destructive influence on many of the defendants, inspired absurd antisocial ideas, and, finally, invited them to take the maxim *the end justifies the means*."
7. Lebeziatnikov is referred to in Part I Chapter 2 of the novel as a benighted wife beater and also, ironically, a "follower of all the new ideas." But he does not come into his own as a character with a name and patronymic until Part V Chapter 1, when Andrei Semyonovich (he shares Sonya's patronymic) emerges as a full-blooded, kind-hearted and sympathetic character, whose natural compassion has been distorted by half-digested English utilitarianism.
8. Dostoevsky, *Crime and Punishment*, 363.
9. Part V was written August–September 24, 1866. Karakozov was hanged before a massed public on September 3, 1866. There is no evidence that Dostoevsky attended the execution.
10. Dostoevskii, *PSS*, 28 b. 2:137; Dostoevsky, *Complete Letters*, 2:174–75.
11. Ibid.
12. Ernest Simmons, *Dostoevsky: The Making of a Novelist*, 153. Simmons is a little self-contradictory on this score, however, since he then admits that "in the novel there is considerable preparation for the preferred denouement, although the fluctuations of Raskolnikov's thought leave us uncertain until the very end."
13. Dostoevskii, *PSS*, 28 b. 2:172. Letter dated December 9, 1866.
14. I am grateful to the participants of the Slavic Seminar on February 5, 2016, at Columbia University for helping me to fine-tune this point.
15. Dostoevsky, *Crime and Punishment*, 273.
16. Dostoevskii, *PSS*, 6:211; Dostoevsky, *Crime and Punishment*, 274.
17. This is not to imply that Dostoevsky was the first to contemplate the aesthetics of murder. Inspired by Sikes's highly effective murder of Nancy in the stage version of *Oliver Twist*, British Romantic writer Thomas De Quincy wrote three essays "On Murder Considered as One of the Fine Arts" (1827, 1839, and 1854). Though De Quincy agreed that the horror of the murder should intensify the emotional and moral effect, he also recognized the possibility that murder scenes would become a mere means of aesthetic pleasure and entertainment. See Joseph Crawford, *Gothic Fiction and the Invention of Terrorism*, 169–70.
18. Dostoevskii, *PSS*, 6:204; Dostoevsky, *Crime and Punishment*, 266. "'Might it not have been some future Napoleon who bumped off our Alyona Ivanovna with an axe last week?' Zamyotov suddenly blurted out from his corner."
19. Dostoevsky, *Crime and Punishment*, 274.
20. Ibid., 275. The quotations are from Pushkin's cycle "Verses from the Koran." Raskolnikov is referring to the battle of November 13, 1795, when Napoleon used artillery to quash an uprising in Paris. See Dostoevskii, *PSS*, 7:381–82.
21. Laqueur, *The Age of Terrorism*, 28; Daniel Bessner and Michael Stauch, "Karl Heinzen and the Intellectual Origins of Modern Terrorism," 144.

22. Benjamin Grob-Fitzgibbon, "From the Dagger to the Bomb: Karl Heinzen and the Evolution of Political Terror," 112.

23. It is possible that Dostoevsky encountered Heinzen's pamphlet during his first trip abroad in 1863: the Underground Man's view of history and Raskolnikov's theory of murder share many points in common with Heinzen. For example, compare Heinzen's "Finally history teaches that crime finishes at the gallows when it is too weak to defend itself, but it becomes 'law' as soon as it has the power to assert itself" to Raskolnikov's observation that "the masses ... punish them and hang them (more or less)," but if they "triumph in their own lifetime," they "start doing their own punishing." See Bessner and Stauch's translation of the 1853 text "Karl Heinzen," 162. Dostoevsky, *Crime and Punishment*, 261.

24. Karl Heinzen, "Murder" [Der Mord], reprinted in Walter Laqueur, *Voices of Terror*, 57.

25. Ibid., 67.

26. Ibid., 60.

27. Susanne Fusso has suggested that Katkov's review of Turgenev's *Fathers and Sons*, "About our nihilism on the grounds of Turgenev's novel" [O nashem nigilizme po povodu romana Turgeneva], provided the inspiration for Raskolnikov's blunder, and I certainly agree. While the nihilist, in Katkov's opinion, is entirely willing to "negate his moral feeling and consciousness of duty at their foundations," "he is repelled by baseness only because of its wretched character, its pettiness, and the fact that it humiliates his person." See Fusso, "Dostoevsky and Mikhail Katkov," 38–39. But as I argue, it is Dostoevsky who in a brilliant stroke of irony frames these objections as "aesthetic."

28. Quoted in Charles A. Moser, *Esthetics as Nightmare*, 79–80.

29. Ibid., 59.

30. Dostoevsky, *Crime and Punishment*, 415.

31. For Dostoevsky's adherence to classical aesthetic standards, see Robert Louis Jackson, *Dostoevsky's Quest for Form: A Study of His Philosophy of Art*, 64.

32. Verhoeven argues against categorizing Karakozov's act as a tyrannicide, contending that Karakozov did not harbor tyrannicidal motives; in other words, his animus was not directed at Alexander II personally, but at autocracy as a political order. See Verhoeven, *The Odd Man Karakozov*, 176.

33. W. J. Leatherbarrow argues that "when Raskolnikov is troubled by the thought of the crime [before the murder], he is disturbed not by its lack of morality, but by its lack of aesthetic form, its ugliness." Leatherbarrow, *A Devil's Vaudeville: The Demonic in Dostoevsky's Major Fiction*, 89. Leatherbarrow puts it too mildly. Raskolnikov is viscerally and physiologically repulsed by the act that his hideous dream has evoked. He has to acquire some Kantian distance, which involves the rationalization of his visceral reactions, before he can contemplate the problem as an "aesthetic" one.

34. Here I refer to Nikolai Solovyev's article "Theory of Ugliness," published in Dostoevsky's journal *Epokha* in July 1864. Solovyev took up Pisarev's gauntlet on behalf of the aesthetic camp by arguing that aesthetic feeling, rather than intellectual calculation (viz. the utilitarian camp), should underpin ethical conceptions. See Moser, *Esthetics as Nightmare*, 50–51.

35. Dostoevsky, *Crime and Punishment*, 519.
36. Dostoevsky, *The Notebooks for "Crime and Punishment,"* 64.
37. Dostoevskii, *PSS*, 6:351; Dostoevsky, *Crime and Punishment*, 460.
38. Dostoevsky, *Crime and Punishment*, 455.
39. Ibid., 475.
40. Ibid., 42.
41. Peter Pozefsky details the famous case of Maria Nozhina, an eighteen-year-old noblewoman who was supposedly abducted by her nihilist brother, Nikolai Nozhin, who was abetted by one of Pisarev's colleagues at *The Russian Word*, Varfolomei Zaitsev. The case was largely fabricated by overzealous anti-nihilist authorities. See Pozefsky, *The Nihilist Imagination*, 119-30.
42. When Dunya pulls a revolver on Svidrigailov to defend herself from ravishment, it turns out that he had been giving her shooting lessons in the country. She shoots to kill twice at three paces: the first shot grazes his head and the second misfires. At two paces, she refuses the shot and throws the revolver down.
43. Pisarev, *PSS*, 8:244-45.
44. Dostoevskii, *PSS*, 6:38-39; Dostoevsky, *Crime and Punishment*, 45.
45. Dostoevsky, *Crime and Punishment*, 551.
46. Ibid., 329.

Part One, Chapter 7. A Gloomier Catechism

1. P. N. Tkachev, *Izbrannye sochineniia na sotsial'no-politicheskie temy*, 1:173-233.
2. "Programma revoliutsionnykh deistvii" in Rudnitskaia, ed., *Revoliutsionnyi radikalizm v Rossii: Vek deviatnadtsatyi*, 204. The Program was published during the trial of the Nechaevtsy in *Pravitel'stvennyi vestnik*, 1871, no 163, 3.
3. "Programma revoliutsionnykh deistvii," 204.
4. Stephen T. Cochrane cites Vera Zasulich's understanding that deception was integral to the Committee's method of radicalizing the students. See Cochrane, *The Collaboration of Nečaev, Ogarev and Bakunin in 1869. Nečaev's Early Years*, 62. See Vera Zasulich, *Vospominaniia*, 23-24.
5. Pisarev's review entitled "The Struggle for Survival" [Bor'ba za zhizn'] purposefully approached Raskolnikov strictly as a social type and his crime as the result of social causes. For Pisarev's emotional reaction to *Crime and Punishment* and his assertion that Raskolnikov's ideas did not in the least resemble those of the radicals, see Lampert, *Sons Against Fathers*, 337.
6. Nechaev's biographer Philip Pomper observes, "In the end, however, Nechaev showed more kinship with Raskolnikov than with Verkhovenskii. He was but a pale criminal." Presumably Pomper means that Nechaev, like Raskolnikov, was but a "pale criminal." Pomper, *Sergei Nechaev*, 219.
7. Cited in Cochrane, *The Collaboration of Nečaev, Ogarev and Bakunin*, 145; Pomper, *Sergei Nechaev*, 80. The original Russian can be found in M. P. Dragomanov, *Pis'ma M. A. Bakunina k A. I. Gertsenu i N. P. Ogarevu*, 478-79.
8. "Nachala revoliutsii" in Rudnitskaia, ed., *Revoliutsionnyi radikalizm v Rossii: Vek deviatnadtsatyi*, 219.

9. Dostoevsky, *Crime and Punishment*, 258.
10. Ibid., 73.
11. Nechaev, "Katekhizis revoliutsionera," 244.
12. Dostoevsky, *Crime and Punishment*, 519. The judgment of the human community is also God's judgment, which shines forth in the eyes of the other. In *The Brothers Karamazov*, Dmitry begs Alyosha for his verdict on Mitya's escape plan but enjoins him for the time being to "Stand and be silent. . . . Not a question, not a movement, agreed? But anyway, Lord, what am I going to do about your eyes? I'm afraid your eyes will tell me your decision even if you are silent." Dostoevsky, *The Brothers Karamazov*, 595.
13. Nechaev, "Katekhizis revoliutsionera," 245.
14. Ibid., 247.
15. F. M. Lur'e, *Nechaev: Sozidatel' razrusheniia*, 156.
16. Pomper, *Sergei Nechaev*, 114-15.
17. Ibid., 118-19.
18. Quoted in ibid., 169.
19. Ibid., 61-62.
20. Lur'e, *Nechaev: Sozidatel' razrusheniia*, 186, 194.
21. Cited in Cochrane, *The Collaboration of Nečaev, Ogarev, and Bakunin*, 71; the original Russian in *Pravitel'stvennyi vestnik*, 1871 no. 163, 2.
22. Ibid., 147.
23. Pomper, *Sergei Nechaev*, 185.
24. Ibid., 212.

Part Two, Chapter 1. "Again, Like Before"

1. For a description of the Nechaev affair, see Part One Chapter 7.
2. *Moskovskie vedomosti*, November 25, 1869, 1.
3. Dostoevskii, *PSS*, 21:125. Also quoted in Frank, *Dostoevsky: The Miraculous Years*, 435. However, in the February 10, 1873, letter accompanying a copy of *Demons* to the heir to the throne Alexander III, Dostoevsky makes a somewhat different claim and terms it "nearly a historical study [pochti istoricheskii etiud], through which I wished to explain the possibility of such hideous phenomena [chudovishchnie iavleniia] in our strange society as the Nechaev movement [dvizhenie]." Dostoevsky, *Pis'ma*, 3:50.
4. For a most thorough account of how Dostoevsky transformed the Nechaev affair into fiction, see Gudrun Braunsperger, *Sergej Nečaev und Dostoevskij's Dämonen*. When it came to the details of the murder, Dostoevsky was almost slavishly faithful.
5. Dostoevskii, *PSS*, 10:508-9; Fyodor Dostoevsky, *Demons*, trans. Richard Pevear and Larissa Volokhonsky, 668. Pevear and Volokhonsky use "another" instead of "again" to render the Russian word *opiat'*.
6. Dostoevskii, *PSS*, 10:374; Dostoevsky, *Demons*, 487.
7. Dostoevskii, *PSS*, 10:392; Dostoevsky, *Demons*, 511.
8. Dostoevsky, however, had imagined bombs and daggers in theaters following the events of 1848, and they make their unlikely appearance in his vaudeville, "The Other Man's Wife and the Husband Under the Bed." See Irina Erman, "Bombing at the Theater: Violence, Performance, and Narrative Rupture

in Dostoevsky's 'Husband Under the Bed' and *The Devils*," unpublished paper, ASEEES, November 18, 2016.

9. Gleason, *Young Russia*, 320; Pomper, however, notes that in late August or early September 1869, Nechaev had tried to insinuate himself into a conspiracy to assassinate the tsar that involved mining the tracks with explosives. See Part One Chapter 7.

10. "It should be noted that Nechaevism is not the most ruthless form of terrorism. Nechaev spoke of the panic that acts of violence against highly placed persons would unleash, but unlike some modern terrorists, he never suggested that innocent victims be selected as targets." Pomper, *Sergei Nechaev*, 85.

11. Nina Pelikan Strauss compares Nikolai Stavrogin to Osama bin Laden, but Stavrogin's position and role cannot be considered comparable to Osama bin Laden's actual active leadership. Straus, "From Dostoevsky to Al-Qaeda: What Fiction Says to Social Science," 197-231.

12. Dostoevskii, *PSS*, 10:325; Dostoevsky, *Demons*, 420-21. Pevear and Volokhonsky translate "moshennik" as "crook," but to the English speaker "crook" implies mercenary ends, whereas "swindler" and its synonyms ("sham," "fraud") emphasize the means—deception—and are a better fit for Peter.

Part Two, Chapter 2. "The Only Possible Explanation of All These Wonders"

1. Dostoevsky, *Demons*, 7.
2. Slobodanka Vladiv first isolated and analyzed this characteristic feature of *Demons*. See Vladiv, *Narrative Principles in Dostoevskij's Besy*, 46-49.
3. Dostoevsky, *Demons*, 50.
4. Ibid., 45.
5. Ibid., 46.
6. Ibid., 51.
7. Ibid., 46.
8. Ibid., 678.
9. Verhoeven, *The Odd Man*, 134.
10. F. M. Dostoevsky, *The Notebooks for "The Possessed,"* 348-49.
11. Quoted in Cochrane, *The Collaboration of Nečaev, Ogarev, and Bakunin*, 140.
12. Stavrogin's actions, however, cause everything from consternation to outright terror. In Madame Liputin's case "the poor frightened woman fainted," while Ivan Osipovich's "mortal terror lasted a full minute, and after it the old man had a sort of fit." Dostoevsky, *Demons*, 48, 51.
13. For example, the peculiar offense of ear-biting appears in Gogol's "The Tale of the Two Ivans."
14. Dostoevsky, *Demons*, 669.
15. Ibid., 670.
16. Quoted in Pomper, *Sergei Nechaev*, 175.
17. Dostoevsky, *The Notebooks for "The Possessed,"* 349.
18. In fact, Katkov had begun singing this conspiracy theory tune immediately following Karakozov's attempt, when it was rumored that the would-be tsaricide was a "foreigner" and Katkov quickly latched onto the Poles as the

most likely suspects. See Verhoeven, *The Odd Man Karakozov*, 45, 47. Even then, Dostoevsky was deeply skeptical of any such connection, and in the same letter in which he defended our "poor defenseless boys and girls" reminded his publisher of the distinctly homegrown nature of Russian nihilism. Frank, *Dostoevsky: The Miraculous Years*, 50–51.

19. Leonid Grossman's provocative argument for *Demons* as "one of the most outstanding interpretations of Bakunin" in world literature was first published as an exchange with his colleague, Viacheslav Polonsky, in 1926. See Frank Goodwin, *Confronting Dostoevsky's "Demons": Anarchism and the Specter of Bakunin in Twentieth-Century Russia*, for a detailed examination of the controversy.

20. *Moskovskie vedomosti*, January 6, 1870, 1.
21. Ibid.
22. As Edward Wasiolek notes, Kirillov comes into being late in Dostoevsky's writing process and was originally conceived for instrumental purposes—to take the blame for Shatov's death. Ultimately, however, Dostoevsky endowed him with "colossal metaphysical significance" and made his suicide an attempt to "dethrone God." In its exalted aspiration and its exalted target, Kirillov's act is closest to tsaricide. Dostoevsky, *The Notebooks for "The Possessed,"* 302.
23. Dostoevsky, *Demons*, 618.
24. Ibid., 619.
25. Dostoevskii, *PSS*, 10:473; Dostoevsky, *Demons*, 621.
26. Dostoevsky, *Complete Letters*, 4:58.
27. Dostoevsky, *The Notebooks for "The Possessed,"* 346.

Part Two, Chapter 3. Tarantulas with a Heart?

1. Dostoevsky, *The Notebooks for "The Possessed,"* 346, 350.
2. Dostoevsky, *Demons*, 76.
3. Ibid., 385.
4. Ibid., 575.
5. Ibid., 305.
6. Carol Apollonio, *Dostoevsky's Secrets: Reading Against the Grain*, 113.
7. Dostoevsky, *The Notebooks for "The Possessed,"* 101.
8. Dostoevskii, *PSS*, 10:312; Dostoevsky, *Demons*, 403–4.
9. Dostoevskii, *PSS*, 10:312–13; Dostoevsky, *Demons*, 404.
10. Dostoevsky, *Demons*, 404.
11. Dostoevsky, *The Notebooks for "The Possessed,"* 140.
12. Oleg Vital'evich Budnitskii, *Terrorizm v rossiiskom osvoboditel'nom dvizhenii*, 35.
13. In fact, in his deposition to the Investigative Committee, Karakozov declared that he first conceived his intention to commit suicide, but did not wish to die in vain [darom], but wanted to be of some use to the people. *Iz pokazanii D. V. Karakozova sledstvennoi komissii po delu o pokushenii na Aleksandra II 4 aprelia 1866g.* http://www.hrono.ru/dokum/1800dok/18660416.html (accessed August 11, 2016).
14. "Studentam universiteta, Akademii, Tekhnologicheskogo Instituta v

Peterburge" in Rudnitskaia, ed., *Revoliutsionnyi radikalizm v Rossii: Vek deviatnadtsatyi*, 208.

15. "Nachala revoliutsii," 221.

16. "Studentam universiteta, Akademii, Tekhnologicheskogo Instituta v Peterburge," 207.

17. Quoted in Mochulsky, *Dostoevsky*, 424.

Part Two, Chapter 4. Dostoevsky's Counterterrorism

1. Joseph Frank, *Dostoevsky: The Mantle of the Prophet*, 14.

2. V. D. Spasovich, *Za mnogo let, 1859–1871, Articles, Excerpts, Histories, Criticism, Polemics, Court Speeches, and Others*, 419–20.

3. Quoted in Frank, *Dostoevsky: The Miraculous Years*, 411.

4. Dostoevsky, *Demons*, 220.

5. Dostoevskii, *PSS*, 11:202.

6. Ibid., 11:207. These two notebook entries are sequential and are dated August 15 and 16, 1870.

7. Frank, *Dostoevsky: The Miraculous Year*, 412. Frank's point is based on Konstantin Mochulsky's famous argument that places Stavrogin at the center of concentric circles of characters. Mochulsky, *Dostoevsky: His Life and Work*, 435–36.

8. Dostoevsky, *Demons*, 419.

9. Prime Minister Stolypin referred to his agricultural reforms, implemented between 1906 and 1914, as a "wager on the strong and the sober" in order to transform Russia and rescue it from backwardness and ultimate dissolution. The reforms were intended to transform Russia's communal agricultural practices into capitalistic ones based on private land ownership. Stolypin was assassinated by Dmitry Bogrov in 1911. Hence, Stolypin lost his wager and Peter won his.

10. Dostoevsky, *Demons*, 420.

11. Nechaev, *Catechism of a Revolutionary*. Quoted in Cochrane, *The Collaboration of Nečaev, Bakunin, Ogarev*, 216.

12. The literary scholar Kate Holland has recently argued for the preeminence of disintegration in Dostoevsky's thinking about Russian modernity and in his approach to the novel as a Western genre in dire need of reform. Although Dostoevsky had progressively become more antipathetic to Westernism in the course of the 1860s, his forced European sojourn in 1867–71 and the destabilizing events of that time (the Franco-Prussian war and the Paris Commune) intensified his mature conviction that Western society was on the verge of collapse, and that the Russian idea of a Christ-centered universal orthodoxy would be the new guiding principle of civilization. Holland illuminates how these ideas shape *Demons* on both a formal and thematic level, but she does not explicitly discuss the role of disintegration at the heart of Peter's tactics and goals. See Kate Holland, *The Novel in the Age of Disintegration*, especially 61–69.

13. Dostoevsky, *Demons*, 421.

14. Oliver Marchart, "The Other Side of Order: Towards a Political Theory of Terror and Dislocation," 101.

15. Dostoevskii, *PSS*, 10:325; Dostoevsky, *Demons*, 421.
16. Cited in Marchart, "The Other Side of Order," 101.
17. Dostoevsky, *Demons*, 422.
18. Ibid., 418.
19. See Part I Chapter 5 for Raskolnikov's aesthetic deliberations regarding murder and terrorism.
20. Dostoevsky, *Demons*, 43.
21. Dostoevskii, *PSS*, 11: 27; Dostoevsky, *Demons*, 710.
22. Ibid.
23. René Girard, *Violence and the Sacred*, 103. Girard wrote extensively about Stavrogin in his earlier work, *Deceit, Desire, and the Novel: Self and Other in Literary Structure*, but here his focus is on Stavrogin as "an internal mediator" of mimetic desire. "The possessed get their ideas and desires from Stavrogin" (60). Girard sees Stavrogin as a false god/antichrist, but he has not yet developed the political-theoretical aspect of mimetic desire that would emerge later in *Violence and the Sacred*. Other literary scholars have followed Girard's lead and read Stavrogin as an internal and empty mediator. See Jostein Børtnes, "The Last Delusion in an Infinite Series of Delusions: Stavrogin and the Symbolic Structure of *The Devils*," 54–68.
24. René Girard, *Violence and the Sacred*, 105.
25. Apollonio also sees Stavrogin in the role of scapegoat, not through his own deeds but by means of words—slander regarding reputed misdeeds that have been committed offstage. Stavrogin is scapegoated by word and by deed, and the effect, in the end, is the same. Apollonio's "against the grain" assertion that his confession to the rape of Matriosha "functions as a self-slandering fiction" demonstrates Stavrogin's active participation in sacrificial enthronement. See Apollonio, *Dostoevsky's Secrets*, 139–41.
26. Girard, *Violence and the Sacred*, 107.
27. Dostoevskii, *PSS*, 29 b. 1:142.
28. Joseph Frank recounts Dostoevsky's agonized attempts to revise "At Tikhon's" so that Katkov would include it and his ultimate realization that the novel would be published without the chapter that provides critical psychological insight into Stavrogin. See Frank, *Dostoevsky: The Miraculous Years*, 431–34.
29. Hans Magnus Enzensberger, "Die Leere im Zentrum des Terrors," 249.
30. Marchart, "The Other Side of Order," 97.
31. Leatherbarrow, *Dostoevsky's "The Devils,"* 49.
32. Apollonio, *Dostoevsky's Secrets*, 128.
33. Kravchinskii (Stepniak), *Underground Russia*, 40–41.
34. Frank describes this mixture in the following way: "Although his 'positive program' has usually been considered 'reactionary' because of its support for Tsarism, the correspondence he received reveals that such support, combined with his harsh denunciation of existing social evils, was by no means felt to be as politically subservient as it has appeared to posterity." Frank, *Dostoevsky: Mantle of the Prophet*, 256.

Part Two, Chapter 5. Dostoevsky's Counterterrorism (Continued)

1. Arnold, *Culture and Anarchy*, 149.
2. Spasovich, *Za mnogo let*, 423. Spasovich begins by likening Nechaev to Goncharov's Mark Volokhov from *The Precipice* (*Obryv*), but he acknowledges that Mark Volokhov was honest, whereas Nechaev "lied mercilessly."
3. Irving Howe, "Dostoevsky: The Politics of Salvation [The Possessed]," 135.
4. Dostoevsky, *The Notebooks for "The Possessed,"* 141.
5. Ibid., 143.
6. Dostoevsky, *Demons*, 216.
7. Ibid., 430.
8. Dostoevsky, *The Notebooks for "The Possessed,"* 129.
9. Dostoevsky, *Demons*, 431–32. In her masterful study of the duel in Russian literature and culture, Irina Reyfman extensively details the Russian nobility's pervasive fear of bodily violation and specifically of flogging. Stories of members of the gentry who had been secretly tortured and flogged, especially under Catherine II's notorious head of the Secret Expedition, Semyon Sheshkovsky (see Prologue) were pervasive through the mid-to-late nineteenth century. In Reyfman's analysis the relatively late rise of the duel in Russian culture was tied to the nobility's attempt to secure for themselves the bodily inviolability and personal dignity that their European peers enjoyed. See Reyfman, *Ritualized Violence Russian Style: The Duel in Russian Culture and Literature*, 113–27. As support for the narrator's skepticism, however, the historian Jonathan Daly argues that in general, Russian political prisoners in the nineteenth century enjoyed lenient, if inconsistent, conditions. This especially pertained to prisoners from the educated classes, but treatment might suddenly worsen according to situational factors such as the political climate or prison commandant. See Daly, "Political Crime in Late Imperial Russia," 87–91.
10. Dostoevsky, *Demons*, 445.
11. Ibid.
12. Ibid.
13. Ibid., 444.
14. Ibid., 449.

Part Two, Chapter 6. The Unity of All Terrorism(s)

1. Alex P. Schmid and Albert J. Jongman, *Political Terrorism*, 196.
2. Schmid does not seem aware that his definition, first proposed in 1984, is completely ahistorical. The very long and seemingly exhaustive definition of terrorism does not take into account the practice of individual targeted terrorism—the form in which terrorism first emerged in pre-Revolutionary Russia. His "definition" describes a later form of terrorism that predominated during the late twentieth century.
3. J. Bower Bell offers a typology specifically of revolutionary terrorism that is cited in Schmid and Jongman, *Political Terrorism*, 50–51.

4. From what we are given to understand, Peter orders the murder so as to simultaneously liberate Stavrogin to pursue his romantic relationship with Liza and to bind him through gratitude/complicity to Peter, so that he will perform his role in Peter's schemes. Stavrogin is in fact complicit; he has an unspoken, intuitive understanding of what Peter intends and gives money to the murderous convict Fedka, which Fedka interprets as blood money for the murder of the Ledbyadkins.

5. Dostoevsky, *Demons*, 8.
6. Ibid., 386–87.
7. Ibid., 429.
8. In relating patchwork biographies of both men earlier in the novel, G___v had given information insinuating that both men had connections to the police, and that such was the prevailing belief among the townsfolk.
9. Dostoevsky, *Demons*, 398.
10. Dostoevskii, *PSS*, 10:309; Dostoevsky, *Demons*, 400.
11. On Balzac as a source for *Crime and Punishment*, see Joseph Frank, *Dostoevsky: The Miraculous Years*, 73.
12. The question has since been posed by the philosophers Philippa Foot and Judith Jarvis Thomson as the famous "trolley dilemma," which pits utilitarianism against deontology. See Judith Jarvis Thomson, "The Trolley Problem," 1395–415.
13. It should come as no surprise that Dostoevsky was right, although he would not be pleased (or perhaps he would be tickled by the irony) with the means of his vindication. The neuroscientist and philosopher Joshua Greene composed scenarios based on the trolley dilemma and exposed subjects to them while their brains were imaged in a fMRI. The results clearly supported Greene's hypothesis—and Shaposhnikov's contention—that deontological judgments are based on emotional reactions (greater activity was recorded in the emotional centers of the brain) whereas utilitarian judgments are cool and calculating. J. D. Green, R. B. Sommerville, L. E. Nystrom, J. M. Darley, and J. D. Cohen, "An fMRI Study of Emotional Engagement in Moral Judgment," 2105–8.
14. Dostoevsky, *The Notebooks for "The Possessed,"* 94–95.
15. Peter's question is as follows: "If any of us knew of a planned political murder, would he go and inform, foreseeing all the consequences, or would he stay home and await events. Views may differ here." "Views may differ here" is obviously Peter's cynical bid to give the semblance of pluralism and choice, when there in fact is none. Dostoevsky, *Demons*, 410.
16. Ilya Kliger argues that the Mandarin dilemma in *Crime and Punishment* offers "the alternatives not merely as moral choices but as modes of self-knowledge." See Ilya Kliger, *The Narrative Shape of Truth: Verediction in Modern European Literature*, 121.
17. In *The Concept of the Political*, Schmitt writes "Only the actual participants can correctly recognize, understand, and judge the concrete situation and settle the extreme case of conflict. Each participant is in a position to judge whether the adversary intends to negate his opponent's way of life and therefore must be repulsed or fought in order to preserve one's own existence." Carl Schmitt, *The Concept of the Political*, 27. In *Theory of the Partisan*, "the enemy" is closely

Notes to Pages 146–152

identified with the self, whose identity is only fully constructed and asserted by means of the enemy. "Historia in nuce. Friend and Enemy. The friend is he who affirms and confirms me. The enemy is he who challenges me (Nuremburg 1947). Who can challenge me? Basically only myself. The enemy is he who defines me. That means in concreto: only my brother can challenge me and only my brother can be my enemy." Schmitt, *Theory of the Partisan*, 85n89.

18. Schmitt's formulation: "Nenne mir Deinen Feind, und ich sage Dir, wer Du bist." Quoted in Claudia Koonz, *The Nazi Conscience*, 293n52.

19. Hannah Arendt is also interested in the distortion of the concepts of enmity and friendship that accompanies totalitarian terror. She sees this as beginning "once totalitarian movements have come to power, they proceed to change reality in accordance with their ideological claims. The concept of enmity is replaced by that of conspiracy, and this produces a mentality in which reality— real enmity or real friendship—is no longer experienced in its own terms but is automatically assumed to signify something else." From this point on, totalitarian regimes prepare their subjects for the interchangeable roles of victim and executioner. Hannah Arendt, *The Origins of Totalitarianism*, 471. Dostoevsky sees this historical moment as occurring earlier.

20. The literal meaning of the idiom (which took off with Shakespeare's *Hamlet*) is "to cause the bomb maker to be blown up with his own bomb." In Shakespeare's day, a petard was a relatively new innovation, a small bomb used to breach fortifications.

21. Quoted in Joseph Frank, *Dostoevsky: Mantle of the Prophet*, 483.

22. Ibid., 482.

Part Three, Chapter 1. A Change of Heart

1. Christopher Ely's new study argues that the urban spaces of the empire's largest cities (St. Petersburg, Moscow, Odessa, etc.) enabled the radicals to create a revolutionary underground. "The formation of this new, organized, and disciplined subversive heterotopia allowed the anti-autocratic movement to congregate and carry out a wide variety of operations in relative safety." Ely, *Underground Petersburg*, 27.

2. For the evolution of the revolutionary movement through its phases from populism to terrorism in the 1870s, see Franco Venturi's *Roots of Revolution: A History of the Populist and Socialist Movement in Nineteenth-Century Russia*; Adam B. Ulam, *In the Name of the People: Prophets and Conspirators in Pre-Revolutionary Russia*; Richard Wortman, *The Crisis of Russian Populism*; and Deborah Hardy, *Land and Freedom: The Origins of Russian Terrorism, 1876–1879*. On August 26, 1879, the Executive Committee condemned Alexander II to death; see Venturi, *Roots*, 658.

3. *Literatura partii "Narodnoi volii,"* 6.

4. The first plot, which consisted of three different attempts (the first entirely abandoned), entailed the mining of the route from the tsar's summer residence in Livadia to the Winter Palace in St. Petersburg. At the first attempt in Alexandrovsk on November 18, the explosive failed to detonate when the wires were joined. On November 19, three versts from the Moscow station, Sophia

Perovskaya and Stepan Shiriaev led a venture to mine and then detonate explosives beneath the rails, but they set the battery too late and destroyed the second baggage train transporting Alexander's servants and retinue. None of the attempts attained their objective, but they served notice to the regime and to the public that systematic attempts were being made on the tsar's life by an organization with the technologically sophisticated means of dynamite. See Venturi, *Roots*, 681–84.

5. Quoted in Zaionchkovsky, *The Russian Autocracy in Crisis*, 92.
6. Ibid.
7. Valuev would know, since he held numerous official positions, including that of Chairman of the Special Conferences established to combat the revolutionary movement that convened for the first time on March 31, 1878, after Vera Zasulich's acquittal. Zaionchkovsky, *The Russian Autocracy in Crisis*, 16.
8. On May 24, 1879, Valuev's report to the tsar on the Special Conference's policy recommendations made no bones about the fact that educated society "was frightened, yet preferred neutrality to working on behalf of the regime." This group, actually, was critical of government policy and opposed it. Zaionchkovsky, *The Russian Autocracy in Crisis*, 58.
9. Dostoevskii, *PSS*, 30 b. 2:37–38.
10. Ibid.
11. Dostoevsky was not alone in seeking to advise the tsar; after the blast at the Winter Palace there was an "understanding of the need for definite political concessions. In the wake of this event there passed a whole stream of memoranda containing various recipes for the 'salvation of Russia.'" Zaionchkovsky, *The Russian Autocracy in Crisis*, 22.
12. Frank, *Dostoevsky: Mantle of the Prophet*, 484.
13. After the attempt on the imperial train on November 19, 1879, the tsar himself initiated discussion of the "family question" and role of religious upbringing, but through the Church, not the press. See Iuliia Safronova's excellent study *Russkoe obshchestvo v zerkale revoliutsionnogo terrora*, 88–90. Safronova notes that Minister of Justice Pahlen had actually broached the subject four years earlier in an extensive report detailing the causes of revolutionary propaganda (the "To the People" movement). In the report, Pahlen had explicitly accused "fathers and mothers" of providing moral and material support for their children's seditious activities and had attributed the propagandists' (and by association, the People's Will's) "success" to the ease with which their teaching infiltrated and elicited society's sympathy. Safronova, *Russkoe obshchestvo*, 89.
14. Ibid., 73.
15. See Safronova, *Russkoe obshchestvo*, especially Part II, Chapter 3, "The Discussion about the School Question," 243–53.

Part Three, Chapter 2. An Original Plan

1. The Zasulich case has received extensive scholarly attention. See Wolfgang Geierhos, *Vera Zasulic und die russische revoluzionäre Bewegung*; Jay Bergman, *Vera Zasulich: A Biography*; Ana Siljak, *Angel of Vengeance: The Girl Who Shot the Governor of St. Petersburg and Sparked the Age of Assassination*; Richard

Pipes, "The Trial of Vera Zasulich," 371–82. The defendants at the Trial of the 193 were those young people who had been arrested for "Going to the People" in 1873–74. Many of them had been held in pretrial detention since their arrest.

2. Jay Bergman points out that although Zasulich makes no mention of it in her memoir, she was fully aware of Land and Freedom's parallel plot to assassinate Trepov. There are conflicting accounts of her reasons for acting independently of her male comrades. See Bergman, *Vera Zasulich*, 37–38.

3. She made sure to change her clothing at the train station prior to the attack so as not to be described in the press wearing a cloak that her landlady would recognize and that would therefore betray her identity. See Vera Zasulich, *Vospominaniia*, 66.

4. Claudia Verhoeven presents the variations and historians' interpretations of them. Karakozov may have countered with his own question to the tsar: "What kind of freedom did you make?" or he may have given the non-explanation "Nothing." Verhoeven credits the latter. See Verhoeven, *The Odd Man Karakozov*, 177–78. It is unlikely that Karakozov was prepared to answer a question put to him by his intended victim.

5. Bergman, *Vera Zasulich*, 39.

6. Ana Siljak gives an excellent account of the conditions obtaining in the House of Preliminary Detention, which, although the most modern prison facility in Russia (based on the British model Pentonville), was a hell for its inmates nonetheless. See Siljak, *Angel of Vengeance*, 176, 177, 184–85.

7. Trepov had in fact obtained the Minister of Justice Pahlen's permission before administering the flogging, so although it was illegal, it was not unauthorized. Bergman, *Vera Zasulich*, 35.

8. Ibid.

9. The Southern Rebels have not yet received the scholarly attention devoted to Karakozov, Nechaev, Zasulich, or the Peoples' Will, but they seem to be a critical evolutionary link in the emergence of revolutionary terrorism. As Venturi emphasizes, "The example of Vera Zasulich and other attempts made at the same time show that this 'terrorism' came from the South and was brought to St. Petersburg by associates of the 'rebels' of Kiev and Odessa. Osinsky had already joined the circles of Zemlia i Volia, but he too came from the Ukraine, as did Popko, Frolenko and Volshenko." Venturi, *Roots*, 597.

10. "Terroristic acts went almost unnoticed in the village: there was no one on whom to observe the effect they produced; unheralded and unmourned, they did not stir even the revolutionists themselves." See Vera Figner, *Zapechatlennyi trud*, 1:68.

11. Pipes, "The Trial of Vera Zasulich," 1–2.

12. In his thorough and insightful investigation of the jury trial and Dostoevsky's incorporation of his experiences of the Kroneberg, Kairova, and Kornilova trials into *The Brothers Karamazov*, Gary Rosenshield repeatedly mentions the profound impact of the Zasulich trial on Dostoevsky. See Rosenshield, *Western Law, Russian Justice: Dostoevsky, the Jury Trial, and the Law*. Frank of course points to the significance of the Zasulich trial, observing that "the tense drama of the Zasulich proceedings . . . served as a model for the atmosphere that Dostoevsky would create two years later in the trial scenes of his novel." Frank, *Dostoevsky:*

Mantle of the Prophet, 374. Leonid Grossman, in a final chapter entitled "Karamazov or Karakozov?," is the first to link Alyosha Karamazov to Dmitry Karakozov (based largely on the similar sounding family names, the novel's setting in 1866, and Dostoevsky's intentions for his hero in the sequel), but he does not mention the Zasulich trial in his extremely abbreviated discussion of the novel. See Grossman, *Dostoevsky: A Biography*, 586–89.

13. See N. F. Budanova and G. M. Fridlender, eds. *Letopis' zhizni i tvorchestva F. M. Dostoevskogo*, 3:262. Quoted in Frank, *Dostoevsky: Mantle of the Prophet*, 375; Siljak, *Angel of Vengeance*, 245 quoting Gradovskii, "Sud," 134–35; Bergman, *Vera Zasulich*, 51.

Part Three, Chapter 3. Emotions on Trial

1. A. F. Koni, *Vospominaniia o dele Very Zasulich*, 193–94.
2. Ibid., 172–73.
3. Siljak, *Angel of Vengeance*, 222–23.
4. Bergman, *Vera Zasulich*, 40–41.
5. Quoted in N. K. Bukh, *Vospominaniia*, 162.
6. Koni, *Vospominaniia*, 138.
7. Ibid., 107–9.
8. Ibid., 101.
9. Ibid., 112.
10. Siljak, *Angel of Vengeance*, 180.
11. Koni, *Vospominaniia*, 132.
12. Ibid.
13. Ibid., 136.
14. Ibid., 139.
15. Ibid.
16. Quoted in Frank, *Dostoevsky: Mantle of the Prophet*, 374.
17. Kessel was third in line for the position, after his superiors V. I. Zhukovskii and S. A. Andreevskii refused to serve as prosecutor. Pahlen rewarded them for their refusal by forcing them to submit their resignations. Bergman, *Vera Zasulich*, 42.
18. Rosenshield, *Western Law, Russian Justice*, 163–64.
19. Koni, *Vospominaniia*, 153–54.
20. Ibid.
21. Ibid., 155.

Part Three, Chapter 4. Emotions on Trial II

1. Rosenshield, *Western Law, Russian Justice*, 17.
2. Dostoevskii, *PSS*, 22:64–65. Quoted also in Rosenshield, *Western Law, Russian Justice*, 39.
3. Siljak, *Angel of Vengeance*, 226–27.
4. Koni, *Vospominaniia*, 162.
5. Frank, *Dostoevsky: The Mantle of the Prophet*, 294.
6. Nikolai Karamzin's "Poor Liza" [Bednaia Liza], a typical sentimental tale, appeared in the *Moscow Journal* in 1792. The title character is a virtuous

young maiden who lives with her widowed mother and is seduced by a likable but shiftless nobleman, Erast. Circumstances force Erast into a marriage of convenience with a wealthy older woman, and when Liza discovers his betrayal, she commits suicide by throwing herself into a pond near the Simonov monastery. That pond became a site of pilgrimage for "Poor Liza" enthusiasts.

7. This reading of Nechaev as Erast is supported by the "romantic" connection between Vera Zasulich and Nechaev. Nechaev and Zasulich became acquainted in St. Petersburg in 1868 when the two frequented the same radical reading circles. Zasulich's sister Alexandra had married Peter Uspensky, Nechaev's most devoted follower and accomplice in the murder of Ivanov. Zasulich records her striking impressions of Nechaev in her *Memoirs*, but by far the most memorable was his nighttime appearance at Zasulich's bedside with a declaration of love and proposal of marriage. Zasulich had good enough sense not to fully trust Nechaev's intentions and so she declined. Nonetheless, she was caught in his snares and suffered arrest and years' long imprisonment with the rest of the Nechaevtsy. See Zasulich, *Vospominaniia*, 59-62.

8. Koni, *Vospominaniia*, 166.
9. Rosenshield, *Western Law, Russian Justice*, 105-6.
10. See Abby Schrader, *Languages of the Lash: Corporal Punishment and Identity in Imperial Russia*, for statutes and practices pertaining to corporal punishment before and after the 1864 reforms.
11. Koni, *Vospominaniia*, 169-70.
12. Dostoevsky, *A Writer's Diary*, 2:1048.
13. Koni, *Vospominaniia*, 171-72.
14. Hunt argues that the self-evidence of abstract notions of human rights rest on their emotional appeal. "We are most certain that a human right is at issue when we feel horrified by its violation." Hunt, *Inventing Human Rights*, 26.
15. Koni, *Vospominaniia*, 176.
16. N. A. Troitsky, "Zasulich ili Figner? (o stikhotvorenii Ia. P. Polonskogo 'Uznitsa')," 183.
17. Ia. P. Polonskii, *Polnoe Sobranie Sochinenii. Stikhotvoreniia 1841-1885*, 1:431.
18. N. A. Troitsky, "Zasulich ili Figner?," 183.
19. Ibid., 184-86. Borovikovskii, one of the defense attorneys at the trial, had himself written a poem titled "K sudiam," inspired by Lydia Figner, who had impressed him with her "stoikost' i obaianie" [firmness and charm].
20. Koni, *Vospominaniia*, 176.
21. Ibid., 178.
22. Ibid., 179-80.

Part Three, Chapter 5. Whose Rebellion?

1. Dostoevskii, *PSS*, 14:216; Dostoevsky, *The Brothers Karamazov*, trans. Pevear and Volokhonsky, 237.
2. Dostoevsky, *The Brothers Karamazov*, 16.
3. Ibid., 241.
4. Ibid., 243.
5. Frank, *Dostoevsky: Mantle of the Prophet*, 431.

6. Quoted in ibid., 433.
7. Ibid., 432.
8. Mikhail Bakhtin, *Problems of Dostoevsky's Poetics*, 18.
9. Robert Belknap, *The Genesis of "The Brothers Karamazov,"* 166.
10. Ibid.
11. Edwin Black, *Rhetorical Criticism: A Study in Method*, 142–43.
12. Richard W. Leeman, *The Rhetoric of Terrorism and Counterterrorism*, 53.

13. After the shooting of General Trepov and Zasulich's acquittal in March 1878, a succession of chiefs of police and governors-general became revolutionaries' favored targets. Kotlyarevsky, Geiking, Totleben, Mezentsev, Drenteln, and Kropotkin were among those whose assassinations were attempted or accomplished before the founding of the People's Will in Summer 1879. See Venturi, *Roots*, 838–39.

Part Three, Chapter 6. False Christs and Little Devils

1. Koni, *Vospominaniia*, 180.
2. Ibid., 181.
3. Dostoevsky, *The Brothers Karamazov*, 245.
4. Ibid., 244.
5. Ibid., 245.
6. Ibid.
7. Koni, *Vospominaniia*, 181.
8. Dostoevsky, *The Brothers Karamazov*, 244.
9. Koni, *Vospominaniia*, 183.

10. M. L. Mikhailov was close to Chernyshevsky and Nekrasov's *Contemporary* from the late 1840s onward. He was one of the founding members of Land and Freedom in its first iteration in the early 1860s, but he and his coauthor Shelgunov were quickly brought to heel and arrested in 1861 for their mini-proclamation campaign, in which they published and tried to distribute three manifestoes. As a result, Mikhailov became one of the first revolutionary-poet martyrs.

11. Koni, *Vospominaniia*, 181.
12. Ibid., 185.
13. Ibid., 186.
14. Ibid.
15. Ibid., 193.
16. Vera Zasulich, *Vospominaniia*, 13–14.
17. Dostoevsky, *The Brothers Karamazov*, 249, 250.
18. Ibid., 258.
19. For Hannah Arendt's reading, see *On Revolution*, 72–75.
20. Ibid., 76.
21. Ibid., 77.

22. Minsky is a fascinating transitional and liminal figure who has been unduly neglected by the criticism. Initially Jewish and Populist, Minsky converted from Judaism to Christianity and was literally at the avant-garde of literary and philosophical modernism. The Russian scholar L. P. Shchennikova has recently

taken up his cause in her dissertation and a series of articles. See especially Shchennikova, "Ispoved' dvukh geroev: Ivan Karamazov i osuzhdennyi N. Minskogo," 222-31.

23. *Literatura partii "Narodnoi voli,"* 17.
24. Near the end of their conversation, Alyosha kisses Ivan on the lips, just as the Christ of Ivan's poema kisses the Grand Inquisitor, giving rise to Ivan's rather pleased accusation of "literary theft!" Dostoevsky, *The Brothers Karamazov*, 263.
25. *Literatura partii "Narodnoi voli,"* 19.
26. Ibid.
27. Dostoevskii, *PSS*, 30 b. 1:68.
28. Ibid., 30 b. 1:70.
29. The Polish painter Henryk Siemiradsky's 1877 painting *Nero's Torches* (*The Torches of Christianity*), which depicts the burning of Christian martyrs before the emperor Nero, was also seen as reflecting the persecution of the radicals. The painting made a tremendous impression on Nikolai Mikhailovsky, who recognized the kinship between the martyrs for Christianity and the martyrs for revolution. See James Billington, *Mikhailovsky and Russian Populism*, 133.
30. Zaionchkovsky, *The Russian Autocracy in Crisis*, 93.
31. Ibid.
32. This is Alyosha's characterization of Ilyusha. See Dostoevskii, *PSS*, 14:503; Dostoevsky, *The Brothers Karamazov*, 557.
33. Dostoevsky, *The Brothers Karamazov*, 203-4.
34. Ibid., 205, 206.
35. Ibid., 207.
36. Dostoevskii, *PSS*, 14:480; Dostoevsky, *The Brothers Karamazov*, 516.
37. Dostoevsky, *The Brothers Karamazov*, 531.
38. Dostoevskii, *PSS*, 14:494; Dostoevsky, *The Brothers Karamazov*, 548.
39. Kolya would have had access to the technological specifications of manufacturing dynamite mines through the Russian press, which published information concerning the manufacture of mines, galvanic batteries, nitroglycerin, etc. during the year and a half in which the People's Will used dynamite. The British press and public would be equally fascinated by explosive technologies during the Fenian dynamite campaign in 1881-85. See Safronova, *Russkoe obshchestvo*, 113; Barbara Melchiori, *Terrorism in the Late Victorian Novel*, 34.
40. Dostoevsky, *The Brothers Karamazov*, 556-57.
41. Ibid., 560.
42. Ibid.
43. Ibid.

Part Three, Chapter 7. "That Is the Whole Answer"

1. Dostoevsky, *The Brothers Karamazov*, 288.
2. Dostoevskii, *PSS*, 30 b. 1:68.
3. In his penetrating study of the elder Zosima, Sven Linnér argues that Zosima's portrait as a "pure, ideal Christian" is drawn through all of his interactions earlier in the novel. I agree entirely; however, Book VI bears a special

burden, and its generic affinities with hagiography establish expectations that Dostoevsky does not meet. See Sven Linnér, *Starets Zosima in "The Brothers Karamazov": A Study in the Mimesis of Virtue,* 23–56.

4. Linnér argues for Hugo's Bishop Myriel as Zosima's most important literary prototype and acknowledges that this connection was made by Dostoevsky's own contemporaries in a review essay by Evgenii Markov in 1879. See Linnér, *Starets Zosima in "The Brothers Karamazov,"* 122–23.

5. Dostoevsky, *The Brothers Karamazov,* 289.

6. Ibid., 299.

7. As Tikhon's formulation makes clear, there is nothing that is only personal and between two people: everything affects the community. "In sinning, each man sins against all, and each man is at least partly guilty for another's sin. There is no isolated sin. And I am a great sinner, perhaps more than you are." Dostoevsky, *Demons,* 708.

8. Dostoevsky, *The Brothers Karamazov,* 74–75.

9. Ibid., 75.

10. Ibid., 262.

11. Ibid., 74.

12. Jackson, *Dostoevsky's Quest for Form,* 2. Jackson cites Prince Myshkin as expressing Dostoevsky's own anxiety that he lacked a "sense of gesture." Prince Myshkin declares to Rogozhin, "I'm always afraid that my absurd manner will compromise the thought and the main idea. I do not have a sense of gesture. I'm always making the opposite gesture, and this evokes laughter and debases the idea."

13. Gary Saul Morson, "The God of Onions: *The Brothers Karamazov* and the Mythic Prosaic," 111.

14. Dostoevsky, *The Brothers Karamazov,* 321.

Part Three, Chapter 8. The Khokhlakov Principle

1. This chapter's title consciously plays upon Safronova's, since her work on Russian society in the mirror of revolutionary terrorism illuminated the role of Madame Khokhlakov for me.

2. Dostoevsky, *The Brothers Karamazov,* 623.

3. On these unprecedented appeals to society, see Zaionchkovsky, *The Russian Autocracy in Crisis,* 47, 97. Safronova thoroughly examines society's response, emphasizing that "one may assert that the cooperation of the government and society was initiated by the government itself, giving [society] permission for that kind of communication." See Safronova, *Russkoe obshchestvo,* 217. Loris-Melikov's appeal "To the Inhabitants of the Capital" was issued on February 15, 1880, three days after the Supreme Administrative Commission had begun to function. Independently of the People's Will, the young Polish Jew I. P. Mlodetsky attempted to assassinate Loris-Melikov five days later, on February 20, and on February 22, Mlodetsky was hanged. Dostoevsky attended the execution that took place on Semyonovsky Square, the place of his mock execution thirty years earlier. Frank suggests that he had hoped to see a sudden reprieve of the type he had received in the Petrashevsky affair. Unfortunately,

despite the young author Vsevolod Garshin's personal appeal to Loris-Melikov, this did not occur. See Frank, *Dostoevsky: Mantle of the Prophet*, 485.
  4. Dostoevsky, *The Brothers Karamazov*, 572.
  5. Ibid., 383.
  6. Ibid., 385.
  7. Since Madame Khokhlakov is a parody of Ivan, she is of course also a parody of the two sides of his nature, Christ and the Grand Inquisitor.
  8. Dostoevsky, *The Brothers Karamazov*, 388.
  9. Belknap, *The Genesis of "The Brothers Karamazov,"* 58–50. Belknap cites B. V. Fedorenko's analysis of the Il'insky trial, which suggests that Il'insky's conviction for parricide was based on circumstantial evidence. While his original sentence was to be sent to the mines indefinitely as a criminal laborer, Nicholas I found the suspicion of parricide so odious that he demanded that Il'insky be "remanded among the convicts in the life category, and lose his membership in the gentry" (61–62).
  10. Dostoevskii, *PSS*, 6:351; Dostoevsky, *Crime and Punishment*, 460.
  11. Dostoevskii, *PSS*, 14:404; Dostoevsky, *The Brothers Karamazov*, 449.
  12. Safronova, *Russkoe obshchestvo*, 73.
  13. Ibid., 159–64.
  14. Dostoevskii, *PSS*, 15:18; Dostoevsky, *The Brothers Karamazov*, 577.
  15. Ibid.
  16. Dostoevsky, *The Brothers Karamazov*, 581.
  17. Ibid.
  18. Ibid., 582.
  19. Ibid., 584.
  20. Dostoevskii, *PSS*, 15:171; Dostoevsky, *The Brothers Karamazov*, 745–46.
  21. Ibid.

Part Three, Chapter 9. Again, Like Before (Again)

  1. Dostoevskii, *PSS*, 30 b. 1:184.
  2. Ibid.
  3. The most thorough treatment of Dostoevsky's remarkable speech is Marcus Levitt's *Russian Literary Politics and the Pushkin Celebration of 1880*, 125.
  4. Ibid., 126. In his polemic with the editor of the liberal paper *Voice* [*Golos*], Grigorii Gradovsky, Dostoevsky emphasized the uniqueness of his speech as a disruptive event. "The seriousness of that moment suddenly frightened many people in our liberal tea-pot, all the more so as it came so unexpectedly." Dostoevsky parodies their alarmed reaction ("Why this a rebellion, let's call the police") and the necessity that "the thing has got to be effaced, as quickly as possible, so that no trace be left."
  5. Robert Louis Jackson, "Alyosha's Speech at the Stone," 238–39.
  6. Quoted in James Rice, *Who Was Dostoevsky? Essays New and Revised*, 165. Rice points out that "the most radical variants" concerning the Karamazov sequel circulated while Dostoevsky was writing Book 10, "The Kids," from January 14 to May 3, 1880.
  7. Dostoevsky, *The Brothers Karamazov*, 774.

8. Dostoevsky's intimate friend and publisher Alexei Suvorin (1834–1912) and the Grand Duke Alexander Mikhailovich found it plausible and attested in their memoirs that Alyosha was to become a revolutionary terrorist. More remarkably, on May 26, 1880, an article appeared in *The Novorossiisk Telegraph* under the byline "Z" that reported certain rumors circulating in St. Petersburg literary circles to the effect that "in time Aleksei will become a village school teacher, and influenced by some special psychological processes taking place in his soul, he will even consider the idea of assassinating the Tsar." See Igor Volgin "Alyosha's Destiny," 271–72.

9. Dostoevsky, *The Brothers Karamazov*, 768.

10. Jackson, "Alyosha's Speech at the Stone," 243.

11. Dostoevskii, *PSS*, 14:223; Dostoevsky, *The Brothers Karamazov*, 245.

12. Rice, *Who Was Dostoevsky?*, 169. Rice infers that Dostoevsky still bore resentment and a desire for revenge against the regime based on a very cryptic remark that he made, one that could mean too many things.

13. As Dostoevsky had made clear in his Pushkin speech, when confronted with the choice of another's suffering or one's own, "the pure Russian soul [exemplified by Pushkin's Tatiana] decides thus: Let me, let me alone be deprived of happiness, even if my happiness be infinitely greater. . . . Finally, let no one . . . know and appreciate my sacrifice." Therefore, to laugh at such people would be wicked, since they are embodiments of the "pure Russian soul." In repurposing Pushkin's *Evgenii Onegin* in terms of his own concerns, Dostoevsky frames Tatiana's choice in the same terms of the Mandarin dilemma, since she is not only sacrificing herself, but "saving" one and "ruining" another. See Dostoevsky, *A Writer's Diary*, 2:1288.

Part Four, Chapter 1. Writing in Blood

1. Venturi, *Roots of Revolution*, 620, 708–10.

2. For details of the assassination, see Venturi, *Roots of Revolution*, 709–13; S. S. Volk, "Narodnaia volia" i "Chernyi peredel," 40; K. Tyrkov, *K sobytiiu 1 marta 1881 goda*; and Edvard Radzinsky, *Alexander II: The Last Great Tsar*, 413–17.

3. Cited in Radzinsky, *Alexander II*, 415.

4. See Iuliia Safronova, *Russkoe obshchestvo v zerkale revoliutsionnogo terrora*, 57–58.

5. Louise McReynolds, *The News Under Russia's Old Regime*, 95; Richard Wortman, "Moscow and Petersburg," 248.

6. Safronova, *Russkoe obshchestvo*, 76. This date is deeply significant for it celebrates the restoration of the veneration of icons after the iconoclast heresy and the triumph of the true faith over heresy.

7. David Footman, *Red Prelude: A Life of A. I. Zhelyabov*, 227.

8. Miliutin, *Dnevnik*, 304.

9. The perception of the People's Will's power and the possibility of another imminent attack was understandably widespread, shared by members of the government as well as by the public. See Zaionchkovsky, *Autocracy in Crisis*, 196–97. Andrei Zhelyabov had planted the seeds of government panic by stating that "the succession to the throne of His Imperial Highness Alexander

Alexandrovich scarcely will satisfy the expectations of the party, which will meet this obstacle without hesitation and will attack the new emperor, too."

10. Vera Figner's reaction as recorded in her memoir has often been quoted to convey the belief of the People's Will and their supporters among the intelligentsia that their act had accomplished this transformation. "I wept as did others that the heavy nightmare that had oppressed young Russia for ten years was over." See Figner, *Zapechatlennyi trud*, 268.

11. Venturi, *Roots of Revolution*, 716–17.

12. Ibid., 718.

13. Hartnett, *The Defiant Life of Vera Figner: Surviving the Russian Revolution*, 125.

14. Safronova, *Russkoe obshchestvo*, 174–75.

15. Ibid.

16. In all of *Narodnaia volia*'s literature, this satirical "feuilleton" that presents itself as the hunted tsar's diary is probably the most disturbing, although it is not devoid of a certain very dark humor.

17. *Literatura partii "Narodnoi voli,"* 38–39.

Part Four, Chapter 2. An Icon with Death

1. Koni, *Vospominaniia*, 191.

2. The editors of Turgenev's *Sobranie sochinenii* quote a study by A. I. Nikitina suggesting that Turgenev attended the Zasulich trial, but no other sources corroborate this. See I. S. Turgenev, *Polnoe sobranie sochinenii i pisem*, 10:497–98 (henceforward *PSS*). In general, Nikitina's statement is too vague to be given any credence, and her assertion that Turgenev was present at one of the court sessions makes little sense since the trial began at 10 a.m. on March 31 and the verdict was announced at 7 p.m. that evening. It is hard to imagine that Turgenev would stay for only part of such a riveting trial. A. F. Koni, the presiding judge of the trial and a close friend of Turgenev, did not mention Turgenev's presence at the trial, although he enumerated all the other dignitaries, including Dostoevsky.

3. Turgenev expresses in the most vehement terms his horror over Dmitry Karakozov and his act, and his gratitude toward the peasant Komissarov, who was singled out as the one who had foiled the attempt by jostling Karakozov's elbow. Turgenev went so far as to request that his friend Annenkov send him a photograph of Komissarov. For letters to Annenkov pertaining to the Karakozov attempt, see Turgenev, *PSS*, 7:26–28.

4. Henri Troyat, *Turgenev*, 120. Donna Oliver gives a concise and perceptive reading of Dostoevsky's, Turgenev's, and Tolstoy's reactions to the Zasulich affair in her chapter "Fool or Saint: Reading the Zasulich Case," 73–95. While our readings have points in common, my reading emphasizes Turgenev's aesthetics as well as his thematics.

5. Turgenev, *PSS*, 10:147–48. The extensive editor's notes to Turgenev's *Stikhotvoreniia v proze* at the end of this edition are in fact the best and most thorough scholarly work available on the collection, and specifically, on the publication history of "Porog."

6. The translation is mine.
7. Turgenev, *PSS*, 10:494.
8. Koni, *Vospominaniia*, 120.
9. Dostoevskii, *PSS*, 27:57.
10. Turgenev, *PSS*, 10:493.
11. Ibid., 10:494.
12. Peter Filipovich Yakubovich (1860–1911) completed his dissertation on Lermontov at St. Petersburg University in 1882 and joined Narodnaia volia in the same year. He attempted to revive the decimated organization by founding the Young People's Will, but was arrested in 1884. After three years' pretrial detention in the dungeon of the Peter and Paul Fortress, he was sentenced to be hanged, but the sentence was commuted to eighteen years hard labor in Siberia. Undaunted, he went on to enjoy a distinguished literary career as a poet and translator of Baudelaire's *Les fleurs du mal* into Russian. Yakubovich did most of the translations while in the Peter and Paul Fortress, and they, along with his own poetry, were smuggled out of prison and published in various legal journals. While some Symbolists derided Yakubovich's translations, others rendered him his due for the service he had done Russian literature. On Yakubovich's career as a translator of Baudelaire, see Adrian Wanner, "Populism and Romantic Agony: A Russian Terrorist's Discovery of Baudelaire," 298–317.
13. Turgenev, *PSS*, 10:495.
14. *Literatura Partii "Narodnoi voli,"* 477.
15. A. I. Baladin, "Zapiska N. M. Gorbova o pokhoronakh I. S. Turgeneva," 140.
16. Avrahm Yarmolinsky observes that since the date on which the poem was written was not included on the flier, people assumed that the Russian girl was Sophia Perovskaya rather than Vera Zasulich. See Yarmolinsky, *Turgenev: The Man, His Art and His Age*, 329.
17. Boris Uspensky, *The Semiotics of the Russian Icon*, 9.
18. *Literatura partii "Narodnoi voli,"* 157.
19. Ibid., 155.
20. Ibid., 156.
21. Quoted in Anna Geifman, *Thou Shalt Kill*, 216.

Part Four, Chapter 3. Celebrity Icons

1. In 1878, two separate attacks on Kaiser Wilhelm I were made by Max Hödel and Karl Nobiling. Although the attacks did not succeed, the crackdown in Berlin was just as severe as anything St. Petersburg had seen, and more than five hundred arrests followed, as well as the suppression of the Social Democratic Party (which had no connection to the attempts). In Italy, both the king and prime minister were wounded when an anarchist attacked them with a knife. In Spain, Juan Oliva Moncasi, a member of the outlawed Spanish anarchist labor organization, fired shots at King Alfonso XII during a royal procession in Madrid. As Randall Law notes, anarchists in Italy expanded their targets to include civilians and threw bombs into crowds gathered to honor the monarchy on various occasions. See Law, *Terrorism: A History*, 99; Miller, *The Foundations of Modern Terrorism*, 113.

2. S. M. Kravchinskii, *Smert' za smert' (ubiistvo Mezentseva)*, 13.
3. Venturi, *Roots of Revolution*, 610.
4. Dostoevskii, *PSS*, 12:141. Letter to Katkov, October 8/20 1870.
5. Ol'ga Liubatovich, who saw him at a secret meeting of the party shortly after the assassination and in the white heat of a police manhunt for him, left this account: "He seemed to draw into himself and saw nothing around him. In general, if you observed carefully, you could note in this man who was to all appearances a healthy, powerful and almost boisterously happy person the symptoms of one who has lived through a deeply unnerving shock, the external signs of which were almost but not quite concealed by the force of his own restraint." See Ol'ga Liubatovich, "Dalekoe i Nedavnee," 213.
6. Volgin, *Poslednii god Dostoevskogo*, 416-18.
7. Kravchinskii (Stepniak), *Underground Russia*, ix.
8. Taratuta, *S. M. Stepniak-Kravchinsky: Revoliutsioner i pisatel'*, 246.
9. Kravchinskii (Stepniak), *Underground Russia*, 39.
10. Ibid., 42.
11. Ibid., 44.
12. Ibid., 42.
13. See Thomas C. Moser, "An English Context for Conrad's Russian Characters: Sergei Stepniak and the Diary of Olive Garnett," 8, on Stepniak's categorical denial in a London *Times* interview that he had ever killed anyone. Olga Novikova, a socialite, salon hostess, publicist, and possibly a tsarist agent, repeatedly tried to unmask Stepniak as Mezentsev's assassin. For more on Novikova, see the Epilogue.
14. See Taratuta, *Istoriia dvukh knig: "Podpol'naia Rossiia" S. M. Stepniaka-Kravchinskogo i "Ovod" Etel' Lilian Voinich*, 72-76, on *Podpol'naia Rossiia*'s reception by Russians after 1905. Leo Tolstoy was also deeply impressed and based his own story "Bozheskoe i chelovecheskoe" on the profile of the revolutionary "saint" (but not terrorist) Dmitry Lizogub.
15. "Pis'ma S. M. Kravchinskogo (Stepniaka) k V. I. Zasulich (ot 1881-1894)," 215.
16. P. David Marshall, *Celebrity and Power*, 5.
17. For a summary of Hazlitt's writing on celebrity, see ibid., 7.
18. This is a much abbreviated synthesis of Marshall's argument concerning the nature of celebrity and its cultural power. For Marshall, the celebrity is an "intertextual sign" that is predicated upon the "domain of interpretive writing on cultural artifacts": on magazine stories, interviews, pinup posters, studio releases, reviews, candid photos... Kravchinsky could be seen as self-consciously participating in this intertextuality.
19. Kravchinskii (Stepniak), *Underground Russia*, 45.
20. Ibid., 106.
21. Ibid., 109.
22. Ibid., 81.
23. Ibid.
24. *Literatura Partii "Narodnoi voli,"* 59-60.
25. For example, in a report of the London *Times* dated April 7, 1881, Perovskaya is described as the "concubine of Jelaboff [sic]." As one scholar notes, "From the appearance of the word 'concubine' her reputation was

steadily degraded and her actions seen only in relation to Zhelyabov . . . her ability to think and act independently was also denied in favor of a male influence." See Cynthia Marsh, "*The Times* (1881) and the Russian Women Terrorists," 57–58.

26. Kravchinskii (Stepniak), *Underground Russia*, 115.
27. Ibid., 117.
28. Ibid., 121.
29. Ibid., 127.
30. Ibid., 132.
31. From a letter to Chaikovsky in the autumn of 1882. Quoted in Senese, *S. M. Stepniak-Kravchinskii: The London Years*, 27.
32. Taratuta, *S. M. Stepniak-Kravchinskii*, 231.

Part Four, Chapter 4. Terror in Search of a Face

1. V. M. Garshin, *Nadezhda Nikolaevna* (henceforward, *N.N.*), 9. The translations from the Russian are mine.
2. John Clubbe, *Byron, Sully, and the Power of Portraiture*, 3. On the regime's effort to erase the Decembrists and their memory from public consciousness "to ban public mention of the Decembrists, to execute the five leaders in secret, and to exile the remaining rebels to Siberia" as well as the "imperial prohibition on the Decembrists' representations (in print and portraiture)," see Ludmilla A. Trigos, *The Decembrist Myth in Russian Culture*, xxii.
3. The painting of her portrait by E. Hauer constitutes a famous episode of Corday's hagiography. The portrait was apparently made at Corday's behest and expense, and it is the subject of an ecstatic ekphrasistic description in Jules Michelet's chapter on Corday's death. See Michelet, *History of the French Revolution*, 129. On artistic and literary images of Corday, see Michael Marrinan, "Images and Ideas of Charlotte Corday: Texts and Contexts of an Assassination"; and Elizabeth R. Kindleberger, "Charlotte Corday in Text and Image: A Case Study in the French Revolution and Women's History."
4. There is no evidence that these rumors are true; rather, the strict sequester of dangerous political criminals was common practice.
5. Footman, *Red Prelude*, 228.
6. See Elizabeth Kridl Valkenier for the artistic cross-fertilization between Ilya Repin and Garshin, *Ilya Repin and the World of Russian Art*, 120. On the intertext between *Ivan the Terrible* and *Nadezhda Nikolaevna*, see in particular "The Writer as Artist's Model: Repin's Portrait of Garshin," 212–13.
7. There is some indication that Garshin had begun the story even earlier, shortly after the Zasulich trial. In a letter to his mother dated December 18, 1879, he describes a plot that closely resembles that of *Nadezhda Nikolaevna* and dates the genesis of the story as a year and a half earlier—that is, June 1878. See letter to E. S. Garshina in V. M. Garshin, *Polnoe sobranie sochinenii v trekh tomakh* (henceforward *PSS*), 3:196–97.
8. As Valkenier points out, the face of the dying tsarevich is in fact a composite, heavily influenced by a study of Garshin made for that purpose, but not exclusively his. Repin combined the study of Garshin, along with a similar

study of another model, the artist Vladimir Menk. Valkenier, "The Writer as Artist's Model," 212.

9. On the uproar and controversy that the painting provoked, see Kevin Platt, *Terror and Greatness*, 111–14.

10. Quoted in Platt, *Terror and Greatness*, 113.

11. "Repin's allegory links up with contemporary events with an intentional looseness—a looseness that revises the present, redirecting attention from prevalent conceptions of political violence to contrasting ones. . . . The painting condemns autocratic violence and calls for a reconciliation before it is too late." Ibid., 114.

12. Garshin, *N.N.*, 9.

13. Ibid.

14. Ibid., 11.

15. Ibid., 10.

16. Ibid., 11.

17. Ibid., 14.

18. See Rivers, *Face Value: Physiognomical Thought and the Legible Body in Marivaux, Lavater, Balzac, Gautier, and Zola*, 79.

19. Garshin, *N.N.*, 16–17.

20. Ibid., 17.

21. Rivers puts it this way: "Physiognomy has no real object. Lavater provides neither method, nor system, nor explanation of how one moves from observations of the physical to assertions of the moral. The work of physiognomy is therefore not the creation of a narrative based on observation and method, but rather the creation of a narrative based on génie or imagination" (102).

22. Henry, *A Hamlet of His Time: Vsevolod Garshin*, 66–67.

23. Garshin, *N.N.*, 63. While it is only foreshadowed at the end of "An Incident," Nadezhda Nikolaevna's full sense of guilt emerges in her confession to Lopatin, and Lopatin accepts her indictment. "She indeed had killed a human being, without herself knowing" (67). Her full transformation is accomplished only after he, like Christ, has judged and forgiven her "everything, that in the opinion of people, requires forgiveness."

24. Jay Bergman, *Vera Zasulich*, 73. Adam Ulam notes, "Poems and radical broadsides celebrated her as another William Tell or Charlotte Corday. The last comparison has always shocked Soviet historians, and rightly so. Charlotte was of course a royalist [in fact, nineteenth-century historiography, namely Michelet's as well as recent historiography cast aspersions on this facile assumption] and Jean-Paul Marat, whom she killed in his therapeutic bath, was what might be called the Tkachev of the French Revolution. But the comparison, used repeatedly by radicals such as Morozov, shows how fascinated revolutionary Populism had become with the idea of individual terror." Ulam, *In the Name of the People*, 270. See also Walter Laqueur, *The Age of Terrorism*, 191–92.

25. Garshin, *N.N.*, 37.

26. Letter to E. S. Garshina in Garshin, *PSS*, 3:196–97.

27. Henry, *A Hamlet of His Time*, 49. The notion of killing while "blinded by an idea" is first expressed in Garshin's 1877 debut story "Four Days," based on

his experiences as a soldier in the Russo-Turkish war. There are striking similarities to the denouement of Nadezhda Nikolaevna. Only when the first-person narrator is inescapably confronted with the rotting corpse of the Turkish soldier that he killed does he realize that he shed blood only because he was "blinded by an idea."

28. After Garshin's visit to Loris-Melikov, he was detained by the secret police and found it necessary to deny any connection to the "social revolutionaries." He repeats this denial in his letter to Loris-Melikov dated February 25, 1880.

29. Garshin, *PSS*, 3:207. Although there were many memoiristic references to Garshin's visit, there was no proof that it was not the product of his disordered imagination until a letter from Garshin to Loris-Melikov dated February 25, 1880, was discovered in 1934. See Henry's account of the mystery in *A Hamlet of His Time*, 110–12.

30. Garshin, *N.N.*, 71–72.

31. In the old Russian folk epics, or *byliny*, Muromets lies crippled until age thirty-three, when he is miraculously healed and endowed with the superhuman strength necessary to defeat terrifying forest monsters such as Nightingale the Robber. Ultimately Ilya Muromets became a monk of the Kiev Pecherski Monastery, accomplishing the transformation from chief warrior to canonized saint of the Orthodox Church.

32. Garshin, *N.N.*, 71–72.

33. Ibid., 3.

34. See the Prologue for an explication of Bakunin's "creative destruction." Of course, Garshin's story runs entirely counter to Bakunin's Hegelian-inspired thesis. In *Nadezhda Nikolaevna*, the passion for destruction is shown to be ultimately only destructive.

35. Garshin, *N.N.*, 82.

36. C. Lombroso and R. Laschi, *Der Politische Verbrecher und die Revolutionen in anthropologischer, juristischer, und staatswissenschaftlicher Beziehung*, 2:62. The translation from the German is mine.

37. Ibid.

38. Ibid., 2:63–64.

39. Valkenier, "The Writer as Artist's Model," 212.

40. Garshin, *N.N.*, 86.

Epilogue: "All of Europe Thrills to the Horror"

1. *Times* (London), January 14, 1881.

2. *Times* (London), March 2, 1881. On the same day, the *Pall Mall Gazette* (*PMG*) also reprinted a report from the *Bristol Mercury* and the *Daily Post* on the situation in the Irish countryside. Deploring the recent activities of the Land League, the paper reported, "The assassins no longer seek to take only the lives of landlords and agents; women and children, labourers and shopkeepers are equally threatened by the hired miscreants of the Terrorists." Prior to the assassination of Alexander II the usage "Terrorists" alternated with "terrorists" and referred both to the Irish and the Russians. *PMG*, March 2, 1881.

3. *Times* (London), March 14, 1881.
4. *PMG*, March 14, 1881.
5. Like many nineteenth-century dailies, the *Pall Mall Gazette* aggregated news from other papers, including ones with rival ideological positions, so as to create a polyphony of views. "The Epitome of Opinion," *PMG*, March 14, 1881.
6. Among other recent studies of the reception of Russian revolutionary terrorism in Britain and the United States, see Choi Chatterjee, "Transnational Romance, Terror, and Heroism: Russia in American Popular Fiction 1860–1917," 753–77; Michael Hughes, "British Opinion and Russian Terrorism in the 1880s," 255–77; and Robert Henderson, "The Hyde Park Rally of 9 March 1890: A British Workers' Response to Russian Atrocities," 451–66.
7. "Epitome of Opinion," *PMG*, March 14, 1881.
8. The *Standard* likened Alexander II to Abraham Lincoln; the *PMG* recalled Henry of Navarre and the Prince of Denmark. *PMG*, March 14, 1881.
9. *Times* (London), December 31, 1881.
10. *PMG*, March 16, 1881.
11. *PMG*, March 23, 1881.
12. *Times* (London), March 18, 1881.
13. *PMG*, January 18, 1881.
14. *PMG*, July 30, 1881.
15. Ibid.
16. *Times* (London), December 31, 1881.
17. *PMG*, April 11, 1881.
18. *PMG*, June 16, 1881.
19. *Times* (London), March 15, 1881.
20. Ibid.
21. *Times* (London), March 14, 1881.
22. *Times* (London), March 23, 1881, 7. See also "The Assassination of the Czar. The Czar's Funeral," *Reynold's Newspaper*, March 27, 1881, 1. Several newspapers ran articles describing the project for international anti-Nihilist legislation by M. F. de Mortens, a professor of international law at the Imperial University of St. Petersburg. The newspapers adopt the characterization of the Nihilists by de Mortens (aka M. Martens) as deriving from Russia's Asiatic barbarism.
23. *Times* (London), May 11, 1881.
24. Anatole Leroy-Beaulieu, *L'empire des tsars et les Russes*, 195. Beaulieu, like Montesquieu before him, correlates the character of a people and its government with their natural environment, the climate and topography. Book III Chapter IV deals with Nihilism and was widely quoted by the press (with and without attribution) in the aftermath of the regicide. The English translation was published as *The Empire of the Czars and the Russians*, translated by Zenaïde A. Ragozin (1898), and I have relied on Ragozin's translation.
25. Leroy-Beaulieu, *The Empire of the Czars and the Russians*, 214.
26. Ibid.
27. Ibid.
28. Ibid., 198.
29. *Times* (London), June 11, 1881.

30. Ibid.
31. *PMG*, June 13, 1884.
32. *Times* (London), June 11, 1881.
33. *PMG*, January 26, 1885. The *Pall Mall Gazette* sought to downplay the attacks and to counter the anti-Irish hysteria fomented by the *Times* and other media outlets by tabulating the economic damage done. "On the whole £20,000 represents the outside damage done by the carefully planned explosions about which all the world is talking this morning."
34. *PMG*, January 26, 1885.
35. *Times* (London), January 26, 1885.
36. Ibid.
37. D. Martens's article in *Golos* entitled "Contemporary Investigation and Regicide" triggered a wide-ranging debate on the European "solidarity of interest in exterminating Nihilist and Socialist terrorists, as in combating ordinary crimes and pestilences." Martens's widely quoted article seems to be the origin of the meme "that Nihilists are the growth of Russian soil, and are characterized by Asiatic barbarity, but are nevertheless offshoots of the same vicious plant which has struck such deep roots in Western Europe." "The Assassination of the Czar. The Czar's Funeral," *Reynolds's Newspaper*, March 27, 1881, 1.
38. "M. F. de Mortens [sic], Professor of International Law," *Western Mail*, March 24, 1881. Once again, the British press is using Martens's own arguments against him. This commentator refers to de Mortens's argument in "Russia and England in Central Asia" in which he is quoted as saying "We contend that international law is only applicable between nations which have attained nearly a like degree of culture and progress."
39. *PMG*, January 15, 1885.
40. *Vera*'s premiere was scheduled for early 1882 but was canceled in November 1881, because of financial concerns, political sensitivities, or both. The play eventually premiered in New York in March 1883, with the diva Marie Prescott as Vera, attired in vermilion silk. But the play bombed so badly that it has been consigned to a historical footnote. See Elizabeth Carolyn Miller, *Framed: The New Woman Criminal in British Culture at the Fin de Siècle*, 194; Miller, "Reconsidering Wilde's *Vera; or, the Nihilists*," 81. In "Reconsidering Wilde's *Vera*," Miller argues that the play clearly expresses Wilde's republican sentiments and sympathy for the Nihilist cause, both of which were nurtured by his friendship with Sergei Stepniak-Kravchinsky. She also reads the play as Wilde's oblique commentary on the Irish question. I am grateful to Professor Miller for making her manuscript chapter available.
41. Mme. Olympe Audouard was a feminist, novelist, and travel writer who was very sympathetic to the Russian socialist revolutionary cause. Her *Voyage au pays des Boyards, etude sur la Russie actuelle, par Olympe Audouard* was one of the pioneering Russian travelogues of the period, antedating both Sutherland's and Beaulieu's more extensive studies. Audouard was thus well acquainted with facts on the ground, and her novel contains extensive arguments, dripping with pathos, in support of nihilism such as the following: "Le nihilisme c'est le désespoir. Nous sommes des désespérés, nous souffrons depuis neuf siècles, depuis neuf siècles nous implorons en vain le Dieu de

justice et de misericorde, mais il ne nous écoute pas: l'autocratie continue, et au nom de cette Divinité de qui elle prétend tenir le pouvoir." Olympe Audouard, *Les soupers de la princesses Louba d'Askoff: Drame d'amour et de nihilism*, 35.

42. Vanessa Schwartz, *Spectacular Realities: Early Mass Culture in Fin-de-Siècle Paris*, 109.

43. Ibid., 111, 113.

44. Ibid., 112.

45. William Eleroy Curtis, *The Land of the Nihilist. Russia: Its People, Its Palaces, Its Politics. A Narrative of Travel in the Czar's Dominions*, 1. Curtis begins his account with the observation that "travel has its fashions like everything else" and that travel to Russia had lately become one of them, "but until then the visitors to the Czar's dominions had been so few that Herr Baedeker, the faithful friend of the travelling public, had not considered it worth his while to issue a Russian guide-book, although he has covered nearly every other country on the globe."

46. Ibid., 264. Conservative explanations for terrorism are based on alterity: *our people* are not terrorists—foreign nationals and "half-baked citizens" are.

47. E. M. de Vogüé, *The Russian Novelists*, 20–22.

48. While he made the odd accusation that the origin of Dostoevsky's enmity toward Turgenev was his envy that Turgenev had been the first to take up the subject of Nihilism, de Vogüé awards Dostoevsky "the prize in the tilting match." Ibid., 192.

49. Ibid., 177.
50. Ibid., 184.
51. Ibid., 193.
52. Ibid., 197.
53. Ibid., 201.
54. Ibid.
55. Ibid., 204.
56. Ibid., 205.
57. Ibid., 206.
58. Ibid.
59. Ibid., 208.
60. Leroy-Beaulieu, *The Empire of the Czars and the Russians*, 217.
61. Ibid., 221.

Bibliography

Newspapers Cited

Kolokol, 1862–1863
Moskovskie vedomosti, 1869–1870
Pravitel'stvennyi vestnik, 1871
Times (London), 1881–1885
Pall Mall Gazette, 1881–1885
Reynold's Newspaper, 1881
Western Mail, 1881

Works Cited

Anderson, Sean, and Stephen Sloan, eds. *Historical Dictionary of Terrorism.* Lanham, MD: Scarecrow Press, 2009.
Anemone, Anthony, ed. *Just Assassins: The Culture of Terrorism in Russia.* Evanston: Northwestern University Press, 2010.
Apollonio, Carol. *Dostoevsky's Secrets: Reading Against the Grain.* Evanston: Northwestern University Press, 2009.
Arendt, Hannah. *On Revolution.* New York: Penguin, 2006.
——. *The Origins of Totalitarianism.* London: Harcourt Brace Jovanovich, 1976.
Arnold, Matthew. *Culture and Anarchy.* Oxford: Oxford University Press, 2009.
Audouard, Olympe. *Les soupers de la princesse Louba d'Askoff: Drame d'amour et de nihilisme.* Paris: E. Dentu, 1880.
Austin, J. L. *How to Do Things with Words.* Oxford: Oxford University Press, 1975.

Babkin, D. S. *Protsess Radishcheva*. Moscow-Leningrad, 1952.
Bakhtin, M. M. *Problems of Dostoevsky's Poetics*. Translated by Caryl Emerson. Minneapolis: University of Minnesota Press, 1984.
Baladin, A. I. "Zapiska N. M. Gorbova o pokhoronakh I. S. Turgeneva." *Filologicheskie nauki* 3 (1962): 138–41.
Belinskii, Vissarion. *Izbrannye sochineniia*. Moscow: Gosudarstvennoe izdatel'stvo "Khudozhestvennaia literatura," 1949.
Bel'chikov, N. F. *Dostoevskii v protsesse Petrashevtsev*. Moscow: Nauka, 1971.
Belknap, Robert. *The Genesis of "The Brothers Karamazov": The Aesthetics, Ideology, and Psychology of Making a Text*. Evanston: Northwestern University Press, 1990.
Bergman, Jay. *Vera Zasulich: A Biography*. Stanford: Stanford University Press, 1983.
Bessner, Daniel, and Michael Stauch. "Karl Heinzen and the Intellectual Origins of Modern Terrorism." *Terrorism and Political Violence* 22, no. 2 (2010): 143–76.
Billington, James. *Mikhailovsky and Russian Populism*. New York: Oxford University Press, 1958.
Black, Edwin. *Rhetorical Criticism: A Study in Method*. New York: Macmillan, 1965.
Børtnes, Jostein. "The Last Delusion in an Infinite Series of Delusions: Stavrogin and the Symbolic Structure of *The Devils*." *Dostoevsky Studies* 4 (1983): 54–68.
Braunsperger, Gudrun. *Sergej Nečaev und Dostoevskijs Dämonen. Die Geburt eines Romans aus dem Geist des Terrorismus*. Frankfurt/New York: P. Lang, 2001.
Budanova, N. F., and G. M. Fridlender, eds. *Letopis' zhizni i tvorchestva F. M. Dostoevskogo*. St. Petersburg: Akademicheskii proekt, 1995.
Budnitskii, O. V. *Terrorizm v rossiiskom osvoboditel'nom dvizhenii: Ideologiia, etika, psikhologiia (vtoraia polovina XIX—nachalo XX v.)*. Moscow: ROSSPEN, 2000.
———. *Istoriia terrorizma v Rossii v dokumentakh, biografiiakh, issledovaniiakh*. Rostov-na-Donu: Feniks, 1996.
Bukh, N. K. *Vospominaniia*. Moscow: Izd-vo Vsesoiuznogo obshchestva politkatorzhan i ssyl'no-poselentsev, 1928.
Burleigh, Michael. *Blood and Rage: A Cultural History of Terrorism*. New York: HarperCollins, 2009.
Cervantes, Miguel de. *Don Quixote*. Translated by Samuel Putnam. New York: The Modern Library, 1998.
Chalmers, David. *Hooded Americanism: The First Century of the Ku Klux Klan, 1865–1965*. Garden City, NY: Doubleday, 1965.
Chatterjee, Choi. "Transnational Romance, Terror, and Heroism: Russia in American Popular Fiction, 1860–1917." *Comparative Studies in Society and History* 50, no. 3 (2008): 753–77.
Chernyshevskii, Nikolai. *Chto delat'? Iz rasskazov o novykh liudiakh*. Moscow: Molodaia gvardiia, 1948.
———. *Polnoe sobranie sochinenii v 15 tomakh*. Moscow: Goslitizdat, 1949.
Chernyshevsky, Nikolai. *What Is to Be Done?* Translated by Michael R. Katz. Ithaca: Cornell University Press, 1989.
Clubbe, John. *Byron, Sully, and the Power of Portraiture*. Aldershot, Hants, England: Ashgate, 2005.

Cochrane, Stephen T. *The Collaboration of Nečaev, Ogarev, and Bakunin in 1869: Nečaev's Early Years*. Giessen: W. Schmitz Verlag, 1977.
Crawford, Joseph. *Gothic Fiction and the Invention of Terrorism: The Politics and Aesthetics of Fear in the Age of the Reign of Terror*. London: Bloomsbury, 2013.
Curtis, William Eleroy. *The Land of the Nihilist. Russia: Its People, Its Palaces, Its Politics. A Narrative of Travel in the Czar's Dominions*. Chicago: Belford, Clarke & Co., 1888.
Daly, Jonathan. "Political Crime in Late Imperial Russia." *Journal of Modern History* 74, no. 1 (2002): 62–100.
Damasio, Antonio. *Looking for Spinoza: Joy, Sorrow, and the Feeling Brain*. New York: Houghton Mifflin Harcourt, 2003.
Deich, Lev, ed. *Gruppa "Osvobozhdenie truda."* Moscow: Gos. izd-vo, 1923.
———. "Iuzhnye buntari." *Golos minuvshego* 9 (1920–21): 44–71.
———. "Valerian Osinskii (K 50-letiiu ego kazni)." *Katorga i ssylka* 54, no. 5 (1929): 22–24.
Denby, David. *Sentimental Narrative and the Social Order in France*. New York: Cambridge University Press, 1994.
Derrida, Jacques. *Specters of Marx*. Translated by Peggy Kamuf. London: Routledge, 1994.
Dietze, Carola. *Die Erfindung des Terrorismus in Europa, Russland, und den USA 1858–1866*. Hamburg: Hamburger Edition, 2016.
Dobroliubov, N. A. *Literaturnaia kritika*. Leningrad: Khudozhestvennaia literatura, 1984.
———. *Pervoe polnoe sobranie sochinenii*. St. Petersburg: Izd. A. S. Panafidinoi, 1911.
Dostoevskii, Fedor. *Polnoe sobranie sochinenii v tridtsati tomakh*. Leningrad: Izd-vo Nauka, 1980.
Dostoevsky, Fyodor. *The Brothers Karamazov*. Translated by Richard Pevear and Larissa Volokhonsky. New York: Farrar, Straus and Giroux: 1990.
———. *Complete Letters: 1860–1867*. 5 vols. Edited and translated by David A. Lowe. Ann Arbor: Ardis, 1989.
———. *Crime and Punishment*. Translated by Richard Pevear and Larissa Volokhonsky. New York: Alfred A. Knopf, 1993.
———. *Demons*. Translated by Richard Pevear and Larissa Volokhonsky. New York: Vintage, 2004.
———. *Pis'ma*. 4 vols. Edited by A. S. Dolinin. Moscow: Moscow: Gos. izd-vo, 1928.
———. *The Notebooks for "Crime and Punishment."* Edited and translated by Edward Wasiolek. Chicago: University of Chicago Press, 1967.
———. *The Notebooks for "The Possessed."* Edited by Edward Wasiolek. Translated by V. Terras. Chicago: University of Chicago Press, 1969.
———. *A Writer's Diary*. 2 vols. Translated and annotated by Kenneth Lantz, with an introduction by Gary Saul Morson. Evanston: Northwestern University Press, 1994.
Dragomanov, M. P. *Pis'ma M. A. Bakunina k A. I. Gertsenu i N. P. Ogarevu*. The Hague-Paris: Mouton, 1968.
Drozd, Andrew Michael. *Chernyshevskii's "What Is to Be Done?": A Reevaluation*. Evanston: Northwestern University Press, 2001.

Dwyer, Philip. *Citizen Emperor: Napoleon in Power*. New Haven: Yale University Press, 2013.
Edelstein, Dan. *The Terror of Natural Right: Republicanism, the Cult of Nature, and the French Revolution*. Chicago: University of Chicago Press, 2009.
Elliott, Robert. *The Power of Satire: Magic, Ritual, Art*. Princeton: Princeton University Press, 1960.
Ely, Christopher. *Underground Petersburg: Radical Populism, Urban Space, and the Tactics of Subversion in Reform-Era Russia*. DeKalb: Northern Illinois University Press, 2016.
Enzensberger, Hans Magnus. "Die Leere im Zentrum des Terrors." In *Mittelmaß und Wahn*, by Hans Magnus Enzensberger, 245–49. Frankfurt am Main: Suhrkamp, 1977.
Fasmer, M. *Etimologicheskii slovar' russkogo iazyka*. Moscow: Progress, 1986.
Festa, Lynn. *Sentimental Figures of Empire in Eighteenth-Century Britain and France*. Baltimore: Johns Hopkins University Press, 2006.
Figner, Vera. *Memoirs of a Revolutionist*. New York: Greenwood Press, 1968.
———. *Studencheskie gody*. Moscow: Golos truda, 1924.
———. *Zapechatlennyi trud. Vospominaniia v dvukh tomakh*. Moscow: Mysl', 1964.
Florensky, Pavel. *Iconostasis*. Translated by Donald Sheehan and Olga Andrejev. Introduction by Donald Sheehan. Crestwood, NY: St. Vladimir's Seminary Press, 1996.
Footman, David. *Red Prelude: A Life of A. I. Zhelyabov*. London: Cresset Press, 1944.
Ford, Franklin F. *Political Murder: From Tyrannicide to Terrorism*. Cambridge, MA: Harvard University Press, 1985.
Frank, Joseph. *Dostoevsky: The Mantle of the Prophet, 1871–1881*. Princeton: Princeton University Press, 2002.
———. *Dostoevsky: The Miraculous Years, 1865–1871*. Princeton: Princeton University Press, 1995.
———. *Dostoevsky: The Stir of Liberation, 1860–1865*. Princeton: Princeton University Press, 1986.
———. *Dostoevsky: The Years of Ordeal, 1850–1859*. Princeton: Princeton University Press, 1976.
Frede, Victoria. *Doubt, Atheism, and the Nineteenth-Century Russian Intelligentsia*. Madison: University of Wisconsin Press, 2011.
———. "Radicals and Feelings: The 1860s." In *Interpreting Emotions in Russia and Eastern Europe*, edited by Mark Steinberg and Valeria Sobol, 62–81. DeKalb: Northern Illinois University Press, 2011.
Freidin, Gregory. "By the Walls of Church and State: Literature's Authority in Russia's Modern Tradition." *Russian Review* 52, no. 2 (1993): 149–65.
Fusso, Susanne. "Dostoevsky and Mikhail Katkov: Their Literary Partnership (*Crime and Punishment* and *The Devils*)." In *New Studies in Modern Russian Literature and Culture: Essays in Honor of Stanley J. Rabinowitz*, edited by Catherine Ciepiela and Lazar Fleishman, 35–69. Stanford: Stanford University Press, 2014.
Garshin, V. M. *Nadezhda Nikolaevna*. Berlin: Erwin Berger Verlag, 1920.
———. *Polnoe sobranie sochinenii v trekh tomakh*. Moscow, Leningrad: Academia, 1930–34.

Geierhos, Wolfgang. *Vera Zasulic und die russische revoluzionäre Bewegung*. Munich, Vienna: Oldenbourg, 1977.
Geifman, Anna. *Thou Shalt Kill: Revolutionary Terrorism in Russia, 1894–1917*. Princeton: Princeton University Press, 1993.
Gertsen, Aleksandr, ed. *O povrezhdenii nravov v Rossii kniazia M. Shcherbatova i Puteshestvie Radishcheva. S predisloviem Iskandera*. London: Trübner, 1858.
———. *Sobranie sochinenii v tridtsati tomakh*. Moscow: Izdatel'stvo Akademii nauk SSSR, 1956.
Ginzburg, Lydia. *On Psychological Prose*. Translated and edited by Judson Rosengrant. Princeton: Princeton University Press, 1991.
Girard, René. *Deceit, Desire, and the Novel: Self and Other in Literary Structure*. Baltimore: Johns Hopkins University Press, 1976.
———. *Violence and the Sacred*. Baltimore: Johns Hopkins University Press, 1985.
Gleason, Abbott. *Young Russia: The Genesis of Russian Radicalism in the 1860s*. New York: Viking Press, 1980.
Gogol, Nikolai. *The Collected Tales*. Translated by Richard Pevear and Larissa Volokhonsky. New York: Penguin Random House, 2008.
Gogol', Nikolai. *Polnoe sobranie sochinenii*. Moscow: Akademiia nauk, 1934.
Goethe, Johann Wolfgang von. *Faust First Part*. Translated by Peter Salm. New York: Bantam Books, 1962.
Goodwin, Frank. *Confronting Dostoevsky's "Demons": Anarchism and the Specter of Bakunin in Twentieth-Century Russia*. New York: Peter Lang, 2010.
Green, J. D., and R. B. Sommerville, L. E. Nystrom, J. M. Darley, and J. D. Cohen. "An fMRI Study of Emotional Engagement in Moral Judgment." *Science* 293 (2001): 2105–8.
Grob-Fitzgibbon, Benjamin. "From the Dagger to the Bomb: Karl Heinzen and the Evolution of Political Terror." *Terrorism and Political Violence* 16, no. 1 (2004): 97–115.
Grossman, Leonid. *Dostoevsky: A Biography*. Translated by Mary Mackler. London: Allen Lane, 1974.
———. "Stilistika Stavrogina: K izucheniiu novoi glavy 'Besov.'" In *Besy: Antologiia russkoi kritiki*, edited by L. I. Saraskina, 606–13. Moscow: Soglasie, 1996.
Hardy, Deborah. *Land and Freedom: The Origins of Russian Terrorism, 1876–1879*. Westport, CT: Greenwood Press, 1987.
Harsin, Jill. *Barricades: The War of the Streets in Revolutionary Paris, 1830–1848*. New York: Palgrave Macmillan, 2002.
Hartnett, Lynne Ann. *The Defiant Life of Vera Figner: Surviving the Russian Revolution*. Bloomington: Indiana University Press, 2014.
Heinzen, Karl. "Murder" [Der Mord]. In *Voices of Terror: Manifestos, Writings, and Manuals of Al Qaeda, Hamas, and Other Terrorists from Around the World and Throughout the Ages*, edited by Walter Laqueur, 57–67. New York: Reed Press, 2004.
Henderson, Robert. "The Hyde Park Rally of 9 March 1890: A British Workers' Response to Russian Atrocities." *European Review of History* 21, no. 4 (2014): 451–66.
Henry, Peter. *A Hamlet of His Time: Vsevolod Garshin. The Man, His Works, and His Milieu*. Oxford: Willem A. Meeuws, 1983.

Hildermeier, Manfred. *The Russian Socialist Revolutionary Party before the First World War*. New York: St. Martin's Press, 2000.

Hobbes, Thomas. *Leviathan, Parts I and II*. Edited by A. P. Martinich. Ontario: Broadview Editions, 2005.

Holland, Kate. *The Novel in the Age of Disintegration: Dostoevsky and the Problem of Genre in the 1870s*. Evanston: Northwestern University Press, 2013.

Hoogenboom, Hilde. "Sentimental Novels and Pushkin: Literary Markets and Russian Readers." *Slavic Review* 74, no. 3 (2015): 553–74.

Howe, Irving. "Dostoevsky: The Politics of Salvation [*The Possessed*]." In *Critical Essays on Dostoevsky*, edited by Robin Feuer Miller, 135–47. Boston: G. K. Hall, 1986.

Hughes, Michael. "British Opinion and Russian Terrorism in the 1880s." *European History Quarterly* 41, no. 2 (2011): 255–77.

Hunt, Lynn. *Inventing Human Rights*. New York: W. W. Norton, 2007.

Iakovlev, V. Ia., ed. *Literatura sotsial'no-revoliutsionnoi partii "Narodnoi Voli."* N.p.: Tipografiia Partii sotsialistov-revoliutsionerov, 1905.

Iangoulova, Lia. "The *Osvidetel'stvovanie* and *Ispytanie* of Insanity: Psychiatry in Tsarist Russia." In *Madness and the Mad in Russian Culture*, edited by Angela Brintlinger and Ilya Vinitsky, 46–57. Toronto: University of Toronto Press, 2007.

Ivanov, Sergei. *Holy Fools in Byzantium and Beyond*. Princeton: Princeton University Press, 2001.

Iz pokazanii D. V. Karakozova sledstvennoi komissii po delu o pokushenii na Aleksandra II 4 aprelia 1866g. http://www.hrono.ru/dokum/1800dok/18660416.html (accessed August 11, 2016).

Jackson, Richard, ed. *Terrorism: A Critical Introduction*. Basingstoke: Palgrave Macmillan, 2011.

Jackson, Robert Louis. "Alyosha's Speech at the Stone." In *A New Word on "The Brothers Karamazov,"* edited by Robert Louis Jackson, 234–53. Evanston: Northwestern University Press, 2004.

———. *Dostoevsky's Quest for Form: A Study of His Philosophy of Art*. New Haven: Yale University Press, 1966.

Jászi, Oszkár, and John D. Lewis. *Against the Tyrant: The Tradition and Theory of Tyrannicide*. Glencoe, IL: Free Press, 1957.

Kahn, Andrew. *Pushkin's "The Bronze Horseman."* London: Bristol Classical Press, 1998.

———. "Self and Sensibility in Radishchev's *Journey from St. Petersburg to Moscow*: Dialogism, Relativism, and the Moral Spectator." In *Self and Story in Russian History*, edited by Laura Engelstein and Stephanie Sandler, 280–304. Ithaca: Cornell University Press, 2000.

Karlinsky, Simon. *The Sexual Labyrinth of Nikolai Gogol*. Chicago: University of Chicago, 1976.

Kindleberger, Elizabeth R. "Charlotte Corday in Text and Image: A Case Study in the French Revolution and Women's History." *French Historical Studies* 18, no. 4 (1994): 969–99.

Kliger, Ilya. *The Narrative Shape of Truth: Verediction in Modern European Literature*. University Park: Pennsylvania State University Press, 2011.

Bibliography

Klioutchkine, Konstantine. "The Rise of *Crime and Punishment* from the Air of the Media." *Slavic Review* 61, no. 1 (2002): 88–108.
Knapp, Liza, ed. and trans. *Dostoevsky as Reformer: The Petrashevsky Case*. Ann Arbor: Ardis Publishers, 1987.
Koni, A. F. *Vospominaniia o dele Very Zasulich*. Moscow: Akademia, 1933.
Koonz, Claudia. *The Nazi Conscience*. Cambridge: Belknap Press, 2003.
Kravchinskii, S. M. *Smert' za smert' (ubiistvo Mezentseva)*. St. Petersburg: Gosudarstvennoe izdatel'stvo, 1920.
Kravchinskii (Stepniak), S. M. *Underground Russia: Revolutionary Profiles and Sketches from Life*. Translated from the Italian. London: Smith, Elder, and Co., 1883.
Kropotkin, P. *Memoirs of a Revolutionist*. Boston and New York: Houghton Mifflin, 1899.
Lampert, Evgenii. *Sons Against Fathers: Studies in Russian Radicalism and Revolution*. Oxford: Clarendon Press, 1965.
Lang, David Marshall. *The First Russian Radical: Alexander Radishchev, 1749–1802*. London: George Allen and Unwin, 1959.
Laqueur, Walter. *The Age of Terrorism*. Boston: Little, Brown, 1987.
———. "The Futility of Terrorism." *Harper's Magazine* 252 (1976): 99–105.
———. *Voices of Terror: Manifestos, Writings, and Manuals of Al Qaeda, Hamas, and Other Terrorists from Around the World and Throughout the Ages*. New York: Reed Press, 2004.
Law, Randall. *Terrorism: A History*. London: Polity Press, 2009.
Leatherbarrow, W. J. *A Devil's Vaudeville: The Demonic in Dostoevsky's Major Fiction*. Evanston: Northwestern University Press, 2005.
———, ed. *Dostoevsky's "The Devils": A Critical Companion*. Evanston: Northwestern University Press, 1999.
Leeman, Richard W. *The Rhetoric of Terrorism and Counterterrorism*. New York: Greenwood Press, 1991.
Leroy-Beaulieu, Anatole. *The Empire of the Czars and the Russians*. Translated by Zenaïde A. Ragozin. New York: G. P. Putnam's Sons, 1898.
———. *L'empire des tsars et les Russes. Tome I, Le pays et les habitants*. Paris: Hachette, 1881.
Levitt, Marcus C. *Russian Literary Politics and the Pushkin Celebration of 1880*. Ithaca: Cornell University Press, 1989.
Linnér, Sven. *Starets Zosima in "The Brothers Karamazov": A Study in the Mimesis of Virtue*. Stockholm: Almqvist & Wiskell International, 1975.
Literatura partii "Narodnoi voli." Moscow: Bor'ba i pravo, 1907.
Liubatovich, Ol'ga. "Dalekoe i nedavnee." *Byloe* 5 (1906): 209–45.
Lombroso, Cesare, and Rudolfo Laschi. *Der politische Verbrecher und die Revolutionen in anthropologischer, juristischer und staatswissenschaftlicher Beziehung*. Translated by Hans Kurella. Hamburg: Verlagsanstalt und Druckerei, 1891–92.
Lotman, Iu. "On the Semiosphere." Translated by Wilma Clark. *Sign Systems Studies* 33, no. 1 (2005): 205–29.
———. *Pushkin*. St. Petersburg: Iskusstvo-OSPB, 1997.
Lotman, Jurij, and Boris A. Uspenskij. *The Semiotics of Russian Culture*. Edited by

Ann Shukman. Ann Arbor: Department of Slavic Languages and Literatures, University of Michigan, 1984.

Lur'e, F. M. *Nechaev: Sozidatel' razrusheniia*. Moscow: Molodaia gvardiia, 2001.

Magun, Artemy. "The Birth of Terrorism Out of the Spirit of Enlightenment: The Subject of Enlightenment and the Terrorist Sensorium." http://www.academia.edu/4084600/THE_BIRTH_OF_TERRORISM_OUT_OF_THE_SPIRIT_OF_ENLIGHTENMENT._The_subject_of_Enlightenment_and_the_terrorist_sensorium (accessed June 16, 2016).

Makogonenko, G. P. *Radishchev i ego vremia*. Moscow: Gos-izd. Khudozhestvennoi literatury, 1956.

Malia, Martin. *Russia Under Western Eyes: From the Bronze Horseman to the Lenin Mausoleum*. Cambridge, MA: Harvard University Press, 1999.

Marchart, Oliver. "The Other Side of Order: Towards a Political Theory of Terror and Dislocation." *Parallax* 9, no. 1 (2003): 97–113.

Marks, Stephen G. *How Russia Shaped the Modern World: From Art to Anti-Semitism, Ballet to Bolshevism*. Princeton: Princeton University Press, 2003.

Marrinan, Michael. "Images and Ideas of Charlotte Corday: Texts and Contexts of an Assassination." *Arts Magazine* 54, no. 8 (1980): 158–76.

Marsh, Cynthia. "*The Times* (1881) and the Russian Women Terrorists." *Scottish Slavonic Review* 21 (1993): 53–70.

Marshall, P. David. *Celebrity and Power: Fame in Contemporary Culture*. Minneapolis: University of Minnesota Press, 1997.

Marx, Karl, and Friedrich Engels. *The Communist Manifesto: A Modern Edition*. London: Verso, 1998.

Mathewson, Rufus W., Jr. *The Positive Hero in Russian Literature*. Evanston: Northwestern University Press, 2000.

Matlaw, Ralph E., ed. *Belinsky, Chernyshevsky, and Dobrolyubov: Selected Criticism*. New York: Dutton, 1962.

McConnell, Allen. *A Russian Philosophe: Alexander Radishchev 1749–1802*. The Hague: M. Nijhof, 1964.

McGee, Owen. *The IRB: The Irish Republican Brotherhood from the Land League to Sinn Féin*. New York: Four Courts Press, 2005.

McLean, Hugh. *Nikolai Leskov: The Man and His Art*. Cambridge, MA: Harvard University Press, 1977.

McReynolds, Louise. *The News Under Russia's Old Regime: The Development of a Mass-Circulation Press*. Princeton: Princeton University Press, 2014.

Melchiori, Barbara. *Terrorism in the Late Victorian Novel*. London: Croom Helm, 1985.

Michelet, Jules. *History of the French Revolution* (abridged version). Translated by Charles Cocks. Chicago: University of Chicago Press, 1967.

———. *History of the French Revolution*. 7 volumes. Translated by Keith Botsford. Wynnewood, PA: Livingston Publishing Co., 1973.

Miliutin, D. A. *Dnevnik general-fel'dmarshala grafa Dmitriia Alekseevicha Miliutina: 1879–1881*. Edited by L. G. Zakharova. Moscow: ROSSPEN, 2010.

Miller, Elizabeth Carolyn. *Framed: The New Woman Criminal in British Culture at the Fin de Siècle*. Ann Arbor: University of Michigan Press, 2008.

———. "Reconsidering Wilde's *Vera; or, the Nihilists*." Unpublished manuscript.

Miller, Martin. *The Foundations of Modern Terrorism: State, Society, and the Dynamics of Political Violence*. Cambridge and New York: Cambridge University Press, 2013.
Miller, Robin Feuer. *Dostoevsky's Unfinished Journey*. New Haven: Yale University Press, 2007.
Mochulsky, Konstantin. *Dostoevsky: His Life and Work*. Translated by Michael A. Minihan. Princeton: Princeton University Press, 1967.
Monoson, S. Sara. *Plato's Democratic Entanglements: Athenian Politics and the Practice of Philosophy*. Princeton: Princeton University Press, 2000.
Morrissey, Susan. *Heralds of Revolution: Russian Students and the Mythologies of Radicalism*. New York: Oxford University Press, 1998.
Morson, Gary Saul. "The God of Onions: *The Brothers Karamazov* and the Mythic Prosaic." In *A New Word on "The Brothers Karamazov,"* edited by Robert Louis Jackson, 107–24. Evanston: Northwestern University Press, 2004.
Moser, Charles. *Esthetics as Nightmare: Russian Literary Theory, 1855–1870*. Princeton: Princeton University Press, 1989.
Moser, Thomas C. "An English Context for Conrad's Russian Characters: Sergei Stepniak and the Diary of Olive Garnett." *Journal of Modern Literature* 11, no. 1 (1984): 3–44.
Murav, Harriet. "From Skandalon to Scandal: Ivan's Rebellion Reconsidered." *Slavic Review* 63, no. 4 (2004): 756–70.
Nabokov, Vladimir. *Lectures on Russian Literature*. Edited by Fredson Bowers. New York: Harcourt Brace Jovanovich, 1981.
Nechaev, Sergei. "Katekhizis revoliutsionera." In *Revoliutsionnyi radikalizm v Rossii: Vek deviatnadtsatyi*, edited by E. L. Rudnitskaia, 244–48. Moscow: Arkheograficheskii tsentr, 1997.
Nietzsche, Friedrich. *On the Genealogy of Morals*. Translated by Walter Kaufmann and R. J. Hollingdale. New York: Vintage Books, 1989.
Offord, Derek. "Alexander Herzen." In *A History of Russian Philosophy 1830–1930: Faith, Reason, and the Defense of Human Dignity*, edited by G. M. Hamburg and Randall A. Poole, 52–68. Cambridge: Cambridge U. Press, 2010.
Oliver, Donna. "Fool or Saint: Reading the Zasulich Case." In *Just Assassins: The Culture of Terrorism in Russia*, edited by Anthony Anemone, 73–95. Evanston: Northwestern University Press, 2010.
Paperno, Irina. *Chernyshevsky and the Age of Realism*. Stanford: Stanford University Press, 1988.
Pipes, Richard. *Russia Under the Old Regime*. New York: Collier Books, 1974.
———. "The Trial of Vera Zasulich." *Russian History* 37, no. 1 (2010): 1–82.
Pisarev, D. I. *Polnoe sobranie sochinenii i pisem v dvenadtsati tomakh*. Moscow: Nauka, 2001.
———. *Selected Philosophical, Social and Political Essays*. Moscow: Foreign Languages Publishing House, 1958.
"Pis'ma S. M. Kravchinskogo (Stepniaka) k V. I. Zasulich (ot 1881–1894)." In *Gruppa "Osvobozhdenie truda,"* edited by Lev Deich. Moscow: Gos. izd-vo, 1923.
Platt, Kevin M. F. *Terror and Greatness: Ivan and Peter as Russian Myths*. Ithaca: Cornell University Press, 2010.

Polonskii, Ia. P. *Polnoe sobranie sochinenii.* St. Petersburg: Tip. R. Golike, 1885.
Pomper, Philip. *Sergei Nechaev.* New Brunswick: Rutgers University Press, 1979.
Pozefsky, Peter C. *The Nihilist Imagination: Dmitrii Pisarev and the Cultural Origins of Russian Radicalism (1860-1868).* New York, Frankfurt: Peter Lang, 2003.
Pushkin, A. S. *Polnoe sobranie sochinenii v desiati tomakh.* Moscow: Izd. Akademii nauk SSSR, 1956.
———. *Sobranie sochinenii.* Moscow: Gos. Izd-vo Khudozhestvennoi literatury, 1960.
Radishchev, A. N. *A Journey from St. Petersburg to Moscow.* Translated by Leo Wiener. Edited, with an introduction and notes, by Roderick Page Thaler. Cambridge, MA: Harvard University Press, 1958.
———. *Puteshestvie iz Peterburga v Moskvu.* Moscow: Khudozhestvennaia literatura, 1964.
Radzinsky, Edvard. *Alexander II: The Last Great Tsar.* New York: Free Press, 2005.
Raeff, Marc. "Filling the Gap between Radishchev and the Decembrists." *Slavic Review* 26, no. 3 (1967): 395-413.
Rahv, Philip. "Dostoevsky in Crime and Punishment." In *Crime and Punishment* by Fyodor Dostoevsky, 543-67. Translated by Jessie Coulson. Edited by George Gibian. New York: W. W. Norton, 1980.
Rapoport, David C. "The Four Waves of Rebel Terror and September 11." *Anthropoetics* 8, no. 1 (2002). http://www.anthropoetics.ucla.edu/ap0801/terror.htm.
Reddy, William M. "Sentimentalism and Its Erasure: The Role of Emotions in the Era of the French Revolution." *Journal of Modern History* 72, no. 1 (2000): 109-52.
Reyfman, Irina. *Ritualized Violence Russian Style: The Duel in Russian Culture and Literature.* Stanford: Stanford University Press, 1999.
Rice, James. *Who Was Dostoevsky? Essays New and Revised.* Berkeley: Berkeley Slavic Specialties, 2011.
Rivers, Christopher. *Face Value: Physiognomical Thought and the Legible Body in Marivaux, Lavater, Balzac, Gautier, and Zola.* Madison: University of Wisconsin Press, 1994.
Rosenblium, N. G. "Peterburgskie pozhary 1862 g. i Dostoevskii." In *Literaturnoe nasledstvo, v. 86: F. M. Dostoevskii. Novye materialy i issledovaniia,* 16-54. Moscow: Nauka, 1973.
Rosenshield, Gary. *Western Law, Russian Justice: Dostoevsky, the Jury Trial, and the Law.* Madison: University of Wisconsin Press, 2005.
Rubin, Barry, and Judith Colp Rubin, eds. *Chronologies of Modern Terrorism.* New York: M. E. Sharpe, 2008.
Rudnitskaia, E. L., ed. *Revoliutsionnyi radikalizm v Rossii: Vek deviatnadtsatyi.* Moscow: Arkheograficheskii tsentr, 1997.
Safronova, Iuliia. *Russkoe obshchestvo v zerkale revoliutsionnogo terrora: 1879-1881 gody.* Moscow: Novoe literaturnoe obozrenie, 2014.
Schapiro, Leonard. *Turgenev: His Life and Times.* New York: Random House, 1978.
Schmid, Alex P., and Albert J. Jongman. *Political Terrorism: A New Guide to Actors, Authors, Concepts, Data Bases, Theories, and Literature.* New York: Transaction Publishers, 2005.

Schmid, Alex P., and Janny de Graaf. *Violence as Communication: Insurgent Terrorism and the Western News Media.* New York: SAGE, 1982.
Schmitt, Carl. *The Concept of the Political.* Translated by George Schwab. New Brunswick: Rutgers University Press, 1976.
———. *Theory of the Partisan.* New York: Telos Press Publishing, 2007.
Schrader, Abby. *Languages of the Lash: Corporal Punishment and Identity in Imperial Russia.* Dekalb: Northern Illinois University Press, 2002.
Schwartz, Vanessa. *Spectacular Realities: Early Mass Culture in Fin-de-Siècle Paris.* Berkeley: University of California Press, 1998.
Senese, Donald. *S. M. Stepniak-Kravchinskii: The London Years.* Newtonville, MA: Oriental Research Partners, 1987.
Shchennikova, L. P. "Ispoved' dvukh geroev: Ivan Karamazov i osuzhdennyi N. Minskogo." *Dostoevskii: Materialy i issledovaniia* 16 (2001): 222–31.
Siljak, Ana. *Angel of Vengeance: The Girl Who Shot the Governor of St. Petersburg and Sparked the Age of Assassination.* New York: St. Martin's Griffin, 2008.
Simmons, Ernest. *Dostoevsky: The Making of a Novelist.* New York: Vintage Books, 1940.
Smith, Douglas. "Alexander Radishchev's *Journey from St. Petersburg to Moscow* and the Limits of Freedom of Speech in the Reign of Catherine the Great." In *Freedom of Speech: The History of an Idea,* edited by Elizabeth Powers, 61–80. Lewisburg: Bucknell University Press, 2011.
Spasovich, V. D. *Za mnogo let, 1859–1871, Articles, Excerpts, Histories, Criticism, Polemics, Court Speeches, and Others.* St. Petersburg: Tip. F. Sushchinskago, 1872.
Straus, Nina Pelikan. "From Dostoevsky to Al-Qaeda: What Fiction Says to Social Science." *Common Knowledge* 12, no. 2 (2006): 197–231.
Taratuta, Evgeniia. *Istoriia dvukh knig: "Podpol'naia Rossiia" S. M. Stepniaka-Kravchinskogo i "Ovod" Etel' Lilian Voinich.* Moscow: Khudozh. lit-ra, 1987.
———. *S. M. Stepniak-Kravchinskii: Revoliutsioner i pisatel'.* Moscow: Khudozh. lit., 1973.
Taylor, Charles. *Sources of the Self: The Making of Modern Identity.* Cambridge: Cambridge University Press, 1989.
Taylor, Michael W. *The Tyrant Slayers: The Heroic Image in Fifth Century B.C. Athenian Art and Politics.* New York: Ayer, 1991.
Test, George A. *Satire: Spirit and Art.* Tampa: University of South Florida Press, 1991.
Thaler, Roderick Page. "Introduction." In *A Journey from St. Petersburg to Moscow,* by Aleksandr Radishchev, 1–37. Cambridge, MA: Harvard University Press, 1958.
Thomson, Judith Jarvis. "The Trolley Problem." *Yale Law Journal* 94, no. 6 (1985): 1395–415.
Tkachev, P. N. *Izbrannye sochineniia na sotsial'no-politicheskie temy.* Edited by B. P. Kuzmin. Moscow: Gosudarstvennoe sotsial'no-ekonomicheskoe izdatel'stvo, 1932–37.
Todorov, Tzvetan. *The Fantastic: A Structural Approach to a Literary Genre.* Translated by Richard Howard. Ithaca: Cornell University Press, 1975.
Tolstoi, Lev. *Sobranie sochinenii L. N. Tolstogo v dvadtsati dvukh tomakh.* Volume 4. Moscow: Khudozhestvennaia literatura, 1979.

Tolstoy, Leo. *War and Peace*. Translated by Richard Pevear and Larissa Volokhonsky. New York: Vintage Classics, 2008.
Trigos, Ludmilla A. *The Decembrist Myth in Russian Culture*. New York: Palgrave Macmillan, 2009.
———. "Historical Models of Terror in Decembrist Literature." In *Just Assassins: The Culture of Terrorism in Russia*, edited by Anthony Anemone, 25–52. Evanston: Northwestern University Press, 2010.
Troitsky, N. A. "Zasulich ili Figner? (o stikhotvorenii Ia. P. Polonskogo 'Uznitsa')." *Russkaia literatura* 20, no. 2 (1977): 183–86.
Troyat, Henri. *Turgenev*. Translated by Nancy Amphoux. New York: Dutton, 1988.
Turgenev, Ivan. *Fathers and Sons*. Translated by Barbara Makanowitzky. New York: Bantam Books, 1982.
———. *Literary Reminiscences*. Translated by David Magarshack. New York: Farrar, Straus, Giroux, 1958.
———. *Polnoe sobranie sochinenii i pisem*. Moscow: Izdatel'stvo "Nauka," 1982.
Tyrkov, K. *K sobytiiu 1 marta 1881 goda*. Rostov-na-Donu: Tipografiia Donskaia rech', 1906.
Ulam, Adam B. *In the Name of the People: Prophets and Conspirators in Pre-Revolutionary Russia*. New York: Viking Press, 1977.
Uspenskaia, A. I. "Vospominaniia shestidesiatnitsy." *Byloe* 18 (1922): 19–45.
Uspensky, Boris. *The Semiotics of the Russian Icon*. Edited by Stephen Rudy. Lisse: Peter de Ridder Press, 1976.
Valkenier, Elizabeth Kridl. *Ilya Repin and the World of Russian Art*. New York: Columbia University Press, 1990.
———. "The Writer as Artist's Model: Repin's Portrait of Garshin." *Metropolitan Museum Journal* 28 (1993): 207–16.
Venturi, Franco. *Roots of Revolution: A History of the Populist and Socialist Movement in Nineteenth-Century Russia*. Translated by Francis Haskell. New York: Knopf, 1960.
Verhoeven, Claudia. *The Odd Man Karakozov: Imperial Russia, Modernity, and the Birth of Terrorism*. Ithaca: Cornell University Press, 2009.
Vinitsky, Ilya. "A Cheerful Empress and Her Gloomy Critics." In *Madness and the Mad in Russian Culture*, edited by Angela Brintlinger and Ilya Vinitsky, 24–45. Toronto: University of Toronto Press, 2007.
Vladiv, Slobodanka. *Narrative Principles in Dostoevskij's Besy: A Structural Analysis*. Bern: Peter Lang, 1979.
Vogüé, Eugène-Melchior de. *The Russian Novelists*. Translated by Jane Loring Edmands. Boston: D. Lothrop Co, 1887.
Volgin, Igor. "Alyosha's Destiny." In *The New Russian Dostoevsky: Readings for the Twenty-First Century*, edited by Carol Apollonio, 271–86. Bloomington: Slavica, 2010.
———. *Poslednii god Dostoevskogo: Istoricheskie zapiski*. Moscow: Sov. pisatel', 1986.
———. *Propavshchii zagovor: Dostoevskii i politicheskii protsess 1849 goda*. Moscow: Izd-vo Libereia, 2000.
Volk, S. S. *"Narodnaia volia" i "Chernyi peredel": Vospominaniia uchastnikov revoliutsionnogo dvizheniia v Peterburge v 1879–1882 gg.* Leningrad: Lenizdat, 1989.

Wanner, Adrian. "Populism and Romantic Agony: A Russian Terrorist's Discovery of Baudelaire." *Slavic Review* 52, no. 2 (1993): 298–317.
Whelehan, Niall. *The Dynamiters: Irish Nationalism and Political Violence in the Wider World, 1867–1900*. London: Cambridge University Press, 2012.
Worobec, Christine. *Possessed: Women, Witches, and Demons in Imperial Russia*. DeKalb: Northern Illinois University Press, 2003.
Wortman, Richard. *The Crisis of Russian Populism*. London: Cambridge University Press, 1967.
———. "Moscow and Petersburg: The Problem of Political Center in Tsarist Russia, 1881–1914." In *Rites of Power: Symbolism, Ritual, and Politics since the Middle Ages*, edited by Sean Wilentz, 244–74. Philadelphia: University of Pennsylvania Press, 1985.
Wyllys, Rufus Kay. "The Filibusters of Amelia Island." *Georgia Historical Quarterly* 12, no. 4 (1928): 297–325.
Yarmolinsky, Avrahm. *Turgenev: The Man, His Art and His Age*. New York: Collier Books, 1959.
Zaionchkovsky, Peter A. *The Russian Autocracy in Crisis, 1878–1882*. Translated by Gary M. Hamburg. Gulf Breeze, FL: Academic International Press, 1979.
Zasulich, Vera. *Vospominaniia*. Moscow: Izdatel'stvo Vsesouiz. obshchestva politkatorzhan i ssyl'no-poselentsev, 1931.
Zulaika, Joseba, and William Douglass. *Terror and Taboo: The Follies, Fables, and Faces of Terrorism*. New York: Routledge, 1996.

Index

act/deed: Nietzsche on, 209; as transformative, 212-13, 299n10; women as terror/ists and, 233. *See also* word and deed (slovo i delo)
activism (acts of fanaticism), 95, 96, 97, 99, 112. *See also* word and deed (slovo i delo)
acts, unheard of: in *Demons* (Dostoevsky), 110-13, 129-30, 283nn12-13; in Gogol's writings, 113, 283n13; Karakozov and, 71, 94, 111-12. *See also* dare to act (audacity)
aesthetics in literature, and "The Threshold" (Turgenev), 216, 222, 223
aesthetics of murder: *The Brothers Karamazov* (Dostoevsky) and, 200-201; in *Crime and Punishment* (Dostoevsky), 82, 85-86, 88-90, 129, 195, 200, 279n17, 280n27; in *Demons* (Dostoevsky), 127, 129, 193, 200; morality and, 89, 279n17; Pisarev on, 88, 280n34; utilitarianism and, 280n34. *See also* murder as/as not terrorism/revolutionary terrorism
"After the Execution of November 4" (Anonymous), 222

Alexander II, Tsar: censorship by, 49-50; death/funeral of, 4-5, 211-12; Dostoevsky as loyal to, 13, 44, 147, 151, 153, 290n11; the Emancipation or new era and, 43-44, 273n10; on filial piety, 290n13; image of, 212, 237, 302n8; jubilee address for, 147, 151, 153, 198, 199-200; liberal reforms under, 43-44, 170, 213; martyr(s)/martyrdom and, 212, 298n6; mourning/celebration of death of, 248-49; murder as/as not terror/ism under, 98-99, 113-14; People's Will or Narodnaia volia and, 213; Supreme Administrative Commission and, 188-89, 198, 242, 296n3; sympathy or sochuvstvie for, 154; Victoria (Queen of England) as relation of, 246; the West on, 247, 248; *Young Russia* (Zaichnevsky) and, 50
Alexander III, Tsar (Alexander Alexandrovich Romanov), 12, 66, 116-17, 188, 213, 241-42, 298n9
Alexandrov, P. A., as defense attorney for Zasulich: corporal punishment digression and, 170-71, 293n14; on flogging

323

Alexandrov, P. A. (*continued*)
of Bogoliubov by Trepov, 161, 162, 174, 175; human dignity/rights and, 171, 293n14; Marian figure, 234; political radical(s)/violence information about Zasulich, 160; religious metaphors and, 169–70, 181–82, 185; sentimentalism strategy by, 292n6; suffering and, 170–71, 293n14; summation by, 161, 168–75, 181–82, 183–85, 215, 292n6, 293n14; witnesses' testimony and, 161–65, 174–75
anarchists/ism: Bakhunin's Hegelian-inspired thesis of, 36, 304n34; Bakunin and, 36; bombs and, 260; *Demons* (Dostoevsky) and, 106, 107, 112; Fenians compared with, 254–55; in France, 108, 260; Nihilists/nihilists as synonym for, 226; terror/ism and, 250, 253; Tolstoy and, 61, 77; Turgenev and, 61; in the West, 224, 258, 300n1
Anderson, Sean, 264n9
Annenkov, Pavel, 219, 270n54, 299n3
anti-colonialism, 12, 264n10
anti-Nihilists/anti-nihilists: about, 83, 272n9; counterterrorism in the West and, 255, 305n22, 306n37; *Demons* (Dostoevsky) and, 107, 127, 129, 132; literature by, 13, 132. *See also* Nihilists/nihilists
Apollonio, Carol, 120, 132, 286n25
Arendt, Hannah, 186, 188, 289n19
Aristogeiton, 19, 88, 267n7
Arnold, Matthew, 134
Arrest of the Propagandist (Repin), 257
arson/arsonists: as Nihilists/nihilists, 45; as terror/ists, 45, 46, 48–51, 60–61, 273n23; word and deed and, 50–51
artistic-political rivalry, 242, 243–44, 246, 304n34
assassination/assassination attempt(s) on Alexander II: aesthetics of murder and, 89; arrests/trials/executions of regicides in, 4, 212, 233, 237, 250–51, 302n4; *The Brothers Karamazov* (Dostoevsky) as allegory and, 153–54, 197, 298n8; censorship of, 154, 212; as

conspiracy versus lone assassin, 71–72, 114–15, 276nn15–16, 283n18; Dostoevsky's writings as influenced by, 71, 72, 82, 83–84, 145, 276n14, 279n9; faith-based hagiography and, 199; by Karakozov, 5–6, 19–20, 33, 71–72, 82, 83–84, 89, 100, 121, 145, 276nn14–16, 279n9, 280n32; Komissarov as foiling, 72, 299n3; media on, 71–72, 212, 247–48, 250, 305n5; by Nechaev, 99, 283n9; by People's Will or Narodnaia volia, 4–6, 12, 33, 66, 112, 146–47, 152, 199, 211–12, 222–23, 264n9, 271n69, 289n4; by Perovskaya, 5, 211, 221, 289n4; public opinion of, 212–13; by Shiriaev, 289n4; terror/ism's origins and, 5–6, 99, 264n9; *Times of London* (newspaper) on, 247; as tyrannicide, 89, 280n32; utilitarianism and, 121, 284n13; the West and, 247–49, 250, 305n5
assassination(s)/assassination attempt(s): on Bourbon monarchs, 19, 267n5; *Don Quixote* (Cervantes) and, 57; by Fenians on Victoria (Queen of England), 5–6, 264n9; *Hamlet* (Shakespeare) and, 57; on Kravshinsky, 132; on Loris-Melikov, 242, 296n3; on Mezentsev, 132, 224–25, 226; on Napoleon I, 19, 267n5; on Stolypin, 285n9; on Trepov, 19, 155–56; as tyrannicides, 19, 89, 267n7, 280n32; tyrannicides and, 19, 26–27, 87–88, 267n7; on Victoria (Queen of England), 5–6, 248, 264n9; *War and Peace/The Year 1805* (Tolstoy) and, 77–78; in the West, 224, 300n1; Zasulich's trial/acquittal as inspiration for, 19, 155, 157, 180, 222, 224–25, 294n13; on Zhelekhovsky by Kolenkina, 155. *See also* assassination/assassination attempt(s) on Alexander II
a-sychrony of terrorists/agency and terror(ism)/activism, 14–15
audacity (dare to act), 78–79, 84–85, 278n22. *See also* acts, unheard of
Audourd, Olympe, 257, 306n41

Index

autocracy/state government. *See* state government/autocracy

Bakhmetev, Pavel Alexandrovich, 64–65, 275n15
Bakunin, Mikhail (Jules Elysard, pseud.), 284n19; anarchists/ism and, 36; behavioral model/s and, 265n19; on *The Brothers Karamazov* (Dostoevsky), 179, 194; "creative destruction" and, 36, 244, 246, 304n34; *Demons* (Dostoevsky) as interpretation of, 115, 123, 284n19; Hegelian-inspired thesis of anarchists/ism by, 36, 304n34; as ineffective political radical, 115; Katkov's portrayal of, 115; Nechaev and, 95, 98, 123; on propaganda, 36; "The Reaction in Germany" (Elysard pseud.), 35–36; word and deed or *slovo i delo* and, 128
Balzac, Honoré de, *Le Père Goriot*, 145, 276n1
Barannikov, Alexander, 211, 225
"Bazarov" (Pisarev), 41, 76
behavioral model/s (social types, new): about, 7, 265n19; Bakunin, 265n19; Byronic, 33, 229, 252; Goethe and, 252; in *Journey* . . . (Radishchev), 22, 23, 27–28, 267n16, 268nn22–23, 268n25, 270n49; Karakozov and, 121; literary critics/criticism and, 23; in literature, 7–8, 33–34, 52, 265n19, 265n26; Nihilists/nihilists and, 252; political radical(s)/violence and, 22–23, 268nn22–23, 268n25; Pushkin on, 22, 27–28, 267n16, 270n49; self-sacrifice as, 23; for terror/ists, 7–8, 61–62, 83, 265n22, 279n6; in *Underground Russia* [La Rossia Sotteranea] (Stepniak pseud./Kravchinsky), 228; Wertherism as, 7, 252; Zasulich's trial/acquittal and, 160, 169, 173, 190, 292n6. *See also* body/image; face/image
Belinsky, Vissarion, 37, 38, 54
Belknap, Robert, 179, 297n9
Bell, J. Bower, 141, 142–43, 145
The Bell [Kolokol] (Herzen), 50, 82
beshenyi (madman). *See* madman (beshenyi)

Black, Edwin, 179
"blinded by an idea," 242, 303n27
body/image: of Alexander II, 212; of female terror/ists, 228, 232, 251, 301n25; of male terror/ists, 227, 228, 251; of state government/autocracy, 227. *See also* face/image
Bogoliubov, Arkhip [pseud.] (Alexei Stepanovich Emilianov): in detention, pretrial, 156, 160–63, 164, 174, 291n7; human dignity/rights, 170, 174, 181, 184, 186; Kurneev and, 161, 163, 164; Land and Freedom membership and, 156; media coverage of flogging of, 156, 160–61, 162, 163, 164, 174, 291n7; self-sacrifice and, 181; suffering of, 182; Trepov's flogging of, 156, 160–61, 162–63, 164, 174, 291n7
Bogrov, Dmitry, 285n9
bomb/s: anarchists/ism and, 260; Dostoevsky and, 107, 146, 147, 282n8, 283n9, 289n20; Fenians's use of, 5, 108, 224, 249–50, 254, 295n39; *Hamlet* (Shakespeare) and, 289n20; People's Will or Narodnaia volia and, 108, 146–47, 152, 199, 258, 289n4, 295n39. *See also* infernal machines
Bourbon monarchs, 19, 267n5
The Bronze Horseman [Mednyi vsadnik] (Pushkin), 6, 28–29, 30–34, 270nn60–62, 271n69
The Brothers Karamazov (Dostoevsky): aesthetics of murder and, 200–201; as allegory, 153–54, 197, 298n8; compassion or *sostradanie* in, 189, 194, 206; corporal punishment in, 177–78; educated society or *obshchestvo* representation in, 198–200, 296n1, 297n7, 297n9; Epilogue in, 205–6; faith-based hagiography in, 192–94, 198–99, 295n3, 296n4, 297n7; the fantastic/fantastical in, 200–201; gesture or emblematic act in, 185, 186–88, 194–95, 206; hero(s)/new hero(s) in, 195, 274n20; icon(s)/iconography(ies) in, 205, 206; and insanity plea, temporary, 200; Mandarin or trolley dilemma in, 145; morality in,

The Brothers Karamazov (continued)
218, 282n12; Nihilists/nihilists and, 200–201; plot of, 153–54; preface to, 204, 274n20; publication of, 153; realism in, 192; religious metaphors in, 185–86, 187, 188, 295n24; revolutionary terrorism and, 13, 44–45, 189–91, 205, 295n39, 298n8; rhetorical genres and devices in, 179–80; satire in, 165–66, 198–99, 297n7; self-sacrifice in, 195, 205, 206–7; sentimentalism in, 205; sequel planned for, 4, 297n6; society as mirror of revolutionary terrorism and, 197–99, 297n7, 297n9; speech as transformative in, 202, 203–7, 297n6, 298n8; state terrorism and revolutionary terrorism relationship in, 185–89, 192, 194, 195–96, 198–99, 297n7; suffering in, 176–77, 182–83, 195, 200, 204–6; suicide in, 197–98; sympathy or sochuvstvie in, 189–90; trial in, 154, 157, 165–66, 176–78, 201, 203, 291n12, 297n9; universal harmony as compared with terror/ism in, 261; word and deed or slovo i delo in, 192–93, 195, 197, 206; Zasulich's trial/acquittal and, 157, 158, 165, 176–78, 185–86, 189, 191, 201, 203, 218, 291n12

"brute fact," terror/ism as, 8, 10, 11, 35, 73. *See also* "social fact," terrorism as

Butashevich-Petrashevsky, Mikhail, and conspiracy, 36–39, 44, 49, 71–72, 114–15, 206, 283n18, 296n3, 298n12

Byronic literature and behavioral models, 33, 229, 252

Café Terminus attack in France in 1893, 260

Catechism of a Revolutionary [Katekhizis revoliutsionera] (Nechaev): about, 121; emotions in, 97; monsters/gloomy monsters in, 6, 264n11; morality in, 96, 97, 127; *Nechaevshchina* affair/conspiracy trial and, 125; political radical(s)/violence described in, 96, 228; terror/ism and, 5–6, 97–98, 128, 264nn9–10, 265n12

Catherine II: censorship by, 20, 28; on *Journey . . .* (Radishchev), 20, 21, 26, 27, 29; literature as crime against, 28, 30; on Martinists, 21, 267n13; as merciful, 28; Pugachev uprising against, 20, 28, 33; punishments by, 20, 287n9; on "right to kill," 27

celebrity(ies), 229–35, 301n18, 301n25

censorship: by Alexander II, 49–50; of assassination/assassination attempt(s) on Alexander II, 154, 212; by Catherine II, 20; and culture of Russia, 198; Dostoevsky and, 38–39, 49–50; *Journey . . .* (Radishchev) and, 20, 28; Pushkin and, 33; society as mirror of revolutionary terrorism and, 199; *What Is to Be Done?* (Chernyshevsky) and, 60, 65

Central Committee/Action Committee, 93–94, 281n2, 281n4

Cervantes, Miguel de. *See Don Quixote* (Cervantes)

Chaadaev, Peter, 62, 75

Chaikovsky, Nikolai, 151, 223

Charushina, Anna, 164

Chernyshevsky, Nikolai: arrest/imprisonment/sentencing of, 60, 66; arson/arsonists as terror/ists and, 49, 60–61, 273n23; Bakhmetev's relationship with, 64–65, 275n15; as literary critic, 43; on realism versus the fantastic/fantastical, 54; and repatriation by People's Will, 66. *See also What Is to Be Done?* (Chernyshevsky)

Christianity: apocalyptical, 36; Dostoevsky and, 193, 206; humility and, 84; icon(s)/iconography(ies) in, 212, 233–34, 298n6; Marian figure in, 216, 234; martyr(s)/martyrdom in, 295n29; Minsky, 294n22. *See also* faith-based hagiography; false god/king; religious metaphors

civilian (soft) targets, 11–12, 108, 199–200, 283n10, 287n2, 300n1

Cochrane, Stephen T., 281n4

compassion (sostradanie): Arendt on suffering and, 186; in *The Brothers Karamazov* (Dostoevsky), 189, 194, 206; in

Crime and Punishment (Dostoevsky), 80, 81, 279n7; Festa on, 268n23; in "The Last Confession" [Poslednaia ispoved'] (Minsky), 187; in *Underground Russia* [La Rossia Sotteranea] (Stepniak pseud./Kravchinsky), 234; for Zasulich's assassination attempt on Trepov, 173
conscience: Corday and, 241; in *Crime and Punishment* (Dostoevsky), 79, 80–81, 86, 92, 165, 213; in *Demons* (Dostoevsky), 120–21, 127, 130; Dostoevsky on, 188; in *A Journey from St. Petersburg to Moscow* (Radishchev), 21; lawyers as served by, 167, 168; in literature, 7; in *Nadezhda Nikolaevna* (Garshin), 241, 246; Perovskaya and, 234; Zasulich's trial/acquittal and, 165, 186, 218, 241
consciousness: about model of, 269n27; in *Crime and Punishment* (Dostoevsky), 64, 79, 85, 86, 213; Enlightenment and, 269n31; in *Journey* . . . (Radishchev), 23–27, 269n31; in *Nadezhda Nikolaevna* (Garshin), 239; Nihilists/nihilists and, 280n27; political radical(s)/violence as provocation for, 12–13, 17; Turgenev on, 55
conservatives: Dostoevsky and, 13, 44, 258; Katkov and, 68, 256; and literature, Russian, 53, 219–20; media and, 212; Pobedonostsev and, 178; sentimentalism and, 23, 268n23; the West's interest in Nihilists/nihilists and, 252, 258, 307n46
conspiracy/ies: assassination attempt on Alexander II as, 71–72, 114–15, 276nn15–16, 283n18; *Demons* (Dostoevsky) and, 106; of family members, 91, 281nn41–42; Petrashevsky affair, 36–39, 44, 49, 71–72, 114–15, 206, 283n18, 296n3, 298n12. See also *Nechaevshchina* affair/conspiracy (Ivanov's murder)
The Contemporary (journal), 29, 43, 54, 55, 57, 59, 60, 61, 294n10
Corday, Charlotte: conscience and, 241; as face/image of revolution/terror, 236, 237, 238–39, 240, 241–42, 244, 245, 246, 302n3; heroine(s)/new heroine(s) and, 251; modern terrorism's origins and, 241, 303n24; "right to kill" and, 246
corporal punishment: Alexandrov on, 170–71; in *The Brothers Karamazov* (Dostoevsky) and, 177–78; Dostoevsky on, 167–68, 170, 174–75; Dzhunkovsky trial/acquittal for, 170; Kroneberg trial/acquittal for, 167, 174–75, 176, 291n12; suffering and, 170–71, 293n14
counterterrorism: in *Demons* (Dostoevsky), 188; state terrorism as, 34, 126–27, 157, 164, 290n7; in the West against Nihilists/nihilists, 255, 256, 305n22, 306n37, 306n38. See also flogging; terror/ism
"creative destruction," 31–33, 36, 79, 244, 246, 304n34
Crime and Punishment (Dostoevsky): aesthetics of murder in, 82, 85–86, 88–90, 129, 195, 200, 279n17, 280n27, 280n33; assassination attempt by Karakozov as influence on, 71, 72, 82, 83–84, 145, 276n14, 279n9; as autobiographical, 68; and "brute fact," terror/ism as, 73; censorship and, 71; compassion or sostradanie in, 80, 81, 279n7; conscience in, 79, 80–81, 86, 92, 165, 213; consciousness in, 64, 79, 85, 86, 213; conspiracy of family members in, 91, 281nn41–42; "creative destruction" in, 79; critiques of, 84, 94, 279n12, 281n5; dare to act or audacity in, 78–79, 84–85; Epilogue in, 73, 75–76, 84, 205; faith-based hagiography in, 44, 84, 193; the fantastic/fantastical in, 67; hero(s)/new hero(s) and political radical(s)/violence in, 72, 78; and insanity plea, temporary, 75–76, 79; justice in, 80–81, 84; literary critics/criticism and, 259; madman or beshenyi in, 75–76; Mandarin or trolley dilemma in, 145, 288n12, 288n16; martyr(s)/martyrdom in, 91; media environment and, 69, 70–71; monsters/gloomy monsters in, 6, 81, 108, 282n8; morality

Crime and Punishment (continued)
in, 78-79, 80, 81, 89, 90, 96-97, 280n27, 282n12; motivation for crime in, 73-76, 78-79, 277n6; murder as/as not terror/ism in, 44-45, 72, 84, 88, 90, 94-95, 99, 129-30, 255, 280n27, 281n6; Nechaev and, 94, 281nn5-6; new man in, 72, 76, 77, 78, 79, 81, 90, 91, 195; Nihilists/nihilists in, 78-79, 83, 89, 253, 280n27; *The Notebooks for "Crime and Punishment"* (Dostoevsky) and, 81, 90, 109, 273n14; plot of, 68, 69-70, 72; political radical(s)/violence in, 72, 75-76, 82-83, 278n2; prostitution in, 69; publication of, 68, 72, 126, 153, 276n10, 277n20; "right to kill" or Napoleonic idea in, 76-77, 78, 84-85, 86, 88-89, 276n14, 279n18, 279n20; self-sacrifice in, 69, 91; and "social fact," terrorism as, 73; success of, 69, 276n10; suffering in, 79, 90-91, 92; suicide and, 88; sympathy or sochuvstvie in, 80-81; and terror/ism, theory of modern, 86-87, 90; utilitarianism in, 86, 279n7; *What Is to Be Done?* (Chernyshevsky) as influence on, 65-66, 68, 83, 275n20, 279n7; word and deed in, 67

crime of murder as/as not terror/ism. *See* murder as/as not terrorism/revolutionary terrorism

"cult of the dagger," 33, 226, 271n70

cultural imaginary: celebrity(ies) in, 229, 231-32, 235; French Revolution terror/ism in, 18-19, 48, 127, 167n6; monsters/gloomy monsters in, 11, 18-19; terror/ism in, 18-19, 35; Underground Russia in, 225

culture and society, Russian. *See* culture of Russia; educated society (obshchestvo)

culture of Russia: censorship and, 198, 199; human dignity/rights in, 198, 287n9; as mirror of revolutionary terrorism, 197-99, 296n1, 296n3, 297n7; Nihilists/nihilists and, 152, 199. *See also* educated society (obshchestvo)

Curtis, William Eleroy, 258, 307n45

Daly, Jonathan, 287n9
Damasio, Antonio, 269n27
Danilov, A. M., 276n10
dare to act (audacity), 78-79, 84-85, 278n22. *See also* acts, unheard of
Decembrist uprising in 1825, 33-34, 78, 236-37, 302n2
deception: in *Demons* (Dostoevsky), 97-98, 108, 126, 283n12; by Nechaev, 97-98, 122, 126, 287n2, 293n7; by political radicals, 94, 281n4; Zasulich and, 122, 281n4
deed and word. *See* act/deed; speech act; word and deed (slovo i delo)
Deich, Lev, 228
Demons (Dostoevsky): about, 15-16; and acts, unheard of, 110-13, 129-30, 283nn12-13; aesthetics of murder in, 127, 129, 193, 200; anarchists/ism and, 106, 107, 112; as anti-Nihilists/anti-nihilists literature, 107, 127, 129, 132; Bakunin as interpreted in, 115, 123, 284n19; bombs in, 107, 282n8, 283n9; conscience in, 120-21, 127, 130; conspiracy/ies and, 106; counterterrorism in, 126-27, 164, 188; deception in, 97-98, 108, 126, 283n12; dedication to Alexander III in, 116-17; Epilogue in, 205; face/image in, 129, 132-33, 244; faith-based hagiography in, 130, 193, 293n7; false god/king in, 116, 124, 129, 130-31, 132-33, 186, 284n22, 286n23, 286n34; the fantastic/fantastical in, 120, 136, 139, 141; filial piety in, 116-17, 124, 153; friend/enemy distinction in, 146-47, 288n17, 289n19; hero(s)/new hero(s) in, 123; ineffective political radical(s)/violence in, 133, 134; irony in, 116, 117, 124, 130, 146; liberalism in, 119, 120, 127, 128, 139; Mandarin or trolley dilemma in, 145-46, 288n15; martyr(s)/martyrdom in, 123-24, 130; monsters/gloomy monsters in, 131, 264n11; morality in, 127, 285n9; murder as/as not revolutionary terrorism in, 106-9, 113, 115-16, 129-30, 131-32, 154, 282n5, 282n8, 283nn9-11; Nechaev as reimagined in, 126-27, 285n7;

Nechaevshchina affair/conspiracy or Ivanov's murder in, 94, 99, 105-6, 113-14, 116-17, 126, 281n6, 282n3; new man in, 129-30, 131; *The Notebooks for "The Possessed"* (Dostoevsky) and, 112, 114, 117, 118, 120-21, 134-35, 136, 145; political radical(s)/violence in, 114-15, 118-19, 120-21, 124, 127-28, 133, 205, 284n19; publication of, 126, 130, 131, 151, 286n28; realism in, 119; satire in, 112-13, 117, 134, 137, 138-39, 142, 143, 144; self-sacrifice in, 123, 124, 130, 131, 132-33, 186, 286n25; sentimentalism in, 119-20, 121, 123, 132-33, 138, 139-40, 228, 286n34; and "social fact," terrorism as, 105-6, 127, 285n9; state terrorism and revolutionary terrorism relationship in, 134-40, 142, 144, 162, 287n9, 288n8; suicide in, 111, 116, 124, 130, 131, 133, 197-98, 284n22; sympathy or *sochuvstvie* in, 119, 120, 135, 136, 138, 139-40; terror/ism as anachronistic in, 108, 142, 143, 283n11; typology of terror/ism in, 141-43, 288n4; and underground, revolutionary, 129; and the West, corruption by, 128-29, 285n12; word and deed or *slovo i delo* in, 106, 282nn3-5

De Mortens, N. F., 305n22, 306n38

De Novikoff (Novikova), Olga, 256

deontology versus utilitarianism, 145, 288nn12-13

De Quincy, Thomas, 279n17

Derrida, Jacques, 18, 266n1

detention, pretrial: of Bogoliubov, 156, 160-63, 164, 174, 291n7; conditions in, 291n6; flogging in, 156, 160-61, 162-63, 164, 174, 291n7; of women, 156, 164, 171-72, 173; of youth from educated society or *obshchestvo*, 151; of Zasulich, 160-61, 164. *See also* state terrorism; trial/s

De Vogüé, Eugène-Melchior, 258, 259-61, 265n14, 307n48

Diary of a Madman (Gogol), 44

Diary of a Superfluous Man (Turgenev), 53

Diary of a Writer (journal), 154, 157, 167, 170, 174-75, 176

Dobroliubov, Nikolai: on behavioral models from literature, 52, 57-59; death of, 59; on hero(s)/new hero(s), 57-59; as literary critic, 52-53; on new man in literature, 54, 55; Nihilists/nihilists and, 59; on *Oblomov* (Goncharov), 52-53; on Oblomovism or oblomovshchina, 52-53, 57; on *On the Eve* (Turgenev), 57-59; on political radical(s)/violence, 95; on renunciation or *otrechenie*, 59, 96; "What Is Oblomovism?," 52, 57; "When Will the Real Day Come?," 57

Don Quixote (Cervantes): assassination(s)/assassination attempt(s) and, 57; the fantastic/fantastical in, 55; hero(s)/new hero(s) in, 57; morality in, 55; new man in, 55-56, 57, 274n20; Nihilists/nihilists and, 59; rulers versus new man in, 57, 274n20; self-sacrifice in, 55; Turgenev and, 56, 57, 59, 62, 93; *What Is to Be Done?* (Chernyshevsky) and, 62, 65

Dostoevsky, Fyodor: arrest/imprisonment/sentencing/commutation for, 37, 38, 206; on arson/arsonists as terror/ists, 49, 273n23; bomb/s and, 107, 146, 147, 282n8, 283n9, 289n20; censorship and, 38, 49-50; Christianity and, 193, 206; on conscience, 188; on consciousness, 13; on corporal punishment, 167-68, 170, 174-75; death/wake/funeral/burial of, 260-61; *Diary of a Writer* (journal) and, 154, 157, 167, 170, 174-75, 176; *Double*, 39; Enlightenment's influences on, 206; *Epokha* (journal) and, 280n34; on fantastic reality/realism, 13, 39; on filial piety and state government/autocracy, 153, 290n11; financial issues for, 68, 125; "The Fires," 48-49; on flogging, 168; on friend/enemy distinction, 146, 147, 289n20; *The Gambler*, 278n2; as gambler/risk-taker, 82-83, 192, 278n2; on gesture or emblematic act, 269n12; on Greek aesthetics, 89; as hero(s)/new hero(s), 39; *House of the Dead*, 199; on human dignity/rights, 206; jubilee

Dostoevsky, Fyodor (*continued*)
address for Alexander II by, 147, 151, 153, 198, 199–200; Katkov's relationship with, 68, 72, 83, 84, 126, 153, 276n10, 277n20; literary critics/criticism in the West on, 258, 259; Liubimov's relationship with, 70, 72, 83; Nechaev's writings and, 112, 125; on new man, 206; on Nihilists/nihilists, 83, 116–17, 147, 153, 259, 283n18, 307n48; *Notes from the House of the Dead*, 68; *Notes from the Underground*, 66, 68, 70–71, 275n20; *Petersburg Visions in Verse and Prose*, 13, 44–45, 272n3; Petrashevsky affair/conspiracy and, 12, 37–39, 44, 49, 206, 296n3, 298n12; on Pisarev, 47; as politically loyal monarchist/conservative, 13, 44, 147, 151, 153, 258, 290n11; on political radical(s)/violence as foreign-born/foreign influenced, 258; *Poor Folk*, 37; on Pushkin Days speech as transformative, 202, 203, 206, 297n4, 298n12; revolutionary terrorism in writings by, 6, 13, 44; revolutionary underground man and, 130, 188, 280n23; rhetorical genres and devices and, 179; on "sedition"/"seditionist" and state government, 215; self-conception of, 14, 39; and "social fact," terrorism as, 49–50; on social relevance of literature, 3–4; on society as mirror of revolutionary terrorism, 198; Stellovsky as publisher for, 83, 278n2; sympathy or sochuvstvie and, 261; *Time* (journal) and, 43, 48, 276n10; on trial lawyers, 167; trips abroad by, 82, 125, 280n23, 285n12; universal harmony as compared with terror/ism and, 260–61; on the West, 3, 128–29, 253, 259–60, 285n12; Zasulich's trial/acquittal as reported by, 157, 168, 203, 291n12, 299n2. See also *The Brothers Karamazov* (Dostoevsky); *Crime and Punishment* (Dostoevsky); *Demons* (Dostoevsky); the fantastic/fantastical, and Dostoevsky
Dostoevsky, Mikhail, 43, 50
Double (Dostoevsky), 39

Douglass, William, 3, 11, 277n17
Drozd, Andrew, 275n7, 275n15
duels, 28–29, 287n9
Dzhunkovsky trial/acquittal, 170

educated society (obshchestvo): *The Brothers Karamazov* (Dostoevsky) and, 198–200, 296n1, 297n7, 297n9; and detention for youth, pretrial, 151; hero(s)/new hero(s) from, 59; political radical(s)/violence relationship to, 43, 151, 153, 198, 290n8; state government/autocracy's relationship to, 151, 153, 189, 198, 213, 242, 260, 290n8, 296n3; state terrorism and, 287n9, 297n9; sympathy or sochuvstvie from, 43, 290n8. See also culture of Russia
Elliot, Robert, 268n21
Ely, Christopher, 289n1
Elysard, Jules [pseud.] (Mikhail Bakunin), "The Reaction in Germany," 35–36. See also Bakunin, Mikhail (Jules Elysard, pseud.)
the Emancipation era, 43–44, 273n10
emblematic act (gesture). See gesture (emblematic act)
emotions, and Nechaev, 95–96, 97, 101. See also suffering; sympathy (sochuvstvie)
empathy. See sympathy (sochuvstvie)
Emperor Hunt. See assassination/assassination attempt(s) on Alexander II
Engels, Friedrich, 264n6
Enlightenment, 22, 23, 24–25, 26, 27, 206, 269n31
Enzensberger, Hans Magnus, 131–32
Epokha (journal), 280n34
Evgenii Onegin (Pushkin), 270n62, 298n13
evildoer (zlodei), 9–10, 46, 120, 153
extraordinary men. See hero(s)/new hero(s); new man

face/image: of Alexander II, 237, 302n8; celebrity(ies) and, 231–33; in *Demons* (Dostoevsky), 129, 132–33, 244; of state government/autocracy, 226; of state terrorism, 237; in "The Threshold" (Turgenev), 214, 221–22, 223. See also body/image

Index

face/image of revolution/terror: of celebrity(ies), 231–33, 235; Garshin as, 245; morality and, 233, 239, 240, 245; as Nihilists/nihilists, 244–45; physiognomic premises and, 239, 240, 244–45, 303n21; women as, 236, 237, 238–39, 240, 245, 302n3

faceless/imageless terror/ists, women as, 214, 221–22, 223. *See also* face/image of revolution/terror

faith-based hagiography: assassination attempts on Alexander II and, 199; in *The Brothers Karamazov* (Dostoevsky), 192–94, 198–99, 295n3, 296n4, 297n7; in *Crime and Punishment* (Dostoevsky), 44, 84, 193; in *Demons* (Dostoevsky), 130, 193, 293n7; Zasulich and, 169–70. *See also* Christianity; false god/king; religious metaphors

false god/king: in *Demons* (Dostoevsky), 116, 124, 130–31, 132–33, 186, 284n22, 286n23, 286n34; Girard on, 130–31, 242, 286n23; terror/ists as, 133. *See also* Christianity; faith-based hagiography; religious metaphors

fanaticism, acts of (activism), 95, 96, 97, 99, 112

the fantastic/fantastical: in *Don Quixote* (Cervantes), 55; realism versus, 54; in terror/ism, 8–9, 13, 44, 50; Zasulich's trial/acquittal and, 173, 185. *See also* fantastic (reality) realism

the fantastic/fantastical, and Dostoevsky: *The Brothers Karamazov* (Dostoevsky) and, 200–201; censorship and, 38–39; *Crime and Punishment* (Dostoevsky) and, 67; *Demons* (Dostoevsky) and, 120, 136, 139, 141; *Petersburg Visions in Verse and Prose* (Dostoevsky) and, 44; terror/ism and, 13. *See also* the fantastic/fantastical

fantastic (reality) realism, 9, 10, 13, 39. *See also* the fantastic/fantastical; the fantastic/fantastical, and Dostoevsky

Fathers and Children/Sons [Otsy i deti] (Turgenev): behavioral model for terror/ists in, 265n22; critiques of, 280n27; hero(s)/new hero(s) in, 59; monsters/gloomy monsters in, 6, 41, 264n11; morality in, 63; Nihilists/nihilists in, 46, 56–57, 59, 259, 264n11, 280n27, 307n48; utilitarianism in, 46

Faust (Goethe), 36, 56

Fedorenko, B. V., 297n9

"Female Prisoner" (Polonsky), 171–73, 183, 218, 221, 223

feminine body/image of terror/ists, 228, 232, 251, 301n25. *See also* women

Fenians (Irish-American Fenians): anarchists/ism compared with, 254–55; in assassination attempts on Victoria (Queen of England), 5–6, 264n9; bombs in arsenal of, 5, 108, 224, 249–50, 254, 295n39; media on terror/ism by, 5, 247, 249–50, 304n2; Nihilists/nihilists' as compared with, 5, 253–56, 263n5; terror/ism in Great Britain by, 5, 247, 249–50, 263n5, 264n6, 304n2; terror/ists or terror/ism and, 5, 249–50, 253, 263n5, 264n6, 264n8; United States and, 5, 254, 263n5, 264n6; *Vera; or the Nihilists* (Wilde) as commentary on, 306n40

Festa, Lynn, 268n23

Fieschi, Giuseppe Marco, 267n5

Figner, Lydia, 172–73, 293n19

Figner, Vera, 118, 156, 172, 291n10, 299n10

filial piety: in *Demons* (Dostoevsky), 116–17, 124, 153; Dostoevsky on, 153, 290n11; literary critics/criticism and, 23; Nechaev and, 122; People's Will or Narodnaia volia and, 290n13; state government/autocracy and, 153, 290n13

Filippeus, K. F., 98–99

Firks, F. I. (pen name Schedo-Ferroti), 60

flogging: Catherine II and, 287n9; in *Demons* (Dostoevsky), 136, 138, 140, 162, 287n9; Dostoevsky on, 168; educated society or obshchestvo and, 287n9. *See also* state terrorism

"Four Days" (Garshin), 242, 303n27

France: anarchists/ism in, 108, 260; Dostoevsky on corruption in the West and, 260; Nihilists/nihilists as perceived in, 257, 258–59, 306n41, 307n48. *See also* French Revolution

Frank, Joseph, and topics/opinions: *The Brothers Karamazov* (Dostoevsky), 153–54, 291n12; Chernyshevsky as influence on Dostoevsky, 275n20; *Demons* (Dostoevsky) publication issues, 286n28; Dostoevsky and Nihilists/nihilists, 283n18; Dostoevsky and Petrashevsky affair/conspiracy, 296n3; Dostoevsky's gamble with publisher Stellovsky, 278n2; Nechaev as reimagined in *Demons* (Dostoevsky), 126–27, 285n7; Nechaev's writings and *Nechaevshchina* affair/conspiracy trial, 125; sentimentalism in *Demons* (Dostoevsky), 286n34

French Revolution: Chernyshevsky's writings as influenced by, 61; cultural imaginary of terror/ism and, 18–19, 48, 127, 167n6; *A Journey from St. Petersburg to Moscow* (Radishchev) as influenced by, 20; justice in political radical(s)/violence during, 23; Marat and, 19, 23, 239, 303n24; revolutionary terrorism origins and, 19; revolutionary underground terrorism compared with, 152; "right to kill" during, 26, 27, 87; sentimentalism during, 23, 268n25; the Terror or "time of Horror" ("vremia Uzhasa") and, 19, 167n6. See also Corday, Charlotte; France

friend/enemy distinction, 146–47, 288n17, 289n19

Fusso, Susanne, 280n27

The Gambler (Dostoevsky), 278n2
Garibaldi, Anita, 58
Garibaldi, Giuseppe, 19, 44, 58, 64, 76, 228, 253–54
Garshin, Vsevolod: on "blinded by an idea," 242, 303n27; as face/image of revolution/terror, 245; "Four Days," 242, 303n27; "An Incident" (Proisshestvie), 240–41, 244, 303n23; mental health of, 243, 304n29; Mlodetsky's stay of execution plea by, 242–43, 296n3, 304nn28–29; People's Will membership and, 242, 304n28; prostitution in writings of, 240–41; religious metaphors in writings of, 303n23; Repin's portrait of, 237, 245, 246, 302n8; utilitarianism and, 242; on Zasulich's trial/acquittal, 240. See also *Nadezhda Nikolaevna* (Garshin)

Gelfman, Gesia, 5
gesture (emblematic act): in *The Brothers Karamazov* (Dostoevsky), 185, 186–88, 194–95, 206; Dostoevsky on, 269n12; Pushkin and, 31, 33
ghosts/terror/ists (specter/spectral metaphor), 18, 19, 34–35, 266n1, 266n3
Ginzburg, Lydia, 7, 265n19, 265n22
Girard, René, 130–31, 242, 286n23
Gleason, Abbott, 276n15, 283n9
Goethe, Johann Wolfgang von: *Faust*, 36, 56; *The Sorrows of Werther*, 7, 252
Gogol, Nikolai: and acts, unheard of, 113, 283n13; *Diary of a Madman*, 44; ghosts/terror/ists or specter/spectral metaphor and, 34–35; on human dignity/rights, 38; *Inspector General*, 115, 126, 134, 165; madman or *beshenyi* and, 35, 44; "The Overcoat," 34–35, 271n73; revolutionary terrorism in writings by, 6, 34; rhetorical genres and devices and, 179; satire and, 35, 137, 139, 142; *Selections from Correspondence With Friends*, 37–38; specter metaphor for terror/ism and, 35; terror/ism in writings by, 35, 271n73
Goloushev, Sergei, 163, 164
Goncharov, Mikhail: *Oblomov*, 52–53, 67; *The Precipice* [Obryv], 165, 287n2
Gorbov, Nikolai Mikhailovich, 220–22
Gothic tropes, 18–19, 266n1. See also ghosts/terror/ists (specter/spectral metaphor); monsters/gloomy monsters
Graaf, Janny de, 277n17
Gradovsky, Grigorii, and *Voice* [Golos] (newspaper), 297n4, 306n37
Granovsky, Timofei, 134–35, 145
Great Britain: counterterrorism against Nihilists/nihilists and, 255, 256, 306n38; Fenians' terror/ism in, 5, 247, 249–50, 263n5, 264n6, 304n2; Ireland's terror/ist attacks and, 247, 253, 254, 304n2; state government/autocracy

Index

of Russia compared with, 256; Victoria (Queen of England) and, 5–6, 246, 264n9. See also *Pall Mall Gazette* [PMG] (newspaper); *Times of London* (newspaper)
Greek aesthetics, 89
Griffith, D. W., 230
Grossman, Leonid, 115, 284n9, 291n12

Hamlet (Shakespeare), 55, 56, 57, 58, 59, 239–40, 289n20
"Hamlet and Don Quixote" (Turgenev), 55, 56–57
Harmodius, 19, 89, 267n7
Hauer, E., 302n3
Hazlitt, William, 229
Hegelianism, 36, 304n34
Heinzen, Karl, 86–88, 90, 280n23
Henry, Émile, 260
Henry, Peter, 240
heroine(s)/new heroine(s): media on female terror/ists in Russia as, 251; in *Nadezhda Nikolaevna* (Garshin), 238; Zasulich as, 157–58, 160, 169, 226, 241, 251. See also women; *and specific heroine(s)/new heroine(s)*
hero(s)/new hero(s): in *The Brothers Karamazov* (Dostoevsky), 195, 274n20; celebrity(ies) as, 229; in *Crime and Punishment* (Dostoevsky), 72, 78; in *Demons* (Dostoevsky), 123; Dobroliubov on, 57–59; Dostoevsky as, 39; from educated society or obshchestvo, 59; *Journey . . .* (Radishchev) and, 23, 30, 268n26; in literature, 33–34, 57–59, 273n10; Pushkin on, 30, 270n61; regicides in assassination of Alexander II as, 4, 251; terror/ists as, 11, 39, 227–28; in *Underground Russia* [La Rossia Sotteranea] (Stepniak pseud./Kravchinsky), 227, 229. See also heroine(s)/new heroine(s); new man; *and specific hero(s)/new hero(s)*
Herzen, Alexander, and topics/opinions: arson/arsonists as terror/ists, 48, 49; Bakhmetev estates, 275n15; behavioral model for terror/ists, 7–8; *The Bell* (Kolokol), 50, 82; literary criticism of Dobroliubov, 52–53; Nechaev as sincere, 98; political radical(s)/violence, 47, 48; Radishchev as martyr, 28, 270n53; Schedo-Ferroti, 60; terror/ism and agency, 50, 82; terror/ism and literature relationship, 7
Hildermeier, Manfred, 12
Hobbes, Thomas, 128
Holland, Kate, 285n12
hostage negotiations, 66, 276n23
House of the Dead (Dostoevsky), 199
Howe, Irving, 134
Hugo, Vicor, 193, 296n4
human dignity/rights: Bogoliubov and, 170, 174, 181, 184, 186; and culture of Russia, 198, 287n9; Dostoevsky on, 206; Enlightenment and, 23; Gogol on, 38; Zasulich's trial and, 170–71, 174, 181, 184, 186, 293n14
Hunt, Lynn, 170

icon(s)/iconography(ies): in *The Brothers Karamazov* (Dostoevsky), 205, 206; in Christianity, 212, 233–34, 298n6; in "The Threshold" (Turgenev), 218, 221–22; in *Underground Russia* [La Rossia Sotteranea] (Stepniak pseud./Kravchinsky), 234–35
image (imaginary construct/s). See behavioral model/s (social types, new); body/image; cultural imaginary; face/image
imprisonment. See detention, pretrial; state terrorism
"An Incident" [Proisshestvie] (Garshin), 240–41, 244, 303n23
infernal machines, 19, 108, 267n5. See also bomb/s
insanity plea, temporary, 22, 75–76, 79, 111–12, 200. See also madman (beshenyi)
Inspector General (Gogol), 115, 126, 134, 165
Ireland, 247, 253, 254, 304n2
Irish-American Fenians (Fenians). See Fenians (Irish-American Fenians)
irony: in *Demons* (Dostoevsky), 116, 117, 124, 130, 146; Marx and, 18
Ishutin, Nikolai, 71, 72, 84, 98, 108, 276n15, 276nn15–16

ISIL attacks in France in 2015, 260
"I. S. Turgenev" (Yakubovich), 219
Ivanov, Ivan Ivanovich, 98, 105. See also *Nechaevshchina* affair/conspiracy (Ivanov's murder)
Ivan the Terrible and His Son Ivan, 16 November (Repin), 237–38, 244, 245–46

Jackson, Robert Louis, 89, 194, 204, 205, 296n7, 296n12
Jongman, Albert J., 141
A Journey from St. Petersburg to Moscow (Radishchev): Catherine II on, 20, 21, 26, 27, 29; censorship and, 20, 28; conscience in, 21; consciousness development and, 23–27, 269n31; French Revolution as influence on, 20; hero(s)/new hero(s) and, 23, 30, 268n26; interpretations and reactions to, 27–28, 270nn47-49, 270n53; justice in political radical(s)/violence in, 26; literature as crime against rulers and, 28, 30; morality in, 23, 24, 25, 27, 28, 29, 30; motivations for publication of, 20, 23, 268n26; narrator in, 22, 268n18, 269n28; political radical(s)/violence in, 22, 23, 24, 38, 268nn20-23; publication and distribution of, 20–21, 27; Pushkin on, 22–23, 27–28, 29–30, 267n16, 270n49; revolutionary terrorism and, 6; "right to kill" in, 24–27, 269n38, 269n41; satire in, 22–23, 268nn20-21; scholarship on, 267n8; sensibilities of author in, 23, 24, 269n28, 269n31, 270n49; sentimentalism in, 22, 23, 27–28, 267n16, 268nn22-23, 268n25, 270n49
justice in political radical(s)/violence: Bakunin/Elysard pseud. on, 36; in *Crime and Punishment* (Dostoevsky), 80–81, 84; during French Revolution, 23; in *Journey...* (Radishchev), 26; in "The Overcoat" (Gogol), 35

Kahn, Andrew, 268n18, 269n28, 270n63
Karakozov, Dmitry: and acts, unheard of, 71, 94, 111–12; arrest/trial/sentencing/execution of, 72, 83–84, 279n9; assassination attempt on Alexander II by, 5–6, 19–20, 33, 71–72, 82, 83–84, 89, 100, 121, 145, 276nn14-16, 279n9, 280n32; biographical information about, 71, 276n16; conspiracy versus lone assassin theory in attempt on Alexander II by, 71–72, 114–15, 276nn15-16, 283n18; Dostoevsky's writings as influenced by assassination attempt by, 71, 72, 82, 83–84, 276n14, 279n9; and insanity plea, temporary, 111–12; media on assassination attempt by, 71–72, 155, 156, 291n4; political radical(s)/violence and, 71, 121; sentimentalism and, 121; suicide and, 284n13; terror/ism's origins and, 5–6, 15, 99, 264n9, 266n39; Turgenev on, 299n3; tyrannicides and, 89, 280n32; utilitarianism in assassination attempt on Alexander II by, 121, 124, 284n13
Karamzin, Nikolai, 119–20, 169, 292n6
Karlinsky, Simon, 265n14
Kartashevskaia, M. G., 48
Katkov, Mikhail: on assassination attempts on Alexander II as conspiracy, 71–72, 114–15, 283n18; on Bakunin, 115; on consciousness, 280n27; conservatives and, 68, 256; *Demons* (Dostoevsky) publication by, 126, 130, 131, 286n28; Dostoevsky's relationship with, 68, 72, 83, 84, 126, 153, 276n10, 277n20; on *Fathers and Children/Sons* [Otsy i deti] (Turgenev), 280n27; *Moscow Gazette* (newspaper) and, 71, 105, 106, 256; on political radical(s)/violence as foreign-born/foreign influenced, 258; *Russian Messenger* (journal) and, 68, 76–77, 126, 153, 276n10, 277n20; Supreme Administrative Commission and, 188; as Tolstoy's publisher, 76–77
Kessel, Konstantin, 161, 164, 165, 166, 168, 292n17
Kibalchich, Nikolai, 5
king. *See* false god/king; state government/autocracy; *and specific rulers*
Kireev, A. A., 152

Kletochnikov, Nikolai, 211
Kliger, Ilya, 288n16
Klioutchkine, Konstantine, 69, 70
Kobylin, Alexander, 276n16
Kolenkina, Maria, 155, 156-57, 168
Komissarov, Osip I., 72, 299n3
Koni, A. A., 159, 160, 161, 162, 163, 164, 181, 218, 299n2
Kovalsky, Ivan, 225
kramola/kramol'nik ("sedition"/"seditionist"). *See* "sedition"/"seditionist" (kramola/kramol'nik)
Kravchinsky, Sergei M. (Stepniak, pseud.): assassination of Mezentsev' by, 132, 225, 226, 301n5, 301n13; biographical information about, 226, 228, 301n13; "cult of the dagger" manifestation and, 226; Lavrov on, 226; media and, 228; on Nihilists/nihilists compared with Fenians, 254; the West on Nihilists/nihilists and, 256; Wilde's friendship with, 306n40; on Zasulich, 226. See also *Underground Russia* [*La Rossia Sotteranea*] (Stepniak pseud./Kravchinsky)
Kroneberg trial/acquittal, 167, 174-75, 176, 291n12
Kropotkin, Peter, 61, 231, 294n13
Ku Klux Klan, 5
Kurneev, Fyodor, 161, 163, 164
Kuznetsov, Alexei, 125, 126
Kviatkovsky, Alexander, 214, 222, 223

Lacenaire, Pierre-François, 276n10
Laclau, Ernesto, 128
Land and Freedom (Zemlia i Volia), 43, 151-52, 155-56, 224, 231, 291n2, 291n9, 294n10
Land League, 253, 254, 304n2
Laqueur, Walter, 6, 7, 241, 264n8, 277n17
Lavater, Johann Kaspar, 239, 240, 303n21
Lavrov, Peter, 151, 226
Law, Randall, 300n1
lawyers tactics, and trials, 167, 170. *See also specific lawyers and trials*
Leatherbarrow, W. J., 280n33
Leeman, Richard, 179-80
Lenin, Vladimir, 65, 94

Leroy-Beaulieu, Anatole, 252-53, 261, 305n24
Leshern, Sophia, 232
Leskov, Nikolai, 273n24
liberalism: under Alexander II, 43-44, 170, 213; in *Demons* (Dostoevsky), 119, 120, 127, 128, 139; media and, 70, 156; public opinion and, 157; Turgenev and, 215
Linnér, Sven, 295n3, 296n4
Liprandi, I. P., 36, 37
literary critics/criticism: *Crime and Punishment* (Dostoevsky) and, 259; filial piety and, 23; new man as birthed by, 7, 52, 54; sentimentalism and, 23; the West's interest in Nihilists/nihilists and, 259-60, 265n14, 307n48. *See also specific literature and literary critics*
Liubatovich, Ol'ga, 301n5
Liubimov, N. A., 70, 72, 83
Lizogub, Dmitrii, 214, 229-30, 231, 301n14
Lombroso, Cesare, 239, 244-45
Loris-Melikov, Count: assassination attempt on, 242, 296n3; Mlodetsky's execution and, 242, 246, 296n3, 304nn28-29; rapprochement with educated society or obshchestvo and, 189, 213, 242, 260; Supreme Administrative Commission and, 188-89, 242, 296n3
Lotman, Yurii, 33-34, 78, 266n29

madman (beshenyi): about, 75, 277n12; in *Crime and Punishment* (Dostoevsky), 75-76; Gogol and, 35, 44; and insanity plea, temporary, 246; in *Journey . . .* (Radishchev), 25, 29; political radical(s)/violence relationship to, 75-76, 97; Pushkin and, 29, 31-32; "sedition"/"seditionist" and, 29
Magun, Artemy, 268n22
Maikov, Apollon, 33
Makhtin, Mikhail M., 179, 194
Makogonenko, G. P., 268n26, 269n31
Malia, Martin, 263n4
Mandarin (trolley) dilemma, 145-46, 288nn12-13, 288nn15-16, 298n13
Marat, Jean-Paul, 19, 23, 239, 303n24
Marchart, Oliver, 128, 132

Marian figure, 216, 234
Marks, Stephen G., 263n3, 265n15
Marshall, P. David, 301n18
Martens, D. (M. F. de Martens), 305n22, 306nn37-38
Martinists, 21, 29, 267n13
martyr(s)/martyrdom: Alexander II as, 212, 298n6; biographies in *Narodnaia volia* (newspaper), 214; in Christianity, 295n29; in *Crime and Punishment* (Dostoevsky), 91; in *Demons* (Dostoevsky), 123-24, 130; Nechaev and, 122-23; political radical(s)/violence and, 122-23, 294n10, 295n29; Radishchev as, 28, 30, 270n53; terror/ists as, 11, 227; *Underground Russia* [La Rossia Sotteranea] (Stepniak pseud./Kravchinsky) and, 228. *See also* self-sacrifice; suffering
Marx, Karl, and topics/opinions, 4, 5, 18, 19, 251, 264n6, 266n1, 266n3
masculine body, and terror/ists, 227, 228, 251
mass media. *See* media
materialism, 9, 18, 46
Mazzini, Giuseppe, 19, 253-54
media: on arson/arsonists as terror/ists, 48-49; on assassination/assassination attempt(s) on Alexander II, 71-72, 212, 247-48, 250, 251, 305n5; assassination(s)/assassination attempt(s) by women terror/ists in, 155-56; celebrity(ies) and, 230; conservative, 212; *Crime and Punishment* (Dostoevsky) in environment of, 69, 70-71; on Fenians's terror/ism, 5, 247, 249-50, 304n2; flogging of Bogoliubov as covered by, 156, 160-61, 162, 163, 164, 174, 291n7; on Karakozov's assassination attempt on Alexander II, 71-72, 155, 156, 291n4; Kolenkina's assassination attempt on Zhelekhovsky and, 157; Komissarov as hero in, 72; Kravchinsky/Stepniak, pseud. and, 228; liberalization of, 70, 156; Marian figure link with Zasulich in, 216; revolutionary terrorism in villages and, 156,

291n10; for revolutionary underground, 213; terror/ism as term of use in, 226; terror/ism's symbiosis with, 7, 48-49, 69, 265n16, 277n17; on trial of regicides in assassination of Alexander II, 251; in the West on Nihilists/nihilists, 250, 251-52, 305n22; in the West on Russian literature, 251-52; on Zasulich, 155-56, 157, 216, 219, 251, 291n3. *See also specific newspapers and journals*
Mezentsev, Nikolai, 132, 198, 224-25, 226-27, 294n13, 301n13
Michelet, Jules, 34, 268n25, 271n70, 302n3, 303n24
Mikhailov, Alexander, 211, 212, 298n8
Mikhailov, M. L., 121, 183-84, 294n10
Mikhailov, Timofei, 5, 212, 251
Mikhailovsky, Nikolai, 213, 295n29
Miliutin, D. A., 212
Minsky, Nikolai, "The Last Confession" (Posledniaia ispoved'), 186-88, 294n22
Mlodetsky, I. O., 242, 296n3, 304nn28-29
Mochulsky, Konstantin, 285n7
modern terror/ism: civilian or soft targets in, 11-12, 287n2; Corday and, 241, 303n24; "Russian method" and, 4, 5, 11, 19, 127, 252, 263n3; theory of, 86-88, 90. *See also* terror/ism
monsters/gloomy monsters: in *Catechism of a Revolutionary* (Nechaev), 6, 264n11; in *Crime and Punishment* (Dostoevsky), 6, 81, 108, 282n8; in cultural imaginary, 11, 18-19; in *Demons* (Dostoevsky), 131, 264n11; in *Fathers and Children/Sons* (Turgenev), 6, 41, 264n11; as Gothic tropes, 18-19, 266n1; as Nihilists/nihilists, 63; Romanticism and, 64, 65; as terror/ist, 11, 63; in *What Is to Be Done?* (Chernyshevsky), 6, 62-63, 64, 65, 275n15
morality: aesthetics of murder and, 89, 279n17; in *The Brothers Karamazov* (Dostoevsky), 218, 282n12; in *Catechism of a Revolutionary* (Nechaev), 96, 97, 127; in *Crime and Punishment* (Dostoevsky), 78-79, 80, 81, 89, 90, 96-97,

280n27, 282n12; in *Demons* (Dostoevsky), 127, 285n9; in *Don Quixote* (Cervantes), 55; Enlightenment and, 23, 24-25; face/image of revolution/terror and, 233, 239, 240, 245; in *Fathers and Children/Sons* [Otsy i deti] (Turgenev), 63; friend/enemy distinction and, 146-47, 288n17, 289n19; in *Journey...* (Radishchev), 23, 24, 25, 27, 28, 29, 30; in literature, 7; Mandarin or trolley dilemma and, 145-46, 288nn12-13, 288nn15-16, 298n13; Pisarev and, 76; Pushkin and, 29; terror/ism as assault on, 11, 12, 19-20, 24; in "The Threshold" (Turgenev), 216, 218, 220-21; in *What Is to Be Done?* (Chernyshevsky), 61; word and deed or *slovo i delo* and, 10; Zasulich's trial/acquittal and, 218
Morozov, Nikolai, 213, 303n24
Morrissey, Susan, 7
Morson, Gary Saul, 194
Moscow Gazette [Moskovskie vedomosti] (newspaper), 71, 105, 106, 256
Murav'ev, M. N., 71, 82
murder as/as not terrorism/revolutionary terrorism: under Alexander II, 98-99, 113-14; in *Crime and Punishment* (Dostoevsky), 44-45, 72, 84, 88, 90, 94-95, 99, 129-30, 255, 280n27, 281n6; in *Demons* (Dostoevsky), 106-9, 113, 115-16, 129-30, 131-32, 154, 282n5, 282n8, 283nn9-11; *Nechaevshchina* affair/conspiracy or Ivanov's murder and, 94-95, 98-99, 100, 106, 113-14, 225, 281n6, 282n5. *See also* aesthetics of murder; terror/ism

Nabokov, Vladimir, 73
Nadezhda Nikolaevna (Garshin): artistic-political rivalry and, 242, 243-44, 246, 304n31, 304n34; "blinded by an idea" in, 303n27; conscience in, 241, 246; consciousness and, 239; "creative destruction" and, 244, 246, 304n34; face/image of Alexander II in, 237, 302n8; face/image of Corday or revolution/terror in, 236, 237, 238-39, 240, 241-42, 244, 246, 302n3; inspiration for, 237, 302n7; *Ivan the Terrible...* (Repin) and, 237-38, 244; morality in, 239, 240, 245; physiognomic premises and, 239, 240, 244-45, 303n21; political radical(s)/violence and, 242; prostitution and, 240; "right to kill" and, 245, 246. *See also* Garshin, Vsevolod
Napoleon I, 19, 229, 267n5
Napoleonic idea, 19, 76-77, 78, 84-85, 86, 88-89, 276n14, 279n18, 279n20. *See also* "right to kill"
Narodnaia volia (newspaper): "After the Execution of November 4" (Anonymous) in, 222; biographies of martyr(s)/martyrdom in, 214; history of, 213-14, 299n16; "I. S. Turgenev" (Yakubovich) in, 219; Osinsky's biographical notes in, 232; propaganda articles in, 152; religious metaphors in, 186-87; satire in, 213-14, 299n16; "The Last Confession" [Posledniaia ispoved'] (Minsky) in, 186-87; Trial of the 16 testimony in, 223. *See also* People's Will (Narodnaia volia)
natural right theory, 26. *See also* "right to kill"
Nechaev, Sergei: on activism or acts of fanaticism, 95, 96, 97, 99, 112; arrest/trial/sentencing/imprisonment of, 100-101, 122, 123, 125, 134, 165; assassination attempt of Alexander II by, 99, 283n9; Bakunin and, 95, 98, 123; biographical information about, 94, 95, 281n6; civilian or soft targets and, 108, 283n10; *Crime and Punishment* (Dostoevsky) and, 94, 281nn5-6; deception by, 97-98, 122, 287n2, 293n7; *Demons* (Dostoevsky) and, 94, 281n6; on emotions, 95-96, 101; filial piety and, 122; Granovsky's conversations with, 134-35; Herzen on, 98; as ineffective political radical, 115, 126, 134, 165; martyr(s)/martyrdom and, 122-23; Ogarev and, 95; People's Will or Narodnaia volia and, 101; political

Nechaev, Sergei (*continued*)
  radical(s)/violence and, 95, 96, 108, 115, 121–23, 126, 134, 165, 283nn9–10, 283n10; *Principles of Revolution* (Nachala revoliutsii, Beginnings of Revolution), 95, 100, 112, 122, 127; "A Program of Revolutionary Actions" (Nechaev and Tkachev) and, 93–94, 281n2; revolutionary underground plan by, 265n12; suffering by, 123; sympathy or sochuvstvie and, 122, 135, 151; "To the Students of the University, . . .," 99–100, 121–23; Uspensky as follower of, 98; utilitarianism and, 97; word and deed or slovo i delo and, 95, 99–100, 128; Zasulich and, 122, 169, 293n7. See also *Catechism of a Revolutionary* [Katekhizis revoliutsionera] (Nechaev)
Nechaevshchina affair/conspiracy (Ivanov's murder), 99, 112, 125–26, 167, 169–70, 259, 281n2, 293n7; arrests/trials/sentencing/imprisonment for, 99, 100–101, 112, 122, 123, 125–26, 134, 165, 169–70, 293n7; deception and, 97–98, 122; Dostoevsky's writings and, 94, 99, 105–6, 113–14, 116–17, 126, 281n6, 282n3; murder as/as not revolutionary terrorism and, 94–95, 98–99, 100, 106, 113–14, 225, 282n5; and "social fact," terrorism as, 105–6, 127; sympathy or sochuvstvie for, 151; as term of use, 95; word and deed or slovo i delo and, 106, 282nn3-4. *See also* Nechaev, Sergei
Nechaevtsy. See *Nechaevshchina* affair/conspiracy (Ivanov's murder)
Nekrasov, Nikolai Alexeievich, 57, 63, 294n10
new man: in *Crime and Punishment* (Dostoevsky), 72, 76, 77, 78, 79, 81, 90, 91, 195; in *Demons* (Dostoevsky), 129–30, 131; in *Hamlet* (Shakespeare), 55, 56; literary characters as prototypes for, 55–56; literary critic as midwife to, 7, 52, 54; Pisarev and, 76–77; political radical(s)/violence as, 95; as prototype in

Don Quixote (Cervantes), 55–56; in Pushkin's writings, 30–31; realism and, 7; rulers versus, 57, 274n20; Tkachev on, 93; Tolstoy on, 76–78; in *What Is to Be Done?* (Chernyshevsky), 60, 63, 64–65, 275n15. *See also* hero(s)/new hero(s)
Nicholas I, Tsar, 33, 37, 297n9
Nietzsche, Friedrich, 21, 209
Nihilists/nihilists: about and definition of, 45–46, 59, 253, 272n9; anarchists as synonym for, 226; arson/arsonists as, 45; *The Brothers Karamazov* (Dostoevsky) and, 200–201; consciousness and, 280n27; in *Crime and Punishment* (Dostoevsky), 78–79, 83, 89, 253, 280n27; Dostoevsky on, 83, 116–17, 147, 153, 259, 283n18, 307n48; face/image of revolution/terror as, 244–45; in *Fathers and Children/Sons* [Otsy i deti] (Turgenev), 46, 56–57, 59, 259, 264n11, 280n27, 307n48; Fenians compared with, 5, 253–56, 263n5; as monsters/gloomy monsters, 63; Pisarev on, 46–47; Romanticism and, 252; "sedition"/"seditionist" versus, 255; sentimentalism and, 252; society's attitude to, 152, 199; speech act and, 59; terror/ism's origins and, 5; Turgenev on, 45, 259, 307n48; *What Is to Be Done?* (Chernyshevsky) and, 63; Zasulich's trial/acquittal and, 256–57. *See also* anti-Nihilists/antinihilists; People's Will (Narodnaia volia); the West's interest in Nihilists/nihilists
Nikitina, A. I., 299n2
Nikol'skaia, Maria Gerasimovna, 232
nonviolence, as Russia's contribution to modernity, 6, 265n15
The Notebooks for "Crime and Punishment" (Dostoevsky), 81, 90, 109, 273n14
The Notebooks for "The Possessed" (Dostoevsky), 112, 114, 117, 118, 120–21, 134–35, 136, 145
Notes from the House of the Dead (Dostoevsky), 68

Notes from the Underground (Dostoevsky), 66, 68, 70–71, 275n20
Nozhin, Nikolai, 281n41
Nozhina, Maria, 281n41

Oblomovism (oblomovshchina), 52–53, 57
Oblomov (Goncharov), 52–53, 67
obshchestvo (educated society). *See* educated society (obshchestvo)
Ogarev, Nikolai, 95, 121, 123
Ognyov, Nikolai, 223
On the Eve (Turgenev), 57–59
Osinsky, Valerian, 214, 231–32, 291n9
otrechenie (renunciation), 59, 96
"The Overcoat" (Gogol), 34–35, 271n73

Pahlen, Konstantin, 157, 160, 165, 290n13, 291n7, 292n17
Pall Mall Gazette [PMG] (newspaper): on assassination of Alexander II, 248, 305n5; on female terror/ists in Russia as heroine(s)/new heroine(s), 251; on Fenians's terror/ism, 247, 254, 304n2, 306n33; on Great Britain compared with Russian state government/autocracy, 256; on trial of regicides in assassination of Alexander II, 251
Paperno, Irina, 54
parody. *See* satire
penal servitude. *See* state terrorism
The People's Vengeance (Narodnaia rasprava), 98
People's Will (Narodnaia volia): Alexander III's relations with, 12, 213; Alexander II's relations with, 213; arrests/trials/executions of members of, 4, 211, 212, 214, 222, 223, 233, 237, 250–51, 302n4; assassination/assassination attempts on Alexander II by, 4–6, 12, 19, 33, 66, 112, 146–47, 152, 199, 211–12, 222–23, 225, 264n9, 271n69, 289n4; bombs in arsenal of, 108, 146–47, 152, 199, 211, 258, 289n4, 295n39; Chernyshevsky's repatriation by, 66; civilian or soft targets and, 199–200; filial piety and, 290n13; Garshin as member of, 242, 304n28; Land and Freedom as precursor to, 224, 231; literature as transformative for, 213–14, 299n10; Marx's praise for, 4, 264n6; Nechaev and, 101; populist politics and, 12, 66; power of, 66, 212–13, 298n9; regicides and, 4, 212, 233, 237, 250–51, 302n4; revival of, 300n12; sympathy or sochuvstvie for, 290n13; terror/ists as term of use by, 222–23; "The Threshold" (Turgenev) and, 220–21; word and deed or slovo i delo and, 213. *See also Narodnaia volia* (newspaper); Nihilists/nihilists
Le Père Goriot (Balzac), 145, 276n1
Perovskaya, Sophia: arrest/trial/execution of, 5, 221, 233–34; assassination/assassination attempts against Alexander II by, 5, 211, 221, 289n4; celebrity(ies) and, 231, 232–34, 301n25; Christian icon(s)/iconography(ies) and, 233–34; compassion or sostradanie and, 234; conscience of, 234; heroine(s)/new heroine(s) and, 258; in media, 232; morality and, 233; suffering and, 234; as terror/ist, 231, 233; "The Threshold" (Turgenev) and, 221, 300n16; visual artists/artworks in the West and, 258; Zhelyabov's relationship with, 232, 301n25
Peter I (Peter the Great), 30, 33, 270n62
Petersburg Visions in Verse and Prose (Dostoevsky), 13, 44–45, 272n3
Petrashevsky affair/conspiracy, 36–39, 44, 49, 71–72, 114–15, 206, 283n18, 296n3, 298n12
Petropavlovsky, Nikolai, 163
Pevear, Richard, 282n5, 283n12
physiognomic premises, 239, 240, 245–46, 303n21. *See also* face/image
Pipes, Richard, 157
Pisarev, Dmitrii: on aesthetics of murder, 88, 280n34; arrest/imprisonment of, 60; "Bazarov" (Pisarev), 41, 76; on *Crime and Punishment* (Dostoevsky), 94, 281n5; on dare to act or audacity, 79, 278n22; on *Fathers and Children/Sons* [Otsy i deti] (Turgenev), 63; as

Pisarev, Dmitrii (*continued*)
   literary critic, 46; on monsters/gloomy monsters in *Fathers and Children/Sons* (Turgenev), 41, 264n11; on morality, 63, 76; on new man, 76-77; Nihilists/nihilists and, 46-47, 59, 264n11; on Nihilists/nihilists in *Fathers and Children/Sons* (Turgenev), 59, 264n11; on perspicacious or pronitsatel'nyi readers, 274n6; on revolutionary overthrow of ruler, 60; Schedo-Ferroti pamphlet critique by, 60; "The Scholasticism of the Nineteenth Century," 46-47, 60; on *What Is to Be Done?* (Chernyshevsky), 60, 91-92, 274n6
Platt, Kevin M. F., 33
Pobedonostsev, Konstantin, 178, 188, 213, 238, 246
Poems in Prose (Turgenev), 217, 219
political radical(s)/violence: artistic-political rivalry and, 242, 243-44, 246, 304n34; in *Catechism of a Revolutionary* [Katekhizis revoliutsionera] (Nechaev), 96, 228; Central Committee/Action Committee and, 93-94, 281n2, 281n4; consciousness as provoked by, 12-13, 17; in *Crime and Punishment* (Dostoevsky), 72, 75-76, 82-83, 278n2; deception by, 94, 281n4; in *Demons* (Dostoevsky), 114-15, 118-19, 120-21, 124, 127-28, 133, 205, 284n19; Dobroliubov on, 95; educated society or *obshchestvo* relationship to, 43, 151, 153, 198, 290n8; as evildoer or zlodei, 46, 153; as foreign-born/foreign influenced, 258, 307n46; Herzen as, 47, 48; as ineffective, 115, 126, 133, 134, 165; in *Journey...* (Radishchev), 22, 23, 24, 38, 268nn20-23; Karakozov and, 71, 121; literature as transformative for, 213-14, 219-20, 299n10; madman or *beshenyi* relationship to, 75-76, 97; martyr(s)/martyrdom and, 122-23, 294n10, 295n29; Mikhailov and, 121, 183, 294n10; Nechaev and, 95, 96, 108, 121-23, 283nn9-10; as new man, 95; populist, 12, 95, 131, 151, 155, 303n24; as profiles in *Underground Russia* [La Rossia Sotteranea] (Stepniak pseud./Kravchinsky), 225, 229-30; propaganda by, 151, 220, 263n5, 290n13; public opinion of, 157, 212-13; satire and, 22-23, 35, 268nn20-21; sentimentalism and, 22-23, 268nn22-23, 268n25; Shelgunov and, 121, 294n10; state government/autocracy's symmetry with, 33; sympathy or sochuvstvie for, 12, 14, 17, 43, 154, 290n13; Turgenev and, 215, 219-20, 299n3; *What Is to Be Done?* (Chernyshevsky) and, 64-65, 275n15; Zasulich as, 160. *See also* detention, pretrial; revolutionary terrorism; revolutionary underground; *and specific radicals, groups, and movements*
Polonsky, Yakov: "Female Prisoner," 171-73, 183, 218, 221, 223; Garshin and, 243
Pomper, Philip, 99, 123, 281n6, 283nn9-10
Poor Folk (Dostoevsky), 37
populist political terror/ism, 12, 95, 131, 151, 155, 231, 303n24. *See also* political radical(s)/violence; revolutionary terrorism
positivism, 8, 9, 166
Pozefsky, Peter C., 272n9, 281n41
The Precipice [Obryv] (Goncharov), 165, 287n2
Prescott, Marie, 306n40
Presniakov, Alexander, 222
pretrial detention. *See* detention, pretrial
Principles of Revolution [Nachala revoliutsii, Beginnings of Revolution] (Nechaev), 95, 100, 112, 122, 127
"A Program of Revolutionary Actions" (Nechaev and Tkachev), 93-94, 281n2
pronitsatel'nyi (perspicacious readers), 62, 63, 274n6, 275n7
propaganda, 36, 132, 151, 152, 220, 263n5, 290n13. *See also specific groups, journals, and newspapers*
prostitution, 69, 240-41
public opinion: of assassination of Alexander II, 212-13; of political radical(s)/violence, 157, 212-13; on "sedition"/

"seditionist," 154; in "The Threshold" (Turgenev), 216; on Zasulich's trial/ acquittal and, 155, 157–58, 160
Pugachev, Emilian, and uprising, 20, 28, 33
Pushkin, Alexander: *The Bronze Horseman* [Mednyi vsadnik], 6, 28–29, 30–34, 270nn60–62, 271n69; censorship and, 33; on "creative destruction," 31–33; "cult of the dagger" manifestation by, 33, 226, 271n70; and death in a duel, 28–29; Decembrists and, 33; *Evgenii Onegin*, 270n62, 298n13; gesture or emblematic act and, 31, 33; on hero(s)/new hero(s), 30, 270n61; on *Journey . . .* (Radishchev), 22–23, 27–28, 29–30, 32, 267n16, 270n49; Lotman on, 33–34; madman or *beshenyi* and, 29, 31–32; on Martinists, 29; morality and, 29; new man in writings by, 30–31; on Peter I, 30, 33, 270n62; publication of writings by, 28–29, 33; Radishchev's biography by, 28–29, 270n54; revolutionary terrorism and, 6; satire and, 22–23; secular biography by, 28–29; on sentimentalism, 22, 27–28, 267n16, 270n49; terror/ism and, 29–34

Radishchev, Alexander: arrest/imprisonment/confessions/sentencing/commutation for, 21–22, 23, 28; biographical information and legacy of, 20, 27, 28, 29–30, 270n46, 270n53; as hero(s)/new hero(s), 30; and insanity plea, temporary, 22; martyr(s)/martyrdom and, 28, 30, 270n53; new men and, 23; Pushkin's biography of, 28–29, 270n54; Raynal's influence on, 21–22, 23; "sedition"/"seditionist" accusations against, 21, 29; sensibilities of, 23, 24, 269n28, 269n31, 270n49. See also *A Journey from St. Petersburg to Moscow* (Radishchev)
Raeff, Marc, 270n46
Rahv, Philip, 72
Rapoport, David, 12
Raynal, Abbé de, 21–22, 23
"The Reaction in Germany" (Bakunin/ Elysard pseud.), 35–36. See also Bakunin, Mikhail (Jules Elysard, pseud.)
readers, perspicacious (pronitsatel'nyi), 62, 63, 274n6, 275n7
the real: literary history of terror/ism and, 9; Nechaev on, 100; terror/ism and, 8–9
real criticism (real'naia kritika), 54
realism: aesthetics versus, 88, 280n34; in *The Brothers Karamazov* (Dostoevsky), 192; in *Demons* (Dostoevsky), 119; the fantastic/fantastical versus, 54; fantastic reality/realism and, 9, 10, 13, 39; in "Hamlet and Don Quixote" (Turgenev), 57; in literary history of terror/ism, 9; new man and, 7
real'naia kritika (real criticism), 54
Reddy, William M., 23
regicides, 4, 212, 233, 237, 250–51, 302n4. See also assassination/assassination attempt(s) on Alexander II; assassination(s)/assassination attempt(s); People's Will (Narodnaia volia)
religious metaphors: in *The Brothers Karamazov* (Dostoevsky), 185–86, 187, 188, 295n24; in Garshin's writings, 303n23; in Minsky's writings, 186–88, 294n22; in "The Threshold" (Turgenev), 216, 221–22; Zasulich's trial/acquittal and, 169–70, 181–82, 185. See also Christianity; faith-based hagiography; false god/king
renunciation (otrechenie), 59, 96
Repin, Ilya: *Arrest of the Propagandist*, 257; Garshin's portrait by, 237, 245, 246, 302n8; *Ivan the Terrible . . .*, 237–38, 244, 245–46, 303n11; *They Did Not Expect Him* (Ne zhdali), 237, 245
revolutionary terrorism: about and origins of, 19–20, 34, 155, 266n39; "blinded by an idea" in, 242; *The Brothers Karamazov* (Dostoevsky) and, 13, 44–45, 154, 189–91, 205, 295n39, 298n8; *Ivan the Terrible . . .* (Repin) as allegory and, 238; *Journey . . .* (Radishchev) and, 6; literature's relationship to, 4, 6, 7, 10–11, 13, 33–34, 44, 252, 265n14; society as

revolutionary terrorism (*continued*)
    mirror of, 197–99, 296n1, 296n3, 297n7;
    in villages and media coverage, 156,
    291n10; word and deed or slovo i
    delo in, 4, 14; after Zasulich's trial/
    acquittal, 19, 155, 157, 180, 222, 224–25,
    294n13. *See also* political radical(s)/
    violence; revolutionary underground;
    state terrorism and revolutionary
    terrorism relationship; terror/ism;
    terror/ists
revolutionary underground: in *Demons*
    (Dostoevsky), 129; Dostoevsky's Un-
    derground Man and, 130, 188, 280n23;
    French Revolution compared with,
    152; history of, 151–53, 289n1, 290nn7–
    8; media for, 213; Nechaev' plan for,
    265n12; society as mirror of revolu-
    tionary terrorism and, 198, 199, 297n9;
    "The Threshold" (Turgenev) and,
    220, 221; Underground Russia and,
    225, 230. *See also* political radical(s)/
    violence; revolutionary terrorism
Reyfman, Irina, 287n9
rhetorical genres and devices, 179–80
Rice, James, 204, 297n6, 298n12
rights, human dignity. *See* human dignity/
    rights
"right to kill": in *Crime and Punishment*
    (Dostoevsky), 76–77, 78, 84–85, 86, 89,
    276n14, 279n18, 279n20; Enlighten-
    ment and, 26, 27; during French Revo-
    lution, 26, 27, 87; in *Journey . . .* (Ra-
    dishchev), 24–27, 269n38, 269n41;
    Nadezhda Nikolaevna (Garshin) and,
    245, 246; natural right theory and, 26;
    or Napoleonic idea, 19, 76–77, 78, 84–
    85, 86, 88–89, 276n14, 279n18, 279n20;
    and terror/ism, theory of modern,
    87–88; tyrannicides based on, 26–27,
    87–88
Rivers, Christopher, 239, 303n21
Romanov, Alexander Alexandrovich (Alex-
    ander III, Tsar), 12, 66, 116–17, 188,
    213, 241–42, 298n9
Romanov, Konstantin Nikolaevich, 152
Le Roman Russe [The Russian Novelists]
    (De Vogüé), 259–61, 307n48

Romanticism: Byronic, 33, 229, 252; dare to
    act or audacity and, 78; French Revo-
    lution historians and, 268n25; Ger-
    man, 36; monsters/gloomy monsters
    and, 64, 65; Nihilists/nihilists and,
    252; in the West, 279n17
Rosenshield, Gary, 157, 165, 170, 291n12
Russia, culture of. *See* culture of Russia
Russian Messenger (journal), 68, 76–77, 126,
    153, 276n10, 277n20
"Russian method," as Russia's contribu-
    tion to modern terror/ism, 4, 5, 11,
    19, 127, 252, 263n3
Russian Nihilists/nihilists. *See* Nihilists/
    nihilists
Russian Wealth [Russkoe bogatstvo] (jour-
    nal), 226
The Russian Word (journal), 60, 84, 91,
    281n41
Rysakov, Nikolai, 5, 211

sacrifice, self-. *See* self-sacrifice
Safronova, Iuliia, 199, 290n13, 296n1, 296n3
satire: in *The Brothers Karamazov* (Dostoev-
    sky), 165–66, 198–99, 297n7; in *Demons*
    (Dostoevsky), 112–13, 117, 134, 137,
    138–39, 142, 143, 144; Enlightenment
    versus, 22; in Gogol's writings, 35,
    137, 139, 142; in *Journey . . .* (Radi-
    shchev), 22–23, 268nn20–21; in *Na-
    rodnaia volia* (newspaper), 213–14,
    299n16; political radical(s)/violence
    and, 22–23, 35, 268nn20–21
Schedo-Ferroti [pen name] (F. I. Firks), 60
Schmid, Alex P., 141, 277n17, 287n2
Schmitt, Carl, 146, 288n17
"The Scholasticism of the Nineteenth Cen-
    tury" (Pisarev), 46–47, 60
"sedition"/"seditionist" (kramola/kra-
    mol'nik): about, 9, 265n26; madman
    or beshenyi as, 29; Nihilists/nihilists
    versus, 255; public opinions on, 154,
    215; Radishchev as accused of, 21, 29;
    state government/autocracy's mis-
    handling of, 215; as terror/ist proto-
    type, 9, 10, 19
Selections from Correspondence With Friends
    (Gogol), 37–38

self-sacrifice: Bogoliubov and, 181; in *The Brothers Karamazov* (Dostoevsky), 195, 205, 206-7; in *Crime and Punishment* (Dostoevsky), 69, 91; in *Demons* (Dostoevsky), 123, 124, 130, 131, 132-33, 186, 286n25; Mandarin or trolley dilemma and, 288nn12-13, 288nn15-16, 298n13; as sentimentalism, 23; of terror/ists, 133; in "The Threshold" (Turgenev), 216, 219, 221; Turgenev on, 55; word and deed or slovo i delo and, 195, 206, 298n13; Zasulich and, 181, 184, 185, 215. *See also* martyr(s)/martyrdom

sentimentalism: in *The Brothers Karamazov* (Dostoevsky), 205; conservatives and, 23, 268n23; in *Demons* (Dostoevsky), 119-20, 121, 123, 132-33, 138, 139-40, 228, 286n34; Enlightenment and, 22; during French Revolution, 23, 268n25

September 11, 2001, attacks, 250

Shakespeare, William, *Hamlet*, 55, 56, 57, 58, 59, 239-40, 289n20

Shchennikova, L. P., 294n22

Shelgunov, Nikolai, 121, 294n10

Sheshkovsky, S. I., 21, 287n9

Shiriaev, Stepan, 223, 289n4

Siemiradsky, Henryk, 295n29

Siljak, Ana, 162, 291n6

Simmons, Ernest, 279n12

Sloan, Stephen, 264n9

slovo i delo (word and deed). *See* act/deed; acts, unheard of; speech act; word and deed (slovo i delo)

sochuvstvie (sympathy). *See* sympathy (sochuvstvie)

"social fact," terrorism as: about, 8, 35, 50; in *Demons* (Dostoevsky), 127, 285n9; Dostoevsky on, 49-50, 73, 105-6; *Nechaevshchina* affair/conspiracy or Ivanov's murder as, 105-6, 127. *See also* "brute fact," terror/ism as

social types, new (behavioral model/s). *See* behavioral model/s (social types, new); body/image; face/image

soft (civilian) targets, 11-12, 108, 199-200, 283n10, 287n2, 300n1

Solovyev, Nikolai, 280n33

Solovyev, Vladimir, 212

The Sorrows of Young Werther (Goethe), 7, 252

Southern Rebels (Iuzhnye buntari), 152, 155, 156, 231, 291n9

Spasovich, V. D., 99, 125-26, 134, 165, 167-68

specter/spectral metaphor (ghosts/terror/ists), 18, 19, 34-35, 266n1, 266n3

speech act: in *The Brothers Karamazov* (Dostoevsky) as transformative, 202, 203-7, 297n6, 298n8; Nihilists/nihilists and, 59; Pushkin Days speech by Dostoevsky as transformative, 202, 203, 206, 297n4, 298n12; transformative effect of verdict during Zasulich's trial/acquittal and, 159-60, 201, 203, 299n2; word and deed or slovo i delo and, 46, 59, 206. *See also* word and deed (slovo i delo)

Stasiulevich, M. M., 171, 218

state government/autocracy, Russian: body/image of, 227; celebrity(ies) and, 229; educated society or *obshchestvo* relationship to, 151, 153, 189, 198, 213, 242, 260, 290n8, 296n3; face/image of, 226; filial piety and, 153, 290n13; Great Britain's government compared with, 256; "sedition"/"seditionist" as mishandled by, 215. *See also specific rulers*

state terrorism: Arnold on, 134; as counter-terrorism, 34, 126-27, 157, 164, 290n7; educated society or obshchestvo and, 287n9, 297n9; face/image of, 237; *Ivan the Terrible* ... (Repin) as allegory and, 238, 303n11; society as mirror of revolutionary terrorism and, 199, 297n9; Zasulich's trial/acquittal and, 162-65. *See also* detention, pretrial; flogging

state terrorism and revolutionary terrorism relationship: in *The Bronze Horseman* [*Mednyi vsadnik*] (Pushkin), 33; in *The Brothers Karamazov* (Dostoevsky), 185-89, 192, 194, 195-96, 198-99, 297n7; in *Demons* (Dostoevsky), 134-40, 142, 144, 162, 287n9, 288n8

Stellovsky, Fyodor, 83, 278n2
Stepniak [pseud.] (Sergei M. Kravchinsky). See Kravchinsky, Sergei M. (Stepniak, pseud.); *Underground Russia* [La Rossia Sotteranea] (Stepniak pseud./Kravchinsky)
Stolypin, Pyotr, 285n9
Strakhov, N. N., 69
Straus, Nina Pelikan, 283n11
suffering: Arendt on compassion and, 186; of Bogoliubov, 182; in *The Brothers Karamazov* (Dostoevsky), 176-77, 182-83, 195, 200, 204-6; *The Brothers Karamazov* (Dostoevsky) and, 176-77; corporal punishment and, 170-71, 293n14; in *Crime and Punishment* (Dostoevsky), 79, 90-91, 92; by Nechaev, 123; in "The Threshold" (Turgenev), 221; in *Underground Russia* [La Rossia Sotteranea] (Stepniak pseud./Kravchinsky), 234; in *What Is to Be Done?* (Chernyshevsky), 64, 91-92; Zasulich's trial/acquittal and, 170-71, 173-75, 181, 182, 293n14. *See also* martyr(s)/martyrdom
suicide: in *The Brothers Karamazov* (Dostoevsky), 197-98; *Crime and Punishment* (Dostoevsky) and, 88; in *Demons* (Dostoevsky), 111, 116, 124, 130, 131, 133, 197-98, 284n22; Karakozov and, 284n13
Supreme Administrative Commission, 188-89, 198, 242, 296n3. *See also* Loris-Melikov, Count
Suvorin, Alexei A., 146, 237-38, 298n8
sympathy (sochuvstvie): for Alexander II, 154; in *The Brothers Karamazov* (Dostoevsky), 189-90; in *Crime and Punishment* (Dostoevsky), 80-81; in *Demons* (Dostoevsky), 119, 120, 135, 136, 138, 139-40; Dostoevsky and, 261; from educated society or obshchestvo, 43, 290n8; Nechaev and, 122, 135, 151; for *Nechaevshchina* affair/conspiracy or Ivanov's murder, 151; for political radical(s)/violence, 12, 14, 17, 43, 154, 290n13; Zasulich's trial/acquittal and, 158, 160-61, 166, 169, 170, 171, 173

temporary insanity plea, 22, 75-76, 79, 111-12, 200. *See also* madman (beshenyi)
the Terror, and French Revolution, 19, 167n6. *See also* French Revolution
terror/ism: about and definition of, 3, 11, 12, 45, 141, 253, 287n2; actor-based approaches to, 8; as anachronistic in *Demons* (Dostoevsky), 108, 142, 143, 283n11; anarchists/ism and, 250, 253; a-sychrony of terrorists/agency versus activism of, 14-15; as "brute fact," 8, 10, 11, 35, 73; *Catechism of a Revolutionary* (Nechaev) and, 5-6, 97-98, 128, 264nn9-10, 265n12; in cultural imaginary, 18-19, 35; Dostoevsky's typology of, 141-43, 288n4; the fantastic/fantastical in, 8-9, 13, 44, 50; fantastic reality/realism and, 9, 13; Fenians and, 249-50, 253; Hobbes on, 128; literature's relationship to, 6, 7, 10-11, 13, 61-62, 265n14; media's symbiosis with, 7, 48-49, 69, 265n16, 277n17; morality as supported by, 11, 12, 19-20, 24; Nihilists/nihilists and, 5; origins of, 4, 5-6, 15, 19-20, 99, 241, 264n9, 266n39, 267n7, 303n24; Pushkin and, 29-34; social constructivist or critical approach to, 8; specter metaphor for, 35; symbolism in literature and, 6, 20, 30; as term of use, 226; Terrorism as term of use versus, 226-27, 229, 231-32; as transnational trend, 250, 255; universal harmony as compared, 260-61; in the West, 250; word and deed or slovo i delo and, 10, 250, 266n29; in *Young Russia* (Zaichnevsky), 47-48. *See also* assassination/assassination attempt(s) on Alexander II; assassination(s)/assassination attempt(s); counterterrorism; modern terror/ism; murder as/as not terrorism/revolutionary terrorism; Nihilists/nihilists; revolutionary terrorism; revolutionary underground; "social

Index

fact," terrorism as; *and specific authors and writings*
terror/ists: arson/arsonists as, 45, 46, 48–51, 60–61, 273n23; a-sychrony of agency and, 14–15; behavioral model/s for, 7–8, 61–62, 83, 265n22, 279n6; as false god/king, 133; feminine body/image of, 228, 232, 251, 301n25; Fenians as, 5, 249–50, 263n5, 264n6, 264n8; ghosts/terror/ists or specter/spectral metaphor for, 18, 19, 34–35, 266n1, 266n3; as hero(s)/new hero(s), 11, 39, 227–28; Ku Klux Klan as, 5; martyr(s)/martyrdom and, 11, 227; masculine body/image of, 227, 228, 251; as monsters/gloomy monsters, 11; "sedition"/"seditionist" as prototype for, 9, 10, 19; self-sacrifice of, 133; as term of use, 222–23, 304n2; Terrorists as term of use versus, 227–28, 233, 304n2; in *Underground Russia* [*La Rossia Sotteranea*] (Stepniak pseud./Kravchinsky), 227–28, 258; women as, 122, 155–56, 186, 223, 231, 232, 233, 241, 301n25; word and deed or *slovo i delo* and, 10, 266n29. *See also* political radical(s)/violence; revolutionary terrorism; terror/ism; *and specific terror/ists*
Test, George A., 268n20
They Did Not Expect Him [*Ne zhdali*] (Repin), 237, 245
"The Threshold" (Turgenev): aesthetics in literature and, 216, 222, 223; icon(s)/iconography(ies) and, 218, 221–22; Koni on publication of, 218; literature as transformative and, 219–20; morality in, 216, 218, 220–21; People's Will or Narodnaia volia and, 220–21; Perovskaya and, 221, 300n16; publication of, 218–19, 223; public opinion in, 216; religious metaphors in, 216, 221–22; revolutionary underground and, 220, 221; self-sacrifice in, 216, 219, 221, 223; Stasiulevich on, 218; suffering in, 221; text/translations of, 216–17, 219–20, 222, 300n12; women as faceless/imageless terror/ists and, 214, 221–22,

223; Zasulich's trial/acquittal and, 221, 300n16
Tikhomirov, Lev, 152, 213
Time (journal), 43, 48, 276n10
"time of Horror" ("vremia Uzhasa"), 19, 167n6
Times of London (newspaper): on assassination of Alexander II, 247; on Fenian terror/ism, 5, 247, 249, 254–55, 306nn22, 306n33; Kravchinsky reports in, 232; on Nihilists/nihilists compared with Fenians, 254–55; Perovskaya in, 232; on political radical(s)/violence as foreign-born/foreign influenced, 258; on Russia and liberal reforms, 247; on Russian literature, 252; on trial of regicides in assassination of Alexander II, 251
Tkachev, Peter N., 93–94, 125, 127, 281n2
Todorov, Tsvetan, 9
Tolstoy, Leo, and topics/opinions: anarchists/ism, 61, 77; *Anna Karenina*, 3; clemency for regicides in assassination of Alexander II, 212; literary critics/criticism in the West, 258; Lizogub, 301n14; new man, 76–78; nonviolence, 265n15; publication of writings, 76–77; rhetorical genres and devices, 179; *War and Peace/The Year 1805*, 77–78; *What Is to Be Done?* (Chernyshevsky), 65
Tomilova, Elizaveta, 125
To the People (*khozhdenie v narod* or "going to the people") movement, 151, 228, 290n13
"To the Students of the University, . . ." (Nechaev), 99–100, 121–23
tourism/travel writers, and the West on Nihilists/nihilists, 257–58, 306n41, 307nn45–46
transnational, terror/ism as, 250, 255
travel writers/tourism, and the West on Nihilists/nihilists, 257–58, 306n41, 307nn45–46
Trepov, F. F. (Fyodor): Bogoliubov's flogging by, 156, 161, 162, 163, 164, 174, 291n7; Land and Freedom or Zemlia i

Trepov, F. F. (*continued*)
Volia assassinations/assassination attempt on, 155–56, 291n3; Trial of the 193 prosecution by, 155. *See also* Zasulich, Vera, and assassination attempt on Trepov
Tretiakov, Pavel, 245
trial/s: in *The Brothers Karamazov* (Dostoevsky), 154, 157, 165–66, 176–78, 201, 203, 291n12, 297n9; Dzhunkovsky trial/acquittal, 170; Kroneberg trial/acquittal, 167, 174–75, 176, 291n12; lawyers' tactics during, 167, 170; *Nechaevshchina* affair/conspiracy, 99, 100–101, 112, 122, 123, 125–26, 134, 165, 169–70, 293n7; Trial of the 16, 222–23; Trial of the 50, 175–76; Trial of the 193, 155, 168, 291n1. *See also* detention, pretrial; Zasulich, Vera, and trial/acquittal
Troitsky, N. A., 172–73, 293n19
trolley (Mandarin) dilemma, 145–46, 288nn12–13, 288nn15–16, 298n13
Turgenev, Ivan: anarchists/ism and, 61; Annenkov's friendship with, 299n3; on consciousness, 55; death/funeral of, 220–21; *Diary of a Superfluous Man*, 53; on *Don Quixote* (Cervantes), 56, 57, 59, 62, 93; *On the Eve*, 57–59; *Hamlet* (Shakespeare) and, 56–57, 58, 59; "Hamlet and Don Quixote," 55, 56–57; heroine(s)/new heroine(s) in writings by, 57–58; on Komissarov, 299n3; on new man, 55–56, 57; on new man versus rulers, 57; on Nihilists/nihilists, 45, 259, 307n48; *Poems in Prose* (Turgenev), 217, 219; political radical(s)/violence and, 215, 219–20, 299n3; politics of, 215, 219–20; revolutionary terrorism in writings by, 6; on "sedition"/"seditionist" and state government, 215; on self-sacrifice, 55; visual artists/artworks in the West and, 258; Zasulich's trial/acquittal and, 215–16, 299n2. *See also Fathers and Children/Sons* [*Otsy i deti*] (Turgenev); "The Threshold" (Turgenev)

tyrannicides, 19, 26–27, 87–88, 267n7. *See also* assassination(s)/assassination attempt(s)

Ulam, Adam B., 303n24
Ulozhenie of 1649, 9–10, 28
Underground Russia, 225, 230. *See also* revolutionary underground
Underground Russia [*La Rossia Sotteranea*] (Stepniak pseud./Kravchinsky): celebrity(ies) and, 229–35, 301n18; compassion or *sostradanie* and, 234; hero(s)/new hero(s) in, 227, 229; icon(s)/iconography(ies) in, 234–35; introduction to, 226; Lombroso and, 244–45; martyr(s)/martyrdom and, 228; preface to, 233; publication of, 225, 228–29, 234, 244–45, 258; sentimentalism in, 228; suffering and, 234; terror/ism as term of use in, 226, 227; terror/ists described in, 227–28, 258; Underground Russia lives in, 230
United States: counterterrorism against Nihilists/nihilists and, 255, 256; Fenians activities/support in, 5, 254, 263n5, 264n6; Ku Klux Klan as terror/ists in, 5; Nihilists/nihilists as perceived in, 257, 258, 306n40, 307nn45–46
universal harmony, as compared with terror/ism, 260–61
Uspensky, Peter, 98, 105, 293n7
utilitarianism: aesthetics of murder and, 280n34; assassination/assassination attempt(s) on Alexander II and, 121, 124, 284n13; in *Crime and Punishment* (Dostoevsky), 86, 279n7; deontology versus, 145, 288nn12–13; in *Fathers and Children/Sons* [*Otsy i deti*] (Turgenev), 46; Garshin and, 242; Nechaev and, 97

Valkenier, Elizabeth Kridl, 302n8
Valuev, P. A., 152–53, 290nn7–8
Vengerov, Semyon, 226
Vera; or the Nihilists (Wilde), 257, 306n40
Verhoeven, Claudia, and topics/opinions:

Crime and Punishment (Dostoevsky), 71, 276n14; Karakozov's assassination attempt on Alexander II, 71, 111, 266n39, 276n14, 276n16, 280n32, 291n4; "The Overcoat" (Gogol) and terror/ism, 271n73; revolutionary terrorism's origins, 266n39; *What Is to Be Done?* (Chernyshevsky), 275n7
Victoria (Queen of England), 5–6, 246, 248, 264n9
visual artists/artworks. See *Nadezhda Nikolaevna* (Garshin); *and specific artists*
visual artists/artworks in the West, and Nihilists/nihilists, 257, 258
Voice [Golos] (newspaper), 297n4, 306n37
Vorontsov, Alexei, 270n48
Vorontsova-Daskhkova, Countess, 270n48
"vremia Uzhasa" ("time of Horror"), 19, 167n6

War and Peace/The Year 1805 (Tolstoy), 77–78
Wertherism, 7, 252
the West: on Alexander II as liberal reformer, 247, 248; Alexander II's death as mourned/celebrated in, 248–49; anarchists/ism in, 224, 258, 300n1; on assassination of Alexander II, 247–49, 250, 305n5; assassination(s)/assassination attempt(s) in, 224, 300n1; civilian or soft targets in, 300n1; counterterrorism and, 255, 256; Dostoevsky on corruption by, 3, 128–29, 253, 259–60, 285n12; and insanity pleas, temporary, 75–76; and literature, Russian, 251–52; literature in, 252; and media on Russian literature, 251–52; media on terror/ism in, 226; on Russia, 3, 5, 252, 263n4, 305n22, 306n37; terror/ism in, 250; *Underground Russia* [La Rossia Sotteranea] (Stepniak pseud./Kravchinsky) as published in, 225; word and deed or *slovo i delo* and, 10; Zasulich's trial/acquittal in media in, 216
the West's interest in Nihilists/nihilists: about and definition of, 253, 305n24; conservatives and, 258, 307n46; conservatives in Russia and, 252; counterterrorism and, 255, 256, 305n22, 306n37, 306n38; De Vogüé's literary criticism on Russian literature and, 259–60, 265n14, 307n48; Fenians compared with Nihilists/nihilists and, 5, 253–56, 263n5; foreign-born/foreign influences and, 258, 307n46; media and, 250, 251–52, 305n22; travel writers/tourism and, 257–58, 306n41, 307nn45–46; *Vera; or the Nihilists* (Wilde) and, 257, 306n40; visual artists/artworks and, 257, 258. See also the West
"What Is Oblomovism?" (Dobroliubov), 52, 57
What Is to Be Done? (Chernyshevsky): as behavioral model for terror/ists, 61–62, 83, 265n22, 279n6; censorship and, 60, 65; as contraband, 65; *Crime and Punishment* (Dostoevsky) as influenced by, 65–66, 68, 83, 275n20, 279n7; critiques of, 60, 62, 65, 91–92, 274n6, 275n7, 275n15; *Don Quixote* (Cervantes) as influence on, 62, 65; French Revolution influence on, 61; hero(s)/new hero(s) in, 65; monsters/gloomy monsters in, 6, 62–63, 64, 65, 275n15; morality in, 61; new man in, 60, 63, 64–65, 275n15; Nihilists/nihilists and, 63; perspicacious or *pronitsatel'nyi* readers of, 62, 63, 274n6, 275n7; political radical(s)/violence and, 64–65, 275n15; success of, 65; suffering in, 64, 91–92; Tolstoy on, 65; as written during imprisonment, 60, 65
Whelehan, Niall, 263n5
"When Will the Real Day Come?" (Dobroliubov), 57
Wilde, Oscar, *Vera; or the Nihilists*, 257, 306n40
women: body/image of terror/ists as, 228, 232, 251, 301n25; as celebrity(ies), 233–34; celebrity(ies) and, 232–34, 301n25; in detention, pretrial, 156, 160–61, 171–72, 173; face/image of

women (*continued*)
  revolution/terror, 236, 237, 238-39, 240, 245, 302n3; as faceless/imageless terror/ists, 214, 221-22, 223; as terror/ists, 122, 155-56, 186, 223, 231, 232, 241, 301n25. *See also* heroine(s)/ new heroine(s); *and specific women*
word and deed (slovo i delo): activism or acts of fanaticism and, 95, 96, 97, 99, 112; arson/arsonists and, 50-51; in *The Brothers Karamazov* (Dostoevsky), 192-93, 195, 197, 206; in *Crime and Punishment* (Dostoevsky), 67; *Demons* (Dostoevsky) and, 106, 282nn3-4; fantastic reality/realism and, 10; morality and, 10; Nechaev on, 95, 99-100, 128; *Nechaevshchina* affair/conspiracy or Ivanov's murder and, 106, 282nn3-5; Oblomovism or oblomovshchina and, 52-53; People's Will or Narodnaia volia and, 213; in revolutionary terrorism, 4, 14; self-sacrifice and, 195, 206, 298n13; speech act and, 46, 59, 206; terror/ism/ists and, 10, 250, 266n29; *Ulozhenie* of 1649 and, 9-10, 28; Zasulich's trial/acquittal and, 184-85. *See also* act/deed; acts, unheard of; speech act

Yakubovich, Peter Filipovich, 219-20, 223, 300n12
Yarmolinsky, Avrahm, 300n16
The Year 1805/War and Peace (Tolstoy), 77
Young Russia (Zaichnevsky), 45, 50-51, 60, 272n6

Zaichnevsky, Peter, *Young Russia*, 45, 47-48, 50-51, 60, 272n6
Zaionchkovsky, Peter A., 188, 290nn7-8, 290n11, 298n9
Zaitsev, Varfolomei, 281n41
Zasulich, Alexandra, 122, 293n7
Zasulich, Vera: celebrity(ies) and, 229, 230-31; compassion or sostradanie for, 173; on deception, 122, 281n4, 293n7; in detention, pretrial, 160-61, 164, 171-72, 173; faith-based hagiography and, 169-70; Kravchinsky on, 226; Nechaev and, 122, 169, 293n7; *Nechaevshchina* affair/conspiracy arrests/trials/imprisonment and, 169-70, 293n7; plays about, 257, 306n40; political radical(s)/violence and, 160. *See also* Zasulich, Vera, and trial/acquittal
Zasulich, Vera, and assassination attempt on Trepov: details about, 161; flogging of Bogoliubov by Trepov and, 156, 160-61, 164; as heroine(s)/new heroine(s), 157-58, 160, 169, 226; media on, 155-56, 251, 291n3; self-sacrifice and, 181, 184, 185; Southern Rebels or Iuzhnye buntari techniques as influence on, 155, 291n9; terror/ism's origins and, 19, 155, 241, 303n24; in Turgenev's writings, 57-58. *See also* Zasulich, Vera
Zasulich, Vera, and trial/acquittal: *The Brothers Karamazov* (Dostoevsky) and, 157, 158, 165, 176-78, 185-86, 189, 191, 201, 203, 218, 291n12; confession of guilt during, 157, 160; conscience and, 165, 186, 218, 241; corporal punishment and, 170-71; Dostoevsky's reports on, 157, 168, 203, 291n12, 299n2; the fantastic/fantastical and, 173, 185; Garshin's response to, 240; human dignity/rights and, 170-71, 174, 181, 184, 186, 287n14, 293n14; jury and, 159-60; Kessel as prosecutor and, 161, 164, 165, 166, 168, 292n17; Koni as presiding judge and, 159, 160, 161, 162, 163, 164, 181, 218, 299n2; Marian figure and, 216, 234; media and, 157, 216, 219; morality and, 218; Nihilists/nihilists and, 256-57; Pahlen and, 157, 160, 165, 290n13, 291n7, 292n17; public opinion on, 155, 157-58, 160; religious metaphors and, 181-82, 185; revolutionary terrorism after, 19, 155, 157, 180, 222, 224-25, 294n13; self-sacrifice and, 215; sentimentalism and, 160, 169, 173, 190, 292n6; state terrorism and, 162-65; suffering and, 170-71, 173-75, 181, 182, 293n14; summations

during, 161, 165–66, 168–75, 171–73, 181–82, 183–85, 215, 292n6, 293n14; sympathy or sochuvstvie and, 158, 160–61, 166, 169, 170, 171, 173; verdict or speech act as transformative during, 159–60, 201, 203, 299n2; witnesses' testimony and, 161–65, 174–75; word and deed or slovo i delo and, 184–85. *See also* Alexandrov, P. A., as defense attorney for Zasulich; Zasulich, Vera; Zasulich, Vera, and assassination attempt on Trepov

Zemlia i Volia (Land and Freedom), 43, 151–52, 155–56, 224, 231, 291n2, 291n9, 294n10

Zhelekhovsky, Vladislav, 155

Zhelyabov, Andrei, 5, 211, 232, 298n9, 301n25

zlodei (evildoer), 9–10, 46, 120, 153

Zulaika, Joseba, 3, 11, 277n17

www.ingramcontent.com/pod-product-compliance
Lightning Source LLC
Chambersburg PA
CBHW070835160426
43192CB00012B/2198